I0124145

Doomed to Repeat?

Terrorism and the Lessons of History

Also by New Academia Publishing

History / International Affairs

FROM PIETY TO POLITICS: The Evolution of Sufi Brotherhoods
by Barbara DeGorge

GOD, GREED, AND GENOCIDE: The Holocaust through the Centuries
by Arthur Grenke

THE SOVIETIZATION OF EASTERN EUROPE: New Perspectives on the Postwar Period, edited by Balázs Apor, Péter Apor, and E. A. Rees, eds.

NATIONALISM, HISTORIOGRAPHY AND THE (RE)CONSTRUCTION OF THE PAST, Edited by Claire Norton

DETECTING THE BOMB: The Role of Seismology in the Cold War
by Carl Romney

TURKEY'S MODERNIZATION: Refugees from Nazism and Atatürk's Vision
by Arnold Reisman

PAN-AFRICANISM, PAN-AFRICANISTS, AND AFRICAN LIBERATION IN THE 21ST CENTURY, by Horace Campbell and Rodney Worrell

PAN-AFRICANISM IN BARBADOS: An Analysis of the Activities of the Major 20th-Century Pan-African Formations in Barbados, by Rodney Worrell

SLAVIC THINKERS OR THE CREATION OF POLITIES: Intellectual History and Political Thought in Central Europe and the Balkans in the 19th Century
by Josette Baer

RED ATTACK WHITE RESISTANCE: Civil War in South Russia, 1918
by Peter Kenez
Peter Kenez

RED ADVANCE WHITE DEFEAT: Civil War in South Russia, 1919-1920
by Peter Kenez

WITNESS TO A CHANGING WORLD, by David D. Newsom

AN ARCHITECT OF DEMOCRACY: Building a Mosaic of peace,
by James Robert Huntley

ECHOES OF A DISTANT CLARION: Recollections of a Diplomat and Soldier,
by John G. Kormann

NINE LIVES: A Foreign Service Odyssey, by Allen C. Hansen

BUSHELS AND BALES: A Food Soldier in the Cold War, by Howard L. Steele

To read an excerpt, visit: www.newacademia.com

Doomed to Repeat?

Terrorism and the Lessons of History

Edited by Sean Brawley

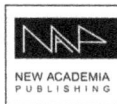

New Academia Publishing
Washington, DC

Copyright © 2009 by Sean Brawley

New Academia Publishing, 2009

All rights reserved. No part of this book may be reproduced or transmitted in any form or by any means, electronic or mechanical, including photocopying, recording, or by any information storage and retrieval system.

Printed in the United States of America

Library of Congress Control Number: 2009925223
ISBN 978-0-9818654-9-2 paperback (alk. paper)

New Academia Publishing
P.O. Box 24720, Washington, DC 20038-7420
info@newacademia.com - www.newacademia.com

The Research Network for a Secure Australia has supported the research forum which produced the collection and the publication of this volume.

Contents

Illustrations

Introduction

Clio Meets CT: The Place of History in Terrorism Studies and Counter-Terrorism

Sean Brawley

In the late 1990s the distinguished American historian Walter Laqueur made a new contribution to "terrorism studies," an academic field he had helped to found with several important studies dating back to the 1970s. Employing a phrase that authors had used since the 1980s to grab attention, Laqueur wrote of the dangers posed by "New Terrorism."[1] Despite Laqueur's own disinclination toward the historian as prophet, his comments foreshadowed eerily the events of 9/11: "much of what we thought about terrorism, including our most basic assumptions, must be reconsidered. The character of terrorism is changing…the threat to human life has become infinitely greater than it was in the past."[2]

Published in the same year as Laqueur's study, a report from Rand Corporation experts also tried to come to grips with New Terrorism from a counter-terrorism (CT) perspective. In his introduction, Ian O. Lesser insisted that the changes in terrorism were profound but that "much of the discussion on terrorism remains tied to images drawn from previous epochs." Such a position was dangerous for CT because "All of this renders much previous analysis of terrorism based on established groups obsolete."[3] Put differently, counter-terrorism had nothing to learn from history.

In the wake of September 11, scholars and commentators in the field have rushed to embrace New Terrorism as the prism through which the field should be examined.[4] Whether it was a ploy to sell their books (by distinguishing them from earlier work) or a genuine conclusion based on the marshaled evidence, many authors pursued the notion (explicitly or implicitly) that history had little to offer the Western world as it dealt with the ensuing crisis. When history was used, it was to illuminate today's unique challenges in comparison with the past, or it was narrowly focused on Osama bin Laden and al Qaeda.

In 2004, Immanuel Wallerstein observed how the twin themes of globalization and terrorism were being imagined in the early twenty-first century as "substantially new phenomena." He cautioned that:

> If we look at globalization and terrorism as phenomena that are defined in limited time and scope, we tend to arrive at conclusions that are as ephemeral as the newspapers. By and large, we are not then able to understand the meaning of these phenomena, their origins, their trajectory, and most importantly where they fit in the larger scheme of things. We tend to ignore their history. We are unable to put the pieces together, and we are constantly surprised that our short-term expectations are not met.[5]

Although Laqueur and other scholars have made efforts to backtrack and problematize New Terrorism by acknowledging history's enduring importance—an "essential key to understanding the phenomenon"—the ahistoric turn in terrorism studies was soon apparent.[6] Osama bin Laden had "wiped the slate clean" and history was seemingly no longer one of the "grand disciplines" of terrorism studies.[7]

The consequences of the turn are exemplified in James Jay Carafano and Marc Sauter's book *Homeland Security: A Complete Guide to Understanding, Preventing and Surviving Terrorism*, published only a year after Wallerstein's warning. The work includes a chapter entitled: "The Transnational Dimensions of Terrorism: The Unique Dangers of the Twenty-First Century."[8]

As with the scholars and commentators, the shock and awe of September 11 left many in political and CT circles believing that history could serve no useful purpose in the new environment. Within the American intelligence community, the castigation and self-flagellation over the failure to predict September 11 also worked against history. History had to take its share of the blame for not having predicted the events of 2001. In defending their records, politicians and the intelligence bureaucracy found comfort in reverting to a rhetoric in which everything was "unprecedented" and "unforeseen."[9] It was a powerful rhetoric that crossed borders and jurisdictions. Speaking in 2004, then Australian Defence Minister Senator Robert Hill informed a conference exploring "Australia's Response to Terrorism" that "The starting point in countering a threat is always to better understand it. Despite a long history of terror, nothing has prepared the world for the 'latest wave,' which we now must confront."[10]

The purpose of this collection of essays is to re-assert the place of history in terrorism studies and its usefulness to CT. The collection seeks to embody Everett Wheeler's 1991 observation that:

> History offers education in the broadest sense: it instructs without dictating a definite course of action, but it provides a perspective from which to make pragmatic decisions. The limits of historical knowledge, Clio's ambiguity, do not reduce history's use for the policy-maker to an inferior role *vis-à-vis* political science, sociology, or psychology.[11]

This publication is the product of a long germination. In 2004 my then PhD student Ian Shaw and I were invited to join the Research Network for a Secure Australia (RNSA), funded by the Australian Research Council (ARC). The RNSA had been conceived as a "multidisciplinary collaboration established to strengthen Australia's research capacity for protecting critical infrastructure (CIP) from natural or human caused disasters including terrorist acts." Its aim was to reach across academia, government and the private sector "to develop research tools and methods to mitigate emerging safety and security issues relating to critical infrastructure."[12] Conceived by engineers, the RNSA identified its academic fields as engineering, science and technology. As the organization grew, however, other disciplines including those in medicine and the social sciences were invited to participate.

For a historian, the various forums conducted by the RNSA proved most interesting. Much of the discussion reflected an absence of historical perspective, and general ignorance about the past. I still recall one conversation over dinner with an academic whose research interest was blast modeling. I learnt much in that conversation about why the twin towers collapsed in 2001 and why they did not collapse in 1993. Having been introduced to a new field I sought to connect the new information to other episodes. Why was Hezbollah's 1983 truck bomb attack on the US Marine barracks in Beirut much more effective than the 2004 car bomb attack on the Australian Embassy in Jakarta? My companion told me about the embassy bombing but he had not heard of the Beirut attack.

The opportunities the RNSA provided for engagement with members of the broad counter-terrorism practitioner community were also thought provoking. Despite the absence of historical knowledge or perspective, the practitioners demonstrated great interest in history. Despite what I had observed in the CT literature, the practitioners who spoke to me had not succumbed to the cargo cult of New Terrorism. Instead, they saw the usefulness of a historical perspective in counter-terrorism, and expressed concern that there was not enough history being published in the area (especially in Australia) to aid their work.

As a consequence of our early participation in the RNSA, and our championing of history as a rich discipline with much to offer, Ian Shaw and I were invited to explore possibilities. With support from the Australian Academy of the Humanities, the first RNSA Terrorism History Research Forum was held in Canberra in November 2006. The brochure for the Forum made some bold claims:

> Terrorism and counter-terrorism history can make a considerable contribution to informing today's national security, defense and anti-terrorism policy makers and practitioners.

It can provide an understanding of context, precedents, lessons learned, failed and successful approaches and how conflicts are concluded.

The Research Forum was a success and led to a conference in June 2007. The gathering brought together a diverse range of academics (both historians and non-historians) and practitioners from government and private enterprise. In addition to short presentations on current research topics, plenary sessions provided opportunities for all attendees to voice their views on a range of issues central to history, terrorism, and counter-terrorism.

An important dimension of these gatherings was that the majority of the participants (both academic and practitioner) were not trained historians (defined for this argument by the absence of formal postgraduate qualifications in history). The fact should have been less surprising than it was given that so few Australian historians have an active research interest in the history of terrorism (either in an international or Australian context) and given that for the overwhelming majority of those with these interests it is not their primary research area. Reflecting the broader international state of the field, when it has not been written by a journalist, terrorism history in Australia has tended to be written by scholars trained in politics and international relations.[13]

It was enlightening to sit, listen, and engage with non-historians passionately speaking about the place of history in terrorism studies and CT. They did great jobs in demonstrating the importance of history to how their discipline or practice engaged (or should engage) terrorism. One powerful example of this was in a talk given by Don Williams, a former Australian Army bomb technician and consulting practitioner. In his presentation, Williams showed an image of the old style globe bomb with burning fuse that most of the participants associated more closely with the cartoons of our childhood than with nineteenth century anarchists. He pointed out that the globe was a piece of "modified military ordinance"; in fact a cannonball altered for terrorist purposes. Many in the audience gasped or chuckled with hitherto unrealized recognition. It was so simple and obvious an observation; here was an IED (improvised explosive device). Williams then proceeded to make a number of practical connections between late nineteenth century anarchist terrorism and al Qaeda.[14]

In his simple but effective presentation, Williams showed how CT communities want and need history. With the stage set, the non-historian academics made similar calls. Academics trained in other disciplines should be able to call on historical studies rather than having to write them themselves before making use of them in their discipline or practice community. Historians, in turn, need people like Don Williams to ensure their work is well informed. To achieve their potential in terrorism studies, historians must reach out in the academy to other disciplines and beyond the academy to the practitioners.

As a result of these gatherings, we instigated the idea of working with a group of scholars and practitioners, historians and non-historians, to further explore and formalize the results of these conversations. The forum and conference had identified that work in Australia was coalescing around three distinct research areas that inform the distinct sections in this collection. The three areas are:

1. Methodological issues
2. International historical case studies, and
3. The Australian experience of terrorism

The collection commences with a section on methodological issues, and an important foundational chapter by a political scientist. Carl Thayer provides an overarching history of the field of terrorism studies that is a valuable anchor for the collection. It allows the reader to better contextualize the place of history in this research area. With the broad field mapped and problematized by Thayer, Lucy Resnyansky focuses her attention on the counter-terrorism community and the meta-discipline of the social sciences that is home to history. In an engaging second chapter of the collection, Resnyansky provides a powerful argument for why social science disciplines such as history must be engaged if proactive and constructive strategies aimed at the prevention of the threat of terrorism are to be realized. Excluding history or not understanding that it is more than a list of facts from the past can produce nothing but "counterproductive counter-terrorism."[15]

Building on the broad understandings of the field of terrorism studies and the needs of CT, I examine terrorism studies' persistent efforts at cross-disciplinary approaches and methodologies. Critiquing these earlier efforts I advocate that a "transdisciplinary" approach to terrorism studies offers the greatest methodological possibilities because it focuses on the "problem" and acknowledges the importance of disciplinary difference. The approach resonates with the most recent developments in teaching and learning in higher education, developments that insist that university graduates exit their studies with ways of thinking and performing informed by their discipline rather than an amorphous set of "generic skills." This realization is an important consideration for counter-terrorism agencies as they employ graduate recruits: transdisciplinarity, complemented by the signature pedagogies of higher education, should become the methodological approach of both the academic and the practitioner. History is but one discipline that will benefit from this reorientation.

The past, however, is not without its own baggage. In the fourth and final chapter in the methodological section, practitioner Brett Peppler provides a cautionary voice as he examines the dead hand of the past on counter-terrorism. His chapter suggests that within Western governments there are "intelligence pathologies" that are the products of mindsets and practices rooted in dated conceptions of terrorism. Having identified the problem Peppler goes on to propose a range of remedies.

As Thomas R. Moctaitis observed in his treatise on the New Terrorism, "much of what passes for the "new" terrorism has a long history."[16] Case studies remain an effective way in which history can be linked to and made meaningful for CT practitioners.[17] Such case studies can focus on past periods and events or they can historicize the present. The four contributions in this section concentrate on current issues and events within an international framework.

Anne Aly's paper explores the way terrorist organizations use the past to legitimize and support their activities, and how this past is often experienced in the "life-history" of prominent members of the organization's leadership. Using the life-history of Ayman al Zawahri as her example, Aly suggests that vital clues as to what should be expected from a terrorist organization can be gained from such case studies and that these insights are central to the creation of holistic approaches to counter terrorism.

Moving from the individual to the nation, Eamon Murphy provides a synthesis that helps the reader to understand Pakistan, one of the most important nations in the "war on terror." Murphy demonstrates how a historian with a solid knowledge of a nation's past, and an awareness of current intelligence needs, can provide foundational observations that contextualize the present. Murphy shows how history can be a crucial tool for background knowledge consolidation. Alexey Muraviev's chapter is a concise history of one of the more neglected theaters of al Qaeda's international operations. Muraviev's examination of Chechnya shows how history can provide a range of "lessons" for consideration.

The final chapter in this section demonstrates how history can play a role in prediction. The South Pacific is not a noted hotspot for religious terrorism but the weak or failing status of several states in Melanesia means it is part of the "arc of instability" to Australia's north. Examining the growth of Muslim communities in the recent past, with the aid of fieldwork, Scott Flower explores the history of, and potential for, religious terrorism in Melanesia.

Reflecting its place of genesis, the third and final section in the collection concentrates on the history of terrorism in Australia. The section opens with Sean Brawley and Ian Shaw musing on what a history of terrorism in Australia—an under-examined field—might look like, and highlights some of the hurdles to overcome in order to achieve a synthesized history of terrorism in Australia. The chapter is followed by another work of broad brush-strokes; Luke Howie examines the roles of discrimination and racism in the way the Australian people and their institutions respond to terrorism. Howie shows that historians and the secondary sources they produce are of vital significance to other scholars in the field but that non-historians, informed by the nature and priorities of their own discipline, will still make their own judgments on the historical evidence.

The third chapter in the section is an Australian case study. Drawing from his PhD thesis, Stuart Koschade—one of the new generation of terrorism scholars who completed their postgraduate studies within the field—provides an examination of the Croatian Revolutionary Brotherhood (HRB). The HRB was the largest terrorist organization ever to operate in Australia and its study is important to understanding the phenomena of terrorism within Australia.

In his study of the High Court of Australia and its responses to terrorism, Andrew Lynch provides not only a case history of the recent decisions of the High Court of Australia but also traces how members of the judiciary and lawmakers use or misuse (depending on your viewpoint) history as a tool in their deliberations. Lynch calls for Australian historians to do more of the heavy historical lifting to support law makers and the legal profession.

The Australian section concludes with a chapter by historian Wayne Reynolds that examines the impact of terrorism on Australian defense planning. Historical trends and assumptions about Australia's place in its region have been challenged but are ultimately reinforced in the new regional strategic environment that appeared after September 11. Reynolds' chapter clearly demonstrates that terrorism studies is not simply about terrorists.

The collection concludes with a short essay by Clive Williams. Williams attended and presented at the earlier research forums and was a part of these conversations. He provides a "critical friend" analysis of the chapters and the collection as a whole. For his overview, Williams was given only two instructions by the editor: remember the term "critical" and remember the term "friend." On behalf of the contributors I thank Clive for his efforts.

In introducing a multi-authored collection it is important to note that the viewpoints as expressed in the chapters are not necessarily those of the editor or other contributors. In this regard one should also recall Alexander Spencer's observation that "The concept of terrorism is one of the most disputed terms in the social sciences."[18] At no stage was an agreed definition sought out or agreed on by the contributors. Where a contributor has felt that definitional precision is important to their chapter they have offered their viewpoint.

The squabbling (quite petty and personal at times) around the emergence of "Critical Terrorism Studies" is another elephant in the room of terrorism studies, especially in Australia. Reflecting the aims and purpose of the RNSA, the application of history for counter-terrorism was a strong motivation behind the organization of the original research forum; though this was not necessarily the motivation behind the contributions of individual participants. In late 2006, no participant at the research forum was discussing the need for a "critical turn." The collection, however, is "critical" because, to borrow Jeroen Gunning's definition, it is "explicitly self-reflexive about assumptions, methodologies and the shortcomings of 'terrorism research.'"[19] This said, I still see enormous merit in engagement with practitioners in CT—a commitment reflected in the presence of practitioners as contributors in this volume. I reject the notion of some advocates of critical terrorism studies that any academic drawn into sharing their ideas with and within the CT industry will inevitably be compromised and have their academic freedom undermined. Of course such consequences are completely possible—the deterioration of the bureaucratic principle of "frank and fearless advice" in several Western nations since the beginning of the "war on terror" is proof enough of the danger—but the academic does his or her profession and nation a disservice if public service only brings compromise.

As with any publication there are many people who deserve thanks. First and foremost, I wish to thank the individual contributors. While it has been a long road, it has been a pleasant journey, thanks to the persistence and good humor of the contributors. This volume was a truly collective effort with many colleagues reading drafts of each other's papers and providing valuable feedback.

Not everyone who attended the original research forum and conference was able to further explore their ideas in this publication. They did nevertheless make some valuable contributions to the process that ensued. Special thanks to Ben Anwyl, Simon Adams and Mark Finnane who helped to make these gatherings a success. Without Athol Yates (RNSA Outreach Manager) and John Byron (Australian Academy of the Humanities Executive Director) none of us would have been in the same room to start the conversations.

My thanks also extend to the Convenor of the RNSA, Priyan Mendis. Priyan's support did not simply end with the research forum and conference. Through his good offices, the RNSA provided financial support to ensure the collection would be published. Chris Dixon was an enthusiastic supporter of the project and I thank him. In realizing the final publication I was greatly assisted in Sydney by Rebecca Sheehan and by Lucy Resnyansky's handy graphic conversions. A final acknowledgement must go to Anna Lawton and her colleagues at New Academia Press. They were quick to see the potential of the collection and their support has resulted in the handsome volume you are reading.

Notes

[1] For earlier examples see the essays in William G. Gutteridge, ed., *The New Terrorism* (London: Mansell, 1986); and Jonathan Harris, *The New Terrorism: Politics of Violence* (New York: Julian Messner, 1983).

[2] Walter Laqueur, *The New Terrorism: Fanaticism and the Arms of Mass Destruction* (New York: Oxford University Press, 2007), 7.

[3] Ian O. Lesser et al. *Countering the New Terrorism* (Santa Monica: Rand Corporation, 1999), 2.

[4] A sample of the academic and popular works include: Andrew Tan and Kumar Ramakrishna, eds., *The New Terrorism: Anatomy, Trends, and Counter-Strategies* (Singapore: Eastern Universities Press, 2002); Simon Reeve, *The New Jackals: Ramzi Yousef, Osama Bin Laden, and the Future of Terrorism* (Boston: Northeastern University Press, 2002); Charles W. Kegley, *The New Global Terrorism: Characteristics, Causes, Controls* (New York: Prentice Hall, 2002); Lee Clarke, ed., *Terrorism and Disaster: New Threats, New Ideas* (Oxford: Emerald, 2003); Doron Zimmermann, *The Transformation of Terrorism: The "New Terrorism," Impact Scalability, and the Dynamic of Reciprocal Threat Perception* (Zurich: Forschungsstelle für Sicherheitspolitik der ETH Zürich, 2003); Richard Pearlstein, *Fatal Future?: Transnational Terrorism and the New Global Disorder* (Austin: University of Texas Press, 2004); Stefan M. Aubrey, *The New Dimension of International Terrorism* (Zurich: vdf Hochschulverlag AG, 2004); D. P. Sharma, *The New Terrorism: Islamist International* (New Delhi: APH Publishing, 2005); John Robb, *Brave New War: The Next Stage of Terrorism and the End of Globalization* (New York: John Wiley and Sons, 2008).

[5] Immanuel Wallerstein, *World-System Analysis: An Introduction* (Durham: Duke University Press, 2004), ix.

[6] See Walter Laqueur, *No End To War: Terrorism in the Twenty-First Century* (London: Continuum, 2004), 7. For other examples of attempts both

within and outside of terrorism studies to historicize September 11, see David C. Rapoport, "The Fourth Wave: September 11 and the History of Terrorism," *Current History*, December (2001): 419-24; Niall Ferguson, "Clashing Civilizations or Mad Mullahs: The United States between Formal and Informal Empire," *The Age of Terror: America and the World after September 11*, ed. Strobe Talbott & Nayan Chanda (New York: Basic Books, 2001): 115-141; Celeb Carr, *The Lessons of Terror: A History of Warfare against Civilians* (New York: Random House, 2002); Andrew Sinclair, *An Anatomy of Terror: A History of Terrorism* (London: Macmillan, 2003); and Sean Anderson and Stephen Sloan, *Terrorism: Assassins to Zealots* (Lanham: Scarecrow Press, 2003).

The ahistorical predilection in terrorism studies and counter-terrorism had been observed for some time. John Bowyer-Bell saw this as a problem in the academic study of terrorism in 1977. In 1987, R. D. Crelinsten had observed the "ahistorical, linear, causal models which ignore the historical and comparative aspects of terrorism and focus selectively on individual actors, their characteristics, their tactics and their stated ideologies." Nearly twenty years later John Horgan suggested this "pitfall" was still a dominant paradigm. See Bowyer-Bell, "Trends on Terror: The Analysis of Political Violence," *World Politics* 29 (1977): 276-88; Crelinsten, "Terrorism as Political Communication: The Relationship Between the Controller and the Controlled," *Contemporary Research on Terrorism*, ed. P. Wilkinson and A. M. Stewart (Aberdeen: Aberdeen University Press, 1987), 3; and Horgan, *The Psychology of Terrorism* (London, Routledge, 2005), 27.

[7] Bruce Hoffman, "Rethinking Terrorism and Counter-Terrorism Since 9/11," *The New Era of Terrorism: Selected Readings*, ed. Gus Martin (Thousand Oaks: SAGE, 2004), 4. The suggestion that history was a "Grand Discipline" is Avishag Gordon's. See "Terrorism as an Academic Subject after 9/11," *Studies in Conflict and Terrorism*, 28/1 (2005): 45-59.

[8] James Jay Carafano and Marc Sauter, *Homeland Security: A Complete Guide to Understanding, Preventing and Surviving Terrorism* (New York, McGraw-Hill), 103.

[9] See Richard Jackson, *Writing the War on Terrorism: Language, Politics and Counter-Terrorism* (Manchester: Manchester University Press, 2005), 96. The "unique challenges" gave some governments—notably the US—a sense of license in the conduct of affairs that many have found troubling. See Jackson Nyamuya Maogoto, *Battling Terrorism: Legal Perspectives on the Use of Force and the War on Terror* (London: Ashgate, 2005), 5.

[10] Robert Hill, "Australia's Response to Terrorism," *Menzies Research Centre Australian Security in the* twenty-first *Century Seminar Series*, Parliament House Canberra, 25 May 2004, http://www.mrcltd.org.au/research/australian-security/Australia_Response_to_Terrorism.pdf (accessed 6/25/08).

[11] Everett L. Wheeler, "Terrorism and Military Theory: An Historical Perspective," *Terrorism Research and Public Policy*, ed. Clark McCauley (Routledge, 1991), 7.

[12] See the RNSA homepage http://www.secureaustralia.org/ (accessed 12/1/08).

[13] For examples see James Crown, *Australia: The Terrorist Connection* (Melbourne: Sun Books, 1986) and Jenny Hocking *Beyond Terrorism: The Development of the Australian Security State* (Sydney: UNSW Press, 1993).

[14] Don Williams, "The lessons from anarchists/nihilists and co-travellers of the late 19th and early 20th centuries," paper presented at "Lessons of the Past: Applications of History for Today's Threats," Canberra, June 14, 2007.

[15] The phrase is borrowed from Colin Flint's "Terrorism and Counter-Terrorism: Geographic Research Questions and Agendas," *The Professional Geographer*, 55/2 (2003): 161-169.

[16] Thomas R. Mockaitis, *The "New" Terrorism: Myths and Reality* (Westport: Greenwood, 2007), xii.

[17] A recent example is Robert J. Art and Louise Richardson, eds., *Democracy and Counterterrorism: Lessons from the Past* (Washington DC: US Institute of Peace Press, 2007).

[18] Alexander Spencer, "Questioning the Concept of 'New Terrorism,'" *Peace Conflict & Development*, Issue 8, January 2006, http://www.peacestudiesjournal.org.uk/docs/Feb%2006%20SPENCER%20version%202.pdf.

[19] Jeroen Gunning, "A Case for Critical Terrorism Studies?" *Government and Opposition*, 42/3 (2007): 363-64.

Part I

Methodological Issues

2
Terrorism Studies: The Dismal Science?

Carlyle A. Thayer

In the aftermath of the terrorist attacks on the United States on September 11, 2001, there has been an outpouring of academic publications on the phenomenon of political violence. According to Andrew Silke, "the five years since 9/11 have probably seen more books published on terrorism than appeared in the previous 50 years. Currently, one new book on terrorism is being published every six hours."[1] After the terrorist bombings in Bali in October 2002, there was a similar surge in publications on terrorism in Southeast Asia. A veritable cottage industry of terrorism experts emerged to offer commentary and analysis on Islamic terrorism and its global reach.[2] But a close scrutiny of these analyses and published writings reveals two disturbing insights. First, most authors were not experts on the countries they were commenting on, although a few could lay claim to being regional security specialists. Second, a close examination of their sources revealed a scant reference to any prior disciplinary body of knowledge related to political violence and terrorism. Most of the academic literature produced by terrorism experts writing about Southeast Asia, for example, was highly empirical and narrowly focused.[3]

The state of the scholarship prompted the author to explore "terrorism studies" as a field of inquiry to see what it could offer methodologically and theoretically to our understanding of political violence in contemporary Southeast Asia.[4] This chapter offers a preliminary report on the endeavor. It seeks to provide an assessment of the contemporary state of terrorism studies and its methodologies by addressing four basic questions: What is terrorism? Who are the terrorists? What are the causes of terrorism? What do terrorists seek to achieve?[5] The chapter also provides an overview of the state of terrorism studies based on a synthesis of several major literature reviews published at intervals over the last two decades. The starting point for this synthesis is Alex Schmid and Albert Jongman's classic survey of six thousand works published between 1968 and 1988.[6] The survey has been updated by incorporating literature reviews published a decade later by Walter Reich as well as more contemporary surveys published by Andrew Silke and Rhyll Valis, Yubin Yang and Hussein Abbass.[7] The chapter concludes with a brief discussion of the utility of history to contemporary terrorism studies and offers a modest proposal for future research.

What is terrorism?

The word *terrorism* is a relatively recent term.[8] It entered the English language as a result of the French Revolution of 1789. It referred specifically to actions of the Committee of Public Safety, as the revolutionary government was known. According to Bruce Hoffman, *régime de la terreur* (1793-94) had a positive connotation compared with its contemporary usage.[9] It was a method to educate the French people on how to govern themselves. Terrorism was deliberately and systematically organized by the state in order to create a better society. Terrorism was also viewed in positive terms by nineteenth century Russian anarchists. In one celebrated example, on 24 January 1878 Vera Zasulick unsuccessfully tried to assassinate a Russian police commander who abused political prisoners. She shot and only wounded her target. Zasulick threw down her weapon and proclaimed, "I am a terrorist, not a killer."[10] And, in a foretaste of later terrorist tactics, Zasulick used the court proceedings to put the Russian political system on trial.

According to Hoffman, terrorism took on a negative connotation in the 1930s and 1940s with the rise of Nazi Germany and Stalinist Russia. Hoffman argues that "terrorism" was now used "to describe the practices of mass repression employed by totalitarian states and their dictatorial leaders against their own citizens."[11]

During the era of decolonization, which began after the First World War, several groups fighting for self-determination actually described themselves as terrorist organizations.[12] But this soon changed. As decolonization quickened after the Second World War, colonial governments used the term terrorism to describe groups fighting for national liberation. Anti-colonial movements, on the other hand, preferred to label themselves freedom fighters. In other words, during the anti-colonial era terrorism regained its revolutionary connotation.[13]

In the modern period some writers have made a distinction between terrorists and guerrilla forces.[14] They argue that guerrillas openly carry their weapons and generally wear an identifying emblem or uniform that obliges a state to treat them as soldiers or at the very least *levée en masse*. Guerrilla movements aim to weaken or destroy their enemy's military forces as their main objective. In the modern era, terrorists, by contrast, observe none of these conventions and strike directly at civilian population in order to undermine their support for the state's armed forces. In these circumstances, some would argue, terrorists are in fact unlawful combatants and as such are not protected by the laws of war.

If the above paragraph appears contentious it is necessary to place its arguments in historical context. Ever since the League of Nations was established in 1920 the international community has been unable to reach agreement on the definition of terrorism. Note the following assessment offered by the Commonwealth of Australia in a 2004 white paper on terrorism:

> There is no internationally accepted definition of terrorism. Not even the United Nations has been able to achieve consensus on this contentious issue. The old adage that 'one man's freedom fighter is another man's terrorist' goes to the root of the ongoing debate. Individual states, therefore, have been compelled to develop their own definitions for the purposes of enacting legislation to counter the threat.[15]

After September 11, the United Nations Security Council adopted Resolution 1267 that made provision for the UN Monitoring

Group to maintain a consolidated list of entities and individuals that were part of or associated with the Taliban and al Qaeda. The UN proscribed two Southeast Asian groups: the Abu Sayyaf Group and Jemaah Islamiyah (JI). All members of the UN were obliged to comply with this resolution. But implementation has been uneven. Indonesia, for example, has not outlawed JI.

Kofi Annan, the then UN Secretary General, proposed that the United Nations adopt an anti-terrorism convention that would define terrorism as any act that is "intended to cause death or serious bodily harm to civilians or non-combatants to intimidate a community, government or international organization."[16] As of this writing, (January 2009), the UN has been unable to reach a definition of terrorism acceptable to the majority of the international community.

Why this is so may be illustrated with reference to the Organisation of The Islamic Conference (OIC). The fifty-seven member OIC met in Kuala Lumpur in 2002. The host, Prime Minister Mahathir, attempted to get the meeting to condemn the use of suicide bombers to kill innocent civilians. After much debate, the OIC Foreign Ministers adopted the following declaration:

> We reiterate...the legitimacy of resistance to foreign aggression and the struggle of peoples under colonial or alien domination and foreign occupation for national liberation and self-determination. In this context, we underline the urgency for an internationally agreed definition of terrorism, *which differentiates such legitimate struggles from acts of terrorism* [emphasis added].
> We reject any attempt to link Islam and Muslims to terrorism as terrorism has no association with any religion, civilization or nationality;
> We unequivocally condemn acts of international terrorism in all its forms and manifestations, including state terrorism, irrespective of motives, perpetrators and victims as terrorism poses a serious threat to international peace and security and is a grave violation of human rights.[17]

Even the United States government cannot agree on a single defini-tion of terrorism.[18] At last count, its various departments and agen-cies employed nineteen separate definitions. President George W. Bush added yet another definition when he issued Executive Or-der 13224 (September 23, 2001) in the wake of 9/11. Each definition reflects the priorities and interests of the agency concerned. The Department of State uses the definition of terrorism found in Title 22 of the US Code. This definition privileges the political aspects of terrorism but makes no reference to its psychological dimensions. By contrast, the FBI's definition stresses the role of intimidation and coercion in terrorism and also recognizes the social and political objectives of terrorist groups.

Not surprisingly, the Department of Homeland Security's defi-nition includes attacks on critical infrastructure—including mass destruction—as terrorist acts. The definition of terrorism employed by the Department of Defense does not include deliberate targeting of individuals for assassination and does not distinguish between attacks on combatant and non-combatant military personnel.

Alex Schmid, head of the UN's Terrorism Prevention Branch, argues that much of what is currently described as terrorism is in reality a legitimate act of war. Schmid then suggests that, since there is general international agreement on what constitutes war crimes, a workable definition of a terrorist could be build around a definition of war criminal.[19]

Who are the terrorists?

There are at least two starting points for the study of contemporary terrorism. The first commences in the late nineteenth century with the emergence of Russian and European anarchists. The second starting point is dated 1968 when the Palestine Liberation Organi-zation (PLO) began hijacking aircraft.[20] It is worth noting, however, that modern terrorism has its roots in ancient times. The precursors to modern terrorism date to the first century when religion-inspired groups such as the Zealots and Siciari (Judaism), Thugi (Hinduism) and the Assassins (Islam).[21]

David C. Rapoport posits that there have been four great waves of terrorism.[22] The first was the anarchist wave in the nineteenth century. The second was the anti-colonial wave lasting from the 1920s to the 1960s. The third was the so-called New Left wave of the 1960s to 1970s. And finally, the religious wave which dates to the Iranian revolution of 1979. Generally, terrorist groups in the first three waves lasted for a generation. There were exceptions, however, and there was some overlap between each wave. The essential point is that terrorism did not begin with al Qaeda but is deeply rooted in modern culture.[23] Each wave has produced its own theorists who have published their views in manuals and books that have become widely available around the globe.

The anarchist wave was marked by the rise of secularism to displace religion as the main motivating force. The anarchists proudly described themselves as terrorists and traced their lineage back to the French Revolution. Terrorism during the first wave was a strategy in which campaigns of targeted assassinations were carried out against prominent individuals, primarily members of the monarchy. So many assassinations were carried out in the 1890s that Rapoport calls this period the "Golden Age of Assassination."

The anarchist wave began in Russia and then spread to Western Europe, the Balkans, and India. Terrorists of this period employed martyrdom to publicize their cause. Assassinations were carried out at close range, and after they were carried out the terrorist stood his or her ground expecting to be killed immediately or taken into custody, and then tried and executed. In court the individual terrorist took personal responsibility for his or her action and used the legal proceedings to put the regime on trial. In the case of Vera Zasulick noted above, for example, she turned her trial into an indictment of the abusive police chief and was let off. A terrorist who was killed at the scene of the crime or later executed achieved the status of martyr or hero.

Terrorism during the anarchist wave was an international phenomenon and a product of globalization. The tactic of martyrdom was adopted by virtually all other anarchist groups during this period. Anarchist groups trained and cooperated with each other in global networks. Russian anarchism spread to the Russian diaspora communities. Russian anarchists also provided training to Armenians and Poles. The transnational character of the anarchist movement is illustrated by The Terrorist Brigade in 1905, which planned its operations in Switzerland, launched attacks from Finland, used arms acquired from an Armenian group that had been trained by Russian anarchists, and was offered funds by the Japanese to be laundered through wealthy Americans.[24]

Why did the first wave occur when it did? Rapoport points to two critical factors.[25] The first factor was the revolution in communications and transportation. During the final quarter of the nineteenth century, public communication was made possible by the daily mass circulation newspapers, the telegraph and the railroads. Terrorist events in one country were quickly reported around the world. Mass transportation enabled large scale migration that resulted in the creation of diaspora communities. The politics of the old country were now inextricably linked with the politics of the new country.

The second critical factor enabling the first wave of terrorism was the development of a doctrine or culture of terrorism. Russian anarchists, such as Sergei Nechaev and Peter Kropotkin, put their strategies, tactics and techniques into print. Kropotkin popularized the expression that terrorism was "propaganda by deed." Sergei Nechaev, in his *Revolutionary Catechism,* argued that terror was the quickest and most effective means to destroy conventions and polarize society.[26]

Terrorism was also designed to force a government to respond in ways that undermined its authority. When society was polarized and the government was left without moral authority, revolution would follow. In sum, Russian anarchists provided the intellectual justification for a strategy of terror that could be transmitted from one terrorist group to another. Each group could modify this strategy to its local circumstances. The written word could also be passed down to future generations.

The second great wave of terrorism began in the 1920s and was motivated by anti-colonialism and the desire to establish new nation-states. Terrorist groups emerged in Israel, Cyprus, Algeria and Ireland and relied on their diaspora communities for support. Terrorism as a strategy was most successful in this period. Terrorist groups even appealed to the League of Nations for support. The anti-colonial struggles following the Second World War also formed part of the second wave.

The third wave of terrorism was generated in the 1960s in reaction to the Vietnam War and the Arab defeat by the Israelis in the Six Day War. New Left groups appeared in the Middle East, Europe, the United States and Latin America. This was the era of hijacking for publicity and kidnapping, and hostage-taking for finance. New Left groups received direct support from sympathetic states that provided funding and safe havens. New Left groups cooperated and trained with each other on an unprecedented scale, even launching joint operations. Foreign embassies were often a target. Most New Left groups were successfully repressed by the state. The Palestine Liberation Organization was a major exception and eventually received special status at the United Nations.

The fourth wave has been termed the "religious wave" because of the importance of religious ideology as a motivating factor for the current generation of terrorist groups. The start of this wave is dated 1979 when two key developments occurred—the Iranian revolution and the Soviet invasion of Afghanistan. But other events have played roles in sustaining the religious wave, including the Israeli invasion of Lebanon in the 1980s, the first Gulf War, the coalition attack on Afghanistan and the invasion of Iraq. The forth wave is characterized by the decline in the number of active terrorist groups and by a rise in the lethality of terrorist violence. The hallmark of the Religious Wave is the suicide bomber.

What are the causes of terrorism?

This is a complex and controversial question that has been explored at multiple levels—individual, group or organization, state, societal and transnational or international system—by a variety of disciplines: criminology, psychology, forensic psychiatry, anthropology, sociology, history, and political science.[27] There is no single cause of terrorism. Richardson argues that "[t]he emergence of terrorism requires a lethal cocktail with three ingredients: a disaffected individual, an enabling group, and a legitimating ideology."[28] This section does not provide a definitive answer on terrorism's causes, but instead sketches out the major methodological approaches necessary to understanding them.

At the individual level psychologists have attempted to identify specific psychological factors that induce a person to become a terrorist.[29] A variant of this approach is known as profiling. In this approach psychologists have attempted to identify a number of factors that individual terrorists have in common in order to create a profile of the standard terrorist personality. These approaches have not been particularly rewarding. As Andrew Silke observed, "[a]fter 30 years of research all that psychologists can safely say of terrorists is that their outstanding characteristic is their normality."[30] A third approach involves analyzing the influence of situational or environmental factors on the individual. A fourth approach focuses on the distinctive characteristics of leaders and followers.[31]

At the group level, social scientists have focused on various aspects of group dynamics as an explanation for the causes of terrorism.[32] One focus is concerned with the role of ideology and indoctrination. Another approach analyzes group identity and how it may be created by peer pressure and mutual reinforcement. This has led to a promising area of research known as social network theory.[33] Finally, social scientists have studied whether terrorist groups are process driven or mission driven.[34]

The third level focuses on the state as the unit of analysis.[35] Here historians and political scientists have studied the state as a terrorist actor through domestic repression. There are two variants of this approach. The first focuses on state sponsorship of terrorism beyond its borders. The second variant considers whether terrorism is caused by the foreign policies of a particular state's (such as the United States) support for repressive non-democratic regimes. Still another approach considers whether terrorism is caused or enabled by weak or failed states.

The fourth level of analysis considers whether some aspect of the international system can explain terrorism.[36] Social scientists have focused on such issues as the clash of civilizations and (religious) ideologies; terrorism as an international movement or ideology; and the impact of globalization.[37] Terrorism is not exclusively a response to external conditions; it is the result of strategic decisions by political actors. Left-wing, right-wing, ethno-nationalist, separatist, and religious terrorist groups are all driven by political motives and oriented towards political ends. In sum, terrorism is fundamentally a political phenomenon.

What do terrorists seek to achieve?

Harvard Professor Louise Richardson has provided a succinct answer to this question. Terrorists, she writes, seek the three Rs — revenge, renown, and reaction.[38] All three objectives are aimed at
intimidating or frightening a target audience, gaining supporters,
and coercing opponents. Richardson argues that "[t]he goals of all
terrorist groups fall into one of two categories: temporal and trans-
formational."[39] Temporal goals are political and can be met without
requiring the overthrow of the existing political system. Transfor-
mational goals, on the other hand, are not amenable to negotiation
and their attainment requires the complete overthrow of the state
system.

First, terrorists seek revenge for real or imagined grievances.
Second, terrorists seek renown in the form of individual glory
(on earth or in heaven) and publicity for their cause. As Margaret
Thatcher once put it, publicity is the oxygen of terrorism.[40] In other
words, terrorism is aimed at gaining publicity in order to recruit
more activists, recognition from the other side for perceived grievances, and attention from third parties who might exert pressure
on the other side. Finally, terrorists seek reaction from the other
side. This may lead to the achievement of their demands. Or terrorism could provoke a counter-productive response by the state that
leads to increased support for terrorists from society.

Richardson distinguishes between demonstrative and destructive terrorism. The former may be characterized as political theater
plus violence, while the latter seeks to inflict real harm or damage.
Suicide bombing represents a special case because it is difficult if
not impossible to deter. The main tactics used by suicide bombers
are the suicide vest and car bomb. Suicide bombing is also highly
lethal because its objective is to kill as many persons as possible
as witnessed in 9/11 when terrorists flew two jet airliners into the
World Trade Center in New York.[41]

Modern suicide terrorism is a product of conflict in Lebanon
in the early 1980s.[42] There are two contending explanations for this
phenomenon that may be characterized as the sacred and the secular. The sacred view argues that what we call "suicide bombing" is
in fact an altruistic act of religious martyrdom carried out because

of a sense of duty to the community. The latter view argues that suicide bombing is rationally motivated and has a strategic logic.

Robert Pape is the foremost proponent for the second thesis.[43] He analyzed 315 suicide terrorist attacks that were carried out globally between 1980 and 2003. Pape determined that over ninety-five percent of these attacks formed part of eighteen separate organized coercive campaigns. They were aimed at forcing a foreign democratic state to give up its occupation of the terrorists' homeland. The Tamil Tigers conducted the most prominent coercive campaigns and executed 171 attacks. Pape found that religious differences between the occupier and the indigenous people served to intensify conflict. However, he concluded that suicide terrorist campaigns were primarily motivated by nationalism and not religion.

In order for a campaign of suicide attacks to be successful it is necessary for three levels to be integrated (see Chart 1 below). At the individual level the suicide bomber has to be motivated by altruism. At societal level, there must be mass support for suicide bombing. And finally, these factors must have coercive impact at the strategic level. When all three conditions are met the strategy of suicide attacks pays off because it works.

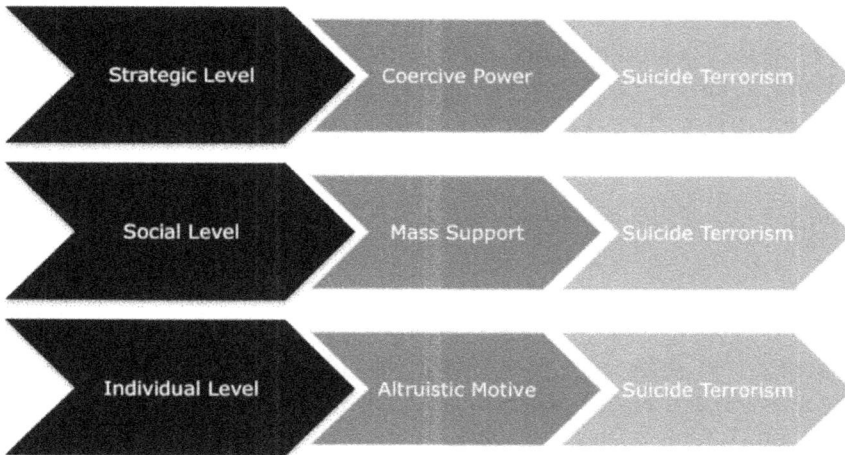

Chart 1. Why Terrorism Works[44]

The argument that suicide terrorism works has recently been contested by Max Abrahms who is critical of Pape's methodology.[45] Abrahms argues that Pape's sample of terrorist campaigns was too small and was based on single case studies or a few well-known terrorist victories (Hezbollah, Tamil Tigers and Palestinian terrorist groups). Ten of the campaigns that Pape analyzed were directed against the same three countries—Israel, Sri Lanka and Turkey. Six were directed against Israel alone.

Abrahms argues that in order to determine whether or not terrorist suicide bombing campaigns are successful, it is necessary to analyze a larger number of these campaigns. And it is essential to specify the antecedent conditions for terrorism to work. To increase the sample size, Abrahms gathered data on all groups listed as foreign terrorist organizations by the US Department of State in its annual reports from 2001. This resulted in a sample of twenty-eight groups. Next, Abrahms identified forty-two separate objectives espoused by these groups. How successful were they in attaining their objectives?

Abrahms discovered that terrorist groups whose attacks on civilian targets outnumbered attacks on military targets systematically failed to achieve their objectives. Their success rate was only seven percent. Target selection was the key variable in determining success. In other words, terrorist groups rarely achieved their policy objectives and their poor success rate was inherent in the tactic of terrorism itself. Contrary to Pape's findings, Abrahams concluded that terrorism does not work.

Overview of terrorism studies

This section presents a snapshot of the state of contemporary terrorism studies by bringing together data from several surveys.[46] Terrorism studies is an extremely broad field of inquiry because there is no general agreement on what constitutes terrorism and because the field does not have an agreed conceptual framework.[47] For example, Schmid and Jongman identified one hundred and nine different academic definitions in their classic study.[48] Two decades later this situation has not improved; the international community still remains divided and the number of definitions of terrorism has also increased.

Does the lack of a definition matter? According to Andrew Silke:

> An agreed definition allows the research world to develop shared methods, approaches, benchmarks and appropriate topics for study. Without a definition, the focus of the field is scattered and fragmented, and an unrealistic range of activities, phenomena and actors have been labeled as terrorist.[49]

Even if there is agreement on the definition of what constitutes terrorism the application of the definition to real life cases is not without difficulty. For example, Australia, the United States and the United Kingdom maintain lists of proscribed terrorist groups. When these lists are compared, the US and UK only agree on thirteen organizations. The US lists fifteen groups not found on the UK list, while the UK list contains eight groups not on the US list. Australia proscribes nineteen terrorist groups two of which are not on the UK list and four of which are not on the US list.[50]

Avishag Gordon argues, however, that differing definitions may signal new vitality in the field of terrorism studies:

> With regard to the study of terrorism, in this process the changing definition of the term plays an important role, which actually signifies a new life cycle each time a new definition arises, since this new definition brings into the field new events, new realities and new research projects and analyses.[51]

The field of terrorism studies is both multidisciplinary and interdisciplinary. But a review of the terrorism studies literature reveals that it is a highly compartmentalized field characterized by weak research methods, and influenced by government agendas and media simplification.[52] Schmid and Jongman, after reviewing 6,000 academic publications issued in the period from 1968–88, concluded that few researchers tried to uncover in an empirical manner the patterns and relationships that exist in terrorist operations. Most of the studies focused on specific events and employed journalistic analysis and in a few cases descriptive statistics. Researchers shied away from the use of inferential statistics. Schmid and Jongman concluded that terrorism studies research scored poorly in terms of validity and objectivity. Silke noted the very heavy reliance on literature review. He estimated that in the 1990s, sixty-eight percent of the research essentially took the form of a literature review and did not add any new data to the field.[53]

Terrorism studies has been heavily influenced by the policy concerns and agenda of the government in power.[54] In these instances research has been carried out solely for the benefit and interest of government. Important research questions, therefore, have been systematically ignored.[55] Silke argues, for example, that there has been an imbalance in the study of terrorist tactics because of an inordinate preoccupation with Chemical, Biological, Radiological and Nuclear (CBRN) weapons. He estimates that prior to 9/11 "nearly six times more research was being conducted on CBRN terrorist tactics than on suicide tactics."[56]

Terrorism studies in general also suffers from the media's need to simplify matters in order to convey its messages. The media reports on what it determines to be news. Some terrorist organizations are ignored while others are reported on in great detail. For example, a survey of media reporting for the decade prior to 9/11 reveals that the media gave overwhelming coverage to the Provisional Irish Republican Army (IRA). Yet al Qaeda did not even make it to the list of the top twenty terrorist groups covered by the media even though its existence was known from at least 1992.[57]

By comparing data compiled prior to 9/11 with data collected in the five years since 9/11, the following sections in turn will examine: the growth in terrorism literature; the disciplines which contribute to terrorism studies; changes in disciplinary output over time; the location of research on terrorism studies; the countries of concern, and the terrorist groups studied.

There has been a considerable growth in social science publications on terrorism over past four decades, but the 1970s was the take-off decade for terrorism studies. There were six core journals published then. The trend continued into the 1980s, which is when the field of terrorism studies stabilized in terms of the number of journals that specialized in the area.[58]

Gordon measured the growth in terrorism literature by counting the number of articles and papers published in forty-two journals identified as belonging to the field between 1987 and 2001.[59] Six disciplinary areas dominated, with "peace studies" at the top of the list, followed by mass communications, psychology, "terrorism studies," comparative politics, and education.

Another survey sought to compare how fast terrorism studies was growing in various disciplines by comparing the publication output by discipline in 1990–94 with 1995–99.[60] These figures show that the fastest growing disciplines for research and publication on terrorism prior to 9/11 were anthropology, history, sociology and psychology. The combined average growth for the six disciplines was 234 percent. Although there was a considerable knowledge growth in terrorism studies publications tended to spill over into non-specialist journals and became dispersed and uncoordinated.[61]

Who writes on terrorism?

Andrew Silke argues that the best way to identify trends in terrorism studies research is to examine the peer reviewed literature published by active researchers. He notes that this is an increasingly difficult task given the growth of terrorism studies in recent years with articles on terrorism appearing in hundreds of academic journals. Silke limits his database to two journals—*Studies in Conflict and Terrorism* and *Terrorism and Political Violence*—which he argues "can be regarded as providing a reasonably balanced impression of the research activity and interests in the field."[62] Data was taken covering the period from 1990 to October 2006.

Silke recognizes that "it would be a mistake to assume that all of the key researchers publish in these journals or that the journals reliably represent the nature of most research on the subject."[63] Having entered this caveat, Silke notes that surveys which have included other journals reveal that articles on terrorism represent between one and three percent of all articles published.

He concludes: "the essential point is that it is extremely difficult to be truly representative in reviewing an interdisciplinary area such as terrorism studies. The approach adopted here is to review only those journals which publish primarily and consistently on terrorism...."[64]

In order to determine their disciplinary backgrounds, Silke surveyed the authors' biographic notes for all articles published in *Studies in Conflict and Terrorism* and *Terrorism and Political Violence,* for the period from 1990 to 1999.[65] His survey identified 490 articles written by 403 individual authors. The average rate of publication was 1.2 articles over the decade with 83 percent of all articles being submitted by first timers.

As the data in Table 1 shows, terrorism studies is dominated by political scientists. It also significant to note that of those working in terrorism studies, government officials constitute the second largest group including politicians, ambassadors, senior civil servants, and internal analysts.

Background	Number of Articles	Percent
Political Science	218	48.6
Government	43	9.6
Consultants	27	6.0
Sociology	26	5.8
Psychology	24	5.4
History	19	4.2
Military	15	3.3
Criminology	13	2.9
Lawyers	10	2.2
Law Enforcement	9	2.0
Academic Law	8	1.8
Economists	7	1.6
Religious Studies	7	1.6
Journalism	5	1.1
Anthropology	4	1.0
Media Studies	4	1.0
Librarian Studies	2	0.5
Medical	2	0.5
Other not classified	19	1.3

Table 1. Who Writes on Terrorism, 1990–99[66]

Prior to 9/11 research on terrorism was rarely conducted by teams of collaborators. Over ninety percent of the published work in terrorism studies was produced by a single researcher working alone. Following 9/11 collaborative work has more than doubled, but terrorism studies lags behind allied disciplines such as forensic psychology and criminology.[67]

Prior to 9/11, terrorism studies suffered both from a chronic lack of researchers in general and from a lack of researchers who took terrorism studies as their main research interest. A 1990 survey revealed that "terrorism studies had 40 percent fewer authors contributing to articles compared to fields such as criminology."[68] Since 9/11 there has been an obvious influx of researchers into terrorism studies but it is too early to tell whether "this growth will be sustained…over the coming decade."[69]

Where are researchers working on terrorism studies based? Silke's survey revealed that seventy-three percent were based in just two countries, the United States and United Kingdom. Nearly three

Country	%
United States	14.9
Northern Ireland	12.3
Israel	7.7
Italy	4.7
United Kingdom	3.8
India	3.8
Russia	3.0
South Africa	2.6
Germany, Spain, Sri Lanka	2.1
Cambodia, Canada, France	1.7

Table 2. Countries of Focus by Terrorism Studies Specialists, 1990-99[71]

and a half times as many terrorism researchers resided in the US as the UK. Seventeen percent of terrorism researchers were based in five countries: Israel, Canada, Australia, Republic of Ireland and the Netherlands.[70]

What are the main countries of focus and what terrorist groups receive the most attention? This data is set out in Tables 2 and 3.

Group	Percent
Provisional IRA	12.1
US militias	7.7
Branch Dravidians, Loyalists (Northern Ireland)	5.5 each
Neo-Nazis, PLO, Red Brigades	4.4 each
Hezbollah, Shining Path	3.3 each
Action Directé, Aum Shinrikyo, Earth First, ETA, FLQ, JDL, Khmer Rouge, Militant Islam, Red Army Faction, Revolutionary Organization November 17, FLN	2.2 each
Others	20.9

Table 3. Major Groups Studied by Terrorism Specialists, 1990-99[72]

One surprising finding revealed in Table 3 is "how little research was focused on al Qaeda in the ten years prior to 9/11."[73] Yet during this period al Qaeda was quickly gaining notoriety for a series of high profile attacks such as the 1998 bombings of US Embassies in Africa and the 2000 bombing of the *USS Cole*. This situation changed dramatically after 9/11 when one in seven articles in the core terrorism studies journals was devoted to al Qaeda. Nonetheless, there are continuities from the past that deserve mention (see Chart 2). The Irish Republican Army was the most studied terrorist group prior to 9/11, and it attracted slightly more attention after 9/11 compared to the 1990s. More attention has been devoted to Hezbollah and the Earth Liberation Front after 9/11. But the most prominent development has been the exponential growth in research on Islamist terrorist groups. According to Silke, "since 9/11, however, Islamist terrorism has completely dominated the field. Nearly sixty-three percent of the literature is on this subject."[74]

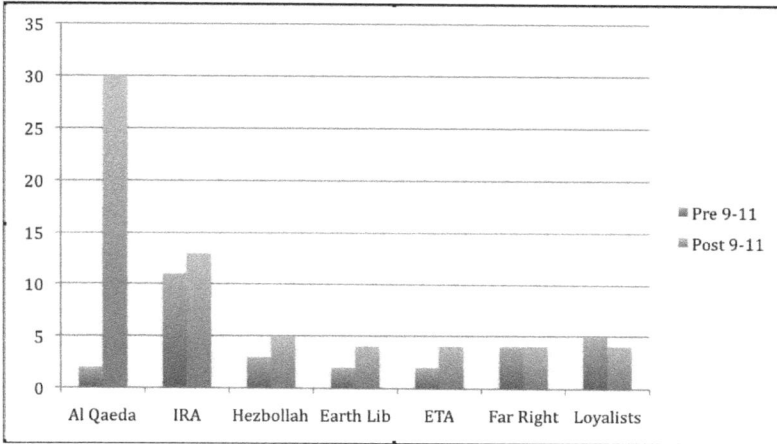

Chart 2. Shift in Research Focus on Terrorist Groups. Pre-9/11 and Post-9/11[75]

The following section discusses the methodology of terrorism research, once again drawing on data derived from Silke's survey of articles published in *Terrorism and Political Violence* and *Studies in Conflict and Terrorism*.[76] To place this discussion in context it is worth referring to the conclusions reached by Schmid and Jongman in their mammoth review of the state of terrorism studies in the 1980s. They argue, "[m]uch of the writing in the crucial areas of terrorism research…is impressionistic, superficial, and at the same time often also pretentious, venturing far-reaching generalizations on the basis of episodal evidence."[77] They further concluded, "there are probably few areas in the social science literature on which so much is written on the basis of so little research" and they estimated "as much as 80 per cent of the literature is not research-based in any rigorous sense; instead, it is too often narrative, condemnatory and prescriptive."[78] A review of the literature on terrorism studies published sixteen years later, concluded "surprisingly little research work of scientific merit has been conducted on the perpetrators of terrorist violence. The activities of terrorist groups, and the nature of their membership, have by and large been studiously ignored by social scientists."[79]

Chart 3 provides information on how terrorism specialists gather their raw data. Chart 4 illustrates how terrorism specialists analyze their data. Chart 5 provides a methodological comparison between terrorism studies and allied disciplines. Collectively, these three tables indicate the limited range of methodologies that dominate research on terrorism.

Chart 3 reveals that secondary sources are the most important source of data consulted by terrorism specialists. Interviews are the second most important source of data. Of all the journal articles reviewed by Silke in his survey, only twenty-two percent relied on interviews. But in half of these cases interviews represented only a minor feature and contributed to no more than four percent of information cited in the articles. Only one percent of the articles that relied on interviews gathered data through systematic and

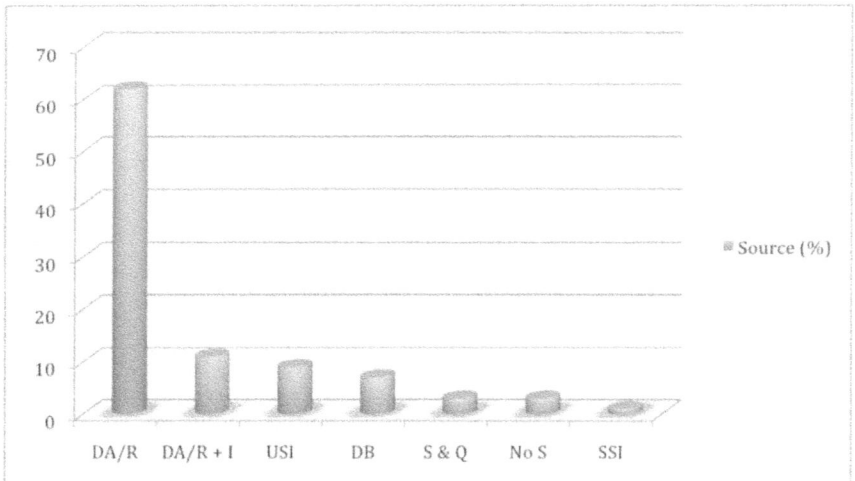

Chart 3. The Sources of Raw Data for Terrorism Studies[80]

Legend: DA/R—documentary analysis/review; DA/R + I—documentary analysis/review plus interviews (<5%); USI—unstructured non-systematic interviews; DB—databases; S & Q—surveys and questionnaires; No S—No sources; SSI—Structured Systematic Interviews.

structured interviews. Ninety-seven percent of interviews in terrorism research were opportunity sampling. Finally, six percent of the articles published on terrorism provided no indication of the sources used in their preparation.

Statistical analysis is important for determining which factors are important and which are not in analyzing complex phenomena. There are two kinds of statistics, descriptive and inferential. Descriptive statistics organize data and summarize it in a meaningful way. Inferential statistics interpret patterns in the data and introduce the crucial element of control to compensate for weak data collection methods. In psychology, for example, experimental design randomly assigns research subjects to experimental and control groups in order to study the impact of various factors on the dependent variable.

Chart 4 provides data on the use of descriptive and inferential statistics by terrorism specialists in their published research. The chart also indicates changes in the use of statistics over a fifteen-year time period beginning in 1995. The data indicate a slight rise in the use of inferential statistics over this period and a drop in the use of descriptive statistics. The vast bulk of published research—eighty percent in 2000—did not rely on statistics to interpret primary data. This leads to the conclusion that terrorism studies researchers relied on weaker uncontrolled data gathering methods and that very little effort has been made to make their methodology more rigorous in the years prior to 9/11.[81]

Prior to 9/11, approximately nineteen percent of the articles surveyed by Silke included either descriptive or inferential statistics.[82] In the five years after 9/11, this situation improved with 28 percent of articles using statistics (see Chart 5). There was a marked increase in the use of inferential statistics but this was from a low base (from 3 percent prior to 9/11 to 10 percent after 9/11). Silke makes the point that he "is not arguing that statistical analysis should be a feature of *every* research study on terrorism… Statistics alone are not the way forward, but neither is avoiding their use to the degree that terrorism research community currently does."[83]

Chart 6 provides an expanded context for assessing the use of statistical methods by terrorism studies researchers with researchers in two allied disciplines, criminology and forensic psychology.[86]

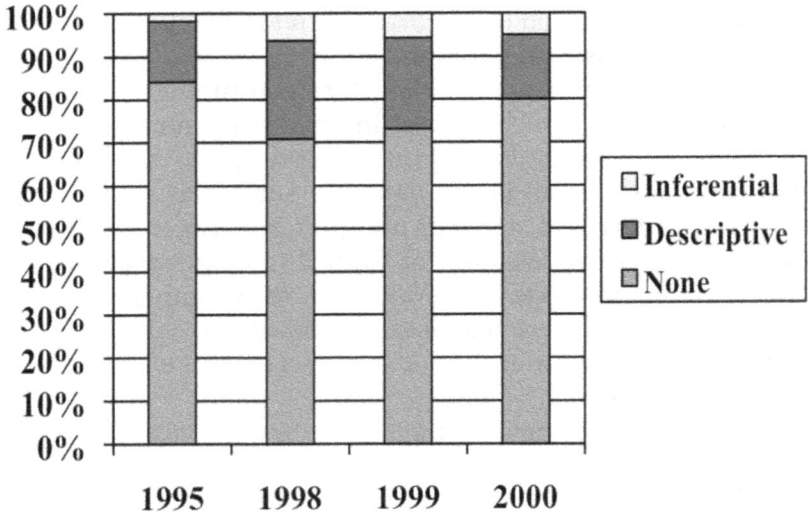

Chart 4. Use of Statistical Analysis by Terrorism Specialists, 1995-2000[84]

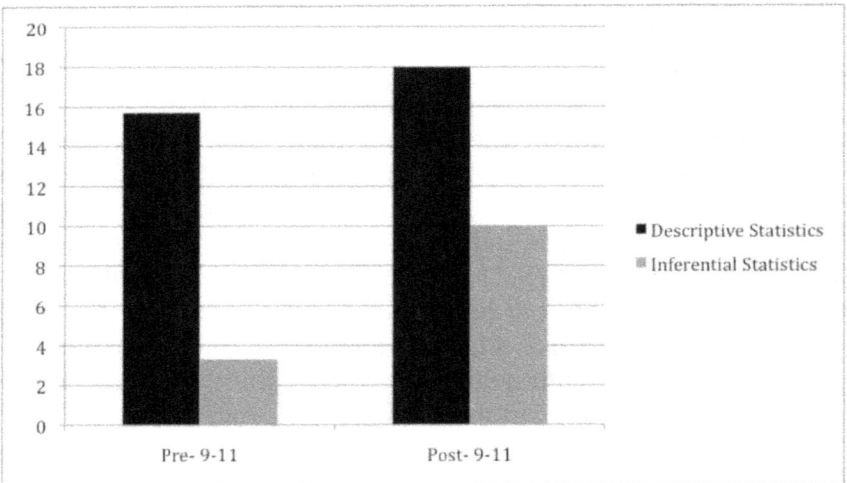

Chart 5. The Use of Statistical Analysis Pre-9/11 and Post-9/11[85]

Terrorism studies shares much in common with criminology and forensic psychology in terms of difficult research populations, real world relevance and human suffering and injustice. But terrorism studies compares poorly with these two allied disciplines. Chart 6 displays data gathered from research papers published in the major terrorism journals over the period 1995–99. Just three percent of published research papers by terrorism specialists involved the use of inferential analysis. This compares to eighty-six percent published by forensic psychologists. At least sixty percent of papers published by criminologists contained some form of statistical analysis with inferential statistics accounting for the majority of analysis. By contrast, terrorism studies specialists rarely incorporated any form of statistical analysis and when statistics were used they were five times more likely to be descriptive statistics.

Terrorism studies today suffer from five main weaknesses. First, terrorism studies rests on a weak methodological foundation. According to one survey, "[t]here is a heavy reliance on qualitative and journalistic approaches which lack the validity and reliability generally expected within mainstream social science research."[88]

Second, terrorism studies is overly dependent on secondary sources and rarely makes use of critical languages.[89] According to

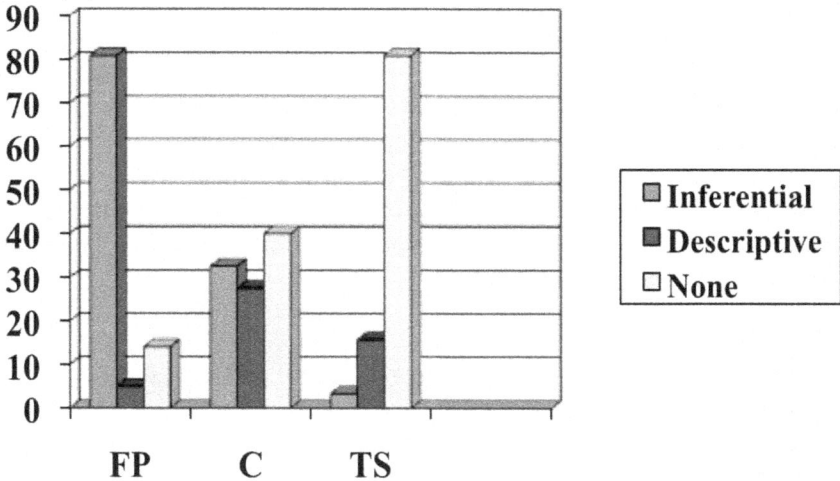

Chart 6. Use of Statistics by Discipline, 1995-99[87]
Legend: C=criminology; FP=forensic psychology; TS=terrorismo studies.

one study, over eighty percent of all research on terrorism is based on English language secondary sources.[90] Data is gathered either solely or primarily from books, journals, or other published documents.

Third, terrorism studies is similarly overly dependent on and uncritical of media reports and media-derived databases. There is little critical reflection on the accuracy, bias and audience context of news reports especially from outside the country of the author's residence.[91] Databases derived from these sources do not control for factual and technical errors and bias arising from ownership, editorial interference, compression of news stories, and journalistic inexperience. Foreign news reports, especially when translated, carry embedded norms, jokes, deliberate mistakes, and irony.

There is also another distortion, events databases lead researchers to focus on the "who, when and where of terrorist activity" at the expense of exploring issues related to the "why and how" of terrorist events.[92] When using media sources or databases derived from media reporting, researchers must share a common frame of reference or serious misinterpretations of these sources can arise.

Fourth, terrorism studies is dominated by "integrators of the literature" and transients. The information produced by most researchers is not substantively new data or knowledge but reworked old material. According to one survey, only twenty percent of articles published on terrorism provide substantially new knowledge that was previously unavailable.[93] Over ninety percent of research studies are planned, conducted and written by just one person working alone.

On the basis of the forgoing analysis it would appear that terrorism studies is indeed the dismal science and still remains at the pre-experimental research design stage. In 2004 Andrew Silke offered this damning evaluation:

> Ultimately terrorism research is not in a healthy state. It exists on a diet of fast-food research: quick, cheap, ready-to-hand and nutritionally dubious. The result of a reluctance to move away from the limited methodologies and levels of analysis of the past is that while the field may appear to be relatively active and energetic, growth in key areas remains stunted and halting.[94]

Bringing history back in

Political scientists who generally employ what might be termed a descriptive-analytic framework dominate terrorism studies. This generates a lot of empirical data on specific case studies. Because political scientists rely so heavily on secondary English-language sources, media reports and media-derived data bases, many of the studies are contemporary and include a heavy focus on policy-related matters. Terrorism studies, especially the literature dealing with terrorism in Southeast Asia, lacks an historical frame of reference.[95] New-timers to the field of terrorism studies reinvent the terrorist wheel as they seek to analyze al Qaeda and its regional networks. Silke provided the telling evaluation that "very little research explores past terrorist conflicts. Before 9/11, only one article in 26 looked at historical conflicts. Since 9/11, interest in historical cases has collapsed and now only one article in 46 is focused away from current events."[96]

As the above discussion on the four waves of terrorism indicates, there are many parallels to be made across the four waves. For example, terrorist groups historically have relied on support from diaspora communities. Terrorist groups have developed distinct strategies and doctrines that other terrorist groups have copied and modified (e.g., suicide bombing initiated by the Tamil Tigers). Terrorist groups have raised funds from groups and sympathetic states well beyond their geographic area of operations. Terrorist groups have cross-fertilized each other through joint training and combined operations. A variety of terrorist groups have used terrorism to provoke the state into a counter-productive response. And historically, terrorists groups have used individual martyrdom as a means of raising both publicity and recruits for the cause.

Al Qaeda and its regional networks are often portrayed in protean terms. The organization has been described as hydra-headed with unique capacities for regeneration. Al Qaeda also has been characterized as an organizational genius for its ability to recruit other terrorist groups to its cause as affiliates or franchises. For example, terrorist groups in Southeast Asia have been viewed through an al Qaeda-centric paradigm.[97] Much of what has been written about al Qaeda's arrival in Southeast Asia lacks an appropriate historical context.[98]

History can serve terrorism studies by providing proper context and laying the basis for comparative studies. For example, most terrorist groups have lasted for no more than one generation, while a few have managed to persist and overlap with terrorist groups in the next wave. But what about the current fourth wave of religiously inspired terrorism: will it fragment and disintegrate with the passing of the generation that fought against the Soviet Union in Afghanistan? Or will it overcome the problem of generational transition?

History, as Audrey Kurth Cronin reminds us, offers examples of how terrorist groups decline and end.[99] Cronin identified seven patterns that could be studied for insights into the current wave of religious terrorism. These patterns are:

1. Decapitation of leadership—Shining Path, Kurdistan Workers' Party, Real IRA, and Aum Shinrikyo.

2. Unsuccessful generational transition—Red Brigades, 2nd June Movement, Weather Underground, Red Army Faction (Bader-Meinhoff Gang), and The Order, and the Aryan Resistance Army.

3. Loss of popular support—Real IRA, ETA, and Shining Path.

4. Successful state repression: People's Will, Shining Path, and the Kurdistan Workers' Party.

5. Transition out of terrorism towards (a) criminality: Abu Sayyaf Group and FARC (Columbia) or (b) full insurgency: Khmer Rouge, Communist Party of Nepal-Maoists, Kashmiri separatist groups (LET and Hizbul Mujahideen), Armed Islamic Group of Algeria, and the Guatemalan Labor Party/Guatemalan National Revolutionary Unit.

6. Transition to a legitimate political process via negotiations—Provisional IRA, Palestine Liberation Organization, The Liberation Tigers of Tamil Eelam, and the Moro Islamic Liberation Front.

7. Achievement of the cause—Irgun/Stern Gang, and the African National Congress.

Finally, David Kilcullen has offered the provocative thesis that jihadism is a globalized insurgency involving a diffuse confederation of Islamist insurgents.[100] He identified nine major theaters of operations where insurgents used violence as part of an integrated politico-military strategy. In his view, violence is instrumental but not central to their approach. Kilcullen argues that countering in-surgency requires a whole-of-government approach that is best pursued by a strategy of disaggregation. By this he means breaking up the global confederation into its localized parts and developing a counter-insurgency, strategy-based, approach to dealing with each separate theater of terrorist operations. If this perspective has valid-ity, it means that past counter-insurgency efforts should be studied for the lessons they reveal about dealing with today's terrorists.

Future research agenda

In order to overcome the deficiencies of terrorism studies identi-fied in this chapter, it is suggested that terrorism specialists form research teams and incorporate the following elements into their future research agenda.[101] Research teams should be formed on an interdisciplinary and multidisciplinary basis and adopt a rigorous methodology. A research team should incorporate individuals with a number of skills such as statistics, critical languages, and religious studies. Every effort should be made to identify primary source ma-terial, such as terrorist websites, in order to overcome dependency on media sources. High priority should be given to developing a research design that explains the causes of radicalization especially in the formation of "home grown terrorists." Research teams need to develop a media strategy in order to more effectively get their academic message across and, of course, the discipline of history must be "brought in from the cold" in order to provide context for political analysis.[102]

Notes

[1]Andrew Silke, "Research on Terrorism: A Review of the Impact of 9/11 and the Global War on Terrorism," *Terrorism Informatics: Knowledge Man-agement and Data Mining for Homeland Security*, ed. Hsinchun Chem, Edna Reid, Joshua Sinai, Andrew Silke and Boaz Ganor (New York: Springer Verlag, 2008), 28.

[2]Rohan Gunaratna, *Inside Al Qaeda: Global Network of Terror* (New York: Columbia University Press, 2002); Peter Chalk, "Al Qaeda and its Links to

Terrorist Groups in Asia," *The New Terrorism: Anatomy, Trends and Counter-Strategies*, ed. Andrew Tan and Kumar Ramakrishna (Singapore: Eastern Universities Press, 2002), 107-128; Andrew Tan and Kumar Ramakrishna, eds., *The New Terrorism: Anatomy, Trends and Counter-Strategies* (Singapore: Eastern Universities Press, 2002); Zachary Abuza, *Militant Islam in Southeast Asia: Crucible of Terror* (Boulder: Lynne Rienner, 2003); Angel M. Rabasa, *Political Islam in Southeast Asia: Moderates, Radicals and Terrorists*, Adelphi Paper 358 (London: Oxford University Press, 2003); Kumar Ramakrishna and See Seng Tan, eds., *After Bali: The Threat of Terrorism in Southeast Asia* (Singapore: World Scientific Publishing, 2003); Justine A. Rosenthal, "Southeast Asia: Archipelago of Afghanistan's?" *Orbis* (2003): 479-493; Andrew Tan, "Southeast Asia as the 'Second Front' in the War Against Terrorism: Evaluating the Threat and Response," *Terrorism and Political Violence* 15:2 (2003): 112-138; and Paul Smith ed. *Terrorism and Transnational Violence in Southeast Asia: Challenge to States and Regional Stability* (New York: M. E. Sharpe, 2005).

[3]Abuza, *Militant Islam in Southeast Asia*; Gunaratna, *Inside Al Qaeda*; Rabasa, *Political Islam in Southeast Asia*; Ramakrishna and Tan, eds., *After Bali*; Rosenthal, "Southeast Asia: Archipelago of Afghanistans?"; Smith, ed., *Terrorism and Transnational Violence in Southeast Asia*; and Tan and Ramakrishna, eds., *The New Terrorism*.

[4]Carlyle A. Thayer, "Political Terrorism in Southeast Asia," *Pointer: Quarterly Journal of the Singapore Armed Forces* 29:4 (2003): 53-62; and Carlyle A. Thayer, "Leadership Dynamics in Terrorist Organizations in Southeast Asia," *Proceedings of the International Symposium on the Dynamics and Structures of Terrorist Threats in Southeast Asia, Held at Kuala Lumpur, Malaysia*, IDA Paper P-4026, eds. John T. Hanley, Kongdan Oh Hassig and Caroline F. Ziemke (Alexandria, VA: Joint Advanced Warfighting Program, The Institute for Defense Analysis, 2005), 76-105.

[5]These questions are taken from: Louise Richardson, *What Terrorists Want: Understanding the Enemy, Containing the Threat* (New York: Random House, 2006).

[6]Alex Schmid and Albert Jongman, *Political Terrorism: A New Guide to Actors, Authors, Concepts, Data Bases, Theories and Literature* (Oxford: North Holland Publishing Company, 1988).

[7]Walter Reich, ed. *Origins of Terrorism: Psychologies, Ideologies, Theologies, States of Mind* (Washington, DC: Woodrow Wilson Center Press, 1998); Andrew Silke, ed. *Research on Terrorism: Trends, Achievements, and Failures* (London: Frank Cass, 2004); Magnus Ranstorp, ed., *Mapping Terrorism Research* (Abington: Routledge, 2006); Rhyll Valis, Yubin Yang and Hussein A. Abbass, *Disciplinary Approaches to Terrorism—A Survey* (Canberra: Defence and Security Applications Research Centre, Australian

Defence Force Academy, 2007); and Hsinchun Chem, Edna Reid, Joshua Sinai, Andrew Silke and Boaz Ganor, eds., *Terrorism Informatics: Knowledge Management and Data Mining for Homeland Security* (New York: Springer Verlag, 2008).

[8]Bruce Hoffman *Inside Terrorism* (New York: Columbia University Press, 2006), 1–20 and Richardson, *What Terrorists Want*, 29–37.

[9]Hoffman, *Inside Terrorism*, 3.

[10]Quoted in David C. Rapoport, "The Four Waves of Modern Terrorism," in *Attacking Terrorism: Elements of a Grand Strategy*, ed. Audrey Kurth Cronin and James M. Ludes (Washington, D.C.: Georgetown University Press, 2004), 50.

[11]Hoffman, *Inside Terrorism*, 14.

[12]Rapport, "The Four Waves of Modern Terrorism," 54.

[13]Hoffman, *Inside Terrorism*, 16.

[14]Ibid., 35-40 and Richardson, *What Terrorists Want,* 6–10.

[15]Commonwealth of Australia, *Transnational Terrorism: The Threat to Australia.* (Canberra: National Capital Printing, 2004).

[16]Kofi Annan, "'In Larger Freedom': Decision Time at the UN," *Foreign Affairs* (2005), Internet edition.

[17] "Kuala Lumpur Declaration on International Terrorism," adopted by the Extraordinary Session of the Islamic Conference of Foreign Ministers, Kuala Lumpur, Malaysia, 3 April 2002.

[18]This section draws on Hoffman, *Inside Terrorism*, 30–33.

[19]Quoted in Andrew Silke, "An Introduction to Terrorism Research," in *Research on Terrorism: Trends, Achievements, and Failures,* ed. Andrew Silke (London: Frank Cass, 2004), 7–8.

[20]Hoffman, *Inside Terrorism*, 63.

[21]Richardson, *What Terrorists Want,* 23-28.

[22]Rapoport, "The Four Waves of Modern Terrorism"; the following account of these four waves is taken from 48–63.

[23]Richardson, *What Terrorists Want,* 23.

[24]Rapoport, "The Four Waves of Modern Terrorism," 52.

[25]Ibid., 48–49.

[26]Ibid., 49.

[27]Audrey Kurth Cronin, "Sources of Contemporary Terrorism," in *Attacking Terrorism: Elements of a Grand Strategy* eds. Audrey Kurth Cronin and James M. Ludes (Washington, D.C.: Georgetown University Press, 2004), 19–45.

[28]Richardson, *What Terrorists Want,* 40.

[29]See the debate between Martha Crenshaw, "The Logic of Terrorism: Terrorist Behavior as a Product of Strategic Choice," and Jerrold M. Post, "Terrorist Psycho-logic: Terrorist Behavior as a Product of Psychological

Forces," in *Origins of Terrorism: Psychologies, Ideologies, Theologies, States of Mind* ed. Walter Reich (Washington, DC: Woodrow Wilson Center Press, 1998), 7–24 and 25–40, respectively.

[30]Silke, "An Introduction to Terrorism Research," 1 and 21.

[31]Richardson, *What Terrorists Want*, 41–48.

[32]Cronin, "Sources of Contemporary Terrorism," 27–30; Richardson, *What Terrorists Want*, 48–49 and Leonard Weinberg and Louise Richardson, "Conflict Theory and the Trajectory of Terrorist Campaigns in Western Europe," in *Research on Terrorism: Trends, Achievements, and Failures*, ed. Andrew Silke, 138–160.

[33]Marc Sageman, *Understanding Terror Networks* (Philadelphia: University of Pennsylvania Press, 2004); Marc Sageman, "The Normality of Global Jihadi Terrorism," *The Journal of International Security Affairs* 8 (2005): 79–89; and Marc Sageman, *Leaderless Jihad: Terror Networks in the Twenty-First Century* (Philadelphia: University of Pennsylvania Press, 2008).

[34]Cronin, "Sources of Contemporary Terrorism," 28–29

[35]Ibid., 30-35 and Richardson, *What Terrorists Want*, 50–59.

[36]Cronin, "Sources of Contemporary Terrorism," 35–39 and Richardson, *What Terrorists Want*, 60–70.

[37]Audrey Kurth Cronin, "Behind the Curve: Globalization and International Terrorism," *International Security* 27:3 (2002-03): 30–58, Michael Mousseau, "Market Civilization and Its Clash with Terror," *International Security* 27:3 (2002-03): 5–29 and Leonard Weinberg and William Eubank, "Everything That Descends Must Converge; Terrorism, Globalism and Democracy," in *Research on Terrorism: Trends, Achievements, and Failures* ed. Andrew Silke, 91–103.

[38]Richardson, *What Terrorists Want*, 71–103.

[39]Ibid., 19.

[40]Quoted in Richardson, *What Terrorists Want*, 25.

[41]General overviews may be found in Hoffman *Inside Terrorism*, 131–172 and Richardson, *What Terrorists Want*, 104–135.

[42]Richardson, *What Terrorists Want*, 112–113.

[43]Robert A. Pape, *Dying to Win: The Strategic Logic of Suicide Terrorism* (New York: Random House, 2005).

[44]Ibid.

[45]Max Abrahms, "Why Terrorism Does Not Work," *International Security* 31:2 (2006): 42–78.

[46]See note seven above.

[47]Silke, "An Introduction to Terrorism Research," 3 and Andrew Silke, "The Devil You Know: Continuing Problems with Research on Terrorism," in *Research on Terrorism: Trends, Achievements, and Failures* ed. Andrew Silke, 59 and Andrew Silke, "The Road Less Travelled: Recent

Trends in Terrorism Research," *Research on Terrorism: Trends, Achievements, and Failures* ed. Andrew Silke, 207.

[48]Schmid and Jongman, *Political Terrorism: A New Guide to Actors, Authors, Concepts, Data Bases, Theories and Literature.*

[49]Silke, "An Introduction to Terrorism Research," 4.

[50]Ibid., 5–6 and Australian Security Intelligence Organisation, *Report of Parliament 2007-2008,* 5 and Appendix A, 121.

[51]Avishag Gordon, "Terrorism and Knowledge Growth: A Databases and Internet Analysis," in *Research on Terrorism: Trends, Achievements, and Failures,* ed. Andrew Silke, 105 and 111.

[52]Silke, "An Introduction to Terrorism Research," and Silke, "The Devil You Know."

[53] Silke, "Research on Terrorism," 34.

[54]Schmid and Jongman, *Political Terrorism,* 177–180.

[55]Silke, "An Introduction to Terrorism Research," 15.

[56]Silke, "Research on Terrorism," 43.

[57]Silke, "An Introduction to Terrorism Research," 22–23.

[58]Gordon, "Terrorism and Knowledge Growth," 110 and Silke, "The Road Less Travelled," 188.

[59]Gordon, "Terrorism and Knowledge Growth," 109.

[60]Silke, "The Road Less Travelled," 190–204.

[61]Gordon, "Terrorism and Knowledge Growth," 106 and 116.

[62]Silke, "Research on Terrorism," 31.

[63]Ibid., 31.

[64]Ibid., 32.

[65]Silke, "The Road Less Travelled," 190–204.

[66]Silke, "The Road Less Travelled," 193.

[67]Silke, "Research on Terrorism," 34.

[68]Ibid., 30.

[69]Ibid., 46.

[70]Silke, "The Road Less Travelled," 196. The remaining ten percent were scattered in twelve countries: France, Germany, Italy South Africa, India, Spain, Austria, Denmark, Norway, Turkey, Brazil, and Japan.

[71]Ibid., 199.

[72]Ibid., 204.

[73]Silke, "Research on Terrorism," 38.

[74]Ibid., 40.

[75]Source: Andrew Silke, "Research on Terrorism: A Review of the Impact of 9/11 and the Global War on Terrorism," in Hsinchun Chem, Edna Reid, Joshua Sinai, Andrew Silke and Boaz Ganor, eds., *Terrorism Informatics: Knowledge Management and Data Mining for Homeland Security* (New York: Springer Verlag, 2008), 40.

[76]Silke, "The Devil You Know," 61-66 and Silke, "Research on Terrorism," 33–46.

[77]Schmid and Jongman, *Political Terrorism*, 177.

[78]Ibid., 179–80.

[79]Silke, "An Introduction to Terrorism Research," 9.

[80] Silke, "The Devil You Know," 62.

[81]Gordon, "Terrorism and Knowledge Growth," 112–114 and Silke, "The Devil You Know," 65–68.

[82]Silke, "Research on Terrorism," 36.

[83]Ibid., 37.

[84]Silke, "The Devil You Know," 66.

[85]Silke, "Research on Terrorism," 36.

[86]Silke, "The Devil You Know," 67.

[87]Ibid.

[88]Silke, "An Introduction to Terrorism Research," 11.

[89]For an outstanding exception see Fawaz A. Gerges, *The Far Enemy: Why Jihad Went Global* (Cambridge: Cambridge University Press, 2005).

[90]Silke, "The Devil You Know," 61.

[91]For an egregious example see: Rohan Gunaratna, Arabinda Acharya and Sabrina Chua, eds., *Conflict and Terrorism in Southern Thailand* (Singapore: Marshall Cavendish, 2005).

[92]Silke, "An Introduction to Terrorism Research," 10.

[93]Silke, "The Devil You Know," 60 and 69.

[94]Ibid., 68–69.

[95]Carlyle A. Thayer, "New Terrorism in Southeast Asia," in *Violence In Between: Conflict and Security in Archipelagic Southeast Asia* ed. Damien Kingsbury (Clayton: Monash Asia Institute, 2005), 53–74.

[96]Schmid, "Research on Terrorism," 44.

[97]Carlyle A. Thayer, "Political Terrorism in Southeast Asia," in *Terrorism and Violence in Southeast Asia: Transnational Challenges to States and Regional Stability* ed. Paul Smith (New York: M. E. Sharpe, 2005), 79–97 and Greg Fealy and Carlyle A. Thayer, "Al Qaeda in Southeast Asia: Problematising 'Linkages' between Regional and International Terrorism," *Re-envisioning Asia-Pacific Security: A Regional-Global Nexus?* ed. William Tow (New York: Cambridge University Press, forthcoming 2009).

[98]For a masterful historical study see John T. Sidel, *Riots, Pogroms, Jihad: Religious Violence in Indonesia* (Singapore: National University of Singapore, 2007).

[99]Audrey Kurth Cronin, "How al-Qaida Ends: The Decline and Demise of Terrorist Groups," *International Security* 31:1 (2006): 7–48 and Audrey Kurth Cronin, *Ending Terrorism: Lessons for Defeating al-Qaeda*, Adelphi Paper 394 (Abington: Routledge for The International Institute

for Strategic Studies, 2008), 23–49.

[100]David Kilcullen, "Countering Global Insurgency," *The Journal of Strategic Studies* 28:4 (2005): 597–617 and David Kilcullen, "Counter-insurgency *Redux,*" *Survival* 48:4 (2006-07): 111–130.

[101]On research agendas see: Martha Crenshaw, "Questions to be Answered, Research to be Done, Knowledge to be Applied," in *Origins of Terrorism: Psychologies, Ideologies, Theologies, States of Mind*, ed. Walter Reich (Washington, DC: Woodrow Wilson Center Press 1998), 247–260 and Gaetano Joe Ilardi, "Redefining the Issues: The Future of Terrorism Research and the Search for Empathy," in *Research on Terrorism: Trends, Achievements, and Failures* ed. Andrew Silke, 214–228.

[102]Adam Roberts, "The 'War on Terror' in Historical Perspective," *Survival* 47:2 (2005): 101–130 and Schmid, "Research on Terrorism," 44–46.

3

Intersections: Social Science Knowledge and Prevention of Terrorism

Lucy Resnyansky

The complexity of the phenomenon of terrorism and the competition between multiple knowledge providers and groups of influence make the meta-analysis of terrorism research more and more important. Researchers examine methods and approaches in terrorism research and highlight the issue of terrorism's definition and taxonomisation.[1] Terrorism studies is constructed as an interdisciplinary, multidisciplinary and transdisciplinary research area.[2] The contribution of social science research on terrorism to political decision making and counter-terrorism practices is considered to be one of the important aspects of terrorism studies.[3]

This paper focuses on the issues related to the interaction between the area of knowledge production on terrorism (research) and the area of the application of this knowledge (practice). It aims to outline an approach to the assessment of social scientific knowledge from the perspective of its contribution to the task of prevention of the emergence of terrorism as a social phenomenon.

In order to solve the problem of terrorism, factual information about terrorist organizations and descriptions of terrorist acts is not enough. The information needs to be perceived within historical and sociocultural contexts and conceptualized within theoretical

approaches known to contemporary social science. As Eugeny Kozhushko argues,

> Even a simple description of all more or less significant ter-
> rorist acts during the last twenty years would take several
> volumes. Meanwhile, society needs not a list of explosions
> and the numbers of corpses but a theoretical analysis of the
> phenomenon of terrorism. People must know what causes
> this phenomenon, understand its nature and methods, and
> clearly realise which ways of fighting terrorism are most ef-
> fective.[4]

Indeed, it is not an easy task to enhance the counter-terrorism practice by theoretical frameworks and social science findings. The
production of knowledge on terrorism is divided by disciplinary
boundaries. This makes it difficult for researchers to offer multidi-
mensional conceptual models of this phenomenon and, in particular, to bring together societal and psychological levels of analysis.
Being divided by disciplinary boundaries, social studies of terrorism share a common ground—the epistemological culture of scientific research. There is an abyss dividing terrorism research from
political, legal and national security practices. As Audrey Cronin
puts it:

> Terrorism is a multidisciplinary challenge: the study of
> sources of terrorism requires the ability to translate between
> the fields of criminology, comparative politics, economics,
> history, international relations, psychology, sociology, theol-
> ogy and arguably others. Moreover, it is not just a matter of
> interdisciplinary differences. There also is an important in-
> tellectual bias related to levels of analyses on which causes
> are evaluated. Revealing those analytical frameworks illu-
> minates areas in which the policy community and academia
> are failing to communicate effectively, to the disadvantage
> of both and to the detriment of the long-term campaign
> against twenty-first-century international terrorism.[5]

This paper offers a critical analysis of some major discourses on terrorism (moral, psychological, and political science) and their contributions both to the understanding of the problem of terrorism and to the adoption of strategies for its solution. This paper also outlines the role of history and historical research in the construction of terrorism as a social phenomenon, and discusses how the social constructivist theory of identity and research on immigration can contribute to the prevention of terrorism. The analysis is preceded by an outline of a methodological approach to the construction of terrorism as an object of interdisciplinary research and practice.

Terrorism as an object of interdisciplinary research and practice: a critical reflexive approach

Social sciences offer multiple explanations of terrorism and a plethora of empirical findings related to specific organizations and individuals. The correctness of knowledge and the validity of data do not guarantee that the consequences of using a particular data set will be beneficial for a specific practice or that there will not be undesirable social implications. Social science knowledge can rarely be applied in the form in which it has been developed by academics.[6] Research on terrorism, particularly, has to undergo significant transformations in the process of its integration into practice because the practitioners tend to acquire social research findings in "compact" forms such as conceptual frameworks, analytical tools, and case-specific recommendations.[7] Therefore, the application of social science knowledge within specific areas of practice needs to be made an object of methodological analysis.[8]

My understanding of the problems that emerge in the process of integrating social sciences in practice is informed by the concept of knowledge as a social construction that is shaped by specific institutional settings and by competing interests and values.[9] This understanding is grounded within a model of interdisciplinary research developed by Georgy Shchedrovitsky.[10] Critical reflection upon theoretical and methodological foundations and the limitations of various "blocks of knowledge" is a necessary element of interdisciplinary research and practice. According to this approach, knowledge on terrorism needs to be assessed both in terms of its heuristic significance (how it contributes to our understanding of an ontological object) and in terms of its utility, or pragmatic significance, which includes an assessment of the potential impact on specific practices, as well as broader sociocultural implications.

The critical reflexive approach has been used to assess the contribution of different social sciences to the analysis of terrorism aiming at the reduction and prevention of the threat of terrorism.[11] This task requires that the following key questions be answered: how to choose between multiple definitions and typologies of terrorism; how to take into account the qualitative aspects of the effects of terrorism; how to bring together different levels of analysis (societal, group, and individual) and different kind of entities (social/human, and physical/resources); how to assess the relevance of specific factors, indicators and data (social, economic, historical, demographic, etc.); how to link the representations of terrorism constructed within different disciplines; and how to incorporate cultural insights and the other/insider's perspective within scientific analysis. In order to solve these problems, three kinds of input from social sciences are required. First, social sciences are sources of empirical data (e.g., anthropology, sociology, history, political science, psychology, and so on). Second, social sciences are sources of general theoretical concepts (social system, activity, and so on). Third, social sciences are sources of methods for the analysis of the epistemological and sociocultural aspects of knowledge production and consumption, the critical examination of theoretical systems and cultural beliefs, and an analysis of symbolic interaction.

The task of terrorism prevention requires the critical analysis of the contested concepts of terrorism. For example, the concepts of terrorism as a form of violence (political science discourse), a threat (discourses of defense and counter-terrorism practice), and a catastrophe risk (discourses of economics and engineering), have been analyzed in order to understand the ways of dealing with terrorism they can encourage and the social consequences of their acceptance.[12] It has been suggested that the conceptualization of terrorism as a threat and a risk may turn the practitioners' attention away from the consideration of the moral aspects of terrorism, and can be misleading in regards to the causes of the emergence of terrorism.

Most importantly, the proliferation of these discursive constructs may contribute to the naturalization of terrorism and encourage the practitioners and the society in general, to adopt a reactive rather than a proactive mindset.

Purpose	**Prevention** of the emergence of the social phenomenon of terrorism
Aspects of assessment	**Heuristic significance** of specific disciplinary approaches for the understanding of terrorism **Relevance** of broader social research for an analysis of terrorism in concrete historical and sociocultural contexts **Utility**: the effects of different concepts of terrorism on practices, and the social implications
Assessment criteria	What strategy is encouraged? **Proactive:** addressing the problem of the emergence of social actors that may be involved in political violence; OR **Reactive:** dealing with those actors' behaviour and its political and psychological effects
Methodology	**Critical analysis** of the representations of terrorism constructed within different discursive fields (research, media, and so on)
Outcomes	**Mapping** the area of knowledge production on terrorism **Extending** the field of relevant knowledge **Incorporation** of different visions of the causes and meaning of terrorism **Linking** conceptual models developed within different disciplines

Table 1. Integration of social science knowledge on terrorism in practice: critical reflexive approach

Table 1 summarizes the critical reflexive approach to the integration of terrorism research in practice.

The critical reflexive approach enables researchers to extend the range of relevant research areas and to map the heterogeneous discourses that can provide conceptual frameworks, as well as affect the practitioners' thinking about the problem of terrorism. For example, the use of open sources of data in intelligence organizations can be affected by different concepts of the Internet. These may be the Internet as an information source, a communication medium, and a social space in which social entities are emerging in the process of discursive interaction.[13] The uncritical adoption of the technological and market-oriented concepts of the Internet may negatively affect the practices of data collection and analysis, as well as an understanding of the contemporary social mechanisms of the emergence and proliferation of radical ideas and identities. The concepts developed within disciplinary areas and the concepts produced within the area of "opinion" (doxa) need to be made an object of critical analysis. This needs to be done because the practitioners' vision of social phenomena and social actors are shaped not only by scientific concepts but, to a substantial degree, by notions constructed in everyday discourse. For example, security-related practices (identification, profiling, surveillance, and policing) draw upon concepts of race and ethnicity developed within such different areas as natural science (biology, physical anthropology), social science (history, sociology), and everyday discourse.

In order to contribute to the prevention of the emergence of terrorism as a social phenomenon, interdisciplinary research on terrorism may need to incorporate those studies that do not directly deal with the phenomenon of terrorism. For example, an understanding of the motivations of suicide terrorists requires not only an examination of the real cases but a broader range of studies—from the sociology of suicide, to studies on altruism, and sociological theories of rationality and community.[14]

In order to be meaningful and effective, the use of social science knowledge needs to be supported by an analysis of the practitioners' needs and activities, and a critical reflection on the competing discourses on terrorism (media, political and academic). These discourses provide assumptions that affect the practitioners' understanding of this phenomenon and their choice of strategies and actions. These assumptions need to be made explicit and assessed in terms of the consequences and effects on the different areas of practice and society as a whole. Current thinking on terrorism is shaped mainly by moral, psychological, and political discourses.[15] The following section tries to assess these discourses in terms of their potential contribution to the prevention of terrorism.

Discourses on terrorism

Terrorism research is an over-politicized and value-laden area of scientific research. On the one hand, social researchers find it difficult to approach acts of violence against innocent people as an object of abstract theoretical and methodological reasoning. On the other hand, attempts to deal with the issue of terrorism from a scientific perspective may be negatively perceived by officials and the public.[16] The perception may be particularly strong when researchers adopt a critical stance and point to these societal misgivings and actions that may contribute to the emergence of terrorism.

The proliferation of moral discourse is an understandable phenomenon. Moral discourse constructs terrorism as a kind of abnormal, non-human behavior. The recent "discovery" that terrorists are rational beings only acts to reinforce the perception of terrorism as a violation of moral norms—because terrorists are able to behave rationally within a distorted, inhuman value system.[17] The moral discourse on terrorism plays an important therapeutic role in a traumatized society. It appeals to the mass consciousness because it gives "us" an opportunity to feel that we are normal, moral, and humane (truly human) beings. The moral discourse also plays an important pragmatic role in the war on terror as it helps obtain public and international support for political decisions and counter-terrorist actions targeting organizations or individuals.

However, the moral discourse on terrorism has very little heuristic significance for the prevention of terrorism as a social phenomenon. The proliferation of the moral discourse on terrorism has the unfortunate implication of imposing a "reactive" mindset. The moral discourse is not a form of *acting* upon terrorism; the moral discourse is a form of *reacting* to terrorism. Its domination is one of the effects of terrorism, along with the feeling of terror and panic.[18] Claims that terrorists are evil cannot solve the problem of the emergence of terrorism. Rather than encouraging societies to pay attention to the systemic conditions that may result in the emergence of political violence, the moral discourse encourages people to compare abstract systems of moral values and metaphysical purposes assigned to different cultures and civilizations (which are also highly abstract theoretical constructions). As a result, the moral discourse can encourage the society to look for large-scale solutions whose effectiveness is highly problematic and the risks and costs are enormous. When the moral discourse is applied to an analysis at the culture/civilization level, it may even become counter-productive. This is because a comparison of cultures and civilizations (or, rather, a comparison of selected constructions of particular cultures and civilizations) can be used in order to undermine the moral justification of the war on terrorism. Similarly, the demonization of certain organizations and their leaders can have a counter-productive effect as it can contribute to some individuals' desire to acquire such "exclusive and powerful" identities.

The moral discourse on terrorism has been critically analyzed as a social practice of *othering*.[19] Potential sociocultural and political implications of the proliferation of the moral discourse on terrorism have been critically examined.[20] This kind of analysis can sometimes be perceived as controversial—as blaming the victims and as challenging moral values, or justifying the use of terrorism as the weapon of the weaker. However, the true significance of the critical analysis of the moral discourse on terrorism is in showing that the problem of terrorism cannot be found within the moral discourse. An adoption of the moral discourse may seem a legitimate and natural reaction of the public consciousness—shaped and affected by desires and phobias and not very enthusiastic about critical self-analysis. However, the contemporary society cannot afford the unquestioning dominance of an evaluative and emotional moral discourse on terrorism at the expense of a rigorous and critical scientific analysis.

Psychology and political science may seem alternative to the moral discourse. For example, a psychological analysis of terrorism at the level of individuals' motivation and background may seem useful within such areas of practice as intelligence and policing. However, a preoccupation with individual motivations and background can result in focusing on those individuals who are already "in the system" (known or suspected members of terrorist organizations or networks) and, therefore, in not knowing how to defend the society against those "self-motivated" individuals who may decide to act independently.[21] In other words, a psychological vision of terrorism may contribute to the imbalance between the reactive and proactive strategies of dealing with terrorism, to the advantage of the former.

Unlike psychology, political science focuses upon external conditions. Political science is interested in terrorism as a strategy that can be acquired by certain actors in a political struggle. The concept implies the importance and priority of the search for causes and goals of terrorism. It is, however, very difficult to reveal the *general* causes of terrorism since political scientists tend to approach terrorism as a response to *concrete* political, economic, and historical circumstances. These circumstances are specific and unique, and are characterized by a multiplicity of variables (including leadership, groups' interests, and so on), which makes it difficult to both identify and generalize the causes of terrorism.[21] The concept of terrorism as a *response* introduces another level of complexity into the analysis of terrorism. As Cronin argues, the action/reaction relationship between counterterrorism and terrorism is very important, and it is necessary to sort out the cause and effect in this relationship. This is difficult to achieve, however, due to multiple factors and interpretations. The political science discourse, therefore, does not seem to be particularly promising in the area of the prevention of terrorism as a social phenomenon. This discourse focuses on the area of policy rather than on the ways in which broader cultural and social factors can contribute to the cause/effect dynamics in relation to the possible emergence of terrorism.

It is not surprising that political science highlights the issue of terrorism definition, as this issue has a great importance within political and legal practices. Politicians and legal practitioners have to deal with specific cases of violent behavior and with concrete individuals who are accused of committing certain acts of violence. In the political arena, it may be very important in some circumstances for the actors, whether individuals or groups, to be labeled as terrorists or as "freedom fighters." However, the issue of categorization does not help to prevent the emergence of groups that may be involved in political violence. The concepts of terrorism developed within the discourse of political science focus on the manifestations of terrorism and on their effects on individuals (the perception of terrorism) rather than on the causes and the mechanism of the emergence of political violence. The conceptualization of terrorism as an effect, response, and/or means used by political actors makes it difficult to understand terrorism as a social phenomenon. It is difficult to reveal the causes of this phenomenon because too many factors and variables affect political behavior and individuals' motivations.

Lessons of history

Historical and sociological approaches to the problem of terrorism are adopted by researchers aiming to analyze the emergence of groups that may be involved in, or provide support to terrorism. These approaches aim to identify the systemic causes of political violence, that is, causes of an ideological and socio-economic nature, such as injustice, poverty, political and social oppression, and so on. Within these approaches, terrorism is studied as an effect, response, or reaction to large-scale sociocultural and historical changes. For example, Castells argues that the more radical the changes that a contemporary society is undergoing—democratization, modernization, and globalization—the stronger the reactive movements aimed to express the interests of those who are unable or unwilling to accommodate themselves to the new systems of values and norms, new lifestyles, and new demands.[22] This is partly due to the lack of necessary resources (financial and cultural capital) and partly due to more successful actors profiting from others' restricted access to power and resources. In the twentieth century, Castells argues, these reactions are manifested in what has generally been perceived by the public consciousness as a rise of religious fundamentalism and nationalism ("new tribalism") and a spread of radicalization and extremist forms of political behavior such as terrorism.[23]

Some researchers believe that contemporary terrorism cannot be explained as an effect of systemic-structural changes and historical and political causes. For example, Laqueur believes that the causes of terrorism have a situational, historical character. He argues that the phenomenon of terrorism in the 19th century and the beginning of the twentieth century can be explained within socio-economic and ideological frameworks.[24] However, at present, the phenomenon of terrorism is better explained within a psychological framework. According to Laqueur, it is not even useful to state the problem of terrorism in terms of causality, since there are no actual conditions that might "objectively" cause some groups to adopt terrorism as a method of political struggle. Rather, it is necessary to ask why people, in spite of the lack of objective causes, may still become terrorists. Laqueur supports his argument via the examination of factors that are usually considered causes of terrorism. He examines—and rejects—factors such as poverty; uncontrolled demographic growth and youth unemployment (Arab countries); the growing frustration about the social and economic stagnation; the clash of civilizations; US military aggression in the post-war world; and the state of Israel and its occupation of Palestine. Laqueur suggests that all these factors may play certain roles, but revealing them does not help us to understand *why* some people become terrorists and others do not. According to Laqueur, at present, the main cause of terrorism is subjective. In the past, terrorists were "idealists" and "selfless heroes," although there were some psychologically unbalanced figures and criminals. Even then, an engagement in terrorist acts was as much a matter of personality (psychology) as of ideological conviction. Towards the beginning of the twenty-first century, psychological factors had started to become more influential than ideological and socio-economic. Nowadays, Laqueur argues, religious fanaticism is the main factor.

Laqueur's explanation is shaped by a substance metaphor which presents an abstract attribute as a substance that has an independent existential status.[25] Can the substance metaphor help practitioners develop an understanding of the causes of terrorism which could be used for the prevention of terrorism? Having been presented as a factor along with, or ahead of socio-economic and political factors, religious fanaticism is constructed as something like an infection currently spread throughout the world, causing a disease called "terrorism."

If there are any lessons that people can learn from history, one of them seems to be that fanaticism is a universal attribute of the human species. A certain percentage of people are more perceptive than others and can become deeply devoted to something or somebody—an idea, project, or individual (or, rather, their images constructed for the public). Also, history teaches us that fanaticism often manifests itself through violent actions regardless of its "filling" (religion, nation, revolution, or sport); and that religious fanaticism, specifically, has been manifested throughout history in various forms, one of which is terrorism.[26] The fact that religious fanaticism is an attribute of certain groups and individuals cannot explain why some of them become terrorists while others do not.

History also teaches us to be particularly careful with the deterministic or causal-effect logic of explanation. It shows, for example, that the emergence of terrorism is not determined by particular socio-economic condition/s and that a reaction to certain hardships, oppression and grievances does not necessarily take the form of terrorism. If there is a certain percentage of people who are fanatically ready to follow somebody and sacrifice themselves in the name of something that is greater than "me," then the question to ask—if one aims to *prevent* terrorism—is: how do social actors access particular fanatic identities? Who is interested in and who has the power and resources for exploiting human ability to become enthusiastic and passionate about something in a destructive way? If terrorism is presented in the collective consciousness as a pattern of behavior that religious fanatics usually acquire (as a modus of "being a religious fanatic"), then asking why some people become terrorists is similar to asking why people with a weak immune system become sick when there is an epidemic. Therefore, the prevention of terrorism requires answers to such questions as: How is terrorism constructed as a legitimate form of religious fanaticism and how is this construction reproduced within specific institutional settings and discursive practices in the contemporary society? In order to answer these questions, we need to explore the patterns of expressing fanatical devotion to those ideas that are available in a given society/culture; the loci of the production and reproduction of those patterns; and the material and symbolic means and resources that can be used for the construction of a fanatic identity and its use as a means of socialization.

So, the contribution of historical science to the analysis of terrorism can be enormous. An analysis of history can provide scholars of terrorism with a broader perspective and comparison, and enable them to re-consider our questions and explanations. History can provide the knowledge that can allow us to identify those societal conditions and patterns of behavior that may lead to terrorism and to understand how to prevent it.

At the same time, historical "facts" and "truths" are shaped by competing interpretations, political agendas, cultural myths and narratives. History may be used as a cultural resource for the construction of collective identities that may encourage people to adopt a terrorist mindset. Knowledge about the historical roots and causes of terrorism, such as lost territories, people's grievances, and large-scale ideological projects, can be used for the legitimization and naturalization of certain identities, attitudes and patterns of behavior. For example, Jordan and Thornburgh's study of Islamic terrorist networks in Spain suggests that the jihadist motivations to attack Spain are grounded in an historical argument where the concept of "Al Andalusia" is used to rationalize violence.[27]

Put differently, the science of history is a social practice that may contribute to the naturalization of certain ways of envisioning the past. Therefore, the use of historical knowledge needs to be accompanied by the critical assessment of the social (discursive) practices that produce historical facts, truths, collective memories, and myths.

Identity

Terrorism can be studied at three levels of analysis: societal, group, and individual. Each kind of analysis has its advantages and disadvantages. The studies of conditions and historical causes of terrorism do not help us understand why certain individuals become engaged in terrorism. Studies focusing upon socio-economic and demographic attributes of individual actors and their motivations, as well as actor networks, do not account for social and cultural factors. Researchers emphasize the necessity of multidisciplinary research on terrorism, research that can reveal external, sociocultural and political factors and internal, psychological attributes causing people to engage in political violence.

The problems related to terrorism require an analysis at the intersections of psychology, history, sociology, political science, law, and other disciplines. In order to conduct interdisciplinary research, it is not enough to make a list of disciplines that could usefully contribute to terrorism research. The main question to answer is: what should be the unit of analysis?

The individual human being is often believed to be such an intersection. However, the fact that individual behavior is affected by external factors and innate characteristics does not mean that focusing on the individual as a unit of analysis is useful for an understanding of how terrorism may be prevented. The intersection of external and internal at the level of an individual is so unique and the cause-effect relationships are so complex that making an individual a starting point of analysis does not seem very promising from the perspective of the prevention of terrorism. Rather, this task can be better informed by the analyses shaped by the social constructivist concept of (social) identity.

Social identity is "those aspects of the individual's self-concept which are derived from membership of and identification with social categories, e.g., race, gender, religion, occupation, and which are made salient in contexts where those social categories assume importance. Associated with each descriptive social identity is an evaluation which imparts positive or negative status."[28] Identity is the social internalized by individuals. The exploration of social identities, therefore, helps understand the norms, values and patterns that shape people's vision of reality and structure their behavior. Social identity is one of the most important concepts used for the explanation of processes such as ethnic conflicts and some groups' resistance against globalization and democratization.[29] Due to the fact that many contemporary terrorist organizations identify themselves with broader social movements based on collective identities, the concept of identity is particularly significant for terrorism research.

Identity has a constructivist nature—it is "the process of construction of meaning on the basis of cultural attribute, or related set of cultural attributes."[30] Castells argues that the rise of the network society is accompanied by the rise of collective identities constructed around ethnicity, nation, religion, or territory. He asks why—in the age of technology-induced globalization—are large groups of people returning to the types of identities that were fundamental for the survival of people in previous ages, but are becoming a threat for the contemporary (global, network, democratic, postmodern) society? The key processes in the construction of a collective identity in the network society are: religious fundamentalism (Islamic and Christian); nationalism (its role in the formation and disintegration of a nation-state); ethnic identity; and territorial identity (urban movements and local communities). Castells also distinguishes between three forms of identity building: legitimizing identity; resistance identity; and project identity. Each form of identity building leads to a different outcome in the constituting society.

The building of a *legitimizing identity* (citizens of a nation state) leads to a civil society, in which political changes are possible without launching a direct, violent assault. The continuity between the civil society's institutions and the power apparatus of the state exists when it is organized around a similar identity (citizens of a nation-state). This identity is offered to the social actors by the dominant social institutions and it helps these institutions extend and rationalize their domination. *Resistance identity* (or defensive identity) is caused by the practice of exclusion supported by the dominant institutions. In order to survive, these social actors build their identities on principles opposite to those of the dominant institutions. So, if the dominant identity is built on the principles of a nation-state (citizen of a nation-state), the identities for resistance are built around ethnicity, religion, territory, and so on. Castells identifies the following major conditions for the formation of a defensive identity: unbearable oppression; a sense of alienation; and resentment against unfair exclusion (political, economical, and social). Phenomena such as: ethnically based nationalism; religious fundamentalism; territorial communities; and nationalist self-affirmation are manifestations of the defensive identity. The proliferation of defensive identities may result in societies' fragmentation into a constellation of tribes. *Project identity* can also result in the transformation of a society. Projects associated with this third type of identity may differ in terms of their content and purposes, varying from a project of a post-patriarchal society to a project of the religious conversion of materialist societies and the reconciliation of all human beings as believers under the guidance of God's law.

According to Castells, conflicts and changes in the global society can be explained by a lack of accordance between the proliferating types of identities and the types of societies. Specifically, the tribal and fundamentalist identities are not in accordance with the global, secular, democratic society. The disjuncture causes conflicts and may result in the formation of radical groups, including those groups which adopt terrorism as a political strategy and communication means. In their search for meaning, social actors reconstruct defensive identities around communal principles. For example, Kaplan argues that the modern terrorism movements "have turned inward, becoming localistic rather than international, and manifest intense ethnic, racial, or tribal mysticism."[31]

Castells focuses mainly on the social conditions that may result in the formation of defensive and project identities (conditions such as industrialization; the emergence of a networked society; the crisis of state, economy, and moral traditions; the impact of technology and culture; and the feeling of uncertainty and hopelessness).[32] Castells suggests that this list can be used to understand fundamentalist, nationalist, and other social movements in such different societies as the Islamic world, the United States, Russia, Mexico, China, or Japan. The main heuristic significance of the concept of identity for terrorism analysis is that it encourages researchers to focus on the process and mechanisms of identity construction. Identity construction depends on the available cultural resources. The exploration of cultural resources available to members of a society should, therefore, be a necessary part of the assessment of a possibility of the formation of particular types of identities. From the perspective of the prevention of political violence, it is important that identities be used as a means of mobilizing certain groups for action. It is necessary, therefore, to know how group identities are constructed and transmitted in a particular society. It is also important to understand who is (what groups are) interested in the (re)production of particular identities, what kind of cultural resources (narratives, myths, stories, discourses) are used in order to reproduce those identities; what are the loci of identity construction (family, school, media, etc); and how can the broader society contribute to the formation of a certain identity, or, rather, to assigning a status of behavior pattern. Such exploration should also involve a critical analysis of the essentialist concept of identity because it plays a very important role in the contemporary discourse on terrorism.

The essentialist concept of identity is widely used in the discussions focusing upon some immigrant groups and, so-called, "home grown" terrorism. Not only the media, but social researchers also may share essentialist concepts of "Muslim" and "European," or "Islam" and "West," thus supporting the legitimization of a culture-based or religion-based divide of the humankind. The traces of the essentialist discourse on identity can be found in recent studies of the processes of Islamization, radicalization, and terrorist events in a number of European cities. For example, Gilles Kepel argues that if those "young second-generation Muslim immigrants who have never lived in a predominantly Islamic country and who have experienced the personal freedom, liberal education, and economic opportunity of democratic societies" were properly integrated into the Western society, they "may become the Islamic vanguard of the next decade, offering their co-religionists a new vision of the faith and a way out of the dead-end politics that has paralysed their countries of origin."[33] This group is constructed as sharing a "Muslim identity" due to their origin. The identity imposes a mission upon them. This mission is to influence and change the minds of their co-religionists all over the world. The assumption seems to be that the descendants of immigrants with a Muslim background are necessarily religious, and being Muslim is how they should identify themselves. The other point is that "Muslim" is seen as a single united identity. The second-generation Muslims, however, are expected to be a special kind of Muslim—loyal to the countries in which they were born, committed to democratic values, and conductors for the transmission of these attitudes and values to the rest of the Muslim world. The essentialist concept of identity, therefore, may open a possibility for thinking about second-generation "immigrants" as a means—i.e., in the same way in which people are constructed in totalitarian discourses. The naturalization of this construction may result in this group feeling like they are a means for achieving certain large-scale historical or political goals. Muslim youth may start perceiving themselves as having to choose which historical purposes to serve, with an unpredictable result, because radical ideas may seem more appealing to this group due to their novelty, and the fleur of cultural depth and social justice.

The essentialist discourse on identity manifests itself through the use of terms such as "second generation immigrants" to refer to citizens within their birth country. Nevertheless, they are called immigrants as if this status was genetic and even birth in a particular country does not change the "inherited" immigrant identity. This idea is manifested through the wide-spread use of such terms as "second or third-generation Muslims," to refer to the descendants of immigrants from Muslim countries. On the one hand, terms such as "second generation Muslim" can be perceived as figures of speech that are used for the sake of brevity. On the other hand, however, this term may—intentionally or unintentionally—contribute to the realization of an ideological project aiming to emphasize the religious element of these immigrants' identity. Becoming aware of the latter case requires theoretical knowledge related to paradigms in social research, as well as discourse analysis skills. Not all readers are able to approach such studies with the necessary degree of criticism, particularly because essentializing identity corresponds to the traditional ideas of social divisions on the grounds of culture, ethnicity and religion.

The essentialist paradigm—critically examined and rejected in discourse theory, postcolonial theory and social constructivism—is reproduced and promoted by "popular science" discourse and media. It can still be found in some writings on particular groups of immigrants and their descendants. The essentialist paradigm cannot, however, help develop constructive strategies aiming to prevent the emergence of particular identities. A social constructivist approach has more heuristic value and is more useful for practitioners, because it enables them to ask concrete questions regarding the mechanisms of social production and the dissemination of identities. The social constructivist concept of identity can usefully inform an assessment of the possibility of the formation and proliferation of particular identities and can help understand how this possibility may be prevented or minimized. The social constructivist concept of identity provides a theoretical ground for the development of analytical frameworks that bring together knowledge related to the social production of identities. It examines:

1. *conditions* (economic, social, political) in which identities are

produced and reproduced;

2.   *mechanisms* of the social construction of identities, including the *loci* of formation and transmission *channels*; and

3.   *resources*—both human and cultural (habitus, discourses, myths, stories, etc)—that can be used in order to construct certain identities.

The adoption of the social constructivist paradigm encourages researchers and practitioners to use a broader range of social research. The paradigm helps link studies that might, at first, seem unrelated. Below, I discuss how research on Muslim immigration in Australia may be used for an analysis of the possibility of the formation and proliferation of identities.

Research on immigration: mapping relevant knowledge

In Australia, Muslim immigrants have been studied within general research on immigrants of non-English speaking background (NESB).[34] These studies draw upon quantitative data and aim to explore socio-economic and demographic variables characteristic of Muslim immigrants. This kind of research reveals systemic (macro-level) factors that are claimed to be relevant for exploring the integration of immigrants: the number and origin of Muslim immigrants in Australia; their settlement patterns; their income in comparison to other groups of immigrants; and marriage patterns. In these studies, identities are defined on a *national* basis; the concept (or, rather, label) of identity is used in order to distinguish between groups of immigrants in terms of their countries of origin.

It is difficult, however, to link these studies to the identity-focused research on immigrants from Muslim countries and their descendants. These studies tend to highlight the religious and ethnic aspects of the identities of Muslim immigrants, while the social aspect is practically silenced. Meanwhile, as Saeed and Akbarzadeh note, the social aspects of Muslim identity seem to have particular impact upon the process of the formation of a unified Muslim identity among Muslim immigrants in Australia.[35] Therefore, an analysis of the social aspect is necessary for the systematic assessment of Muslim immigrants' identity formation and integration into the mainstream Australian society. Also, this research gap may contribute to the construction of immigrants from Muslim countries in public consciousness as well as among Muslim immigrants themselves.

Existing qualitative studies of immigrants from Muslim countries and their descendants can provide valuable information regarding the cultural resources that may be used for identity construction, the loci of identity formation, the channels of the dissemination of ideal constructs of certain identities, and the cultural resources that may be used in identity construction. On the one hand, these studies reveal the role of different versions of Islam as a cultural resource that may be used by certain actors. On the other hand, they show that so-called youth culture may become such a cultural resource.

Qualitative research on Islam and Muslims in Australia provides critical analyses of the past and present representations of Islam and Muslims in the mainstream political, media, and public discourses. These studies reveal the interactive nature of identity and show the significant role that the mainstream society plays in the process of forming and spreading certain identities. Specifically, the acquisition of a civilization's (culturalist) paradigm in political and media discourses may result in silencing the differences within Muslim immigration—ethnic, cultural, religious, and social. As Saeed and Akbarzadeh argue:

> [I]t has to be asked whether Australia is home to a single Muslim community. Mainstream public opinion in Australia, the media and policy makers have tended to answer this question in the affirmative. Misconceived assumptions about the social and ethnic background of Muslims have often led to a neglect of their diverse social and ethnic heritage. This, in turn, has reinforced the idea that there is a single Muslim community with uniform needs and aspirations.[36]

The mainstream public opinion, therefore, may contribute to the naturalization of such constructs as *umma* (the unified community of Islam) and to the proliferation of a unified Muslim identity. The mainstream public perception of Muslims as a culturally homogeneous group, however, ignores the differences between Muslim immigrants. This difference needs to be put forward in order to avoid the stereotyping of immigrants.

Muslim immigrants and their descendants do not perceive themselves as a unified ethnic or cultural group: "In reality the diversity of the Muslim population in Australia is the reflection of the diversity of the world. On the contrary the image of a Muslim in the minds of the majority of Australians would be quite uniform and universal."[37] Concepts such as Muslims or Westerners represent *ideal types*, social resources of meaning construction. Reality is more complex and being a member of a community/group/society does not imply sharing all the qualities assigned to this community. Theoretical speculations about Muslim community/ies need to be complemented by and verified against an empirical study of individual views and opinions. This may be difficult to do, however, due to the dominance of community-based methods in research on Muslims in Australia. The complex and dynamic picture of identity building of Muslim immigrants and their descendants may not be revealed entirely because certain views and opinions may be excluded from analysis, as their bearers are not considered to be true members of a community, or do not qualify as representatives of the "minority." The concept of *community* plays an important role in the studies of radicalization and political violence in recent times, in spite of the fact that this is a highly contested and criticized concept.[38] The concept of community needs to be critically assessed particularly due to the trend to use it for the construction of new identities. For example, a "unified Muslim community" may be constructed that ties Muslim immigrants together regardless of their geographical distribution in the post-modern urban environment, and irrespective of the differences generated by their origin, languages, and socio-economic and cultural background.

Studies that focus on Islam and Muslim communities in Australia are characterized by the use of both quantitative and qualitative data (statistical data are combined with case studies and analysis of narratives).[39] These studies are often conducted by "insiders"—researchers linked to Muslim communities and engaged in their social, cultural and political projects, a fact that enables them to draw upon their cultural experience and reach a deep understanding of the analyzed phenomena. These insights are a valuable source of knowledge about the types of identities acquired by Muslim immigrants and the social mechanisms of identity construction and proliferation.[40]

A substantial body of Australian research related to Muslim immigrants focuses on how Muslim identity is constructed and perceived within the mainstream Australian society. It aims to reveal prejudices and racism towards the Muslim "Other."[41] The media and/or official discourses are the usual object of this research. The discourses employed in everyday life by "ordinary people" are explored less, which means that there may be a substantial gap in our knowledge about the perception of immigrants by different groups. As a result, the attitudes of the silent majority may remain largely unknown until they are manifested in actions.

Table 2 presents an example of how research on immigration can be mapped and assessed in terms of its heuristic significance. However, it is not the intention here to provide a detailed picture of all research on immigration conducted in Australia. This paper seeks to illustrate the idea that the problem of the prevention of terrorism may require a substantial extension of what can be considered relevant knowledge. For example, it may require an analysis of the discursive construction of different identity types (secular, religious, national, ethnic) within specific societies. It may require knowledge about such processes as integration, alienation, marginalization, and acculturation; as well as knowledge about strategies and patterns used by social actors in order to reposition themselves and others in terms of power relations and access to the economic and cultural capital. It also requires a systematic exploration of the factors, conditions, and resources that may contribute to the construction and proliferation of different types of identities. Among them are: structural-systemic conditions (demographics, wealth distribution, relative deprivation); historical and political factors (perceived grievances, symbolic events, conflicts); resources to draw upon (cultural norms and values, religious beliefs, collective memories, myths and narratives, discourses, language, stereotypes and prejudices); loci and channels of identity construction and transmission (school, family, church, media, etc); and actors (groups and individuals) who may benefit from the proliferation of different types of identities.

Focus	Approach	Heuristic significance
NESB immigrants: Socio-economic background; education; qualification; marriage patterns	Quantitative approach	Provides comprehensive quantitative data on NESB immigrants, covering all groups
		Identities are defined formally - on a national basis (country of origin).
		The level of immigrants' integration into the host society is explained as being determined by systemic factors (socioeconomic variables)
		Quantitative data need to be complemented by the qualitative research findings
Islam and Muslim communities in Australia: Historical and sociocultural issues	Qualitative approach Case studies of selected groups and communities	Provides knowledge on the types of identities acquired by Muslim immigrants and the social mechanisms of their construction
		The majority of studies draw upon the concept of multiculturalism and community studies
		Provides useful data on the types of identities, social projects, and mechanisms of identity formation in immigrant communities
		Can provide valuable insider's perspective
Second generation immigrants Focus on the groups of youth, located mainly in Sydney	Qualitative interpretative research	Provides deep insight into everyday life, the nature of hybrid identities and the resources that are used for the formation of such identities
		Research is conducted on a limited sample and often focuses on negative experiences and phenomena
		Can be enhanced by a broader range of research on youth cultures and needs to be linked to an analysis of systemic variables (socio-economic factors)
Immigrants' integration	Research is conducted within the strategic essentialism and exclusion framework	Highlights such phenomena as racism and exclusion – on the part of the mainstream society
		Needs to take into account the interactive nature of cultural identities
Identity construction	Interpretative research, discourse analysis	Provides analysis of discourses shaping the representation of particular groups of immigrants in media and public discourses
		Reveals the mainstream culture's prejudices and attitudes to 'other'
		Insignificant attention is paid to the everyday discourse; the interactive nature of representations is largely ignored

Table 2. Australian studies of Muslim immigration: heuristic significance

Conclusion

The solution to the problem of terrorism can focus either on those who have already become terrorists, or on the conditions that result in the emergence of groups and individuals that may support and/or be involved in political violence. The relevant knowledge emerges at an intersection of different discourses reflecting the interests and views of various stakeholders and groups. Social sciences are one of the providers of such discourses and conceptual frameworks; media and everyday commonsensical (collective) consciousness are the other two major influences. The use of social science knowledge in practice, therefore, requires an assessment of this knowledge in terms of its impact upon the balance of narrow professional and organizational interests and goals as well as broader social interests and long-term strategic goals. It also requires critical reflection upon the discourses as social practices that may either problematize or naturalize certain interpretations and categorizations of reality.

Horgan notes, quite rightfully, that, in spite of the exponentially growing number of publications on terrorism, we still do not know much about this phenomenon and are very far from understanding what goes on in the minds of those who are capable of committing acts of terrorism.[42] Nevertheless, contemporary social science has produced a substantial body of knowledge that can be used in order to develop more effective sociocultural, economic and international policies aiming at the prevention of terrorism. There are studies that can inform security-related practices, such as research on the integration of immigrants, the spread of fundamentalism, the radicalization of youth, and so on. The majority of these studies, however, have not been conducted from a security perspective. Having been shaped by needs and concerns unrelated to security practices, these studies need to be critically re-examined in terms of their heuristic significance for the counter-terrorism practice. The critical reflexive approach to the construction of terrorism as an object of interdisciplinary research and practice can also help researchers and practitioners understand the relevance and significance to Australian conditions of studies on threatening identities, radicalization, and political violence in different countries and times.

In order to develop proactive and constructive strategies aimed at preventing terrorism, different levels of analysis (societal, group and individual) need to be brought together. The development of such strategies requires an assessment of the means and resources used for mobilizing certain groups for action, revealing the actors' interests and, most importantly, identifying those groups that are successfully integrated into the larger society, and promoting their experience.

The social constructivist concept of identity can help bring together the micro- and macro-levels of analysis. The adoption of this approach can help develop proactive strategies aiming to prevent the emergence of threatening identities. The social constructivist concept of identity encourages researchers and practitioners to focus on the social mechanisms of identity formation and proliferation, and the cultural resources that may be used by interested actors, including such resources as history and religion. At the same time, it enables the use of knowledge from the broader socio-economic, historical, cultural and discursive contexts (e.g., research on immigrant integration, youth cultures, and media constructions).

To summarize, the selection of social science knowledge to be used in practice has to be governed by the following criteria and purposes:

1. *The local perspective*
There is an experience of studying radicalization, involvement in terrorist activities, and political violence. In order to draw upon this experience, it is necessary to understand whether it is applicable to the local (Australian) conditions and whether solutions found elsewhere may have similar results in this country. Therefore, it is necessary to know which factors and societal and group characteristics to examine in order to assess their relevance for the proliferation of certain types of identities.

2. *Relevance of a broader range of social research*
Studies that have not been conducted from a security perspective may be very relevant from the perspective of terrorism prevention because they help reveal the positive experience. For example, the majority of studies on Muslim immigrants have been

conducted from the perspective of the immigrants' socio-economic integration and acculturation. Having been shaped by needs and concerns unrelated to those of security and counterterrorism, these studies need to be critically re-examined in terms of their heuristic significance for the prevention of the emergence of groups that may be engaged in political violence.

3. *Proactive strategies and constructive solutions*

It is necessary to assess the utility (pragmatic significance) of social science studies and to understand whether they may help develop proactive and constructive strategies or, on the contrary, contribute to the naturalization of undesired phenomena. It is necessary to assess them in terms of their contribution to (a) an understanding of those conditions that contribute to the emergence of groups that may feel disintegrated and acquire radicalized identities versus the groups that are successfully integrated within the broader society; and (b) revealing social and cultural mechanisms of identity production, resources that the social actors draw upon, and the channels of identity dissemination.

Notes

[1] John Horgan, *The Psychology of Terrorism* (London: Routledge, 2005); David C. Rapoport, "The Four Waves of Modern Terrorism," *Attacking Terrorism: Elements of a Grand Strategy*, ed. Audrey K. Cronin and James M. Ludes (Washington, D.C.: Georgetown University Press, 2004), 46–73; Alex P. Schmid, "Framework for Conceptualising Terrorism," *Terrorism and Political Violence* 16(2) (2004): 197–221.

[2] Sean Brawley, "Transdisciplinarity, Signature Pedagogy and the Place of History in Terrorism Studies and Counter-Terrorism," in this volume; Audrey K. Cronin, "Sources of Contemporary Terrorism," *Attacking Terrorism: Elements of a Grand Strategy*, ed. Audrey K. Cronin and James M. Ludes (Washington, D.C.: Georgetown University Press, 2004), 19–45; Mathieu Deflem, ed., *Sociology of Crime, Law and Deviance. Volume 5. Terrorism and Counter-Terrorism: Criminological Perspectives* (Amsterdam: Elsevier, 2004); Lucy Resnyansky, "Social Modelling as an Interdisciplinary Research Practice," *IEEE Intelligent Systems* 23(4) (2008): 20–27; Andrew Silke, ed., *Research on Terrorism: Trends, Achievements & Failures* (London: Frank Cass, 2004); Carlyle A. Thayer, "Terrorism Studies: The Dismal

science?," in this volume; Leonard Weinberg, Ami Pedahzur, and Siran Hirsch-Hoefler, "The Challenges of Conceptualizing Terrorism," *Terrorism and Political Violence* 16(4) (2004): 777–794.

[3] Ronald D. Crelinsten, "The Discourse and Practice of Counter-Terrorism in Liberal Democracies," *Australian Journal of Politics and History* 44, no. 1 (1998): 389–413; Avishag Gordon, "Terrorism as an Academic Subject After 9/11: Searching the Internet Reveals a *Stockholm Syndrome* Trend," *Studies in Conflict and Terrorism*, 28(1) (2005): 45–59; Gary LaFree and Laura Dugan, "How Does Studying Terrorism Compare to Studying Crime," in *Sociology of Crime, Law and Deviance. Volume 5. Terrorism and Counter-Terrorism: Criminological Perspectives*, ed. Mathieu Deflem (Amsterdam: Elsevier, 2004), 53–74; Edna O.F. Reid, "Terrorism Research and Diffusion of Ideas," *Knowledge and Policy: The International Journal of Knowledge Transfer and Utilization*, 6(1) (1993): 17–38.

[4] Eugeny P. Kozhushko, *Modern Terrorism: An Analysis of Major Trends* (Minsk: Harvest, 2000), 7.

[5] Cronin, "Sources of Contemporary Terrorism," 20.

[6] John Law, *After Method: Mess in Social science Research* (London: Routledge, 2004).

[7] Lucy Resnyansky, "Technology in Foreign Policy and National Security: A Factor, a Tool, and a Mediator," in *Australia and the New Technologies: Towards Evidence Based Policy in Public Administration*, ed. Katina Michael and M.G. Michael (Wollongong, NSW: University of Wollongong), 74–79; Zuleyka Zevallos, "Sociology As 'Other' Representing Sociological Knowledge Within a National Security Context," in *Public Sociologies: Lessons and Trans-Tasman Comparisons: TASA/SAANZ 2007 Joint Conference Proc.*, ed. B. Curtis, S. Matthewman and T. McIntosh (Auckland: University of Auckland, 2007).

[8] Resnyansky, "Social Modelling as an Interdisciplinary Research Practice."

[9] Michel Foucault, *The Order of Things: An Archaeology of the Human Sciences*, trans. Alan M. Sheridan Smith (New York, NY: Random House, 1970); Michel Foucault, *The Archaeology of Knowledge*, trans. Alan M. Sheridan Smith (London: Tavistock, 1972); G. Nigel Gilbert and Michael Mulkay, *Opening Pandora's Box: A Sociological Analysis of Scientists' Discourse* (Cambridge, UK: Cambridge University Press, 1984); Erving Goffman, *Strategic Interaction* (Philadelphia, PA: University of Pennsylvania Press, 1969); Karin D. Knorr Cetina, *The Manufacture of Knowledge: An Essay on the Constructivist and Contextual Nature of Science* (Oxford: Pergamon Press, 1981); Bruno Latour, *Science in Action: How to Follow Scientists and Engineers through Society* (Cambridge, MA: Harvard University Press, 1987); Robert K. Merton, *The Sociology of Science: Theoretical and Empirical Investigations*

(Chicago: The University of Chicago Press, 1973); Michael J. Mulkay, *Science and the Sociology of Knowledge* (London: Allen & Unwin, 1979).

[10] Georgy P. Shchedrovitsky, *Selected Works* (In Russian) (Moscow: School of Cultural Policy, 1995). For a more detailed description of Shchedrovitsky's model of interdisciplinary research and its application within the field of terrorism research and counter-terrorism practice, see Resnyansky, "Social Modelling as an Interdisciplinary Research Practice."

[11] Lucy Resnyansky, *Integration of Social Sciences in Terrorism Modelling: Issues, Problems and Recommendations. DSTO-TR-1955* (Commonwealth of Australia, 2007), http://www.dsto.defence.gov.au/publications/5099/DSTO-TR-1955.pdf.

[12] Lucy Resnyansky, "Conceptualisation of Terrorism in Modelling Tools: Critical Reflexive Approach," *Prometheus* 24(4) (2006): 441–447.

[13] Lucy Resnyansky, "The Internet as a Communication Medium and a Social Space: A Social Constructivist Approach to the Use of Open Data," in *From Dataveillance to Überveillance and the Realpolitik of the Transparent Society: Proc. 2nd RNSA Workshop on the Social Implications of National Security*, ed. Katina Michael and M.G. Michael (Wollongong, NSW: University of Wollongong, 2007), 147–168.

[14] Zuleyka Zevallos, "What Would Durkheim Say? Altruistic Suicide in Analyses of Suicide Terrorism," in *Sociology For A Mobile World: Proceedings Of The Annual Conference of The Australian Sociological Association 4–7 December*, ed. V. Colic-Peisker and F. Tilbury (Perth: University of Western Australia, 2006), http://www.tasa.org.au/conferencepapers06/papers/Law,%20politics,%20crime%20and%20deviance/Zevallos.pdf.

[15] Crelinsten, "The Discourse and Practice of Counter-Terrorism in Liberal Democracies"; Schmid, "Framework for Conceptualising Terrorism," Weinberg et al., "The Challenges of Conceptualizing Terrorism."

[16] Horgan, *The Psychology of Terrorism*.

[17] For example, suicide terrorism can be interpreted as being rationally motivated within a so-called "strategic" logic. See Thayer comments in the preceding chapter on the "sacred view" on suicide bombing as an altruistic act of religious martyrdom inspired by a sense of duty to the community.

[18] Victor E. Kappeler and Aaron E. Kappeler, "Speaking of Evil and Terrorism: The Political and Ideological Construction of a Moral Panic," *Sociology of Crime, Law and Deviance. Volume 5. Terrorism and Counter-Terrorism: Criminological Perspectives*, ed. Mathieu Deflem (Amsterdam: Elsevier, 2004), 175–197.

[19] Jean Baudrillard, The Spirit of Terrorism and Other Essays, trans. C. Turner (London: Verso, 2002); John Edwards and R.J. Martin, ed., *Discourse*

& *Society (Special Issue: Interpreting Tragedy: The Language of 11 September 2001)* 15, no. 2–3 (2004).

[20] Crelinsten, "The Discourse and Practice of Counter-Terrorism in Liberal Democracies"; Resnyansky, "Conceptualisation of Terrorism in Modelling Tools: Critical Reflexive Approach"; Resnyansky, "The Internet as a Communication Medium and a Social Space: A Social Constructivist Approach to the Use of Open Data."

[21] Kelly R. Damphousse and Brent L. Smith, "Terrorism and Empirical Testing: Using Indictment Data to Assess Changes in Terrorist Conduct," *Sociology of Crime, Law and Deviance. Volume 5. Terrorism and Counter-Terrorism: Criminological Perspectives*, ed. Mathieu Deflem (Amsterdam: Elsevier, 2004), 75–90.

[22] Cronin, "Sources of Contemporary Terrorism." Manuel Castells, *The Power of Identity* (Malden, MA: Blackwell, 1997).

[23] Ibid.

[24] Walter Laqueur, *No End to War: Terrorism in the Twenty-first Century* (New York, N.Y.: Continuum, 2003).

[25] George Lakoff and Mark Johnson, *Metaphors We Live By* (Chicago: The University of Chicago Press, 2003).

[26] Michael Burleigh, *Sacred Causes: The Clash of Religion and Politics from the Great War to the War on Terror* (Harper Collins, 2007); Gabriel A. Almond, R. Scott Appleby, and Emmanuel Sivan, *Strong Religion: The Rise of Fundamentalisms Around the World* (Chicago and London: The University of Chicago Press, 2003); J. Harold Ellens, ed., *The Destructive Power of Religion: Violence in Judaism, Christianity, and Islam*, Condensed and Updated Edition (Psychology, Religion, and Spirituality) (Westport, CT: Praeger, 2007).

[27] Javier Jordan and Nicola Horsburgh, "Mapping Jihadist Terrorism in Spain," *Studies in Conflict and Terrorism*, 28, no. 3 (2005): 169–191.

[28] David Jary and Julia Jary, *Collins Dictionary of Sociology*, 3rd Edition (Glasgow: Harper Collins, 2000), 565–566.

[29] Thomas S. Szayna, ed., *Identifying Potential Ethnic Conflict: Application of a Process Model* (Santa Monica, CA: RAND, 2000).

[30] Castells, *The Power of Identity*, 6.

[31] Jeffrey Kaplan, "The Fifth Wave: The New Tribalism?" *Terrorism and Political Violence,* 19(4) (2007), 545.

[32] Castells, *The Power of Identity.*

[33] Gilles Kepel, *The War for Muslim Minds: Islam and the West* (Cambridge, MA: The Belknap Press, 2004), 8–9.

[34] Robert Birrell and Siew-Ean Khoo, *The Second Generation in Australia: Educational and Occupational Characteristics* (Canberra: Australian Govt.

Pub. Service, 1995); Toni O'Loughlin and Ian Watson, *Loyalty is a One Way Street: NESB Immigrants and Long Term Unemployment* (Sydney, Australia: University of Sydney, 1997); Wafia Omar, Philip Hughes, and Allen Kirsty, *The Muslims in Australia* (Canberra, Australia: Australian Govt. Pub. Service, 1996); Janet Penny and Siew-Ean Khoo, *Intermarriage: A Study of Migration and Integration* (Canberra, Australia: Australian Govt. Pub. Service, 1996).

[35] Abdullah Saeed and Shahram Akbarzadeh, "Searching for Identity: Muslims in Australia," in *Muslim Communities in Australia*, ed. Abdullah Saeed and Shahram Akbarzadeh (Sydney, Australia: UNSW Press, 2001), 1–11.

[36] Saeed and Akbarzadeh, "Searching for Identity: Muslims in Australia," 2.

[37] Whid A. Razi, "The Islamic World and Its Search for Identity in Modern Times: A Socio-political Study of Modern Islamic Communities with an Investigation of Muslim Settlement in Australia" (PhD diss., Macquarie University, 2001), 215.

[38] Graham Allan, "Community," in *Sociology: The Key Concepts*, ed. John Scott (Routledge, 2006), 35–8; Graham Day, *Community and Everyday Life* (Routledge, 2006).

[39] Shahram Akbarzadeh and Samina Yasmeen, ed., *Islam and the West: Reflections from Australia* (Sydney: UNSW Press, 2005); Abdullah Saeed and Shahram Akbarzadeh, ed., *Muslim Communities in Australia* (Sydney, Australia: UNSW Press, 2001); Nahid A. Kabir, "The Muslims in Australia: An Historical and Sociological Analysis, 1860–2002" (PhD Diss., The University of Queensland, 2003).

[40] See, for example, Nadia Jamal and Taghred Chandab, *The Glory Garage: Growing up Lebanese Muslim in Australia* (Crows Nest, NSW: Allen & Unwin, 2005).

[41] See, for example, Scott Poynting et al., *Bin Laden in the Suburbs: Criminalising the Arab Other* (Sydney, Australia: The Sydney Institute of Criminology and Federation Press, 2004).

[42] Horgan, *The Psychology of Terrorism*.

4

Transdisciplinarity, Signature Pedagogy, and the Place of History in Terrorism Studies and Counter-Terrorism

Sean Brawley

In 2004 the American Congress passed the Intelligence Reform and Terrorism Prevention Act. Within the new public law the National Intelligence Director was instructed to establish "Cross-disciplinary Education and Training…in order to promote a more effective and productive intelligence community." The directive was a response to the complaint that, in the wake of September 11, American counter-terrorist agencies had not been good at "cross-disciplinary work."[1]

The political response reflected a similar scholarly discussion within the field of "terrorism studies."[2] While the field has not expended much effort reflecting on its own practice (Ranstorp suggests less than a dozen dedicated works in 30 years), when scholars have referred to matters methodological their fleeting utterances have often centered on issues of disciplinarity and cross-disciplinarity.[3] Ganor's study of counter-terrorism (CT) observed that:

> In order to fully understand the phenomena of terrorism, the tools of a single research discipline do not suffice. Almost all academic disciplines are relevant to one aspect or another of terrorism. In order to understand just how complex this

phenomenon is, all we need to do is remind ourselves of some of the disciplines that are directly or indirectly related to terrorism.[4]

Many advocates of "cross-disciplinary" approaches in the post September 11 world sought to justify the inclusion of their discipline into the field of terrorism studies. With a perception that the terrorism studies "club" held a narrow discipline constituency, many scholars shared Nelles' conclusion that the field actively *discouraged* cross-disciplinarity.[5] In their advocacy of the importance of political economy to terrorism, Enders and Sandler were insistent: "To better understand terrorism and to counter its threat, society must apply varied techniques and knowledge from many disciplines—for example, history, sociology, law, psychology, statistics, and economics."[6]

In examining the place of psychology in terrorism studies, Taylor observed:

> The challenge is for behavioral scientists to...be open to contributions from different academic disciplines about the causes and consequences of terrorism, and consider whether the outcome might help them to unravel more of the complexities of the problems they face.[7]

Lia made similar claims, and identified other "ignored" disciplines, in his study of globalization and terrorism.[8]

When advocating what other fields of study have labeled an "integrative dialogue" between disciplines, scholars of terrorism studies have tended to use the term "interdisciplinarity."[9] Smelser's recent study advises: "For the study of terrorism I regard interdisciplinarity as a strength, because the topic itself knows no disciplinary boundaries and spreads into all of them."[10] Ganor insisted that the new generation of CT practitioners required a capacity to "make decisions on an interdisciplinary basis."[11] In 2009, Routledge and the Society for Terrorism Research will launch their new journal, titled *Interdisciplinary Research on Terrorism and Political Violence.*

Ross has also suggested applying another variant of "cross-disciplinarity": "In order to understand terrorism, we need to use an interdisciplinary or *multidisciplinary* [authors italics] approach that integrates, at the very least, the fields of criminology, criminal justice, history, law, philosophy, political science, psychology, religion and sociology."[12]

The call for scholars in the field of terrorism studies to look beyond their own disciplines when researching and writing is a call worthy of amplification. Yet there is little clarity about the meaning of "cross-disciplinary" approaches. What does Smelser mean when he uses the phrase "interdisciplinary"? Ross suggests interdisciplinarity and multidisciplinarity are either/or methodological propositions but what is the difference between them?

For most scholars in terrorism studies their understanding of these terms is vague at best and their application superficial. Enders and Sandler assert they are "interested in the history of terrorism" and that their study has "drawn insights" from a range of disciplines. There is, however, no explanation of how these insights have been secured or applied to, what remains, a work of political economy.[13]

For a field so invested in definitions (what terrorism studies scholar has not defined the term "terrorism" in their writings or public utterances?), the imprecision associated with cross-disciplinary methodology is somewhat surprising. More important, the imprecision compromises methodological possibilities. Scholars in the field know they want to look outside their disciplinary silos to enhance their individual contributions but they have no methodological framework for approaching the task. As a consequence motherhood statements and little else sit in monograph and article introductions; staying inside disciplinary boundaries is bad, looking to other disciplines is good.

A closer examination of cross-disciplinary terms such as "interdisciplinary" or "multidisciplinary" problematizes their methodological usefulness in terrorism studies. Multidisciplinarity has tended to be constructed as an approach that brings together scholars from different disciplines but does little more than ask them to turn their attention to the same issue.[14] The hope is that some form of disciplinary osmosis might then occur but little effort is made to encourage it. Certainly the current field of terrorism studies is multidisciplinary. Yet placing scholars from different disciplines under the one roof does not necessarily produce new outcomes. Indeed, Crenshaw asserts that multidisciplinarity can produce a negative result in terrorism studies: "Multidisciplinarity made it hard to build a unifying set of theoretical assumptions that could coordinate different approaches to understanding the threat of terrorism or analyzing responses."[15]

By contrast, interdisciplinarity seeks to meld two or more disciplines to produce a hybrid that could then provide new insights, and that can range from simply transferring methods across disciplines to generating new disciplines.[16] Environmental studies and film studies are cited as examples of new fields that emerged through the melding of traditional disciplines, examples that have inspired similar calls for terrorism studies[17]. Before 9/11 it could have been asserted that the narrower version of terrorism studies that existed then was an interdisciplinary field of study. Reflecting its origins, the field was mostly confined to what Avishag Gordon has labeled the "grand disciplines" of history, political science, sociology and religious studies.[18] Much writing did reflect a melding of these disciplines.

Even when dealing with complementary disciplines, some commentators have observed that interdisciplinarity is not unproblematic. As Kanbur has noted in his examination of economics and development studies, some scholars are concerned that "creating a true hybrid might lose the strengths of each approach, with the gains lost in disciplinary and methodological confusion."[19] Such issues are compounded many times over as more disciplines seek inclusion in the area of study. Interdisciplinarity is simply impractical in a field such as terrorism studies; its constituency has mushroomed in the twenty-first century. How could the current field merge not just disciplines (history and geography for example) but wider academic cultures (the humanities and the natural sciences for example)?[20] The task is beyond interdisciplinarity.

Transdisciplinarity

There is one variant of cross-disciplinarity that possesses greater possibilities for a viable methodological framework applicable to terrorism studies. It has been suggested that in an evolutionary sense multidisciplinarity occurs before interdisciplinarity, and that "transdisciplinarity" follows.[21] To quote Nicolescu: *"transdiscipli-narity concerns that which is at once between the disciplines, across the different disciplines, and beyond all discipline. Its goal is the un-derstanding of the present world*, of which one of the imperatives is the unity of knowledge."[22]

An important dimension of transdisciplinarity is its potential to "obtain a better outcome."[23] Tracing the rise of cross-disciplinary research to defense-related fields in World War II, Klein has noted that the power of transdisciplinarity is best revealed when focused on "important problems."[24] The need for "joint problem solving" produces the favored outcome at a time in world history when the problems are many but the answers are few.[25] Klein insists, "To-day's transdisciplinary initiatives demand movement beyond older forms of interdisciplinary cooperation."[26] It is the problem rather than the methodology itself which drives such a need.[27] As Chilean economist Max-Neef has observed:

> If we go through a list of some of the main *problematiques* that are defining the new Century, such as water, forced mi-grations, poverty, environmental crises, violence, terrorism, neo-imperialism, destruction of social fabric, we must con-clude that none of them can be adequately tackled from the sphere of specific individual disciplines. They clearly repre-sent transdisciplinary challenges.[28]

Despite much talk, application of transdisciplinary research meth-ods is "still fairly young…[and is] still being developed."[29] Accord-ing to Stehr and Grundmann, there have been many attempts to es-tablish transdisciplinary frameworks in a variety of fields of study, but, "despite the best intentions," they have been failures.[30] A lack of institutional support has been cited as one of the main impedi-ments. This chapter is not in a position to offer a "best practice" transdisciplinary methodological approach for terrorism studies. A good starting point for designing such a methodology is the *Hand-book of Transdisciplinary Research* published by a group of European scholars in 2008. Showcasing a number of approaches in a range of areas (none of them terror-related), the authors remain reluctant to formalize a preferred approach but they do conclude their work by identifying fifteen propositions to be adhered to when approaching transdisciplinary practice.

Transdisciplinarity also holds resonance for scholars in terrorism studies because in looking beyond disciplines the methodology also encourages collaborations beyond the academy. Because the problem-focused approach of transdisciplinarity deals with "life-world" issues, academics have to "overcome the mismatch between knowledge production in academia, and knowledge requests for solving societal problems."[31] Stehr and Grundmann have observed that in transdisciplinary research, boundaries between "universities and industry, seem to be less and less relevant."[32] Giovannini and Revéret note that "close collaboration of academics with stakeholders from society on a problem involving different disciplines in a complex was one of the methods that has led to a true transdisciplinary attitude from the academic participants."[33]

Collaboration between academics and practitioners is informed by the notion that, fundamentally, a society's tertiary education system is about producing knowledge as a "public good" and that the "problems" they address are also often under investigation by other "stakeholders" and their "practitioners."

Attempts to connect scholarly terrorism studies with practitioners in CT have gained great momentum since September 11. The moves have generated heated discussions about the involvement of academics in counter-terrorism. The new "Critical Terrorism Studies" sees these external connections with stakeholders and practitioners as counter-productive to the role and purpose of scholarship in the maintenance of liberal democracy and the rule of law.[34] Because most of these external connections are with government, Herman and Sullivan fear that important questions are simply not asked because the academic can be intellectually straight-jacketed or fall victim to government biases.[35]

This chapter asserts that transdisciplinarity can produce rigorous, critical and conceptually innovative research. At the same time, the approach is at odds with the stated position of many who have inspired or become advocates of "Critical Terrorism Studies," because of the suggestion that the "predominance of problem solving" as an approach to the field accounts for "many of the observed methodological and conceptual shortcomings of terrorism research."[36] Such commentary—along with the wider ideological fracas associated with calls for a "critical turn"—leaves transdisciplinarity with a challenge if it is to become a useful methodology for terrorism studies.[37]

Signature pedagogy

Whereas interdisciplinarity has sometimes been heralded as the logical end of disciplinarity, transdisciplinarity holds no such allusions. Reading from the "Charter of Transdisciplinarity"—devised by a group of scholars meeting on the subject in Portugal in 1994— transdisciplinarity does not weaken or threaten but "complements disciplinary approaches."[38] Disciplinary training therefore remains a central component of the transdisciplinary enterprise. Before a scholar can perform in the transdisciplinary, he or she must be trained in the disciplinary. Such a viewpoint places transdisciplinarity as a research methodology in close relationship with some of the most recent developments in teaching and learning in higher education.

In the last five years university teaching across the English-speaking world has been challenged by a disciplinary-based approach to university teaching known as the Scholarship of Teaching and Learning (SOTL).[39] SOTL acknowledges the centrality of the disciplines and the nexus between teaching and research in higher education.[40] Disciplines are more than simply outmoded repositories of knowledge and method. They are not simply sites of chauvinism that have stood in the way of new ideas; a claim that has often been used to justify cross-disciplinary approaches.

Detailed studies across a range of disciplines have done much to emphasize that disciplines produce their own unique ways of thinking and performing that are then reflected and perpetuated in their teaching and research methodologies.[41] These disciplinary ways of thinking and performing produce what American scholar Lee Shulman has labeled "signature pedagogies."[42]

Signature pedagogies (especially in the humanities and social sciences) challenge the notion—which had become popular into the 1990s—that university students graduate with little more than some quickly forgotten content and a range of "generic skills." In fact, research is showing that university graduates have a range of transportable skills but that these skills are grounded in their disciplinary ways of thinking and performing.[43] Yes an English graduate has "critical thinking skills" but these skills have been developed and reinforced by that discipline. They are not the same critical thinking skills gained by a biologist. In essence the student undertakes a "cognitive," "practical," and "moral" apprenticeship in their discipline.[44]

The consequences of this new approach to teaching and learning have been profound. For many discipline communities it has provoked widespread calls for major curriculum review and change. Given the power of the discipline in shaping the graduate, more attention is being given to what academics teach, how students learn and the broader educational context.[45] Such change is not only important for the student but for the wider society. In championing major curriculum review in history for example, Calder insists that the poor teaching of history in the United States must "share in the blame for Americans' deplorable ignorance of history."[46]

An important development in teaching and learning has been the continuing work on "threshold concepts." In addition to the scholarly conventions and techniques of the discipline community, students should be introduced to the "threshold concepts" that they need to successfully complete the major. Traditionally these concepts have been rarely discussed explicitly with students; teachers either assume that the student has been introduced to the concepts in their secondary education or they fail to recognize them as new ideas for a student new to the discipline. This tacit/implicit approach produces "bottlenecks" which impair student learning because the "troublesome knowledge" for a novice can be conceptually difficult, counter-intuitive or "alien."[47] Removing these bottlenecks by specifically addressing threshold concepts has been seen to improve student learning and satisfaction and to strongly ground the student in their discipline.

To recap, a history graduate has a different knowledge and skill set to a graduate of English literature or a graduate of geology. Successful teaching and learning in the discipline allows the student to effectively deal with a series of threshold concepts that in turn enable the student to assume disciplinary ways of thinking. Their acquired knowledge and abilities have been filtered and are understood through the signature pedagogy of the discipline. Geology students might have some of the same content knowledge as history students, but their discipline does not approach such content in the same way because they have not been trained to "perform" as historians. Of course, very few history graduates become historians and very few biology graduates biologists but in whatever career they pursue their basic educational default is their discipline training. As new material is presented before them they will approach it from their disciplinary perspective whether or not they are conscious of this fact.

What is happening in teaching and learning in higher education has a profound impact on the state's efforts in CT. Because of the nature of their training, historians working in terrorism studies and their graduates working as practitioners in the field of CT bring to the study of terrorism ways of thinking and performing that are not replicated by other disciplines. This is not to suggest that historians or history graduates are necessarily more important than other scholars or graduates; they are simply different. Returning to the touchstone of transdisciplinarity, various disciplines and their graduates will bring their own ways of thinking and performing to the research environment. An intelligence officer with a mathematics degree will perform his or her role differently to an intelligence officer with a history degree even when completing the same task; education predetermines such an outcome. The key to fully realizing a graduate's potential is making the most effective use of the disciplinary skills—whether in history or mathematics—in a transdisciplinary environment.

Accepting the significance and power of a discipline's signature pedagogy, must, therefore, shape the working environment. Education cannot be viewed in generic terms. A graduate recruitment scheme that sees all graduates as equal is important but a scheme that assumes they come to the job with the same skills and abilities is misguided. Are agencies in the field of CT making the best use of the disciplinary skills and ways of thinking of their graduates? For a true transdisciplinary CT environment to succeed the differences of the various disciplines cannot be subsumed by some overarching approach that pays no heed to disciplinary difference. A graduate's disciplinary background is important and should be considered when tasking them in a CT environment.

CT's ability to harness the full potential of their graduates is currently compromised by the fact the disciplines are still coming to grips with their signature pedagogies. In history, Sipress and Vockler have observed that there is currently no agreed definition of what constitutes a signature pedagogy; "critics agree that students must be asked to 'think historically,' [but] a common understanding of what exactly constitutes historical thinking, let alone how to promote it, has yet to emerge."[48] This said, there is a range of models on thinking historically that are of immediate use. American scholars Andrews and Burke have identified the "Five Cs" of historical thinking: "change over time, context, causality, contingency and complexity."[49] English scholars Booth and Hyland have identified ten characteristics of "high-caliber" learning in history. These are:

1. The ability to seek out knowledge
2. The ability to manage large, disparate and often incomplete bodies of information from a wide range of courses
3. The ability to understand and evaluate the conceptual and methodological frameworks which form the basis of historical knowledge and interpretation
4. The ability to describe and explain the nature of past societies, and the forces of historical change and continuity within them
5. The ability to use historical knowledge and skills to develop one's own insights and interpretations
6. The ability to address and resolve problems
7. The ability to think creatively within and beyond one's historical studies
8. The ability to work and learn with others
9. The ability to manage one's one learning within and beyond academic studies
10. The ability to use knowledge and skills in a socially responsible and constructive manner.[50]

Although many of these ten characteristics are not peculiar to history, they comprise the signature pedagogy of the discipline. Much of the current work focuses on how universities can train students in disciplinary ways of thinking through course learning outcomes and program attributes.[51]

Historians and history can make an important contribution to the academic field of terrorism studies and to CT. Such contributions would be best made in transdisciplinary environments that recognize the historian or history graduate's unique skills. Historians have been quite resilient in protecting their disciplinary integrity, and, as a result, they tend to be placed on the margins of cross-disciplinary endeavor. History graduates in CT have certainly far more exposure than their teachers to cross-disciplinary environments. This is both an opportunity and curse if not handled correctly. Subsuming the discipline or subverting the signature pedagogy in the name of CT "cross disciplinary education and training" does not use a history graduate to their full potential. Creating a transdisciplinary research environment that recognizes and encourages the unique ways of thinking and performing of the history graduate (or any graduate) will produce a better outcome. Better to train the history graduate to be a better historian in a transdisciplinary environment than to engage in some form of "cross-disciplinary education and training" that fails to appreciate difference and does not know how to use that difference to its advantage.

Notes

[1] Charles W. Wessner, *Partnering Against Terrorism: Summary of a Workshop* (Washington: National Academies Press, 2005), 90.

[2] Some scholars in the field are reticent to use the term "terrorism studies" because it might denote a discipline and hence have a limiting effect. This study sees the term as useful shorthand and an acceptable nomenclature to refer to this broad field of study. See John Horgan "Understanding Terrorism: Old Assumptions, New Assertions, and Challenges for Research," *Tangled Roots: Social and Psychological Factors in the Genesis of Terrorism*, ed. J. Victoroff (Amsterdam, IOS Press 2006), 2–3.

[3] Magnus Ranstorp, "Mapping Terrorism Research—Challenges and Priorities," *Mapping Terrorism Research: State of the Art, Gaps and Future*

Direction, ed. Ranstorp (London: Routledge, 2006), 4.

[4] Boaz Ganor, *The Counter-Terrorism Puzzle: A Guide for Decision Makers* (Edison, NJ, Transaction Publishers, 2005), vxi. Repko notes that a *discipline* "refers to a particular branch of learning or body of knowledge such as physics, psychology or history." The "defining elements"—which include assumptions, perspective, worldview, epistemology, concepts, and theories, distinguish disciplines from one another. Disciplines are social and intellectual constructs that are not "rigid and unchanging" and can evolve over time. See Allen F. Repko, *Interdisciplinary Research* (London, Sage, 2008), 3–5.

[5] Wayne Nelles "Theoretical Issues and Pragmatic Challenges for Education, Terrorism and Security Research," *Comparative Education and Human Security From Critical Pedagogy to Peace Building?* ed. Wayne Nelles (London, Palgrave McMillan, 2003), 12.

[6] Walter Enders and Todd Sandler, *The Political Economy of Terrorism* (New York: Cambridge University Press, 2006), xii.

[7] A. J. W. Taylor, "Defusing the Terrorism of Terror," *Psychology of Terrorism*, ed. Bruce Bongar et al. (New York: Oxford University Press US, 2007), 391.

[8] No scholar has been as bold as geographer Colin Flint to suggest that their discipline has not been ignored but, rather, has been disinterested in contributing to the scholarship of the field. See Flint, "Terrorism and Counter-Terrorism: Geographic Research Questions and Agendas," *The Professional Geographer*, 55/2 (2003): 161-169.

[9] See for example Jones Irwin, *War and Virtual War* (Amsterdam: Rodopi, 2004), 1.

[10] Neil J. Smelser, *The Faces of Terrorism* (Princeton: Princeton University Press, 2007), 4.

[11] Ganor, *The Counter-Terrorism Puzzle*, xvi.

[12] Jeffry Ross, *Political Terrorism: An Interdisciplinary Perspective* (New York: Peter Lang Publishing, 2006), 5. Bunge has suggested that interdisciplinary and multidisciplinary are variants of cross-disciplinarity. See Mario Bunge, *Emergence and Convergence: Qualitative Novelty and the Unity of Knowledge* (Toronto: University of Toronto Press, 2003), 169.

[13] Enders and Sandler, *The Political Economy of Terrorism*, xii.

[14] For a detailed discussion see Michael Gibbons et al., *The New Production of Knowledge* (Thousand Oaks: Sage, 1994).

[15] Martha Crenshaw, "Terrorism, Strategies, and General Strategies," *Attacking Terrorism: Elements of a Grand Strategy*, ed. Audrey Kurth Cronin and James M. Ludes (Washington DC: Georgetown University Press, 2004), 78.

[16] For recent studies providing strong advocacy for interdisciplinary work see Sharon J. Derry et al., *Interdisciplinary Collaboration: An Emerging Cognitive Science* (London: Routledge, 2005); and Repko, *Interdisciplinary*

Research.

[17] John Horgan, "Understanding Terrorism," *Tangled Roots: Social and Psychological Factors in the Genesis of Terrorism*, ed. Jeffrey Victoroff (Amsterdam: IOS Press, 2006), 75.

[18] Avishag Gordon, "Terrorism as an Academic Subject after 9/11," *Studies in Conflict and Terrorism* 28 (2005), 45. This said, Gordon had earlier noted a broadening of the field out of the social sciences into other areas such as the life sciences. See Gordon, "The spread of terrorism publications: A database analysis," *Terrorism and Political Violence*, 10/4 (1998): 190–193.

[19] Ravi Kanbur, "Economics, Social Science and Development," *World Development*, 30/3 (2002), 484.

[20] Holger Hoffman-Riem et al., "Idea of the Handbook" in *Handbook of Transdisciplinary Research*, ed. Gertrude Hadorn et al. (New York: Springer, 2008), 5.

[21] Stephen H. Cutliffe, *Ideas, Machines, and Values: An Introduction to Science, Technology, and Society Studies* (Lanham: Rowman & Littlefield, 2000), 45.

[22] Basarab Nicolescu, *Manifesto of Transdisciplinarity* (Albany: State University of New York Press, 2002), 44.

[23] Helga Notwotny, "The Potential of Transdisciplinarity," http://www.interdisciplines.org/interdisciplinarity/papers/5 (accessed August 5, 2008).

[24] Julia Klein, "Moving Past Dichotomies in Brussels," http://www.interdisciplines.org/interdisciplinarity/papers/5 (accessed August 5, 2008).

[25] Notwotny, "The Potential of Transdisciplinarity." See also Margaret A. Somerville and David Rapport, *Transdisciplinarity: Recreating Integrated Knowledge* (Montreal: McGill-Queen's University Press, 2003). This approach also deals with the concerns of scholars like Horgan who believe that disciplinary focus and scholars finding niches in a new field can produce "rigidly held perspectives." See Horgan, "Understanding Terrorism," 75.

[26] Julia Klein, "Moving Past Dichotomies in Brussels."

[27] Repko, *Interdisciplinary Research*, 15.

[28] Manfred A. Max-Neef, "Foundations of Transdisciplinarity," *Ecological Economics*, 53/1 (2005), 5.

[29] Urs Wisemann et al. "Enhancing Transdisciplinary Research: A Synthesis in Fifteen Propositions," *Handbook of Transdisciplinary Research,* 433.

[30] Nico Stehr and Reiner Grundmann, *Knowledge: Critical Concepts* (London: Taylor & Francis, 2005), 285.

[31] Hoffman-Riem et al., "Idea of the Handbook" in *Handbook of Transdisciplinary Research,* 3.

[32] Stehr and Reiner Grundmann, *Knowledge: Critical Concepts*, 286.

[33] Cited in Shimshon Belkin and Shoshana Gabbay, *Environmental*

Challenges (New York: Springer, 2000), 478.

[34] The danger of the academic not being able to see past the biases with a resulting distortion to their scholarship has been raised by Sharon Pickering, Jude McCulloch and David Wright-Neville, *Counter-Terrorism Policing: Community, Cohesion and Security* (New York: Springer, 2007), 10. The discussion point, however, is not a new one. See Paul Wilkinson, *Terrorism and the Liberal State* (London: Wiley, 1977).

[35] See Edward Herman and Gerry O'Sullivan, *The Terrorism Industry: The Experts and Institutions That Shape Our View of Terror* (New York, Pantheon, 1990).

[36] Jeroen Gunning, "A Case for Critical Terrorism Studies?" *Government and Opposition*, 42/3 (2007): 363–64. Gunning suggests that terrorism studies has become fixated with the "terrorism problem" which has been framed by the state and been accepted "uncritically" by scholars. This view has been long held and his article provides a useful introduction to this argument.

[37] For a negative reaction to "Critical Terrorism Studies" see Mervyn F. Bendle, "Hijacking Terrorism Studies," *Quadrant*, 52/9 (2008), http://www.quadrant.org.au/magazine/issue/2008/9/hijacking-terrorism-studies (accessed October 3, 2008).

[38] Pierre Gilles Weil, *The Art of Living in Peace: Guide to Education for a Culture of Peace* (Paris: UNESCO/Unipaix, 2002), 98.

[39] The inspiration for SoTL is seen to lie in the seminal 1989 work of Ernest Boyer. See Boyer, *Scholarship Reconsidered: Priorities of the Professoriate* (San Francisco: Josey Bass, 1990).

[40] For important contributions on disciplines and teaching and learning see Alan Jenkins "Discipline-based Educational Development," *International Journal for Academic Development*, 1/1 (1996), 50–62; Mick Healey, "Developing the Scholarship of Teaching in Higher Education: A discipline-based approach," *Higher Education Research and Development*, 19/2 (2000) :169–187; Healey and Jenkins, "Educational Development through the Disciplines," *The Scholarship of Academic Development*, ed. H. Eggins and R. Macdonald (London: Open University Press and the Society for Research into Higher Education, 2003), 47–57; Mary Huber and Sherwyn P. Morreale, *Disciplinary Styles in the Scholarship of Teaching and Learning* (Washington DC: American Association for Higher Education, 2002); and George Lueddeke, "Professionalising Teaching Practice in Higher Education: a study of disciplinary variation and teaching-scholarship," *Studies in Higher Education*, 28/2 (2003): 213–228. For an introduction to debates around the teaching/research nexus consult Alan Jenkins, Rosanna Breen and Roger Lindsay, *Reshaping Teaching in Higher Education: Linking Teaching with Research* (London: Routledge, 2003). Much of the discussion of the

nexus examines the flow from research to teaching. This paper asserts and demonstrates that the flow can also be important in the opposite direction.

[41] A notable contribution in history is A. Booth, "Rethinking the Scholarly: Developing the scholarship of teaching in history," *Arts and Humanities in Higher Education*, Vol. 3, No. 3 (2004): 247–266.

[42] Lee Shulman, "Signature Pedagogies in the Professions," *Daedalus*, 134 (2005): 52–59.

[43] For a recent discussion of this field see Nancy L. Chick, Aeron Haynie and Regan A.R. Gurung, "From Generic to Signature Pedagogies," in Regan A.R. Gurung et al., *Exploring Signature Pedagogies: Approaches to Teaching Disciplinary Habits of Mind* (Sterling VA: Stylus, 2009), 1–18.

[44] Early work around the notion of a cognitive apprenticeship was conducted by A. Collins, J.S. Brown, and S.E. Newman, *Cognitive Apprenticeship: Teaching the Craft of Reading, Writing and Mathematics* (Cambridge MA: BBN Laboratories, 1987). Shulman expanded this work into the three apprenticeships. See Lee Shulman, "The Signature Pedagogies of the Professions of Law, Medicine, Engineering, and the Clergy: Potential Lessons for the Education of Teachers," Delivered at the "Teacher Education for Effective Teaching and Learning" Workshop Hosted by the National Research Council's Center for Education, 8 Feb 2005, http://hub.mspnet.org/index.cfm/11172 (accessed 11 June 2008). For a study utilizing this framework consult Dai Hounsell and Charles Anderson "Ways of Thinking and Practising in Biology and History: Disciplinary Aspects of Teaching-Learning," *Higher Education Colloquium*, University of Edinburgh, 10–11 June 2005.

[45] A notable contribution in history has been by David Pace "The Amateur in the Operating Room: History and the Scholarship of Teaching and Learning," *American Historical Review*, 109/4 (2004): 1171–1192.

[46] Lendol Calder, "Uncoverage: Toward a Signature Pedagogy for the History Survey," *Journal of American History*, 92/4 (2006), 1362.

[47] Jan Meyer and Ray Land, "Threshold Concepts and Troublesome Knowledge: Linkages to Thinking and Practising Within the Disciplines," *Improving Student Learning: Ten Years On*, ed. C. Rust (Oxford: Oxford University Centre for Staff and Learning Development, 2003); J. J. Bonner, C. Lotter, and W. S. Harwood, "Improving Student Learning, One Bottleneck at a Time," *The Science Teacher*, Dec. (2004): 26–29.

[48] Joel M. Sipress and David J. Voekler, "From Learning History to Doing History: Beyond the Coverage Model," *Exploring Signature Pedagogies: Approaches to Teaching Disciplinary Habits of Mind*, ed. Regan A.R. Gurung et al. (Sterling VA: Stylus, 2009), 25.

[49] Thomas Andrews and Flannery Burke, "What does it mean to think historically," *Perspectives: The Newsmagazine of the American Historical As-*

*sociatio*n, 45/1 (2007): 32–35.

[50] Alan Booth and Paul Hyland, "Introduction: Developing Scholarship in History Teaching," *The Practice of University History Teaching*, ed. Booth and Hyland (Manchester: Manchester University Press), 2000, 8.

[51] Joan Middendorf and David Pace, "Decoding the Disciplines: A Model for Helping Students Learn Disciplinary Ways of Thinking," *New Directions for Teaching and Learning*, ed. Middendorf and Pace, 98 (2004): 1–11; Arlene Diaz, Joan Middendorf, David Pace, and Leah Shopkow, "The History Learning Project: A Department "Decodes" Its Students," *Journal of American History*, 94/4 (2008): 1211–24.

5

Intelligence Pathologies in Terrorism Analysis

Brett Peppler

National intelligence priorities can be fickle, often reflecting urgent rather than important considerations. During the 1980s, a debate raged within the US intelligence community over whether or not the Soviet Union was the principal supporter of terrorism. In the early 1990s, following the collapse of the Soviet Union, counter-proliferation and the challenges presented by failed or rogue states were the most important intelligence priorities. Terrorism was considered important but it had not yet engaged policymakers in a strategic sense in the post-Cold War security environment.[1] The lack of focused strategic attention led to early confusion and uncertainty about the capabilities, intentions and vulnerabilities of contemporary terrorism.

Understandably, many were quick to pronounce the 9/11 attacks a failure of intelligence analysis. Intelligence analysis is the most fascinating and yet the least understood or recognized part of the intelligence process.[2] Intelligence failures, however, are difficult to define and often resist simple explanations. For example, intelligence analysis does not occur in isolation of a broader policy, planning, or operational context. An examination of a series of apparent analytic failures to foresee terrorism events, including the bombing of the USS *Cole* in 2000, suggested that the US intelligence analytic community had demonstrated "organizational rigidity, poor planning, insufficient use of outside sources, and isolation of intelligence providers and consumers."[3] In terms of 9/11, the same observer noted that "although many [US Government] officials were aware of the threat of al Qaeda [before 911], and the [Director of Central Intelligence] had instructed the intelligence community to follow the group more closely, intelligence organizations did not respond effectively."[4]

While the 9/11 Commission's final report addressed institutional failures in detail, it had little to say about intelligence analysis in general. However, the 9/11 Commission did conclude that the core analytic failure was one of a "lack of imagination."[5] In addition to organizational failures within the intelligence community, recent literature on intelligence practice, spawned from the 9/11 catharsis, has paid particular attention to weaknesses in analysts' cognitive processes and methodologies or so-called "intelligence pathologies" — especially analytic pathologies made apparent by the threat of contemporary terrorism.[6]

The paper argues that the rapid evolution of terrorism has created intelligence pathologies in Western governments arising from legacy mindsets and practices rooted in dated conceptions of conflict in general and terrorism in particular. With an emphasis on the 9/11 experience, the paper examines contemporary terrorism, noting its growing complexity, and the resulting transient competitive advantages it enjoys over the Western intelligence community. Next, the paper illustrates a range of systemic weaknesses acting upon and within the intelligence community that precipitate so-called intelligence pathologies. Finally, the paper proposes remedies to overcome these pathologies, and foster more effective intelligence support for terrorism analysis.

Threat perception

Statecraft is experiencing a "revolution in intelligence affairs." However, many of the concepts and practices around which intelligence organizes and operates are anything but revolutionary. Some observers have characterized these concepts and practices as "familiar relics from another era."[7] A pervasive "relic" is the conception of threat developed during the Cold War, which comprises both an estimated intent and an estimated capability, displaying the relationship as a quasi-mathematical model: Threat Perception = Estimated Intent x Estimated Capability, or more commonly, *Threat = Intent + Capability*.[8] The "threat equation" seemingly offers a simple and convenient approach to threat analysis.

The Cold War threat equation gained widespread acceptance in key Western defense and intelligence communities over the following decades. During this period, the threat equation has undergone limited modification, remaining recognizable in its numerous appearances, despite challenges to an underpinning and often unstated assumption; namely that threat is considered in a rather well-defined or "tight" bi-polar system, with the most crucial policy decisions being taken in Washington and Moscow. In a more complex time, the threat equation's underpinning assumption does not hold in a contemporary threat environment dominated by the pervasive but intangible threat of terrorism.

Defining contemporary terrorism is fraught with danger. Contemporary terrorism is not easily understood in terms of traditional nationalist or political campaigns such as Irish, Basque or Tamil separatist movements. While these previously known forms of terror continue, they are essentially peripheral to the nature and scale of the security challenge posed by the threat from al Qaeda.[9] Some observers have side-stepped the definitional challenge by describing a number of characteristics of contemporary terrorism.[10] However, for the purposes of this paper, contemporary terrorism may be defined as politically motivated (including ideologically, religiously or socially—but not criminally) violence by sub-state actors directed generally against non-combatants, intended to shock and terrify, and to achieve a strategic outcome.[11] This definition excludes state-sponsored terrorism, with its divisive, value-laden comparative assessments throughout the international community.

The definition of contemporary terrorism given above highlights a shift from an "event-focus" to an "effect-focus" in the planning and execution of terrorist operations. Effect-based operations (EBO) are "conceived and planned in a systems framework that considers the full range of direct, indirect, and cascading effects, which—with different degrees of probability—may be achieved by the application of military, diplomatic, psychological, and economic interests."[12] EBO constitute asymmetric threats, that is, those threats that achieve disproportionate effects by attacking vulnerabilities not appreciated by the target, or that capitalize on the target's limited preparation against the threat.[13] The targets selected for the 9/11 terrorist attacks, for example, seem to meet these twin criteria of vulnerability and limited preparation.

The dynamic character of contemporary terrorism has limited the utility of concepts such as "intent" and "capability." In contemporary terrorism, intent is often "nested"; that is, multiple layers of intent co-exist at varying scales, such as the transnational intent of some terrorist movements, and the embedded intent of supporting, aligned or inspired individual acts of terrorism. Capability typically refers to action or events, rather than the effects intended to be created by terrorist events, and associated terrorist vulnerabilities are highly situation-dependent. Added complexity is imposed on terrorism analysis by the effects-based nature of its planning, as well as its ability to adapt and employ novelty in its operations. Contemporary terrorism arguably outpaces the capacity of intelligence communities to adapt to a new operating environment.

Intelligence pathologies

The rapid evolution of contemporary terrorism and the corresponding cognitive and methodological challenges have created a range of "intelligence pathologies" in Western intelligence communities. Specifically, these intelligence pathologies arise from legacy mindsets and practices rooted in dated conceptions of terrorism and a failure of imagination in shaping and interpreting the current operating environment. These intelligence pathologies are present at the intelligence system, intelligence organization, and individual intelligence analyst levels.

1. *Intelligence System Level*

Robert Clarke's (then National Coordinator for Counterterrorism) description of his first meeting with Condoleezza Rice in 2001 is insightful. At that time, Rice was the newly appointed National

Security Advisor in the first George W. Bush Administration. Clarke said:

> [I] gave her the same briefing on al Qaeda that I had been using with the others [Cheney, Powell, and Hadley—Deputy National Security Advisor]...her reaction was very polite [but] her facial expression gave me the impression that she had never heard the term before...Rice looked skeptical [then] she focused on the fact that my office staff was large by NSC standards....[14]

Clarke surmised that Rice was still operating within the old Cold War paradigm from when she had previously worked in the NSC as a staffer for three years (1990–92) dealing with the Warsaw Pact and the Soviet Union. Rice had not worked in government on new post-Cold War security issues dealing with other than nation-state threats, where the boundaries between foreign and domestic policy were increasingly blurring.[15] Intelligence expertise arising from formative experiences can get in the way of anticipating and appreciating departures from the norm.[16]

The nature of the international response to contemporary terrorism—the "war on terror"—risks politicizing the intelligence function. The Bush-imposed dichotomy of "right" and "wrong" discourages consideration of root local causes and trigger factors for acts of terrorism, and the production of strategic analyses that may challenge state interests.[17] The "war on terror" ideology produces moral hazards in the intelligence community that are likely to follow state interests and outweigh analytical objectivity. The CIA's National Intelligence Officer responsible for the Middle East (2000-05) described a "dysfunctional and acrimonious relationship between the intelligence community and senior policy makers," which he believed, arose from alleged efforts to politicize intelligence at that time.[18]

The 9/11 Commission Report observed that the government keeps too many secrets. There is growing evidence that an increasing amount of information is being withheld from the public through the proliferation of handling caveats such as "sensitive but unclassified," "sensitive homeland security information," and "sensitive security information."[19] To address this problem, especially the apparent atavistic behavior of the Executive Branch of the US Government, the 9/11 Commission recommended that:

> ...the culture of agencies feeling they own the information they gathered at taxpayer expense must be replaced by a culture in which the agencies instead feel they have a duty...to repay the taxpayers' investment by making that information available.[20]

2. *Intelligence Organization Level*

Bureaucratization of intelligence is characterized by internal barriers that stifle communications and collaboration, a resistance to engage external centers of expertise, and the absence of a truly multidisciplinary analytic effort able to develop creativity. George Tenet's (then CIA Director) unclassified testimony to the Senate Select Committee on Intelligence (SSCI) on February 7, 2001 highlighted the global danger posed by al Qaeda. He argued:

> Terrorists are also becoming more operationally adept and more technically sophisticated in order to defeat counterterrorism measures. For example, as we have increased security around government and military facilities, terrorists are seeking "softer" targets that provide opportunities for mass casualties.[21]

While Tenet was hinting at emerging al Qaeda threats to the American homeland, the dominant Cold War paradigm (mentioned above), enduring bureaucratic politics, and internal organizational struggles for resources were apparently more influential in shaping debates in the intelligence community and security policy. Insightful analysis suffered. These tensions are present when national security and foreign policy responsibilities often have competing geographical and functional interests.

An intelligence organization has a duty of "professional care" to both external clients, and its analysts. Without a commitment to a duty of professional care, intelligence pathologies emerge such as an inattention to the environment and to internal procedures where people slip into routines, fail to notice changes in a larger context, see new phenomena in old categories, and use incoming information (even if it indicates significant variances) to confirm expectations. Rigid concepts and closed perceptions that enshrine untested assumptions as received wisdom have been a persistent feature of national intelligence work.[22] Yet despite frequent authoritative advice about the dangers of these institutionalized cognitive weaknesses, the pathologies endure.[23] For example, in the late 1990s, the US counterterrorism agenda was shaped by three dominant assumptions:

1.   That terrorism against US interests would continue to be conducted only outside the borders of the United States;

2.   That Sunni Islamic terrorist organizations [al Qaeda is Sunni] were less political and therefore less inclined to attack the United States; and

3.   That such terrorist groups were too splintered and poorly equipped to mount a major attack against the United States.[24]

The findings of the 2002 Joint Inquiry seem to support the influence of these untested assumptions on intelligence analysis:

> Prior to September 11, the Intelligence Community's understanding of al-Qaeda was hampered by insufficient analytic focus and quality, particularly in terms of strategic analysis...there was a dearth of creative, aggressive analysis targeting Bin Laden and a persistent inability to comprehend the collective significance of individual pieces of intelligence.[25]

The findings of the Joint Inquiry also highlighted a pathology at the heart of intelligence analysis, namely, a bias towards "seeing is believing" that may anchor an intelligence organization to prior analytic judgments. "Seeing is believing" is a dominant cognitive process in modern intelligence analysis. The proposition appears self evident, so much so that it has been captured in popular culture.[26] "Seeing is believing" is exemplified by the hypothetico-deductive method.[27] "Seeing is believing" is effective when a problem is familiar, or when a problem is likely to develop in a certain way or ways, but without context, new events that do not fit existing mindsets may not be used to test underlying assumptions. The Joint Inquiry found that:

> From at least 1994, and continuing into the summer of 2001, the Intelligence Community received information indicating that terrorists were contemplating, among other means of attack, the use of aircraft as weapons. This information did not stimulate any specific Intelligence Community assessment of, or collective US Government reaction to, this form of threat.[28]

3. *Individual Intelligence Analyst Level*

The effects-based nature of modern terrorism is problematic for intelligence analysts due to the scope and magnitude of uncertainty associated with the achievement of intended and unintended effects. This level of uncertainty limits the utility of dominant methods of analysis and modeling used in the intelligence community.[29] For example, risk management techniques underpin threat assessment, and the importance of risk management for the nation's security posture is reflected in its centrality in various government national security planning documents.[30] Risk assessments are the product of judgments about the likelihood and consequence of specific threats; however, these judgments are normative and become meaningless under conditions of high uncertainty.[31]

Intelligence analysts are encouraged to avoid false analogies, especially "mirror thinking," where the cultural mores and decision-making rationale of the analyst are transposed onto the target.[32] However, differences in culture and decision-making are real—not all human actions are determined by Western notions of rational thought, and these differences affect societal and individual preferences for action.[33] These differences suggest that the dominant intelligence challenge is not to penetrate denied areas but to understand denied minds.[34] This shift in targeting has implications for the types of information needed, the nature of the information gathering necessary to provide that information, and associated information processing.

The adaptive nature of contemporary terrorism demands an equally agile and imaginative response from intelligence analysts.[35] Intelligence analysts are challenged to provide judgments on complex and often unfamiliar adversaries, especially their likely behavior, based on fragmentary and frequently ambiguous information.[36] To date, successful attacks by Islamic extremists have been characterized *inter alia* by novelty, networked structures, deception, and good operations security, effectively creating "history-less" events. Forecasting "history-less" events is a challenge when intelligence analysts have no intimate understanding of a target's future behavior, few concrete indications of emerging intent or capability, and no conventional trail of premises to construct a robust inference. Under these circumstances, intelligence analysis quickly confronts the limits of knowability.

The novelty employed by contemporary terrorism challenges the analysts' ability to "think outside the box," particularly in bureaucratic cultures more familiar with "groupthink."[37] Analysts need to understand how a terrorist group would employ a threat in novel ways. Inability to "think outside the box" may constrain projections of asymmetric effects, limiting options for influencing the shaping and operations of friendly forces. Also, the underestimation of terrorist threats may contribute to increased surprise when the threat is executed. This analytic challenge may contribute to a pattern of conflict that unfolds as "a dialectic of challenge and response, with each side creating challenges for the other and responding to the other's challenges in turn."[38]

Remedies for intelligence pathologies

To its credit, the US intelligence community has reflected on the lessons of 9/11, recognizing the imperative for unconventional thinking to overcome the Joint Inquiry's charge of a "failure of imagination."[39] For example, the Central Intelligence Agency recently sponsored a comprehensive and authoritative study to examine ways to deal with intelligence pathologies.[40] Also, improving the analytic function has been a key theme in recent intelligence literature.[41] However, at an intelligence system level, dominant practices tend to anchor perspectives to the present where they become victim to past experiences and hostage to rigid interpretations of particular operating environments. Thus robust remedies for intelligence pathologies should go beyond narrow training interventions at the individual level to shaping culture and thinking at the organizational level.

The intelligence community (and its clients) needs to deal explicitly with the complexity of contemporary terrorism rather than effectively excluding complexity from its deliberations. One approach to deal with the complexity of contemporary terrorism could involve shifting perspectives from a "monochronic" view of time to a "polychronic" view.[42] A "monochronic" view conceptualizes time as a line extending into the future, which can be divided into equal segments. A "polychronic view" creates temporal signatures or "social ages" based on social relationships that coordinate, orient, and regulate interactions between people and groups. The distinction reduces the risk of negative unintended consequences arising from inappropriate targeting of threat groups in different but co-existing social ages.

The intelligence community should adopt ways of knowing that shift thinking from an "atomistic approach" to a "holistic approach." An atomistic approach embraces mechanical, reductionist thinking that breaks a complex problem down to understand it, while a holistic approach employs systems thinking to understand the bigger picture by focusing on the relationship between the parts and the emergent behavior produced by such interactions. Also, an atomistic approach is incremental in character, assessing new evidence in piecemeal fashion in terms of its effect on the body of judgments already made, while an holistic approach assesses evidence in a "stock-take" fashion in which the entire collection of evidence is reviewed.[43] A holistic approach to intelligence analysis requires institutionalizing a process for capturing the lessons of experience, interrogating those lessons, and advancing organizational learning that fosters "mindfulness." Weick and Sutcliffe define the approach as:

...the combination of ongoing scrutiny of existing expectations, continuous refinement and differentiation of expectations based on new experiences, willingness and capability

to invent new expectations that make sense of unprecedented events...and identification of new dimensions of context
that improve foresight and current functioning.[44]

The intelligence community should shift its thinking from a "seeing is believing" approach to a "believing is seeing" approach. "Believing is seeing" helps free up frozen mindsets and move beyond
the existing observation, intelligence, or evidence base to build a
new context for analysis. Before 9/11, for example, terrorist attacks
involved actions such as siege, assassination, and bombing, usually
on a localized scale, admittedly often with wider asymmetric effects.
This was the dominant mindset in the intelligence community, and
there was little reason to believe that things would be any different
in the near future.[45] The failure to recognize the few available intelligence indicators during the preparations for 9/11—such as the
abnormal flight training requests—arose from a lack of context. The
dominant mindset could not perceive that terrorists could fly passenger jets into multiple high-value targets in the American heart-
land. As a result, the small pieces of available information were not
contextualized into intelligence, and they remained "noise" rather
than becoming a "signal."

The intelligence community should embrace the new body of
alternative analysis (AA) methodologies.[46] While traditional intelligence analysis logically processes available evidence, alternative analysis seeks to help analysts and policy-makers stretch their
thinking through structured techniques that challenge underlying
assumptions and broaden the range of possible outcomes considered.[47] Alternative analysis embraces the process of "sense-making," which is a continuous, iterative, largely informal effort by
members of organizations to understand, or "make sense" of what
is going on in the external environment that is relevant to their
goals and needs.[48] By aggregating and refining intuitive judgment
through conversations within the intelligence community, analysts construct interpretations of reality that account for perceived
anomalies, which is very useful for problems characterized by high
ambiguity or uncertainty.

Conclusion

Intelligence pathologies are present in modern intelligence practice principally from the disparity in the rate of change in the operating environment, which has become revolutionary, and the rate of change in the intelligence community, which is essentially evolutionary. In particular, intelligence pathologies limit the ability of the intelligence community to respond to this disparity, especially in the face of systemic weaknesses in culture and practice. The more intense the policy making environment, the more urgent the need for analytic agility in the intelligence community. However, an emphasis on expanded intelligence production at the expense of wider sense-making and learning may be counterproductive. Employing alternative analysis methodologies that seek to understand adversary worldviews, mindsets, and ways of fighting, would be more useful for counter-terrorism problems characterized by high ambiguity or uncertainty.

Notes

[1] Louise Richardson, *What Terrorists Want: Understanding the Terrorist Threat* (London: Murray, 2006), 20-23.

[2] A.S. Hulnick, *Fixing the Spy Machine: Preparing American Intelligence for the Twenty-First Century* (Westport, CT: Praeger, 1999), 13.

[3] Bruce Berkowitz, "Better Ways to Fix US Intelligence," *Orbis* 45, no. 4 (Fall, 2001), 609-619.

[4] Bruce Berkowitz, "National Security: The Information War," *Hoover Digest* (2003), http://www.hoover.org/publications/digest/3058346.html (accessed January 1, 2009). One reason posited by the 9/11 Commission to explain the apparent poor response to the emerging threat from al Qaeda was that intelligence support to counterterrorism had placed too much emphasis on tactical requirements and not enough on predictive, strategic intelligence.

[5] US Congress, *The 9/11 Commission Report: Final Report of the National Commission on Terrorist Attacks upon the United States* (New York: Norton, 2004), 339–344.

[6] In particular, see J.R. Cooper, *Curing Analytic Pathologies: Pathways to Improved Intelligence Analysis.* Washington, D.C.: Centre for the Study of Intelligence, 2005.

[7] Bruce Berkowitz and A.E. Goodman, *Strategic Intelligence for American National Security* (Princeton: Princeton University Press, 1989), 56.

[8] D.J. Singer, "Threat Perception and the Armament-Tension Dilemma," *Journal of Conflict Resolution* 2, no. 1 (March, 1958): 90-105.

[9] For example, al Qaeda poses an adaptive threat, in that it has regrouped, generated new leadership at all levels, shifted geographic focus, adjusted tactics, and reorganized into a collection of networks and cells quite different from its pre-9/11 condition.

[10] Richardson, *What Terrorists Want*, 9-10. Richardson notes also that the study of terrorism was a marginalized field in academe at this time, focusing at the level of individual terrorist groups rather than on terrorism as a global phenomenon.

[11] This definition is adapted from a definition developed by Clive Williams. See Clive Williams, *Terrorism Explained: The Facts About Terrorism and Terrorist Groups* (Sydney: New Holland, 2004), 7.

[12] P.K. Davis, *Effects-Based Operations: A Grand Challenge for the Analytical Community* (Santa Monica: RAND, 2001), 7.

[13] B.W. Bennet, C.P. Twomey, and G.F. Treverton., *What are Asymmetric Strategies?* (DB-246-OSD) (Santa Monica: RAND, 1999), 33.

[14] R.A. Clarke, *Against All Enemies: Inside America's War on Terror* (New York: Free Press, 2004), 229-230.

[15] Ibid., 229-230.

[16] Richard Betts, "Fixing Intelligence," *Foreign Affairs* 81, no. 1 (January / February, 2002): 49*ff.*

[17] Terrorism can be seen as an attitudinal phenomenon manifested at an individual level, driven by political, economic and social forces; so an objective that seeks to defeat or eliminate terrorism is unlikely to be achieved.

[18] Paul R. Pillar, "Intelligence, Policy and the War in Iraq," *Foreign Affairs* 85, no. 2 (March/April, 2006), http://www.foreignaffairs.org/20060301faessay85202/paul-r-pillar/intelligence-policy-and-the-war-in-iraq.html (accessed January 1, 2009).

[19] George W. Bush, "Disclosures to the Congress," Presidential Memorandum (October 5, 2001), http://www.fas.org/sgp/bush/gwb100501.html (accessed January 1, 2009).

[20] US Congress *The 9/11 Commission Report*, 46.

[21] George Tenet. "Current and Projected National Security Threats to the United States." Testimony to the US Senate Select Committee on Intelligence (SSCI) (Washington, D.C., February 7, 2001), http://intelligence.senate.gov/107-2.pdf (accessed January 1, 2009).

[22] Roy Godson, "Avoiding Political and Technological Surprises in the 1980s," *Intelligence Requirements for the 1980s: Analysis and Estimates,* ed. Roy Godson (London: Transaction Books: London, 1980), 85.

[23] For example, see J. Davis (1992); and Richards J. Heuer, *The Psychology of Intelligence Analysis* (Washington, D.C.: Centre for the Study of Intelligence, 1999).

[24] M. A. Turner, *Why Secret Intelligence Fails* (Potomac Books: Dulles, TX, 2005), 115.

[25] US Congress, *Joint Inquiry Into Intelligence Community Activities Before and After the Terrorist Attacks of September 11, 2001* (Washington, D.C.: US Congress, 2003).

[26] For example, consider the popular expression "show me the money"—meaning when I see the money I will believe you are serious.

[27] The hypothetico-deductive method is based on the scientific method but the term is better suited to intelligence analysis because it explicitly describes the problem-solving process. The method incorporates inductive reasoning to discover and build testable generalizations or hypotheses that guide the analyst's information collection, while deductive reasoning is used to test and verify the inductive generalizations formed previously. So induction allows us to "see" within the available evidence, and deduction in verifying the hypothesis, allows us to "believe."

[28] US Congress, *Joint Inquiry Into Intelligence Community.*

[29] P.K. Davis, *Effects-Based Operations*, xiii.

[30] Athol Yates, *National Security Practice Note: The Beginning of the End for Risk Management?* (Canberra: Australian Homeland Security Research Centre, September, 2005), 1. Yates cites *Protecting Australia Against Terrorism* and the *Critical Infrastructure Protection National Strategy* as examples of national security planning documents that are constructed around risk management principles.

[31] The risk management principles and methodology observed by the Australian Government are explained in Standards Australia, *Australian / New Zealand Standard (AS/NZS) 4360:2004 Risk Management* (Sydney: Standards Australia, 2004).

[32] See George Packer, "Knowing the Enemy," *The New Yorker*, December 18, 2006, http://www.newyorker.com/archive/2006/12/18/061218fa_fact2 (accessed January 1, 2009).

[33] See National Security Coordination Centre, *The Fight Against Terror: Singapore's National Security Strategy* (Singapore: Singapore Government, 2004). This document makes it clear that Singapore views the modern terrorist threat posed by jihadi groups as being far more profound and sustained than anything seen in the past. Recognizing that "...communists fought to live, whereas the Jihadi terrorists fight to die, and live in the next world" appeared to be a shocking revelation by the Singaporean Government after it arrested the first of a number of Jemaah Islamiyah (JI) members in December 2001, who were accused of plotting to bomb various targets around the island.

[34] Cooper, *Curing Analytic Pathologies*.

[35] The growing sophistication of individual terrorists is aiding their adaptation to changing circumstances at an individual and group level.

[36] Cooper, *Curing Analytic Pathologies*, 41.

[37] Irving L. Janis, *Groupthink*, 2nd edition (Boston: Houghton-Miffin, 1982), 174-197.

[38] Peter Chalk, "Terrorism, National Security and the New Realities" (paper presented at the Global Executive Forum, University of Colorado at Denver, October, 2001).

[39] The discussion of remedies focuses on pathologies associated with intelligence analysis, especially at the organizational and individual analyst levels.

[40] Cooper, *Curing Analytic Pathologies*.

[41] For example, see C.M. Grabo, *Anticipating Surprise: Analysis for Strategic Warning* (Lanham, MA: Massachusetts University Press, 2004); Turner, *Why Secret Intelligence Fails*; and R.Z. George and R.D. Kline, eds., *Intelligence and the National Security Strategist: Enduring Issues and Challenges* (Lanham, MA: Rowman and Littlefield, 2006).

[42] See http://timestructures.com/tutorial.html.

[43] Emphasis on collection that holds that new information will appropriately correct earlier judgments, a practice based in Bayesian logic, depends on prior observations that may never be carefully re-examined.

[44] Karl E. Weick and K.M. Sutcliffe, *Managing the Unexpected: Assured High Performance in an Age of Uncertainty* (Michigan: Jossey-Bass, 2001), 25.

[45] Even terrorism scholars such as Louise Richardson, when consulted by the US intelligence community before 9/11, offered the same prognosis for the future of intelligence. Richardson bravely admits this in her 2006 book.

[46] See George and Kline, *Intelligence and the National Security Strategist*. The most powerful alternative analysis (AA) methodologies include key assumption checks, Devil's advocacy, Team A / Team B, Red Cell exercises, Contingency "what-if" analysis, high impact / low probability analysis, and scenario development.

[47] W. Fishbein and G. Treverton, "Rethinking Alternative Analysis to Address Transnational Threats," *Sherman Kent Center for Intelligence Analysis* (2004), https://www.cia.gov/library/kent-center-occasional-papers/vol3no2.htm (accessed January 1, 2009).

[48] Ibid.

Part II

International Case Studies

6

Lessons from the Past: The Historical Roots of Militant Islamic Ideology and its Influence on Contemporary Jihadist Movements

Anne Mahmoud Aly

Islamist movements in the Arab world were born in the age of imperialism with the aim of establishing an Islamic order. The collapse of the Ottoman Empire and subsequent westernization of the Arab world marked the beginnings of militant Islamism in Egypt as Islamic Jamaat (groups) began organizing themselves with the vision of overthrowing the government and establishing an Islamic state. Da'wa, or the Islamic tradition of spreading Islam through words and deeds, was the original path chosen in their endeavor. Gamal Abdul Nasser's program of modernization presented a barrier to the achievement of the Jamaats' aims, most notably those of Al Ikhwan al Muslimeen (Muslim Brotherhood). As public support for Nasser's aspirations for Egypt dwindled with events such as the loss of the June war in 1967 (resulting in the loss of the Sinai Peninsular to Israel), the Islamist movement gained popular support as a viable and attractive alternative to Nasserism among disgruntled Egyptian youth.

The death of Nasser in 1970 and the installation of Anwar al Sadat as his successor marked a shift in the political activity of the Islamist movement. Unlike Nasser, Sadat attempted to appease the Jamaat and win their support by lightening the restrictions on their political activities put in place by his predecessor. In the more politically free environment during Sadat's leadership, a number of organizations and splinter groups developed with the aim of overthrowing the government and instilling sharia law and governance.

While terrorism is essentially a political tool, Islamic terrorism has evolved into an ideological quest for support for the Islamist cause aided by a powerful religious discourse designed to legitimize itself to the masses. Traditionally, counter-terrorism strategies have tended to focus on neutralizing threat and capability for terrorism and on crisis management. However, pressing questions remain about the history and origins of militant Islamism, the objectives and strategies of al Qaeda, and the globalization of the jihadist movement. This paper traces the history of and developments in the militant Islamist movement through an examination of Ayman al Zawahri's (al Qaeda's principal ideologue) jihadist discourse.

Rather than offer further analysis of the various explanations of the origins of militant Islamism in Egypt, this chapter examines the discursive construction of al Zawahiri's ideology in order to analyze the proliferation of militant Islamism in the contemporary context of global terrorism. In doing so this chapter proffers two arguments. The first argument is that Zawahiri's major contribution to the current jihadi movement, and in particular to the ideology espoused by al Qaeda, is discourse — a discourse which has gained legitimacy among the Muslim Ummah, galvanized mass support, and which has a regenerative capacity. Zawahiri's message, embodied in this discourse of jihad, has succeeded and continues to succeed because it has become ontogenetic such that the message has taken on a life, or indeed many lives, of its own. The ontogenetic power of this discourse resides in its core message that Islam is under attack and that Muslims are the victims of a conspiracy to undermine Islam as a global religion. It is a message that resonates with the personal and communal situations of Muslims of all ages, nationalities and backgrounds. Most importantly, it is a message that has permeated the identity construction of Muslim youth. For some, the victim identity is so entrenched that the allure of fighting Islam's opponents is almost impossible to resist. It is therefore no longer enough to stop the messenger: attentions must also focus on diffusing the message.

The second argument this chapters offers, is that understanding the discursive construction of the jihadi discourse and its appeal offers a basis for developing a terrorist profiling model that moves beyond intelligence gathering and capability management to one that addresses intent and antecedent. The hazards of terrorist profiling are well established in the literature with a general agreement that there is no particular psychological or personality attribute that is distinctive of terrorists.

Russell and Miller profile terrorists as single males aged between twenty-two and twenty-four with some university education or, at the least, a college degree: "Whether having turned to terrorism as a university student or only later, most were provided an anarchist or Marxist world view, as well as recruited into terrorist operations while in the university."[1] Edgar O'Ballance's profile leans more towards psychological characteristics. These characteristics include: dedication—including unconditional obedience to the leader of the movement; personal bravery; the absence of any pity or remorse even though victims are likely to include innocent men, women, and children; above average intelligence, and a reasonably good educational background including a good grasp of general knowledge.[2] The ability to speak English as well as one other language and a university degree are also mandatory. The US Federal Research Division also suggests that terrorists are generally people who feel alienated from society and have a grievance or regard themselves as victims of an injustice. Many are dropouts, they are devoted to their political or religious cause and do not regard their violent actions as criminal. The sophistication of the terrorist will vary depending on the significance and context of the terrorist action.[3]

What is clear from the literature is that profiling terrorists on psychological, social or even religious and racial lines is inadequate. There may be some value in some established approaches to criminal profiling such as the model of antecedent, method and manner, body disposal and post-offensive behavior.[4] Certainly, body disposal and post-offensive behavior do not apply in the case of terrorism; particularly suicide terrorism. Method and manner are not constants as ongoing conflicts in Iraq and Afghanistan provide fertile ground for terrorists to learn and perfect new methods of attack. This leaves antecedent or intent. Traditionally counter-terrorism responses such as border control, intelligence, legislative amendments and crisis management tend to be primarily concerned with managing threat and capability rather than addressing motivation or intent. However, the global proliferation of al Qaeda's discourse of jihad indicates that counter-terrorism measures including profiling, policing and intelligence-gathering need to focus on signifiers of intent and on diffusing intent.

Ayman al Zawahiri: a brief history

Ayman al Zawahiri was born into an aristocratic family in 1951 in the upper middle class Cairo suburb of El Maadi. He was a serious and studious student who followed in the footsteps of his strict Muslim family. By some accounts Zawahiri led an unnamed clandestine cell in 1966 at the age of just fifteen, notably also the year that Sayyid Qutb, Zawahiri's primary ideological influence, was executed. By Zawahiri's own accounts, he was part of a group that established the cell but did not take over leadership of the cell until after 1974 when the cell consisted of eleven members. Their objective was to topple the government and instill Islamic rule in Egypt. Zawahiri's cell understood jihad to mean "removing the current government through resisting it and changing the current regime to establish an Islamic government...through a military coup."[5] Members of Zawahiri's group were arrested in connection with the assassination of President Sadat in 1981. At least one went on to establish jihadist training camps in Pakistan. Abdul Azeez, as he is known, along with Zawahiri established the first *Islamic Jihad* in Peshawar with Zawahiri eventually taking leadership in 1992. Zawahiri's greatest criticism of the early jihadist movement in Egypt was its ideological focus on the "far enemy" while neglecting the ruling regime. On this matter he was influenced by the writings of Sayyid Qutb who affirmed that the primary ideological issues for the Islamist movement were unification against the "enemies of Islam," and recognition of the ruling regime—the "internal enemy"—as a co-conspirator in the repression of Islam.[6]

Zawahiri graduated with a degree in medicine in 1974 and then went on to attain a Master's degree in surgery and a PhD in surgery while he was living in Peshawar. He was arrested in connection with the assassination of President Sadat on October 15 1981 (one week after the assassination on October 6) and sent to Turrah prison where he was allegedly tortured into confessing the whereabouts of certain individuals—among them Esam al-Qamari, an officer in the Egyptian Armed Forces who had joined Zawahiri's group.

After his acquittal and subsequent release from Turrah in 1984, Zawahiri traveled to Saudi Arabia in 1985 where he worked at a hospital in Jeddah before moving to Afghanistan in 1986. It was here that he first came into contact with Osama bin Laden. Between 1987 and 1990 he gained prominence among jihadi groups in Afghanistan where his efforts were focused on regrouping the jihadi movement, and on training and preparing foreign (Arab) fighters in the Afghan jihad against the Soviets. During this time he maintained links to Cairo and the jihadi movements there. In 1992, along with other Arab mujahideen leaders, he was forced out of Afghanistan having splintered from the Afghan mujahideen who had turned against them. Under the hospitality of bin Laden, Zawahiri fled to Sudan. He eventually returned to Afghanistan when the Taliban took control and welcomed back the Arab mujahideen. The Taliban enjoyed the support of the Islamic jihad and in turn offered protection to Arab jihadists fleeing intolerant regimes in countries like Egypt. This agreement allowed jihadi movements to flourish under the protection of the Taliban regime and Bin Laden.

Zawahiri was already familiar with Afghanistan having spent four months there in 1980 and another two months in 1981 at Al Sayiddah Zeinab clinic run by the Muslim Brotherhood. By his own account, this precipitous event, over a decade before he was to ally himself with bin Laden, marked the beginning of Zawahiri's connection with Afghanistan and opened his eyes to the opportunities for coordinating jihadi activities in Egypt from a remote base in Afghanistan. Zawahiri saw the Afghan arena as a model example for jihad; the victory over the Soviet superpower provided not just a blueprint but, more importantly, renewed hope and affirmation that the jihadi could emerge victorious from a battle with the world's other superpower, namely the United States:

...I saw this as an opportunity to get to know one of the arenas of jihad that might be a tributary and a base for jihad in Egypt and the Arab region, the heart of the Islamic world, where the basic battle of Islam was being fought.[7]

Although Zawahiri is cautious not to admit it, his efforts to co-ordinate the Egyptian Islamic Jihad from abroad failed dismally. Between 1988 and 1997 jihadi groups attempted a series of assassinations that failed. During this volatile period clashes between jihadi groups and police were increasingly common, resulting in the imposition of curfews and mass arrests of Islamic group members. In essence the campaign of continued confrontation with the government went against the philosophy of Zawahiri who had maintained that the core activity of his Islamic Jihad group should be to recruit and train members in preparation for the overthrow of the regime. However, his members argued that Jemaa Islamiya was continually launching attacks against the government and winning new recruits: for Islamic Jihad to gain support, it too would have to put into practice the tactics learnt at the Afghan training camps.

The failed operations damaged the public opinion and support for the Islamic groups particularly when two of the failed assassinations resulted in the death of innocent bystanders, one a young school girl. In 1998 Zawahiri joined bin Laden in forming the International Islamic Front for Jihad on the Jews and Crusaders. The principles and aims of the Front, it would seem, are markedly different from those that Zawahiri had developed for Islamic Jihad. Importantly, the Israel-Palestine issue (though a central issue of ongoing concern in much of the Arab world) was never a focus for Zawahiri. Zawahiri's focus had always been on the internal enemy: the regime, and in particular on toppling the Egyptian regime as he stated repeatedly with the catchcry "The way to Jerusalem passes through Cairo."[8] The liberation of Palestine and enmity of the US would come only after the battles in Egypt had been won and Cairo opened. It is not completely clear why Zawahiri joined bin Laden in forming the Front and apparently shifted his focus from the internal to the external enemy. At least one analysis suggests that major factors influencing his decision included waning public support for Islamist movements in Egypt, dwindling financial funds, increasing crackdowns on jihadi activities by the police (including the handing down of the death penalty in absentia for Zawahiri),and serious losses and internal fracturing of Islamic Jihad.[9]

In *Knights Under the Banner of the Prophet*, written three years after the formation of the alliance with bin Laden, Zawahiri continues to make clear his vision for the militant Islamist movement in Egypt. In reference to the jihadi movement in Egypt, Zawahiri issues this powerful caveat "the battle has not stopped in the past 36 years. The fundamentalist movement is either on the attack or in the process of preparing for attack."[10] Under the banner of al Qaeda and with the financial support of bin Laden, he could continue to coordinate the activities of Islamic Jihad to covertly recruit members in Egypt. Zawahiri makes further reference to the establishment of an Islamic caliphate in Egypt when he states:

> If God will it, such a state in Egypt, with all its weight in the heart of the Islamic world, could lead the Islamic world in a jihad against the West. It could also rally the world Muslims around it. Then history would make a new turn, Insha Allah, in the opposite direction against the empire of the US and the world's Jewish government.[11]

The emerging phenomenon of militant Islamism

Explanations about the emergence of the Islamist phenomenon in Egypt abound.[12] Some underscore the role of the state in motivating political orientations among youths (particularly on university campuses) that were ideologically aligned to annihilating leftist trends. Secularists tend to attribute the emergence of militant Islamism to increasing religiosity primarily fuelled by a rejection of Western dominance and secular influence. Social analysts argue that repression and poverty compelled disgruntled youth to seek ontological security in organized religion. However, like many of the members of jihadi groups in Egypt, Zawahiri and his confidantes were not poor. They were not economically disadvantaged. They were not uneducated. They were doctors, engineers, pharmacists, professionals—middle or upper middle class or, like Zawahiri, from an aristocratic background. Militant Islamism flourished not among the poor, underprivileged, or the masses, but often among the elite. Many of those recruited by Zawahiri for his cell between 1967 and 1981 were students.

Despite their differences, the various (at times conflicting) explanations for the emergence of the militant Islamist phenomenon in Egypt share the view that militant Islamism is what Ansari calls an "alien and transient intruder in the body politic of Egypt."[13] Arguably, as Ansari asserts, this analysis prefers to deal with militant Islamism in Egypt as a passing phenomenon rather than confront it as widespread and deeply entrenched.

Ironically, Zawahiri's writings support the arguments espoused by secularists and liberal critics who trace Islamic militancy to the growing religiosity among disgruntled youth in response to the decline of modern secularism. Disenchanted by the promises of Nasserism which failed to provide viable solutions to social and economic repression, and galvanized by the demoralizing defeat of the June war in 1967, youth turned to the political ideologies of Islamism as an alternative. Zawahiri's own words support this analysis when he describes the 1967 defeat, known as the "naksa" or setback, as a galvanizing event for Muslim youth: "The direct influence of the 1967 defeat was that a large number of people, especially youths, returned to their original identity: that of members of an Islamic civilization."[14]

The potential to galvanize large numbers of people on the basis of a shared Islamic identity figured prominently in the development of Zawahiri's ideology and strategy. The apparent shift from the near to the far enemy in his strategy is therefore not all it appears to be. Zawahiri recognized the immense potential that focusing on the US and Israel had for achieving his highly desired goal of mass support for the Islamist movement and inspiring the Muslim Ummah in a global wave of resistance:

> The fruits of the jihad resistance go beyond inspiring hope in the hearts of the Muslim youth. The resistance is a weapon directed against the regime's henchmen, who are demoralized as they see their colleagues falling around them. Furthermore, stepping up the jihad action to harm the US

and Jewish interests creates a sense of resistance among the people, who consider the Jews and Americans a horrible symbol of arrogance and tyranny.[15]

The significance of this statement and the centrality of this notion to al Qaeda's ideology—an ideology created, disseminated and promoted through a discourse of jihad—cannot be underestimated. The transformation of al Qaeda from a "base" to what has repeatedly been described as "a global movement," an "ideology," and a "phenomenon," continues to be the subject of analysis and debate.[16] Al Qaeda's ideology of political Islam generates and regenerates itself through a discourse of jihad that offers a counter-hegemonic discourse for Muslims around the globe, collectively identified as the West's "other." Sayyid contends that it is through Khomeini's political thought that "Islamism makes the transition from an opposition and marginalized political project to a counter-hegemonic movement."[17] Through Zawahiri's discourse of jihad, al Qaeda makes a similar transition.

Al Qaeda's discourse of jihad

In a Foucauldian sense, discourse is conceptualized as the social construction of reality facilitated through language. Discourse then, imposes frameworks of understanding about reality through which people experience reality and construct meaning. Each discourse defines what can be said or done in relation to an experience. The central element of this notion of discourse is that reality can only ever be referential: discourses create effects of truth which are not necessarily true; realities that may not necessarily be reality. In its current usage, discourse refers to "socially and institutionally originating ideology, encoded in language."[18] Discourses attain dominance as truths because they are uncontested: they have achieved the status of "common sense," and are legitimized and naturalized as socially shared ideologies. One way that discourses do this is by configuring certain socially shared understandings or socially embedded categories into chains or narratives about reality.

Zawahiri's discourse of jihad has as its principal audience Muslim youth. Effectively, the discourse serves the ultimate purpose for

al Qaeda: that of galvanizing popular support for the Islamist movement and ultimately recruiting for violent jihad. The core elements
of this discourse are delineated clearly in Zawahiri's own writings.
In *Knights under the Banner of the Prophet*, Zawahiri sketches his vision for the future of jihadist movements both within Egypt and
globally. His blueprint for terrorism draws not on Qur'anic teachings but on a political analysis of Middle Eastern politics. Notably, Zawahiri rarely quotes Qur'anic verses in his book. Rather he
delivers a detailed historical narrative of political events and the
historical evolution of the Islamist movement as a counter political force. The key messages embedded in his discourse are based
on two key constructs: a shared Islamic identity of victimhood and
self-efficacy. By constructing the Muslim Ummah as a monolithic
nation bound in a global struggle and emphasizing that victory is
achievable, Zawahiri employs a potent mix of messages that has
mass appeal.

The battle is universal. It involves two opposing forces: the West
(US, Israel and Russia) in alliance with the United Nations, Muslim states, multinational corporations, the media and relief agencies and the jihadist movement. The jihadist movement represents
a growing alliance of Muslim youth prepared to defend Islam and
seek retribution for various injustices against Muslims.

Jihad is the only solution. Peaceful dialogue is a failed option.
The 1997 ceasefire of all armed operations by Jemaa Islamiya drew
strong criticism from Zawahiri who had been critical of the Muslim
Brotherhood's non-violent approach to jihad and firmly believed
that there was no dialogue with the ruling regime. According to
Zawahiri the Brotherhood had committed political and ideologi-
cal suicide in pledging allegiance to Egyptian President Hosni
Mubarak.

Endurance, patience and perseverance are the keys to victory.
Strong and steadfast leadership are key to fulfilling the goal of establishing a Muslim state as a base for launching the battle to restore
the Caliphate. Here, Zawahiri stresses loyalty to the leadership and
cautions against diverting attention away from the original principles of militant Islamism.

The nation must be mobilized to participate in the movement.
The reach of the militant Islamists must move beyond the elites to

the masses. They must be motivated to defend their honor and fight injustice against Muslims around the globe, the nation must own jihad, and there must be unity before the single enemy. Public discontent is a condition for public support. Palestine is "a rallying point for all the Arabs, be they believers or non-believers, good or evil" because every Muslim in Palestine is a part of the global Muslim community.[19]

Every person is capable of killing and inflicting terror. Zawahiri favors suicide missions for their ability to inflict maximum damage with minimal effort and loss. His message attempts to build a sense of self-efficacy among Muslims who identify with the cause. "Tracking down the Americans and the Jews is not impossible. Killing them with a single bullet, a stab, or a device made up of a popular rod is not impossible. Burning down their property with Molotov Cocktails is not difficult. With the available means, small groups could prove to be a frightening horror for the Americans and the Jews."[20]

The discourse of jihad provides a narrative basis for a shared Islamic identity. In this narrative the imagined nation of Islam is under attack from the West—constructed as the US and Israel—which seeks to destroy it by infiltrating the Muslim world both politically and ideologically. It is a powerful narrative for unifying the masses. It is not the shared Islamic identity that is at the center of the issue here. Indeed the Ummah has long been a unifying concept for Muslims all over the world who find ontological security in the idea of belonging to an imagined community of believers. What is at issue here is the basis for that shared identity. In the discourse of jihad that basis is victimhood and injustice. This is both the locus and focus of power in the discourse of jihad that has enabled the key messages to proliferate and permeate the world views of Muslims around the globe and become subsumed into their understandings of what it means to be Muslim. Importantly it is not a message that appeals only to the poverty stricken, disaffected and marginalized youth, it is a message that appeals to Muslims of all ages everywhere.

The global appeal of the jihad discourse

There are several reasons that can be put forward to explain the global appeal of the messages embedded in the jihad discourse. One of the most compelling reasons is that the underlying message of Islam under attack resonates with the real or imagined experiences of Muslims around the globe. The narrative of victimhood is one that is easily subsumed into the real life or imagined experiences of Muslims in the diaspora and in the Muslim world. Discrimination, vilification, marginalization, negative media reporting on issues involving Muslims, Bosnia, Chechnya, Palestine: all are evidence of a Western led attempt to destroy Islam.

In the aftermath of the terrorist attacks in New York in 2001 and the ensuing "war on terror," the notion of Muslims as the "common enemy" became the framework for understanding the experiences of Muslims in diasporic communities in the US, UK, Europe and Australia. Underlying this construction of the victim identity is a widespread perception that Muslims are the targets of negative media, negative public opinion and negative political rhetoric.[21] This perception is embedded in a broader framework in which Australian Muslims who see themselves as part of a global community of believers identify with a notion that Muslims around the globe are under attack, and that they are the victims of a larger conspiracy aimed at undermining Islamic identity and eradicating Islam as a world religion. The following quotes from interviews with Australian Muslims demonstrate the extent of this notion:

> —*They [the West] are aiming to destroy us and we are not aware of it but now we are under attack we are being destroyed. What about realizing we are being attacked by purpose not by our people. And now there are terrorists- all these crimes that are happening under the name of the Muslims. Who are really behind them?*

> —*Because we have something different we have Islam, and that is the difference. They want that we must not lead that way of life.*

> —*Decades ago people revolted against oppression as such we labelled them freedom fighters. Now we all even looking at the media so much we even said terrorists. But who's instilling the fear?*

*Who is actually terrorising? It's not the people that are being op-
pressed...But they're not the terrorists. They're not instilling the
fear. They're not terrorising.*[22]

The growing identification with the perception of a global war
against Islam and the construction of an Islamic identity based on
the notion of shared victimhood fulfills the requirements for the
propagation of the jihadist message and Zawahiri's vision to breach
the chasms of understanding between militant Islamism and the
"common people."[23]

The video message left by London bomber Mohammed Siddique Khan is a striking reminder that the concept of a hostile divide between "us" and "them" is a powerful message for vulnerable minds:

> Your democratically elected governments continuously per-
> petuate atrocities against my people all over the world. And
> your support of them makes you directly responsible, just
> as I am directly responsible for protecting and avenging my
> Muslim brothers and sisters...
> Until we feel security, you will be our targets. And until you
> stop the bombing, gassing, imprisonment and torture of my
> people we will not stop this fight. We are at war and I am a
> solider.

Despite being born and raised in the United Kingdom, Siddique
Khan's reference to "my people" is a potent articulation of the ability of the militant Islamist message of unity to transcend nationalism. The Report of the Official Account of the Bombings in London
on July 7 2005 asserts that British intelligence has been unable to
establish a link between al Qaeda and the four young British citizens who carried out the bombings in 2005. It also asserts that there
is little evidence of overt compulsion by an individual or organization concluding that "the extremists appear rather to rely on the
development of individual commitment and group bonding and
solidarity."

Countering the jihadi discourse

One of the main reasons that the jihadi discourse has resounded and continues to resound with particular individuals and groups of Muslims is the dismal failure by Western governments and media to counter the key messages in the jihadi discourse. Rather than challenge the message of Islam under attack, the political rhetoric employed in the lead up to the coalition-led "war on terror" provided confirmation of an ideological battle between the West and Islam.

There is a remarkable resemblance in the language used by both sides of the divide to garner collective support for their respective agendas. The language of war became the primary language for describing counter-terrorism efforts whether in terms of homeland security, foreign policy or offshore operations. This language legitimates al Qaeda's message and speaks directly to those who have internalized the message and perceive themselves not as violent terrorists, but as mujahideen fighting a just battle for a just cause against the oppressors.

The terrorist attacks on the United States on September 11, 2001 set the scene for the Western media's distinct role in the developing discourse on terrorism and counter-terrorism. The emerging media discourse on terrorism reinscribed the binary of Islam and the West and perpetuated the notion of ideological opposition between the forces of "good" (the West) and "evil" (fundamentalist Islam).[24] Importantly, the tendency for the media discourse to use religion as the primary marker of identity for Muslims contributed to the construction of a new, de-ethnicized, identity among Muslims in Western nations: an identity that is primarily religious and that is shaped by a shared perception that the media is a complicit player in a global conspiracy to undermine Islam.[25]

There is no counter-hegemonic discourse that challenges the notion of a global battle forged along religious and ideological fault lines. The terrorist attacks on New York and Washington in September 2001 were galvanizing events designed to inspire Muslim youths around the world to take up the cause of violent jihad. What has transpired since then—most notably the war in Iraq, the revelations of mistreatment at Abu Ghraib prison, the Lebanon-Israel war, and the emerging media discourse on terrorism—inveterate key points in al Qaeda's jihad discourse and reinforce the image of the US and the West in general as the enemy. In the absence of a counter-hegemonic discourse, the jihadi discourse gains legitimacy as an irrefutable truth.

Paradoxically, both defeat and victory serve as powerful motivators to action for the jihadi cause. Just as the humiliating defeat of Egypt in June of 1967 rallied together Muslim youth searching for a viable alternative to the failed promise of Nasserism, so too the September 11 terrorist attacks in the United States inspired various splinter groups to emulate the "victory" of violent Islamism. This paradox presents a challenge to counter-terrorism efforts and highlights the need to develop counter-terrorism messages that undermine the notions of victory and defeat in violent conflict.

Conclusion

The phenomenon, tactics, demands, and political motives of contemporary terrorism are not new. What *is* perhaps new about this current wave of terrorism is the proliferation of the message of militant Islamists (referred to variously as jihadists, mujahideen, fundamentalists, radicals) to a globalized audience and the ability of that message to motivate individuals and groups to commit violent acts of terrorism for a cause that, apparently, has little if anything, to do with their everyday lives: second generation youth, professional and homegrown terrorists living and working in the diaspora who fall under the influence of the militant Islamist message.

Al Qaeda's stated objective is to create a single Islamic nation to which bin Laden refers repeatedly in his speeches when he addresses the Islamic nation, bringing to an end what they perceive as the oppression of Muslims by the West. Propaganda used by Islamist groups including al Qaeda nurtures a belief among Muslims that Muslims around the world are being "victimized." Indeed one of the central methods Islamists use to recruit people to their cause is to expose them to propaganda about perceived injustices to Muslims across the world with international conflict involving Muslims interpreted as examples of widespread war against Islam and conspiracy theories abounding.

The basis of al Qaeda's ideology embodied in its jihad discourse has, to a large extent, become entrenched as the primary basis for the formation of an Islamic identity of shared injustice and victim-hood. There are now generations of Muslim youth both in the Muslim world and the diaspora who are increasingly identifying with this notion of victimhood and who are growing up with this defini-tion of what it means to be a Muslim in today's world. What is most problematic here is that if individuals or groups identify with the notion of Islam under attack they are exponentially more likely to also identify with the notion of the West as the infidel enemy. They may also be more likely to identify with the notion that the Um-mah must unite against this enemy and with the notion that violent jihad is not only their duty but also easily achievable. The bridge that spans ideas, notions and beliefs and behavioral responses is therefore, narrowed.

One of the most important lessons we can learn from the his-torical development of al Qaeda is how Ayman al Zawahiri's dis-course of jihad developed from an ideological viewpoint to a global message that resonates with increasing numbers of Muslims. Those who sympathize with the jihadists believe that they have a cause: the cause of freeing Islam from the infidel shackles. The "war on terror" has failed to generate a counter-discourse that challenges this notion and to regain the power of language and persuasion.

Notes

[1] C.A. Russell and B. H. Miller, "Profile of a Terrorist," *Terrorism: An International Journal* 1.1 (1977), 32.

[2] Edgar O'Ballance, *The Language of Violence: The Blood Politics of Terror-ism* (California: Presidio Press, 1979).

[3] Rex Hudson, *The Sociology and Psychology of Terrorism: Who Becomes a Terrorist and Why?* (Washington: Library of Congress, 1999).

[4] L. Winerman, "Criminal Profiling: The Reality behind the Myth," *Monitor on Psychology* 35 (2004): 66.

[5] Ayman al Zawahiri cited in Montasser Al Zayyat, *The Road to Al- Qa-eda: The Story of Bin Laden's Right-hand Man*, trans. Ahmed Fekry, ed. Sara Nimis (London: Pluto Press, 2004), 43.

[6] Ayman al Zawahiri, "Knights under the Prophets Banner," in *His*

Own Words: A Translation of the Writings of Dr. Ayman al Zawahiri, trans. Laura Mansfield (USA: TLG Publications, 2006), 47.

[7] *Ibid.*, 28.

[8] *Ibid.*

[9] Al Zayyat, *The Road to Al- Qaeda.*

[10] Al Zawahiri, "Knights Under the Prophets Banner."

[11] *Ibid.*, p. 113.

[12] H. N. Ansari, "The Islamic Militants in Egyptian Politics," *International Journal of Middle East Studies,* 16.1 (1984): 123-144.

[13] *Ibid.*, p. 125.

[14] Al Zawahiri, "Knights Under the Prophets Banner," 55.

[15] *Ibid.*, p. 109.

[16] Karen J. Greenberg, ed., *Al Qaeda Now: Understanding Today's Terrorists* (New York: Cambridge University Press, 2005).

[17] S. Sayyid, A Fundamental Fear: Eurocentrism and the Emergence of Islamism (New York: Zed Books Ltd, 2003), 89.

[18] R. Fowler, *Language in the News: Discourse and Ideology in the Press* (New York: Routledge, 1991), 42.

[19] Al Zawahiri, "Knights Under the Prophets Banner," 211.

[20] *Ibid.*, p. 212.

[21] Anne Aly, "Australian Muslim Responses to the Discourse on Terrorism in the Australian Popular Media," *Australian Journal of Social Issues* 42.1 (2007): 27-40.

[22] The quotations used here were expressed during interviews with Australian Muslims as part of a research project on the construction of terrorism and the fear of terrorism among Australian Muslims and the broader Australian community.

[23] Al Zawahiri, "Knights Under the Prophets Banner."

[24] Anne Aly and David Walker, "Veiled Threats: Recurrent Anxieties in Australia," *Journal of Muslim Minority Affairs*, 27.2 (2007): 203-214.

[25] Anne Aly, "Australian Muslim Responses to the Discourse on Terrorism in the Australian Popular Media."

7

Combating Religious Terrorism in Pakistan

Eamon Murphy

The image of Pakistan, perpetuated in part by the images that appear in the Western media, is that of a highly dangerous state that is rife with religious extremism. Pakistan consequently is viewed as a natural home for Islamic terrorism. An analysis of the growth of religious extremism and terrorism in Pakistan demonstrates, however, that Pakistan historically has not been particularly receptive to extremism and violence perpetuated in the name of Islam. Indeed, an explanation for the rise of religious terrorism and the problems inherent in combating terrorism in Pakistan must take into account not only religion but, more importantly, the efforts by power groups within Pakistan bureaucrats, military leaders and politicians—to foster and support religious extremism for political goals. In addition, the policies of foreign governments, particularly Saudi Arabia and the United States, have had a major impact on the internal politics of Pakistan and in so doing have contributed, in a very major way, to the rise of religious terrorism. Successfully combating religious terrorism in Pakistan is a major goal of the Pakistan government and its main ally the United States. The implications of the fight against religious terrorism in Pakistan are also extremely important for the international community.

While it would be unwise to minimize the threat of religious terrorism in Pakistan, the historical context provided by an understanding of the modern history of the state can offer a more satisfactory explanation for the rise in religious terrorism. In so doing, this chapter draws upon insights from the new field of critical terrorism studies, particularly the need to critically examine the root causes of terrorism and to consider how the state itself creates conditions that are conducive to the rise of religious terrorism.[1] An historical approach addresses a criticism of ahistorical traditional terrorism studies that views terrorism as a very recent phenomenon that started only after 9/11.[2] It is essential to examine the rise of religious terrorism in the context of "power relations at a local and global level" which will be a central theme of this chapter.[3] Simply trying to explain terrorism as a consequence of religious beliefs gets us nowhere. In particular, crude attempts to explain religious terrorism in cases such as Pakistan as purely a product of the teachings of Islam are simplistic and superficial. Instead, they have merely contributed to the unfortunate rise of prejudice and violence towards Muslims living in Western countries.

A central argument of this chapter, therefore, is that religion *per se* has not been the dominant factor in the growth of religious terrorism in Pakistan and that the majority of Pakistanis are not susceptible to Islamic extremism. In other words, religion is largely a cloak to hide the manner in which both the deliberate and unplanned activities of powerful groups in Pakistani society have led to the rise of religious terrorism. While Islamic extremism and religious terrorism still pose a threat to the internal security of Pakistan and to the international community, the threat may not be as severe as many analysts predict. This chapter argues that the most effective way of combating religious terrorism in Pakistan lies in addressing the underlying political, social and economic problems facing Pakistan. Simply jailing or killing terrorists as part of the global war on terrorism merely addresses the symptom not the root cause of religious terrorism in Pakistan.

Islam in Pakistan

In explaining contemporary religious extremism in Pakistan, it is important to understand the nature of Islam in Pakistan and its historical roots. Islam was initially brought to the part of the Indian subcontinent that was to become Pakistan in the eighth century by

Arab invaders from Iraq who long had been in contact with other religious traditions in the Middle East. The Islam that they brought with them, therefore, was a tolerant, inclusive form. The Arab conquerors of Sind—the region that is now southern Pakistan—did not attempt to impose Islam by force. Conversion of the indigenous Hindus and Buddhists was gradual over a long period of time. Many of the original converts to Islam were strongly influenced by Sufism with its belief in miracles, saints and holy men. Early Islam was also syncretistic, being tolerant towards the existing Buddhist and Hindu religions and incorporating pre-Islamic beliefs and religious practices. In addition, communities adhering to the Shia minority sect of Islam settled throughout Pakistan.[4]

Pakistan's northern Punjab region was more exposed to iconoclastic invaders from Afghanistan and Central Asia. However, later Muslim rulers of the region showed little interest in persecuting non-Muslims or in imposing Islam by force. Again, as in Sind, the process of Islamization was generally gradual and peaceful. Beside the numerically dominant Sunni sect, communities of Shias (the minority Muslim sect), as well as Hindus and Sikhs lived in relative harmony with each other until the catastrophic communal violence that took place during the partition of the subcontinent in 1947. In the western tribal regions bordering Afghanistan—Baluchistan, the Northwest Frontier Province and the Federal Administered Tribal Areas—a simple form of Islam developed that reflected the conservative tribal society in which it took root. In such regions, tribal customs, such as the seclusion of women and honor killings, became interwoven with Islam to produce a socially and religiously highly conservative society.[5] The region that now is Pakistan, therefore, embraced different religions and religious sects which generally lived in harmony until recently. The legacy of tolerance has survived in the modern state of Pakistan despite the growth of religious extremism and sectarian violence particularly over the past twenty years.

Terminology is a major problem in analyzing religious terrorism generally.[6] For example, the term "fundamentalist" is often used to describe the ideology of those committed to using violence in the name of religion. Most Muslims in Pakistan and elsewhere who follow a fundamentalist approach to their religion do not support nor are involved in religious terrorism. Indeed, pious Muslims would argue that the activities of religious extremists, particularly in targeting innocent civilians, are contrary to the teachings of their religion.[7] Salafism is often used to describe fundamentalism. It is a term used to describe those Muslims who seek to revive a simplified, purified version of Islam that existed during the lifetime of Mohammed and his immediate successors. It emphasizes a strong monotheism and condemns as un-Islamic practices such as venerating the graves of prophets and saints. As such, Salafists disagree with both the Sufis and their mystical approach to Islam, and with the Shias and their deep veneration to Ali, Mohammed's son-in-law and cousin, whom they regard as the rightful successor to Mohammed. Salafism is associated with the puritanical Wahhabi Islam of Saudi Arabia.[8] Beside its strict monotheism, Salafism places great emphasis on the proper rituals not only in prayer but in everyday activities such as dress.

But it is incorrect to identify the majority of Muslims in Pakistan who follow Salafist traditions as being terrorists or supporters of violence in the name of religion just as most Christian or Jewish fundamentalists are not likely to resort to violence to spread their religious beliefs.

The main doctrinal division among Pakistani Muslims is between the Deobandis and the Barelvis. The Deobandis see themselves as belonging to a more orthodox and true form of Islam and hence can be described as Salafi. Originally opposed to the formation of Pakistan, the Deobandis regard themselves as the main voice of Sunni Islamic orthodoxy in Pakistan. In their beliefs and practices, particularly in their emphasis on law and ritual, the Deobandis echo many of the beliefs of the puritanical Sunni Wahhabi school of Islam, which is dominant in Saudi Arabia, and which has become influential in Pakistan and Afghanistan in recent years.[9]

Unfortunately, a minority of religious extremists who hold to Salafist views are intolerant, viewing both non-Islamic religions and divergent Muslim sects as heretics or infidels. Attacks on Shias and the tiny Christian community have become more common in recent times in Pakistan. Deobandism has produced many outstanding Asian leaders, but a minority of breakaway groups have played a key role in promoting Islamic extremism in Pakistan and elsewhere.[10]

Until recently at least, the majority of Pakistanis followed the Barelvi School which is less conservative and more inclusive. In particular, the Barelvis are very close to Sufism with its central messages of veneration for the prophet, love, and mysticism. Followers of this inclusive school of Islam are far less likely to be influenced by religious terrorists than those who preach a very narrow, literal form of Islam.

It must be pointed out again that being a follower of the more conservative forms of Islam does not necessarily imply a tendency towards terrorism and violence. For most conservative Muslims in Pakistan, their religion is a private affair: a matter of strictly obeying the law and carefully carrying out prescribed rituals as set out for a good Muslim.[11] Nevertheless, the growth in influence of the Salafist schools of Islam in Pakistan has been a factor in the emergence of religious terrorism in recent times promoted by those who hold to the most extremist Salafist views.

Islam and the foundation of Pakistan

One of the popular misconceptions about Pakistan is that it was established as an Islamic state to be ruled according to sharia, Muslim law. However, the foundation of Pakistan had very little to do with religious beliefs or religiously motivated politics. Attempts to rewrite Pakistan's history by placing Islam as the driving force for the creation of the new state are historically incorrect.

The credit for the formation of Pakistan goes to Mohamed Ali Jinnah known as Quaid-e-Azam or Great Leader. As a secular, rationalist nationalist, he was a strong supporter of Hindu-Muslim unity but ironically he was to become the driving force for the foundation of the Muslim state of Pakistan. There is a great deal of historical debate about Jinnah's motivations behind his drive for an independent Muslim Pakistan.[12] A major factor was his growing disillusionment with, and fears of, the Indian National Congress which he saw increasingly as representing the interests of the Hindu majority. He became firmly convinced that a partition of India along religious lines was the only way to protect Muslim interests and preserve Muslim political and economic power. In his drive for Pakistan, Jinnah and his supporters received little support from Muslim religious leaders particularly those from the conservative followers of the Deoband School. The religious elite had little in common with the urbane, westernized Jinnah, and generally were either opposed or indifferent to the concept of Pakistan altogether. Instead, Jinnah's initial power base was a small group of Muslim professionals and administrators, mainly from the Muslim minority provinces. It is only very late in the Pakistani movement that the powerful Muslim landlords who dominated politics in the Muslim majority areas in Punjab, Sindh, and East Bengal, came to support Pakistan.[13]

The most convincing explanation for the landed interests' belated support for Pakistan was that they came to believe that in a Muslim state they would have the best opportunity to protect their vested interests. Land reforms initiated by socialist minded Congress leaders such as Jawaharlal Nehru came to be seen as a major threat to their economic and accompanying political power. History has shown that as far as their interests were concerned, the feudal nobility made the right choice—the descendents of the large feudal landholders who belatedly came to support Pakistan still dominate Pakistan politics today. Their power, particularly in the rural areas, is a major obstacle to the development of democracy in Pakistan and frustration and opposition to their dominance of society and politics has been a factor in the rise of religious extremism and terrorism.[14]

In his inaugural address to the Pakistan Constituent Assembly on the 11th of August 1947, Jinnah clearly called for the establishment of Pakistan as a state that gave full rights to all citizens irrespective of religion. He stated:

> You may belong to any religion or caste or creed…. in the course of time Hindus would cease to be Hindus and Muslims will cease to be Muslims, not in the religious sense, because that is a personal faith of each individual, but in the political sense, as citizens of the state.[15]

Over time, however, Jinnah's vision of Pakistan as a tolerant state in which religion is the private concern of citizens has been threatened by the growth of more rigid intolerant strains of Islam and by the pressure to create a Sunni Islamic state similar to Saudi Arabia ruled strictly according to sharia, Muslim law. Not only has there been a disturbing growth in hostility to non-Muslims, but sectarian divisions among Sunnis and Shias themselves have become wider in recent years. These developments and the rise of religious terrorism are closely linked.

Towards an Islamic state

Pakistanis brought up in the 1950s and 1960s remember a very relaxed and liberal society where religion was largely the concern of the individual, but, as in other parts of the Islamic world, Pakistan has become much more outwardly Islamic. More Pakistanis attend the mosque regularly and strictly observe the fast of Ramadan. Many more women wear the burka or hajib while the full length beard is becoming more common among men. The sale and consumption of alcohol is now illegal for Muslims.[16] Nevertheless, while Pakistanis have become more outwardly religious, this does not mean that they are necessarily more susceptible to religious extremism. The support for Islamist parties and for the creation of an Islamic state governed according to sharia, while growing, is still weak. For example, during the first national elections held in 1970, Zulfikar Ali Bhutto's secular Pakistan People's Party soundly defeated a coalition of right wing Islamic parties in western Pakistan.[17]

Unfortunately, as has happened all too often in Pakistani politics, religion has been used for political objectives. Bhutto's electoral victory gave him a unique opportunity to develop democracy in Pakistan. His rhetoric of socialism and democracy, however, belied the fact that his rule was personal and authoritarian—hardly surprising given his position as an all-powerful feudal landlord. In his attempts to appeal to all sections of Pakistani society, Bhutto began to actively court the religious parties. He banned alcoholic beverages, gambling and nightclubs. More significantly, he caved in to pressure from the religious parties and amended the Constitution declaring the minor Shia Islamic sect, the Ahmadiyas, to be non-Muslim.[18] Bhutto's banning of the Ahmadiyas led to outbreaks of violence against them and encouraged attacks on other Shia sects in Pakistan.[19]

Bhutto's rule was to have two long-term consequences that encouraged the growth of religious terrorism in Pakistan. He failed to take the opportunity to develop strong democratic institutions, and he encouraged, for political reasons, the growth of religious sectarianism in Pakistan. Other prime ministers, including his daughter Benazir Bhutto, were also authoritarian and were also prepared to play the Islamic card when it suited them.[20]

Military rule and jihad: Zia ul-Huq and resistance to the Soviet occupation of Afghanistan

The move towards a more conservative Islam in Pakistan accelerated greatly during the reign of General Zia ul-Huq. The general was a devout Muslim who conspired with hard-line religious groups to overthrow Bhutto's democratically elected government through a military coup on July 5, 1977. During his rule, a close alliance grew between the more conservative orthodox Sunni mullahs and the military.[21] A major consequence of this alliance and of the reign of Zia was that Pakistan became a much stronger Islamic society—at least in appearance if not always in reality.[22]

The invasion of Afghanistan by the Soviets in 1978 and their propping up of the Marxist government was an extremely important catalyst in the growth of religious conservatism, militant Islam, and religious extremism in both Pakistan and Afghanistan. During Zia's rule, Pakistan became the center of a religious crusade—a *jihad* or a holy Islamic war—against the godless Soviet occupiers of Afghanistan. The armed resistance to the Soviets was financed to a large extent by the United States, which saw the opportunity to defeat its main ideological and political opponent, the Soviet Union.[23] The other main financial supporter for jihad in Afghanistan was Saudi Arabia, keen to export its particular exclusivist narrow form of Wahhabi Islam in part to counter Iranian-backed Shia influence in the region.[24]

The long term consequences of the involvement of the US and Saudi Arabia were to be disastrous for both the internal security within Pakistan and, in the long-run, for the United States and its struggle against religious terrorism. It can be argued that 9/11 was in part a long-term consequence of the US policies in Afghanistan, particularly during the Zia period.

The war in Afghanistan and support by the United States also greatly strengthened Zia's power. Zia was an authoritarian ruler who attempted to destroy Jinnah's dream of a religious state and turn Pakistan into a Sunni Islamic state ruled by strict Islamic sharia laws. He also had more pragmatic goals in using Islam to consolidate his personal power and that of the military. He encouraged the orthodox clergy, particularly the Sunni mullahs, by attempting to introduce a rigid interpretation of sharia. By aligning himself with the mullahs and by taking up the cause of an Islamic state, Zia attempted to provide an ideological justification for military rule: he and the military were the protectors of Islam. He was supported by many of the religious parties that already had close ties with the military.

Islamists were appointed to important government positions in the judiciary, the civil service and educational institutions. Sharia courts were established to try cases under Islamic law, while Islamization was promoted through the government supported media.[25] In addition, education was Islamicized. The narrow Islamic model of citizenship taught in schools, particularly since the rule of Zia, has helped create a climate conducive to sectarian violence and religious intolerance by marginalizing non-Muslim citizens and those belonging to minority Muslim sects.[26] For example, history books in Pakistani government schools stereotyped and demonized Hindus as untrustworthy, treacherous and backward.[27]

During Zia's reign a close alliance developed between the conservative mullahs, Islamic clerics and mosque leaders, and the military which was to become a persistent factor in Pakistani politics. The mullahs and support for conservative Islam were important factors in providing an ideological justification for the dominant role that the military played in Pakistani politics. The mullahs and religious parties were to be an effective counter to secular opposition politicians. Military dictators courted religious parties as a counter to secular opposition groups and political parties.[28] This policy strengthened Islamic forces in Pakistan.

Under General Zia, attempts were also made to Islamize the
military. Islamic education became incorporated into the curriculum for officers. Increasingly more religiously conservative officers
were promoted. Mullahs belonging to the conservative Deoband
School were appointed to work among the troops. Radical Islamic
ideas influenced some of the younger officers and rank-and-file.
According to one source some 25–30% of officers had fundamentalist leanings. Nevertheless it appears that only a minority were
radicals. An attempt by radical Islamic officers in the mid-1980s to
bring about an Islamic revolution and theocratic state was easily
crushed.[29]

A major factor in the Islamization of Pakistan was the rapid
growth in the number of *madrassas* (religious schools), during the
1980s. In 1971 there were 900 madrassas in Pakistan but by the end
of the Zia era in 1988 there were 8,000 registered and 25,000 unreg-
istered madrassas.[30] The madrassas provided education, food and
housing and a very narrow Islamic education for the very poor.
Many of these madrassas preached a narrow form of Sunni Islam.
They were financed to a large extent by Saudi Arabia and, ironically, as it turned out, by funds from the United States. While only a
minority of madrassas preached violence, a long-term consequence
of the growth of the madrassas was the development of a narrower
less tolerant form of Sunni Islam particularly among the poor.[31] A
minority of madrassas became indoctrination and training schools
for jihad especially in the tribal areas although according to terrorism expert Rashid Ahmed, many militants who have fought in
Afghanistan and Kashmir, especially from the North West Frontier
Provinces and from the Federally Administered Tribal Areas, never
have been students of madrassas.[32]

For the mullahs, the support of the military was to provide them
with the means to increase their influence in all aspects of Pakistani
society. The Soviet invasion of Afghanistan in 1979, therefore, was
a key factor in strengthening the alliance between the mullahs and
the military. This alliance was a major factor in the drift to Islamic
fundamentalism in Pakistan. Religious fundamentalism, as has already been observed, does not imply religious extremism but splinter extremist groups who misinterpret fundamentalist doctrines
have emerged who are violent.

The ten-year conflict in Afghanistan between the Soviets and Afghan rebels, therefore, became a key factor in the growth of Islamic extremism both in Pakistan and Afghanistan. For many in the Islamic world, Pakistan became a frontline state against godless communism. For a while the struggle provided a common ground for two very different strategic and ideological objectives. For the United States, it was an extension of the Cold War between the two superpowers: the US and the Soviet Union. For many pious Muslims, it was jihad or holy war against the unbelievers. Ultimately, the very divergent ideological goals of the US and the Islamists emerged after the defeat of the Soviet forces and their withdrawal from Afghanistan.

The struggle against the Soviets in Afghanistan also greatly strengthened the power and authority of the main Pakistani intelligence organization: the Inter-Services Intelligence (ISI). The ISI controlled the secret operations in Afghanistan against the Soviets. ISI officers controlled the distribution of weapons and trained the Afghan commanders. The ISI worked closely with the US Central Intelligence Agency (CIA) which provided a huge amount of funds and military equipment. Saudi funding and jihadi volunteers were also controlled by the ISI. In addition, the Afghan war placed huge resources at the disposal of the organization which became highly intrusive and interfered not only in the domestic politics of Pakistan but also in spying on the military itself. In the training of the jihadis, the ISI established very close links with Muslim militant groups, while many individual officers sympathized with religious militants.[33] However, the death of General Zia in the mysterious plane crash in 1988 and the withdrawal of Soviet troops from Afghanistan in 1989, greatly weakened the uneasy and unnatural alliance between the CIA and the Pakistan military particularly the ISI. No longer having a common enemy, both organizations became distrustful of each other.

In 1990 the United States imposed sanctions against Pakistan for its nuclear weapons program. The mistrust that the Pakistanis felt towards the United States re-emerged as it was considered that the United States was prepared to walk away from Afghanistan and from Pakistan now that the common enemy, the Soviets, had been defeated. All sections of the Pakistani public bitterly resented what was regarded as treachery and betrayal by the United States. The short sighted policies of the US which led to a power vacuum in Afghanistan were in large part responsible for the emergence of the most formidable opponents of the US in Afghanistan and Pakistan: the Taliban.

Pakistan, religious extremism and the rise of the Taliban in Afghanistan

The defeat of the Soviet forces in Afghanistan and the withdrawal of the United States from the region created a vacuum of power that was to be filled by the Taliban. These were ultraconservative religious students educated in the many madrassas financed by Pakistan and by Saudi Arabia.[34] The students who came out of madrassas, particularly those in the tribal regions of Pakistan, were generally very poor. They were provided with a basic education and were taught a very literal and narrow interpretation of Islam. Puritanical and fanatical, the Taliban established a strict Islamic state in Afghanistan.[35]

For a variety of reasons, Pakistan supported the Taliban which in 1996 seized Kabul. The Taliban were initially viewed as a force that could bring peace to Afghanistan; at the time Afghanistan was being fought over by the various rival warlords who had been involved in the struggle against the Soviets. Pakistan also saw that its long-term economic and strategic interests would be best served by supporting what they saw as a friendly regime in Kabul. Again the ISI was closely involved in supporting Taliban commanders. In Pakistan itself many Islamists, particularly those belonging to Pakistan's Islamic parties, were highly supportive of the Taliban and its imposition of a strict Islamic regime.

The success of the Taliban in Afghanistan attracted thousands of Pakistani students from the madrassas especially those in the tribal border areas of the Northwest Frontier Province and Baluchistan. In addition, Afghanistan and the frontier border regions of Pakistan became the base for Islamic militants from throughout the Islamic world. The best-known of these was Osama bin Laden who, along with many members of his al Qaeda network, made Afghanistan and Pakistan's frontier regions their home and base.[36]

The rise of the Taliban, and Pakistan's support for the Taliban, contributed strongly to the growth of Islamic extremism in Afghanistan and Pakistan. Pakistan's rulers had little ideological commitment to the Taliban. Their main concern was the strategic benefits to be gained from supporting the Taliban. Nonetheless, the longer consequences for Pakistan were disastrous. Pakistan has become more radicalized religiously especially in the frontier regions adjoining Afghanistan. In particular, the defeat of the Taliban by the US-led coalition after 9/11 led to an exodus of hardened jihadis, both Pakistani and foreign, from Afghanistan into Pakistan. These exiles have remained a serious security risk ever since.[37] Involvement with the Taliban also radicalized a number of ISI officers especially those of junior rank. The rift between the more senior officers within the military who were concerned primarily with strategic and personal interests, and those more junior officers committed to the goals of the jihadis emerged within the ranks of the Pakistani military. After the defeat of the Taliban in Afghanistan, the jihadis and the Pakistani military—particularly the ISI—turned their attention to another struggle: rebellion in the Indian-occupied part of Kashmir.

Islamic militancy and rebellion in Kashmir

After the defeat of the Soviets in Afghanistan, Kashmir became the main target of Islamic militancy in the region. It was an ideal opportunity for the Pakistani military to channel the religious zeal previously directed against godless communism towards an old enemy: the Hindu state of India. The military saw the opportunity to tie up the numerically superior Indian military by supporting the movement of the highly trained tough jihadis who had fought in Afghanistan. Religious militants—offshoots of the groups sponsored by the US and Pakistani intelligence during the war in Afghanistan—were used to destabilize Kashmir. It was a dangerous game, however, which was to have very important consequences for Pakistan's relationship with India and with the US. It also further strengthened the influence and the power of Islamic militancy within Pakistan itself.

It is difficult to overstate the importance of the Kashmiri issue for Pakistan. Indian control of two thirds of Kashmir and its incorporation into the Indian state is bitterly resented by all sections of Pakistani society. Most Pakistanis believe that Kashmir rightly belongs to Pakistan and that India is illegally occupying Pakistani territory. The dispute between Pakistan and India over Kashmir has been the key factor in the tension between the two countries. It has led to three wars and the very real threat of a nuclear war between the two countries. The outbreak of a rebellion in Kashmir in 1988 by local Kashmiris resentful of the neglect of their regional interests was a unique opportunity for Pakistan trained militants to become involved in the rebellion.

As in Afghanistan, the ISI trained and equipped various militant Islamic groups which had been active in Pakistan and in Afghanistan to do their dirty work in Kashmir. From the mid-1990s, Pakistan-based hardline Islamic militant groups, such as Lashkar-e-Taiba, infiltrated Indian-controlled Kashmir heightening tensions between India and Pakistan. Since the organization first appeared in Kashmir in the early 1990s, Lashkar-e-Taiba, along with many other similar groups, has carried out ambushes, bombings and assassinations against the Indian army and police. Lashkar-e-Taiba and other militant groups also targeted local secular resistance fighters.[38]

The activities of the Pakistan-based militants in Kashmir divided the Kashmiri resistance movement which was being waged against the excesses of the Indian administration. Initially, resistance to Indian rule in Kashmir had been largely non-religious. The goals of the various resistance movements differed, but in general most Kashmiris wanted a greater degree of regional autonomy in Kashmir. They wanted free and open elections and protection against the excesses of the Indian Army. Increasingly, however, the growing power of the militants from Pakistan was to lead to a sharp division largely between the local Kashmiris and infiltrators from Pakistan. This development led to increased communal terrorism and communal violence in Kashmir involving not only attacks on the Hindu and Sikh minorities but also clashes between the militants from outside and the local Muslims. Up to that period, relations between Muslims and the other communities had been generally very good as the Kashmiri form of Islam was generally inclusive and tolerant coming from its Sufi roots.

The Pakistani-backed infiltration of Indian-controlled Kashmir presented long-term dangers to regional stability and created serious security problems for Pakistan's rulers. The strategy certainly tied up large sections of the Indian military but by encouraging and supporting militant activity in Indian controlled Pakistan, the Pakistan military were playing a dangerous game. Not only was it creating highly dangerous tensions with India and Pakistan, but before 9/11 Pakistan was in danger of being portrayed by the outside world as a rogue state supporting terrorism. The terrorist tactics of the various jihadi groups not only threatened the security of Kashmir but also intensified religious extremism in Pakistan itself.[39]

Musharraf, 9/11, and the global war on terrorism

Disillusionment with what was seen as the corrupt and ineffectual government of Nawaz Sharif led to yet another military takeover by General Musharraf and his supporters among the military in 1999. A former commando officer, Musharraf was regarded as a hardliner in his hostility towards the Indian occupation of Kashmir.[40] Musharraf was regarded as a religious liberal, but under his rule Pakistan continued to support Islamic militants in fighting a proxy war in Kashmir. Until 9/11, the military under Musharraf through the ISI supported terrorist groups that proliferated in Pakistan.

However, following 9/11, General Musharraf and his government were given a clear choice: either to join the US and its allies in the global war against terrorism or Pakistan would be declared a terrorist state. To resist the demands of the United States would have been disastrous for Pakistan, but the alliance between the two countries, imposed under threat, has always been fragile. Musharraf had to play a very delicate balancing act of trying to meet the demands of the US to crack down hard on terrorism while, at the same time, recognizing the dangers of alienating Muslim radicals and their supporters at home.[41] This dilemma has never been resolved satisfactorily and has continued to play a key role in Pakistan's efforts to combat terrorism even after the overthrow of Musharraf.

After 9/11, Pakistan's intelligence cooperated with US intelligence to track down and arrest al Qaeda suspects in Pakistan. In

October 2001, Pakistan provided the United States with the use of four air bases to attack Taliban strongholds in Afghanistan. In January 2002 Musharraf imposed a clampdown on religious extremists and banned five Islamic extremist organizations. In October 2003, the Pakistani army under US pressure attacked Afghan Taliban and al Qaeda bases in the Federally Administered Tribal Areas in Waziristan on the border with Afghanistan. These attacks were met with fierce resistance by the fiercely independent tribes in Waziristan and, in conjunction with other actions against the extremists, saw Musharraf and his government branded as anti-Islamic stooges of the US by many in Pakistan, particularly extremist Muslims.[42]

Despite these and other crackdowns on Islamic extremism, Musharraf and his government had to attempt to balance the internal politics of Pakistan with the demands of the US to clamp down hard on militants. As support for his regime faded, Musharraf needed allies among the religious political parties even more. Yet, at the same time, he had to crack down on the activities of the more violent and extreme religious terrorists. In his attempts to hang on to power, Musharraf suppressed the activities of rival political parties, undermined the independence of the judiciary, and attempted to browbeat the media. In so doing he pleased nobody. Musharraf's war on al Qaeda as well as against Pakistani terrorists made him an enemy for Islamic militants and the target of assassination attempts. For the United States and its allies, Musharraf's efforts against the militants were seen to be too little and ineffective. For the mass of the population and Pakistan, Musharraf became increasingly seen as a power-hungry dictator protecting his own power and that of the military. This uncertain and unstable political climate further encouraged religious extremism to flourish.

Combating terrorism in Pakistan: an analysis

A new generation of Muslim militants has emerged in Pakistan. Their goal has been to turn Pakistan into what they see as a pure Islamic state and they are prepared to use violence to achieve this. They are opposed to the rampant corruption which has long plagued Pakistani politics and society. They opposed the invasion of Afghanistan by the US and its allies, which they view as part of a global offensive against Islam led by the US. They hate the West and what they see as its corrupting influence. Besides acts of terrorism, such as the assassination attempts on Musharraf, the assassination of Benazir Bhutto, and attacks on government personnel and institutions, Islamic militants run schools, operate charities, and publish newspapers. Their leaders also are able to bring out large mobs onto the streets in protest against crackdowns on militants. Some of these Sunni extremist groups target Christians and Shias.[43] Suicide bombings, attacks on politicians and government servants and civilian targets, hostility and violence towards other Islamic sects, and noisy demonstrations in the streets have created fear and uncertainty in Pakistan itself. It has given the country the reputation to the outside world of being a dangerous country at the mercy of religious extremists. Former Prime Minister Benazir Bhutto stated that, "Pakistan today is the most dangerous place in the world."[44]

The major question is: to what extent do the Islamic militants reflect the views and have the support of the majority of Pakistanis? Pakistan's history since independence has shown that support either for an Islamic state or for Islamic extremism and violence has been confined to a minority of the population. Islam in Pakistan, as we have seen, has traditionally been flexible in its beliefs and tolerant towards different sects and religions. Islamic parties, even when supported by the military, have polled badly in elections. Even in the 2002 elections, which were rigged by the military, their religious allies did poorly except in the North West Frontier Province. In the 2008 elections they were routed everywhere including the North West Frontier Province.

Support for religious parties has been regional, confined mainly to the North West Frontier Province, western Baluchistan, and the Federally Administered Tribal Areas. Outside these regions the strongest support for an Islamic state has come from the very poor, generally unemployed, graduates of the numerous madrassas, influenced by extreme Deobandism or Saudi-funded Wahhabism. This chapter argues that the support for Islamic parties and for Islamic militants arises not out of religion but primarily out of frustration at the poverty, corruption, and failure of democratic institutions in Pakistan.

A major factor that hampered Musharraf's efforts to clamp down on religious militants has been his need to use religious parties in an attempt to neutralize mainstream secular political parties that challenged his personal authority and the authority of his government. In particular, he was strongly dependent on religious allies to counter the mass appeal of the late Benazir Bhutto's Pakistan People's Party and to a lesser extent the support given to the Pakistan Muslim League led by Nawaz Sharif. As he became increasingly unpopular among a large section of the Pakistani public, Musharraf had to be careful not to alienate the traditional supporters of the Pakistan military: the mullahs and their followers.

The military is another major factor to consider when analyzing attempts to counter terrorism in Pakistan; its political power and economic resources. The Pakistani military see themselves as having an historical right to protect the state and to play a major role in government and foreign policy in part because of the perceived failure and corruption of the political parties. A more mundane goal, however, is the determination to protect the vested interests of the military, particularly its huge financial empire. The military run many lucrative businesses. On retirement from the military, senior officers have been able to gain access to land and to a variety of positions in government bodies. Many are multimillionaires living in vast mansions.[45] The last thing that many in the military want is a cleansing of Pakistani society. As such, they are hardly likely to support the introduction of a strict Islamist regime which would threaten their vested interests. As a last resort, the military has the capacity to crush resistance except in the border states of the North West Frontier Province and the Federally Administered Tribal Areas.

Some analysts have stressed the growing influence of Islamists among the junior officers especially those serving in the ISO who are exposed to militant Islamic views.[46] One of the doomsday scenarios proposed is that there will be a military coup by Islamist junior officers who would then have access to nuclear weapons. While this possibility cannot entirely be ruled out entirely, it would seem that this is extremely unlikely to happen given the conservatism of the Pakistani military high command and their vested economic interests. Various stakeholders, including India with its nuclear capacity and far superior military force, and the US and Israel, would not permit a hostile Islamic state with access to nuclear weapons to become a serious threat to peace in the region. Similarly, the majority of Pakistanis who oppose religious extremism would not accept a narrow Islamic state.

Most analysts agree that the best way to combat Islamic militancy in Pakistan is to encourage the growth of democracy and a democratic tradition in Pakistan.[47] It is argued that such a development would undercut much of the support for the Islamic militants from individuals motivated by frustration and anger. They are not necessarily religious zealots but see the militants as one of the few forces willing to combat the rampant corruption and misuse of power by military dominated governments and corrupt politicians. Redressing the endemic economic and political wrongs that have plagued Pakistan since independence is a major strategy to curb the bitterness and frustration that has contributed so much to religious extremism.

According to many analysts, the madrassas that have proliferated in Pakistan in recent times are a primary source of religious extremism and violence. It is correct that many of these madrassas provide a very narrow Islamic education. Conditions in many are primitive, and even brutal. Many graduates leave committed to a narrow form of Islam and with limited employment opportunities. The products of such a narrow education are graduates susceptible to religious intolerance and sectarianism. Many of the Taliban in Afghanistan, for example, were educated in Pakistani madrassas which continue to turn out jihadis. But the madrassas provide a basic education particularly for the very poor. Most of the graduates are pious individuals. While some have had links with al Qaeda and its Islamic militant groups, the majority simply provide the basic education not provided by the state. Attempts to reform the narrow education provided by the madrassas will be a key concern of Pakistan's new government.[48]

While scholars argue that the development of a democratic Pakistan, with free elections and effective and responsible government, would undercut religious militancy, extremism, and bitterness, few analysts or Pakistanis citizens would argue that the transition to a variable functioning democracy in Pakistan will be either simple or immediate. The military will continue to play a major role in politics protecting their vested interests and what they see as their rightful role as rulers. Another major obstacle to the development of a true democracy is the domination of the major political parties by the very powerful feudal landlords such as the Bhuttos. Nepotism, factionalism, and corruption are unfortunately still rife among the major Pakistani political parties.

Nevertheless, despite the weaknesses and imperfections in the Pakistani political system and political processes, somehow they need to be made to work. Reforms of institutions such as education, the judiciary, and law and order, are essential, as is the passing down of economic benefits to the majority of the population. Issues such as the cost of living, the price of basic foodstuffs, and economic opportunities, are major concerns of the Pakistani people just as they are in other countries. If economic and political grievances are at least partly resolved, then the support for religious extremists will evaporate. If not, deep anger and frustration may move many to support extreme forms of resistance to the state which could lead to widespread violence.

In the painful transition to democracy, the United States in particular with its economic and political power can play a constructive role particularly in encouraging the military to withdraw from politics. The threat to cut off support for military equipment would be one such weapon.

The 2008 elections in Pakistan offered some hope for democracy and the defeat of religious extremism. The solid vote against the Pakistan Muslim League–Q, which has supported Musharraf, indicates clearly that the majority of Pakistanis were disillusioned with his authoritarian rule and that of the military. The newly appointed Pakistani Chief of Staff appears to be attempting to divorce the military from politics, a difficult if not impossible task. The main vote in the elections went to the secular parties: the Pakistan People's Party now led by Benazir Bhutto's husband, Asif Ali Zardari, and the Pakistan Muslim League. During the 2008 elections, Pakistani voters shunned the Islamic parties. In particular, the stunning defeat of the Muslim parties in the North West Frontier Province suggests that most Pakistanis are concerned more with mundane everyday issues such as the cost of living than with religion.

It remains to be seen, however, whether the corruption, factionalism and personal differences within the main political parties will allow the survival of the current government led by Zardari and the efforts to address Pakistan's urgent political, social and economic problems. The major question is whether the dominance of the military and feudal politicians who have cowed the judiciary and bureaucracy can be broken. The outcome will be crucial not just for Pakistan but for South Asia and the world generally. Leading Pakistani political commentator Professor Rasul Bakhsh Rais was cautiously optimistic about political reform in Pakistan after the February 18, 2008 elections when he commented on the emergence of "new politics" in Pakistan. He pointed to the "resolve and grit of the democratic forces and civil society to reshape Pakistan as a modern democratic state."[49] For the sake of Pakistan and the stability of South Asia one hopes that he is correct.

It would be foolish to underestimate the threat of religious terrorism and extremism to Pakistan's stability and growth. However, as has been argued throughout this chapter, it is also necessary to understand the reasons for the growth of religious terrorism and why it presents such a problem to Pakistan today.

Religious extremism did not naturally grow out of Pakistani society or the type of Islam that had taken root in the country. Rather, it has been fuelled by such events as the jihad against the Soviets in Afghanistan, the obsession with fighting a proxy war with India in Kashmir, and the support of Islamic extremists by sections of the military and by politicians. In other words, religious terrorism is a symptom, not the main cause, of the ongoing crises in Pakistani politics. Using military force alone to combat religious terrorism will not work unless the basic underlying problems facing Pakistan are tackled effectively. Making some real progress in economic and political reforms that will reduce poverty and give people hope for the future may well demonstrate that the support for Islamic extremism and militancy in Pakistan is shallow and narrow. But that is an even greater and long term challenge than combating religious extremism.

154   *Eamon Murphy*

Notes

[1] See the collection of articles on aspects of critical research in *European Political Science*, no 6 (2007).

[2] See the comment by Richard Jackson, "The Core Commitments of Critical Terrorism Studies," *European Political Science*, 6, issue 3 (2007), 244.

[3] Marie Breen-Smyth, "A Critical Research Agenda for the Study of Political Terror," *European Political Science* 6, issue 3 (2007), 263.

[4] See Hamza Alavi, "Pakistan and Islam: Ethnicity and Ideology," *State and Ideology in the Middle East and Pakistan*, ed. Fred Halliday and Hamza Alavi (London & New York, 1998), 10-13 in

http://ourworld.compuserve.com/homepages/sangat/Pakislam.htm.

[5] Although dated, S.M. Ikram's book remains one of the best balanced accounts of the spread of Islam in South Asia. See *Muslim Civilization in India* (New York: Columbia University Press, 1964).

[6] For a discussion of the problems in using terminology to describe movements in Islam see Filippo Osella and Caroline Osella, "Introduction: Islamic reformism in South Asia," *Modern Asian Studies*, 42 nos 2 &3 (2008): 247-57.

[7] The students that I interviewed at Quaid-i-Azam University and the University of Peshawar in March 2008 saw themselves as religious but strongly rejected any suggestion that their religious views made them in any way susceptible to religious extremism or terrorism. Some of these students, especially at Peshawar, came from very conservative religious tribal backgrounds.

[8] Some Salafists, however, regard Wahhabism as a heretical sect.

[9] For a clear concise overview of the Deobandi movement in Pakistan see Ahmed Rashid, *Taliban: Militant Islam, Oil and Fundamentalism in Central Asia* (New Haven: Yale University Press, 2000), 88-90.

[10] For the first time, the Darul Uloom, the most important seminary of the Deobandi school of Islam, recently denounced all forms of terrorism as un-Islamic. See Aoun Sahl "Religious edicts bars terrorism," *Daily Times* (Lahore), March 9, 2008.

[11] See Frederic Grare, "Pakistan: The Myth of an Islamist Peril," *Carnegie Endowment Policy Brief*, No. 45, February 2006, http://www.carnegieendowment.org/publications/index.cfm?fa=view&id=1799.

[12] Jinnah has been the subject of many monographs and articles. See for example, Akbar S. Ahmed, *Jinnah, Pakistan and Islamic Identity: The Search for Saladin* (London: Routledge, 1997).

[13] East Bengal became part of the state of Pakistan in 1947 but in 1971 seceded and formed the state of Bangladesh.

[14] For a clear discussion of the politics of partition with an emphasis on class interests see Alavi, "Pakistan and Islam," 6–10.

[15] Husain Haqqani, *Pakistan: Between Mosque and Military* (Washington DC: Carnegie Endowment for International Peace, 2005), 12–13.

[16] On a recent research trip to Pakistan I found that restrictions on the sale of alcohol seem to be easing.

[17] Haqqani, *Pakistan: Between Mosque and Military*, 13.

[18] Orthodox Muslims consider them heretics because of the semi-divine status that they allocate to their founder. They also hold that all religions contained elements of the divine truth.

[19] Haqqani, *Pakistan: Between Mosque and Military*, 14.

[20] For a criticism of the perception of Benazir Bhutto as a savior of democracy, see William Dalrymple "Bhutto's Deadly Legacy," *International Herald Tribune*, January 4, 2008, http://www.iht.com/articles/2008/01/04/opinion/eddalrymple.php

[21] Haqqani offers an excellent study of the nexus between Islamists and the military. See Haqqani, *Pakistan: Between Mosque and Military*.

[22] For a study of the limited impact of Islamization in a rural community see Richard Kurin, "Islamization in Pakistan: a view from the countryside," *Asian Survey*, 25 no.8 (August 1985): 852–62.

[23] Haqqani, *Pakistan: Between Mosque and Military*, especially 183–189.

[24] Ahmed Rashid, *Taliban: Militant Islam, Oil and Fundamentalism in Central Asia* (New Haven, Yale University Press, 2000), especially chapter 15.

[25] Haqqani, *Pakistan: Between Mosque and Military*. See, for example, 132.

[26] See Iftikhar Ahmad "Islam, democracy and citizenship education: an examination of the social studies curriculum in Pakistan," *Current Issues in Comparative Education*, vol 7, no 1, December 15, 2004, especially 13–14.

[27] For a discussion of the inaccuracies and biases in Pakistani public school history textbooks see Waqar Gillani, "History books contain major distortions: SDPI, *Daily Times* (Lahore), June 13, 2005.

[28] This is the central theme of Haqqani, *Pakistan: Between Mosque and Military*.

[29] Haqqani, *Pakistan: Between Mosque and Military*, 21.

[30] Rashid (2000), op. cit, 89.

[31] For a balanced discussion of Pakistani madrassas see William Dalrymple "Inside Islam's "terror schools," *New Statesman*, March 28, 2005, http://www.newstatesman.com/200503280010

[32] As quoted in Aoun Sahl "Religious Edicts Bars Terrorism," *Daily Times* (Lahore), March 9, 2008.

156   *Eamon Murphy*

33 Haqqani, *Pakistan: Between Mosque and Military*, 12.

34 The best study of the Taliban is Rashid, *Taliban: Militant Islam*.

35 For a highly critical analysis of the role that Saudi Arabia has played in spreading religious intolerance see William Dalrymple, "Saudi Arabia created the monster now devouring it; The US and Britain are straining to shore up a hated autocracy," *The Guardian*, June 14, 2004.

36 Jessica Stern, "Pakistan's *jihad* culture," *Foreign Affairs* (November/December 2000): 115–126, http://ksghome.harvard.edu/~jstern/pakistan.htm

37 Ibid.

38 Ibid.

39 Ziauddin Sardar, "Pakistan: The Taliban takeover," *New Statesman*, April 30, 2007, http://www.newstatesman.com/200704300025.

40 He was criticized as being largely responsible for the disastrous intrusion of Pakistani troops into the Kargil region which very nearly resulted in an all-out war with India. For Musharraf's version of the events, see Pervez Musharraf, *In the Line of Fire* (London: Simon & Schuster, 2006), especially 80.

41 Musharaff's dilemma is succinctly discussed in Ziauddin Sardar, "Pakistan: The Taliban takeover," *New Statesman*, April 30, 2007, http://www.newstatesman.com/200704300025.

42 Ibid.

43 C. Christine Fair, "Military recruitment in Pakistan: implications for Al Qaeda and other organizations," *Studies in Conflict & Terrorism*, vol 27 no 6 (July 2007), 491.

44 Benazir Bhutto, *Reconciliation Islam: Democracy and the West* (London: Simon and Schuster, 2008), 210; *Timothy D. Hoyt, "US policy shifts can encourage dawn of new era Pakistan," World Politics Review, February 29, 2008, http://www.worldpoliticsreview.com/article.aspx?id=1697*.

45 See Ayesha Siddiqa, *Military Inc. Inside Pakistan's Military Economy* (London: Pluto Press, 2007).

46 For a very pessimistic scenario, see Subodh Atal, "Extremist, nuclear Pakistan: an emerging threat?" Cato Institute, Cato Policy Analysis No. 472, March 5, 2003 http://www.cato.org/pubs/pas/pa-472es.html.

47 Rasul Baksh Rais, "New Politics," *Daily Times* (Lahore), March 11, 2008.

48 William Dalrymple, "Inside Islam's '"terror schools'"

49 Rais, "New Politics."

8

Al Qaeda's Eastern Front: The Russian Vector in the Network's International Activity

Alexey D. Muraviev

In mid-October 2008, Aleksandr Bortnikov, the Director of the FSB—Russia's Counter-Intelligence Agency—announced that during July and August national security services prevented several large-scale terrorist attacks against the Black Sea resorts of Sochi (the host city of the 2014 Winter Olympic Games) and Anapa. The attacks were reportedly planned by Umarov—one of the key leaders of the Chechen extremists—and Mohammed, al Qaeda's current representative in Russia.[1] The report did not receive much coverage but it did highlight al Qaeda's continued interest in Russia's North Caucasian region.

Eight years after the historic September 11, 2001, multiple terrorist attacks against the eastern seaboard of the United States, the international security community is watching Central and West Asia, the Afghanistan-Pakistan geopolitical nexus, and Iraq and the Near East. The once debated conflict in Russia's North Caucasian republic of Chechnya and neighboring areas, particularly after the successful end of the second campaign by the Russian federal forces, has been effectively transformed into a historical "case study" of peripheral significance.

Throughout the 1990s, the analysis and discussions of the Chechen security dilemma were largely based on the understanding that the origins of the conflict were driven by ethnic separatism;

the struggle of the once oppressed minority for independence from a regional colonial empire. The growing terrorist activity in the North Caucasus and larger Russia was attributed to heavy-handed tactics that Moscow employed to crack down on the separatists, while significant connections with the growing transnational extremist Islamic networks, united by the militant expansionist al Qaeda ideology (later the Green International), were ruled out. As a result, to date there is little professional and public analysis and debate of the role that international Islamic extremists played in transforming the conflict from a localized struggle for independence into one of major battlegrounds of the Green International at the turn of the new millennium.

Al Qaeda's involvement in the area has evolved through three major phases: first (1992–1994)—preparations and strategic reconnaissance; second (1995–2002)—engagement and establishing control; and third (from 2003)—declined interest and capacity but retaining links. This chapter seeks to chart this transformation, to explain why it has happened, and to analyze strategic lessons that could be learned from the analysis of al Qaeda's operations in south-western Russia.

The beginning 1994–97

Former Soviet Transcaucasia and its most turbulent provinces— Chechnya, Dagestan and neighboring areas—emerged on the radar screen of the Green International and its principal power broker—al Qaeda—in the early 1990s, soon after the Iron Curtain came down and the once mighty Soviet empire broke apart. The collapse of the Soviet Union in December 1991 did not solely mean the disappearance of the second most powerful actor in Cold War international politics. The crisis of the official state ideology—largely based on the notion that the world's first socialist power would be cemented by the centrally controlled idea of atheistic communist internationalism, alongside accelerating economic hardships and the USSR's declining status—exposed hidden wounds that the Soviet state inherited from the Russian empire and also inflicted on itself. The nation's strategic transformation, which occurred over a dramatically short period, included a crisis in both state ideology and established norms of morale; corruption that penetrated government structures and law enforcement; a struggle for regional power, which often fuelled separatism and religious intolerance; and finally the trauma of the Afghanistan war, which in the words of Russian analyst Vitiuk, "revived the thought that the use of armed violence is the norm of social life."[2]

The speedy break up engulfed several glowing conflicts, primarily along the former Soviet southern and south-western periphery. Among those conflicts were the civil war in Islamic Tajikistan— which conveniently shares a land border with Afghanistan, and the war between Christian Orthodox Armenia and Muslim Azerbaijan over the Nagorny Karabakh. It seems that during that period al Qaeda identified the once Soviet Eurasia as one of its spheres of interest. With the final withdrawal of Soviet forces from Afghanistan in 1989, the once principal theater of operations of the Green International (theater of jihad, ToJ) was transformed into a localized battlefield. Human *mujahideen* resources that were massed in the country to challenge Soviet "infidels" were freed up, and many fighters began returning home or seeking new jihadi battlegrounds.

The situation provided an opportunity for intervention in Eurasia's internal conflicts, intervention also driven by a religious agenda. Human and financial resources were mobilized, and groups of fighters and advisors were dispatched to the emerging ToJs in Eurasia. In Azerbaijan alone, by mid-1994, al Qaeda's office in Baku facilitated a force of up to 2,500 Afghan "veterans."[3] The ceasefire reached between Armenia and Azerbaijan in 1994 occurred at a time when the conflict in neighboring Chechnya was entering its hot phase—in December then Russian President Boris Yeltsin authorized the military operation against the separatist regime of the former Soviet Air Force General Dzhokhar Dudayev. The end of hostilities in the Bosnian ToJ in 1995, where the combined forces of Bosnian Croatians and local Muslims (the later, with the generous support of the Green International) were fighting the offensive campaign of Christian Orthodox Serbs, served as another trigger for the redeployment of mujahideen human resources and the influx of individual volunteers into the Caucasus.

However, the timing (the beginning of the First War in Chechnya coinciding with the suspension of hostilities in Nagorny Karabakh,

Bosnia, and also Algiers) and the convenient geographical location (sharing border with Azerbaijan and being en route from Central Asia to the Balkans) were not the only reasons for the involvement of foreign Islamic militants in the conflict. The troubled history of the Chechens and the Ingush, forced out of their land under Joseph Stalin in the mid-1940s, is a long one, stretching back to the armed resistance in the nineteenth century when the Russian empire was expanding its regional influence. The high levels of unemployment in the 1980s and the rapid criminalization of the republic that followed, contributed to the emergence of a separatist and later, an extremist agenda at the turn of the 1990s. Adding to that, in the early 1990s the republic was hit by waves of criminal and ethnic terrorism directed against opposition to Dudayev, local law enforcement and Russian Armed Forces (RusAF) elements stationed in Chechnya, ethnic Russians and other minorities that resided in the area before the First Chechen War.[4]

Vahhabist extremist ideology has also played a significant role. Attempts to import this ideology into the area occurred as early as the 1970s. According to an unnamed FSB senior officer, the "peak of the first active penetration of the Chechen-Inguish Autonomous Soviet Socialist Republic (ASSR) by the vahhabists falls within 1977–1980."[5] For example, in 1978 Chechen farmer Saleh Susayev was recruiting local youth into an extremist group, which had a strategic goal of seceding from the Soviet Union.[6]

In addition to the factors discussed above, the rise of a separatist militancy in Chechnya can also be attributed to the massive availability of weaponry and ammunition left by RusAF after their withdrawal from the republic in 1992. The enormous stockpiles of military hardware (over 42,000 light firearms alone) combined with available human resources (many of whom saw military service, including in Afghanistan) enabled Dudayev to form a potent standing force comprising 2 brigades, 7 independent regiments, and 3 independent battalions of 5,000–6,000 personnel (with additional 15,000 in reserve). These forces were heavily armed, with 42 main battle tanks (MBTs), 66 armored vehicles, 123 mortars and guns, and 40 air defense systems. In addition, Dudayev's forces could be reinforced by about 30,000 militia-men.[7] This combined force, comprising highly motivated nationalist-inspired and often experienced fighters, posed a serious military challenge to opponents of the self-proclaimed Republic of Ichkeriya (Chechnya).

A number of individuals believed to be linked to the Green International began arriving in Chechnya as early as 1991. However, al Qaeda did not pioneer in linking Chechen separatists with Islamic militants. In 1994, Dudayev's representatives established formal links with the Islamic Party of Afghanistan (*Hezb-i-Islami*), which allowed mobilization of the Afghani mujahideen to join the fight in Chechnya.[8] A year later contacts were established with al Qaeda and Osama bin Laden, bin Laden's personal envoy Amir Ibn al-Hattab (Table 2) and, perhaps, the most notorious Chechen warlord, Shamil Basayev. Each played critical roles in facilitating the links.

Al-Hattab played the decisive role in the eventual transformation of the secular ethno-centric separatist struggle in Chechnya into an extension of al Qaeda's globalized fight for influence and control over strategically important areas. A veteran of the Afghani resistance against Soviet occupation, Saudi-born al-Hattab was fighting in Tajikistan before arriving in Chechnya.[9] Gunaratna describes him as bin Laden's "protégé," a man who had apparently fought with bin Laden in several engagements against the Soviets.[10] According to General Troshev who commanded the Russian Army Group in Chechnya during the second campaign, in January 1995 al-Hattab arrived in Grozny with a group of 18 mujahideen.[11]

The arrival of bin Laden's trusted envoy initiated the process of sending experienced Arab fighters into the newly emerged North Caucasian ToJ via al Qaeda's office in Baku. Burke, in his reputed monograph, noted, "Fighters were…dispatched to Chechnya via an office set up in Azerbaijan."[12] By mid-1995, according to Gunaratna estimates, approximately 300 foreign mujahideen were fighting Russian forces in the republic, though Russian open source data suggests that 500 Islamic insurgents, including 425 Afghani instructors and fighters, joined the resistance.[13] The majority of Islamic insurgents formed an independent unit, the *Jamaat* Battalion, under the command of al-Hattab. Towards the end of the First War, al-Hattab took control of all foreign militants operating in Chechnya, formally under Basayev. Throughout the war, he also acted as the principal foreign military advisor to the separatists.

The role of Basayev in bringing al Qaeda into Chechnya was also significant. He was one of the few key figures of the Chechen resistance who traveled to both Afghanistan and Pakistan to meet with al Qaeda's leadership, including bin Laden. According to open Russian and Arab sources, in 1995 Basayev traveled at least twice to both countries to set up links with al Qaeda and the *Taliban*. In particular, on one occasion he visited Pakistan's Peshawar province before inspecting the *Abu Khuldan* terrorist training camp (TTC) in Khost, southern Afghanistan. Arrangements were made to allow selected Chechen fighters to be trained in TTCs controlled by the network. By mid-1995, about 40 Chechen militants were undergoing specialized paramilitary training in the area.[14] According to Gunaratna, several hundred ethnic Chechens were trained in Afghani camps.[15] Some Chechens were sent to al Qaeda's TTCs located in Pakistan and Sudan; collaborative contacts were established with the Lebanon-based *Hezbollah* and Palestinian groups; the latter provided fighters and instructors.

Despite these developments, throughout the First War the overall impact of al Qaeda's activities in the area was limited. During the first campaign, the Green International supplied Chechen separatists with experienced fighters (the Afghani "veterans"), organized recruitment of volunteers and fundraising, and provided ideological, technical, financial, and other support and advice. In particular, between 1995 and 1996, the actual presence of foreign mujahideen in Chechnya during did not exceed several hundred active personnel. Apart from the *Jamaat* battalion, another significant unit was the *Fatah* battalion (about 300 fighters from Palestine and elsewhere) under the command of Abu Bakar (a.k.a. Berkan Yashar, a Turkish-born ethnic Chechen).[16] Other groups manned with foreign Islamists had no more than 15 to 20 men.

At the same time, it is important not to underestimate the influence that the fighters of the Green International gained during that period. For once, established Islamic links turned into important channels that provided much needed financial support to the Chechens. According to Russian open sources, in 1995 alone, foreign Islamic donors raised over US$ 45 million for the Chechen cause.[17] As Williams points out:

While Hattab's fighters were few, they brought the out-gunned Chechen resistance access to the immense financial resources of his powerful supporters, the quasi-official charities of Saudi Arabia, such as the wealthy Al Haramein foundation. While the hard-drinking Sovietized Chechen Sufis initially found Hattab's bearded jihadi-puritan Wahhabis to be something of an oddity, the scrappy Chechens soon came to appreciate the contribution these professional infidel-killers could make to their cause.[18]

The mujahideen have also distinguished themselves as effective and often ruthless fighters. Whilst being a relative small fighting force, they brought with them extensive combat experience, particularly in asymmetric warfare, including high impact terrorist attacks (Table 1).

However, the First War was fought primarily under the banner of ethnic nationalism and separatism with the green color of anti-infidel jihad being quite marginal. It is only after Yeltsin's personal envoy General Aleksandr Lebed signed the 1996 Khasaviurt Agreement with Dudayev's successor Aslan Maskhadov, which

Target	Date	Type of attack
Budyenovsk, Southern Russia	14–19 June 1995	Mass hostage taking
Kizlyar, Pervomaiskoe, Dagestan	9–10 January 1997	Mass hostage taking
Moscow	9, 13 September 1999	Apartment bombing
Kaspyisk, Dagestan	9 May 2002	Bombing of Victory Day parade
Moscow	23 October 2002	Mass hostage taking
Moscow	5 July 2003	Suicide bombing at a rock concert
Mozdok, North Ossetia	1 August 2003	Suicide bombing at military hospital
Pyatigorsk, Stavropol region	3 September 2003	Train bombing
Yessentuki, Stavropol region	5 December 2003	Suicide train bombing
Moscow	6 February 2004	Suicide bombing of a metro train
Moscow	24 August 2004	Suicide bombing of two passenger planes
Moscow	31 August 2004	Suicide bombing of a metro station
Beslan, North Ossetia	1–3 September 2004	Mass hostage taking
Nalchik, Kabardino-Balkariya	13 October 2005	Multiple attacks on the city

Table 1. Most Significant Terrorist Attacks Facilitated by al Qaeda Operatives

effectively saw Chechnya's departure from Russia, that al Qaeda's golden hour has come.

The peak 1997–2002

During the interwar years (1997–99), Chechnya became the lawless enclave of Russia's North Caucasian region. The republic was divided into several spheres or areas of influence, each controlled by a local family clan (*teip*), an alliance of *teips*, or a powerful warlord.

Chechnya and neighboring Dagestan became areas of strategic interest for both bin Laden and his close aid, Egyptian-born Dr. Ayman al-Zawahiri, because of convenient geography such as tuff mountainous terrain (in the south) and large areas covered by forests and bush, complemented by the developed ground infrastructure; strategic location (at the cross roads of a major route connecting Central Asia with the Transcaucasus and the Balkans); the inclination of some locals (particularly, militant youth to endorse al Qaeda's extremist ideology); and the absence of a centralized authority. Al-Zawahiri traveled the area in 1996 and was even arrested by the FSB but later released after spending six months in jail, sparking speculations about the motives that drove Russian authorities to free him.[19]

Critical analysis of al Qaeda's linked activities in the area in the second half of the 1990s suggests that the network and like-minded or affiliated groups and organizations were pursuing three major objectives:

1. Ideologically indoctrinating local sympathizers, also through propaganda of militant *neo-Salafism* (Wahhabism)

2. Preparing organized armed reserve for strategic operations in the Transcaucasia and elsewhere (the first two could also be identified as the preparatory phase); Assuming complete control over Chechnya and neighboring regions (active phase).

As discussed earlier, the first attempts to import Wahhabism into the republic date back to the late 1970s. However, it was not until the troubled 1990s that foreign religious influence began penetrating local Muslim communities. With the assistance of foreign charities and missionaries, a large number of mosques and madrassas that taught Salafi Islam were opened. Religious literature circulated widely among the local population that challenged established local religious norms and practices. Speckhard and Ahkmedova note:

> Many Wahhabist mosques and schools were opened in Gro-zny and over time numerous rural regions became domi-nated by non-indigenous Wahhabi influences that instituted non-local practice of covering women and sharia law. Finan-cial rewards in these regions were often used to bind Mus-lim clerics and their constituents to adhering to this newly imported politicized version of Islam. Likewise, madrassas (religious schools) for children were opened in the capital Grozny and elsewhere and children of fathers killed in war were specifically targeted for recruitment. Unbeknownst to their families these schools and mosques promoted radical Islamic values very unlike those of the indigenous popu-lation and encouraged the children onto a militant jihadi path—to fight for national and religious independence and indeed worldwide jihad using terrorism as a method.[20]

Wahhabists began winning the hearts and minds of many be-cause the majority of the adult population was born and lived dur-ing secular atheist Soviet times and thus did not have a comprehen-sive understanding of all Islamic norms and practices, and because the local youth was largely religiously illiterate.

Foreign Islamic charities also played important roles in posi-tioning Chechnya as a regional center of religious education. Young Russian Muslims residing in Tatarstan, parts of Siberia, and his-torical places of concentration of Muslim population, were encour-aged to travel to the republic. Many of these trips were funded by foreign sponsors. After arriving in Chechnya, these young recruits were subjected to intensive introduction to Wahhabist ideas, often combined with paramilitary training in one of TTCs.[21] This trend was particularly evident between 1997 and 1999.

Al Qaeda played a noticeable role in promoting the ideas of mil-itant Wahhabism. For example, al-Hattab controlled the so-called Islamic Institute of the Caucasus, a paramilitary religious regional educational establishment of the Muslim Brotherhood international network. According to Russian intelligence, the institute had about

160 selected "students" and 40 instructors, primarily Afghanis and Arabs. The militant training was undertaking at the Institute's *Said ibn Abu Vakas* TTC.[22] Most successful graduates were later sent for further training to Pakistan and Turkey. Another paramilitary-religious facility, the madrassa in the settlement of Khacharoi, was also under al-Hattab's control.

However, al-Hattab was not the leading provider of al Qaeda's ideological operations and information warfare campaign in the North Caucasus. According to Russian intelligence, the network's main ideologue in the area was Shekh Abu Omar Muhammad As-Seif (Table 2), who was apparently sent to the region by the directive of bin Laden around 1995–96.[23] Working under the banner of the *al-Haramein* Islamic Foundation As-Seif played a significant role in spreading the idea of militant Wahhabism in Chechnya and Ingushetiya, and from 2005, in Dagestan, where he was killed in November of that year during a special counter-terrorist (CT) operation.

Another important figure who contributed to the promotion of militant *neo-Salafism*, particularly in Dagestan, was the Jordanian cleric Khabib Abdurrakhman, who arrived in the republic in the early 1990s.[24] Dagestan was equally important for the Green International, and tremendous effort was made not just to destabilize the security situation in the republic but to radicalize the local population. In 1995 alone, Islamic charities raised US$17 million in support of propaganda of Wahhabism.[25] Abdurrakhman played

Name	Portfolio	Status
Ibn al-Hattab (a.k.a Samer ben Saleh ben Abdallah al Sweleim)	Commander (Amir) of Islamic insurgents in Chechnya; IIPB Commander (1998–2002); Principal figure in the area	Assassinated on 20 March 2002
Sheikh Abu Omar Muhammad As-Seif (a.k.a. Abu Omar or bin Abdallah As-Seif)	AQ's principal ideologue/ Mufti of the Chechen *mujahadeen*; coordinator of financial support; Second most significant figure in the area	Killed in November 2005
Abu al-Walid al-Ghamidi (a.k.a Abd al-Aziz Bin Ali Bin Said al-said al-Ghamdi)	Al-Hattab's deputy; IIPB Commander (2002–04)	Killed on 16 April 2004
Abu Hafs Al-Urdani (a.k.a. Faris Yusef Amirat)	Successor of al-Hattab and al-Walid; coordinator of financial support	Killed on 26 November 2006
Abu Dzeit (a.k.a. Abu Omar Al-Kuwaiti)	Abu Hafs' Deputy; coordinator of financial support	Killed on 16 February 2005
Abu Atiy[y]a (a.k.a Adnan Muhammad Sadik)	Main representative of al-Zarqawi in Georgia	Detained in Azerbaijan in 2003
Abu Kuteiba Jammal	AQ's special instructor/explosives expert	Killed in summer 2004

Table 2. Al Qaeda's Key Figures (Chechen Arabs) in the North Caucasus 1995–2007

one of the key roles in this campaign, actively working in neighboring Chechnya's mountainous areas of Dagestan. By and large, he was responsible for the creation of militant Islamic enclaves in the southwest of the republic, which were turned into terrorist strongholds in August 1999 during a large-scale insurgent invasion from Chechnya.

Among major initiatives undertaken by al Qaeda's affiliates in Chechnya was the decision to set up a comprehensive TTC network with an objective to train local militants, as well as recruits from overseas, in conventional military operations, specialized terrorist activities, and asymmetric operational methodologies. The network was controlled primarily by al-Hattab and Basayev.

Militant training infrastructure was established in Chechnya under Dudayev. But it was mujahideen influence that transformed existing facilities and opened new ones in support of the Green International strategic agenda. As Speckhard and Ahkmedova argue, "The politics and practices of many rebel camps during the 1990s transitioned from a major emphasis on nationalistic aims into terrorist bases with a more international religious agenda similar to those operating in Afghanistan during the Taliban regime."[26]

In December 2001, the FSB released information that between 1997 and 1999, the financial and other logistical assistance of the Green International enabled the establishment of seventeen TTCs in the republic. The primary goal of these TTCs was to "train international terrorists from…Chechnya, Southeast Asia, Africa and Europe."[27] Russian intelligence claimed that the external financial assistance for terrorist training activities in Chechnya in that period often reached US$5 million per month.[28]

Al-Hattab managed the largest and most sophisticated terrorist training network, which was organized in Chechnya. Codenamed *Kavkaz* (also known as the *Islamic Center Caucasus*), the network consisted of seven major permanent TTCs with the main being located near the Serzhen'-Iurt settlement. Specialized courses in urban and field warfare, including the use of heavy armaments such as main battle tanks, armored vehicles, artillery systems and other, special terrorist activities, were taught by Pakistani and Arab instructors. About 2,000 militants were trained at any given time in the *Kavkaz*.[29] By the end of July 1999, a month before the invasion of Dagestan, al-Hattab's terrorist training network managed to train, perhaps, up to 4,000 militants.

While analyzing the *modus operandi* of the international terrorist training network in Chechnya, Troshev noted:

> At the end of the 1990s Hattab's training centers, which were turned into a preparatory base of international terrorists, occupied a special place in the plans of international extremist organizations. Together with young men from Central Asia, the Volga region, North Caucasus, young people from Saudi Arabia, Jordan, China, Egypt, Pakistan, Malaysia, other countries were trained there.[30]

In support of their principal activities in Chechnya, by the turn of the new millennium, militant Islamists were able to establish a relatively firm presence in neighboring Russia territories, notably Azerbaijan and Georgia. Prior to September 2001, when Baku joined the United States in a globalized fight against terrorism, Azerbaijan played an important role as a transit base for human resources, arms, and other material supplies en route to Chechnya and Dagestan, linking these areas with Central Asia, including Afghanistan. The measures undertaken by Azerbaijani authorities reduced the operational flexibility of al Qaeda affiliated jihadists in the country, and neutralized several terrorist plots aimed against Western, Russian, and national interests.[31]

Compared with Azerbaijan, the extent of the activities of the Green International in Georgia was considerably greater. Georgia's complex geography, vast border with Chechnya and large concentration of Chechen refugees in border areas, as well as the poor state of national law enforcement and high levels of corruption, made Georgia an attractive fallback solution; initially for the Chechen militants and, later, for foreign mujahideen.

The center of Chechen and al Qaeda-linked activities in Georgia became the mountainous Ahmed region, including the Pankisi Gorge. By 2001, with al Qaeda's assistance and support coming from other sources, the militants developed a good support base in the area, which included training and recreational facilities, and the *Assalam* military hospital.[32] Apparently, Abu Musab al-Zarqawi, chief commander of al Qaeda in Iraq, had strong links to the Pankissi. In particular, al Qaeda's main person in the area—Abu Atiyya—was al-Zarqawi's personal envoy in Georgia (Table 2).[33]

However, it was the training operations that sparked the most serious concern among international intelligence and law enforcement communities. The analysis of various publications suggests that in Pankissi the Green International have organized what some media reports described a "terrorist academy," a training outlet for local and foreign recruits who have volunteered to join anti-Western and anti-Russian jihadist struggles. One of the specific functions of the Pankissi training center was preparation of experts in unconventional terrorist operations, including combat employment of poisons and toxins.[34] According to Brisard and Martinez, it was Abu Atiyya that managed unconventional terrorist warfare (UTW) training in the Pankissi, including several Algerians who attempted to stage a large scale terrorist attack in Paris in 2002.[35]

The problem of UTW in the context of the Chechen terrorism is of special significance. Contrary to some other newly-emerged terrorist movements, the Chechens expressed an interest in UTW almost right from the beginning of their armed separatist movement. According to some open sources, Dudayev sanctioned a plan to hijack one of the Russian Pacific Fleet nuclear-powered submarines using a special infiltration team in order to engage in nuclear blackmail with Moscow.[36] On November 23, 1995, Chechen terrorists deployed a crude radioactive device (the so-called "dirty bomb") to Moscow's Ismailovskiy Park but did not detonate it.[37]

After 1996, Chechens, with the help of Arab experts (most of them with links to al Qaeda) set up crude production facilities, primarily aimed at producing ricin and other toxins. Russian sources claimed that between 1997 and 1999, the *Al Risal* special UTW facility was functioning in Chechnya, a claim that was vigorously denied by the separatists.[38] It is hard to independently verify whether the *Al Risal* was in existence. However, throughout the Second War in Chechnya (later the Second War) the Russian military reported several findings of large quantities of poisons and toxins, as well as special instructions on how to use them against combatants and civilians. For example, in April 2004, a Russian Special Forces unit, whilst searching through a compound at an abandoned terrorist base near the settlement of Pervomaiskoye, found a container with combat poison sufficient to kill up to 100,000 people.[39] The Russian military have also uncovered documentation concerning production of crude versions of weapons of mass destruction (WMD).[40]

However, perhaps the most significant and alarming outcome of the Chechen-al Qaeda-UTW partnership was the attempt to acquire Soviet military nuclear technology, particularly small atomic demolition munitions (SADM), more popularly known as "suitcase N-bombs." There has been quite a bit of speculation in recent years about al Qaeda's possible acquisition of several SADMs, also possibly from the former Soviet Union. The most sensationalist claim was made by Bodanskiy, who has recently published a monograph on the Chechen jihad. He writes:

> The Chechen leaders' greatest service to Osama bin Laden and the jihadist movement was helping al Qaeda acquire a number of nuclear "suitcase bombs." Between 1996 and 1998, bin Laden had spent $3-million trying to purchase an ex-Soviet nuclear suitcase bomb, but his efforts were futile. The Chechen *Mafiya*, on the other hand, found better sources for such weapons. Back in 1994, a Moscow-based Palestinian Islamist named Shaaban Khafiz Shaaban claimed to have purchased two suitcase bombs with the help of the Chechen *Mafiya*.[41]

Interestingly enough, Russian fugitive businessman Boris Berezovskiy, whom Russian law enforcement agencies accused of aiding Chechen terrorists, also claimed that the Chechens had at least one SADM at their disposal.[42] For obvious reasons, these allegations continue to be categorically denied by Russian authorities, as well as some reputable security analysts.

It is hard to verify whether or not Chechen terrorists and/or al Qaeda managed to acquire ex-Soviet SADMs, but what is absolutely clear is that with the Chechen assistance, the network trained a small cohort of UTW experts, a fact that must be taken into serious consideration.

Indeed, training of ex-Soviets (volunteers from former Soviet republics, including Russia) and foreigners was an important element of al Qaeda's operational philosophy. However, it seems that the main strategic end was the preparation of a combat ready force for operations in the North Caucasian ToJ in support of al Qaeda's regional agenda—the transformation of the regional geopolitical map through the eventual creation of the TransCaspian Caliphate. In April 1999, Basayev announced the formation of the so-called Islamic Legion, which eventually embraced all major terrorist units/groups operating in and from Chechnya, among them the Islamic International Peacekeeping Brigade (IIPB), Special Purpose Islamic Regiment (SPIR), and the *Riyadus-Salikhin* Reconnaissance and Sabotage Battalion of Chechen Martyrs.[43]

Apparently, the Islamic Legion was formed on the basis of SPIR, which was formed around 1996. It is possible that the *Jamaat* and *Fatah* units provided the foundation for the creation of a larger combat formation linked to al Qaeda—the IIPB. After its formation, the Brigade was the principal mujahideen combat unit operating in Chechnya. The fact that the IIPB was commanded by Arab nationals (initially by al-Hattab, and after his death in 2002, by Abu al-Walid, Table 2), also suggests a close link to al Qaeda.

Perhaps at the height of its power between 1999–2000, the Legion represented al Qaeda's second most significant combat unit after the elite 055 Brigade based in Afghanistan.[44] Comprising several units mentioned above, it had about 4,000 fighters (up to 2,000 under command of al-Hattab; up to 1,500 under command of Basayev; about 500 under command of Salman Raduyev) armed with an array of weapons, including several pieces of artillery, 6 MBTs, and several armored vehicles.[45] The *Riyadus-Salikhin* had a special *shakhid* unit for suicide attacks against military and civilian targets. In fact, the revolutionary introduction of suicide-style operations signaled the increasing influence that al Qaeda-minded insurgents had on the local resistance. Overall, the formation of the Legion signaled that the preparatory phase in the North Caucasus was coming to an end.

Whilst gathering strength in terms of popularity of the globalized jihadist course as well as assembling a standing paramilitary force, the supporters of the Green International in Chechnya challenged Maskhadov's secular regime. The peak of the confrontation occurred in 1998 when the rivalry between Maskhadov's supporters for a nationalist-driven course came into an open armed confrontation with Wahhabists headed by al-Hattab, Basayev, and another charismatic Chechen terrorist Salman Raduyev, then commander of the so-called Army of Dzhokhar Dudayev (about 1,000-strong force).[46] The Wahhabists had a chance of assuming authority by force—in late 1998 their total strength was about 3,000 (see the Islamic Legion), whilst Maskhadov's forces had over 7,000 troops with 60 pieces of heavy equipment.[47] When the *Kavkaz* terrorist training network finished training of all its recruits, the fighting strength of the Wahhabist opposition in Chechnya grew considerably. The real threat posed by the al-Hattab-Basayev Islamic coalition forced Maskhadov in 1999 to declare that sharia law would be introduced during the following three years.[48]

The submission of Maskhadov to Wahhabist demands, and the August 1999 armed invasion of neighboring Dagestan, marked the beginning of the second phase of al Qaeda's regional strategy: the physical expansion of its sphere of influence through establishing control over the whole of Chechnya and key areas of Dagestan, with an aim of eventually extending the Transcaucasus areas of responsibility from the Pankissi Gorge to the shores of the Caspian Sea. At the same time, efforts were made to formalize relations between al Qaeda, the *Taliban* and Chechnya. In particular, at the time of the invasion of Dagestan, a special envoy from Grozny by the name of Abdul Vahid Ibrahim, held secret talks with the *Taliban* representatives in Kandahar, Afghanistan. The issues discussed included the establishment of formal "diplomatic ties" between Taliban-controlled Kabul and Grozny, and the possibility of bin Laden's relocation to Chechnya.[49] An agreement to establish formal contacts between the *Talibs* and Chechen separatists was reached a year later, during talks between mullah Mohammed Omar and former President of Ichkeriya Zelimhan Yandarbiyev. This agreement also meant formalization of contacts between the Chechens and bin Laden.[50]

The formalization of strategic relations between the transformed Chechen resistance on one hand, and *Taliban* and al Qaeda on the other, led to the increase of financial aid coming into Chechnya. According to Russian intelligence, between 2000 and 2004, the Green International provided the Chechens with financial assistance exceeding US$60 million.[51] Attempts to coordinate military operations against Russia, the Northern Alliance and, later, the US-led coalition, were made as well, at least between 2000 and 2001. However, the ambitious plans to synchronize operations in both North Caucasian and Central Asian ToJs failed with terrorist forces suffering defeats on both fronts.

During the second phase of engagement, al Qaeda managed to revolutionize the nature of the Chechen armed resistance to Russia. Not only have foreign insurgents played a role in inflicting military and political defeat on Moscow, they have transformed what was a secular ethnic struggle driven by strong local nationalist agenda into a regional battlefield of globalized neo-Salafi jihad against Western and Eastern (e.g., Russian) infidels. The Alqaedanization of the Chechen conflict was the main strategic outcome of the second phase.

The decline 2003

If the First War stimulated the flow of human and other resources of the Green International into the republic, the Second War trigged the opposite effect. Some volunteers were still making their way to the theater. For example, in September 2004 Major-General Ilia Shabalkin noted that groups of 5–10 insurgents were still infiltrating Chechnya.[52] Likewise, couriers continued to channel financial aid. However, the flow of human and financial resources into the North Caucasian ToJ was incomparable with the situation at the end of the 1990s. The principal causes of this change were:

1. The effectiveness of Russia's second CT campaign (the "push" factor)
2. The need to redeploy available combat-ready resources to different ToJs (the "pull" factor).

Contrary to the political situation during the First War, during which Yeltsin's team displayed contradictory approaches due to internal power politics and external political pressures, Vladimir Putin's administration was consistent right from the beginning, giving the military *cart blanch* to deal with the security challenge swiftly, and mobilizing full political and societal support. As a result, RusAF were able to achieve consistent military successes throughout campaigns in 2000, 2001 and 2002, during which all major combat units of the Chechen resistance were eliminated, and the majority of support-ground infrastructure—including bases, training facilities, and armored depots—was either captured or destroyed.

There is no doubt that Russia's successes in breaking up command-and-control structures (including through elimination of key figures such as al-Hattab, Abu al-Walid, Maskhadov, Basayev and others), dismantling the fighting capacity of the international militancy in Chechnya, and securing the territory, stimulated the flux of fighters—including foreign mujahideen—from the area. However, another stimulus was the emergence (or re-emergence) of ToJs in the Middle East, and Central and South Asia, where reinforcements of experienced fighters, among them Chechen veterans, were urgently required.

In late-September 2000, after the outbreak of the second *intifada* against Israel, al-Hattab and Basayev ordered a relocation of about 150 experienced Chechen veterans to Palestine. A year later, they were joined by more Chechens arriving to the area from the Afghanistan-Pakistan ToJ.[53]

From 2000, there was a steady redeployment of fighting resources from Chechnya to the Afghanistan-Pakistan ToJ. Several hundred Chechen veterans ended in Afghanistan and Pakistan where they joined the ranks of al Qaeda and Taliban units. In particular, Chechen militants reinforced the 055 Brigade.[54] Chechen veterans proved to be potent, ruthless fighters, hard to fight on a battlefield, and hard to bargain with when captured.

The successes of the combined air and ground offensive of the United States and the Afghani Northern Alliance in late 2001 (*Operation Enduring Freedom*) led to the military defeat of Taliban and al Qaeda forces with many of their fighters fleeing into the Federally Administered Tribal Area (FATA) and other border regions of neighboring Pakistan. Those Chechen militants, who were not killed or captured in 2001, reinforced jihadist forces in Pakistan. For example, in early March 2002, Pakistani security officials claimed that they had surrounded an al Qaeda militant unit comprising 150 Arab and 250 Chechen fighters.[55]

The role of the Chechen veterans in raising the new generation of Islamic fighters was noted in the special United Nations (UN)

Secretary General report to the Security Council on the security situation in Afghanistan: "The Al-Qaeda affiliated trainers in these facilities [TTCs outside of Afghanistan] reportedly include Chechens and Uzbeks, as well as Yemenis and other Arab nationals."[56]

Other regional groups like the Pakistani-based *Lashkar-e-Taiba* (LeT) benefited from the flux of experienced fighters from Chechnya. The group offered their expertise in support of its associated activities in Pakistan, South Asia and countries including Australia. In particular, the investigation of a Sydney-based LeT cell supervised by Willie Brigitte uncovered alleged plans to invite the Chechen explosive expert known as Abu Salouh as an advisor to local extremists.[57] In Southeast Asia, concerns were raised about possible links between the Chechen veterans and the *Jemaah Islamiah* (JI) regional terrorist network.[58]

In the Iraq ToJ, local Islamists and foreign insurgents utilized Chechen operational methodologies to the full. Among them were tactics of engaging mechanized regular units in the urban environment, ambushing military convoys, suicide attacks, hostage-taking, and videotaped executions. The Chechen veterans that made their way to the theater proved to be highly effective and dangerous fighters, who took part in a number of major engagements, including the Battle of Fallujah. Pool, the author of *Militant Tricks*, described the effectiveness of Chechen veterans during that battle: "After two Chechen snipers killed 15 Marines during a single day in Fallujah, US officers said that "the remaining rebels are smart, and adapting to changing battle conditions."[59] Just like Islamic insurgents revolutionized the nature and conduct of the Chechen separatists in 1995–96, the Chechen veterans were injecting combat "adrenalin" in the veins of Islamic resistance in the first eight years of the twenty-first century.

In the North Caucasian ToJ, between 2001 and 2003, successes were achieved in Azerbaijan and Georgia. During the first stage of the Second War in Chechnya, militants operating in the latter used the Pankisi Gorge as a safe haven avoiding attacks by Russian forces. In 2002, various reports suggested that between 600 and 800 militants under the command of the Chechen warlord Ruslan Gelayev, including a unit comprising up to 100 mujahideen were based in Pankissi.[60] However, after the destruction of Gelayev's unit after increased CT measures undertaken by the Georgian authorities with US support, the activities of the Green International in Pankissi were severely curtailed. In Azerbaijan, though, after initial successful CT efforts in 2001 and 2002, the threat of Islamic terrorism was on the rise again.[61]

After 2003, the presence of the Green International (including al Qaeda) in Chechnya was minimal, although Russian authorities continued to insist that al Qaeda is intensely involved in regional terrorism. For example, after the September 2004 Beslan school siege (Table 1), Russian intelligence claimed that ten al Qaeda operatives were active across the North Caucasus, including in Chechnya.[62] However, these claims could not be verified independently. In late 2006–early 2007, Russian intelligence estimated that the total strength of extremist forces in Chechnya was approximately 450 to 500 active militants, including 30-60 foreign fighters, organized into 34 to 37 groups.[63]

Bodanskiy explained a change of heart for Chechnya by priority shifts:

> With the collapse of the popular jihad in Chechnya, the jihadist leadership abandoned realistic hopes for regional achievements and instead committed to furthering the global jihadist causes as articulate by Osama bin Laden, Ayman al-Zawahiri and the supreme leadership.[64]

Between 2006 and 2009, major areas of terrorist activity in Russia's North Caucasus shifted into Chechnya's neighboring republics of Ingushetiya and Dagestan; to date, the latter continued to be viewed as a potential hotspot. In late 2008, the Ministry of Internal Affairs of Dagestan released its statistical data concerning Wahhabist extremism in the republic. According to the Ministry's information, 1370 active Wahhabists were residing in Dagestan; seven active militant groups (each comprising seven to fifteen active members) were involved in terrorist related activity in the area.[65]

According to FSB Director Bortnikov, in 2008, Russian law enforcement agencies thwarted 69 terrorism-related criminal acts, including thirty-six potential mass casualty attacks.[66] By comparison, in 2006 national security services prevented 884 terrorism-related acts.[67] Among the factors that contributed to the significant reduction of terrorism-related incidents in Russia was the ability of the authorities to reduce considerably the level of insurgency in the ongoing security dilemma in the North Caucasus, and to win the support of the majority of the local population. Nevertheless, Moscow continues to emphasis the al Qaeda link to the current instability in the area. On January 21, 2009, Arkadiy Edelev, the Deputy Minister of Internal Affairs of the Russian Federation, announced that al Qaeda has retained its presence in Chechnya and Dagestan by offering logistical support and advice to local extremists, a claim that once again could not be validated independently.[68] Perhaps al Qaeda continues to have an interest in the area. However, for the time being the Russian vector of the network's globalized operational strategy is no longer of considerable significance.

Lessons learned

Fifteen years ago, the standoff between the separatists under Dudayev and the Russian authorities transformed into a full-scale military operation. The standoff sparked a worldwide debate and criticism of Russia's heavy-handed and often brutal tactics against what seemed to be a band of rebels fighting against the tyranny and oppression of a once-mighty empire.[69] The phenomenon of Chechen terrorism that arose from the conflict continues to divide the security and terrorism studies communities. The role of the Green International, including al Qaeda, whilst acknowledged, was often underestimated, and the overall Chechnya security dilemma was viewed in the context of the separatism trends that accelerated with the collapse of the Soviet Union, rather than as one of several jihadist fronts that emerged in the 1990s.[70]

The conflict in Chechnya, including issues concerning terrorism and CT, is a complex security problem. The high politicization of this problem, by both Russia and the West, is one of the main factors that make the task of undertaking an impartial research and analysis so challenging. In the post-1998 environment, following attacks on US diplomatic posts in Kenya and Tanzania, and when the al Qaeda-inspired menace became a publicly debated matter in the West, Moscow tried to earn as much political capital as possible by linking security problems in Chechnya and the Green International. After September 11, Russian authorities have stepped up their information campaign.

In fact, the conflict in Chechnya proves to be an excellent case study of a full-scale information war, involving traditional (states) and non-traditional actors such as non-government organizations, ranging from human rights and humanitarian assistance groups to terrorist groups and networks. One of the main driving factors behind the politicization of the Chechnya security dilemma was the regional Great Game: the geopolitical rivalry between Russia and the West on one hand, and Russia and regional players on the other, for control and influence over the strategically important Transcaucasia.

The conflict in Chechnya, particularly its terrorism dimension, highlights once again the old-new dilemma for the international community: the politics of double-standards and CT. Often, Chechen separatism was used as a bargaining chip in a power struggle with Russia for influence over the North Caucasus and larger Transcaucasia. For Western players it was, (and still is), a combination of geo-strategic and economic interests, among them the geopolitics of pipelines.[71] The Russians are convinced that by encouraging separatist tendencies in Chechnya, Dagestan and neighboring areas, the external players aim to weaken Russia's position in the area and force the nation eventually to abandon it.

The involvement of Muslim players like Turkey, Saudi Arabia or Iran, is also driven by the desire to expand influence into predominantly Muslim areas of the former Soviet Union. Even former Soviet republics, like Azerbaijan and—to a greater extent—Georgia, used the factor of Chechen terrorism as a card in their game against the Kremlin. Likewise, the Russians paid them in kind by using the very same factor to impose their political will upon the above nations.

Critical analysis of al Qaeda's role in Chechen affairs suggests the need to pay close attention to what may seem to be only an isolated "hot spot." The deployment of RusAF units into the breakaway republic of Chechnya marked the beginning of a long and

painful struggle for Russia, initially with ethno-nationalism driv-
en forces that endorsed secession, and eventually with organized
armed resistance, which endorsed Islamic radicalism imported into
a conflict zone by foreign insurgents.

It would be a mistake to argue that insurgency in Chechnya was
comprised entirely of Afghani veterans and Arab volunteers. The
ranks of the Chechen resistance, particularly during the First War,
were reinforced by ethnic Ukrainians, nationals from the former Soviet Baltic republics, and even ethnic Russians—different cohorts of
militants that joined the fight driven either by Russo phobic agenda, or as mercenaries. Altogether, 5,000 foreign militants ended up
in Chechnya in 1995.[72] Neither of these "interest groups" had any
significant impact on the nature of Chechen resistance.

The same is not true of Islamic insurgents. For the analyst who
examines terrorism developments in the twenty-first century, it is
worthwhile remembering that, back in the 1990s, Chechnya was as
important for the Green International as Afghanistan was in the
1980s, and Iraq has been since 2003.[73] Initially arriving in smaller
numbers, the mujahideen soon established themselves as potent
assets to the Chechen resistance, fighting and funding their way
through the ranks, eventually assuming strong positions in the
Chechen command hierarchy. Towards the end of the First War, Islamic insurgents were able to revolutionize the anti-Russian resistance. Burke makes the point, "The Arabs who made their way to
Chechnya galvanised groups there."[74]

Why did al Qaeda and its top command (bin Laden and al-Zawahiri) express so much interest in Chechnya and its neighborhood
in the late 1990s? Why did the Chechen resistance, which initiated
the fight against Russia under the banner of secular ethnic separatism, receive generous financial and other logistical support from
the network, often greater compared to amounts of aid provided to
sympathizers in Africa or Southeast Asia?

Neither philanthropical feelings nor personal interest (for example, preparation of the Caucasian *Wolfsschanze*) seem likely motivations. A more logical approach is to understand al Qaeda's Russian vector in the context of its global offensive strategy.

After the end of hostilities in 1996, al Qaeda acquired in Chechnya and neighboring Georgia important recruitment points and

regional training bases for preparing organized fighting forces for local theaters of operation as well as for terrorist campaigns in Europe, the Middle East, and Asia. In 2003, in a *Washington Post* interview, Gunaratna argued that, "Chechnya and the Pankisi Gorge in Georgia partially replaced Afghanistan as a center for terrorist training. The initial wave of terrorists who are now coming to Europe trained in Chechnya or Algeria."[75] The developed regional terrorist training network (notably, the *Kavkaz*) assisted al Qaeda in assembling its regional standing fighting force, the Islamic Legion, which is perhaps the second most potent fighting formation after the 055 Brigade.

In the Chechen ToJ, Islamic militants mastered guerrilla warfare tactics, particularly urban combat, ambush, and attacks on aerial targets, which they now effectively use in Afghanistan, Pakistan, and Iraq. Brutal terrorist tactics, among them various types of bombings, suicide attacks, hostage takings, videotaped interrogations and executions were introduced and widely practiced before the West confronted some of these methodologies in Iraq and elsewhere.

Favorable conditions in Chechnya and Georgia allowed al Qaeda to initiate experimentation with asymmetric means of terrorist warfare. The fact is that North Caucasus was one of the few areas outside Afghanistan where al Qaeda pursued WMD research and production programs. Attempts to produce ricin and chemical warfare agents, to train personnel for unconventional attacks, and to employ chemical and biological agents in combat conditions, all support the hypothesis that Chechnya featured strongly in al Qaeda's operational and strategic plans. Adding to that, the network also tried to use Chechen criminal links to acquire Russian-borne WMD technologies.

Finally, in the North Caucasus al Qaeda attempted to establish physical control over strategically important territories. This two-step strategic move initially triggered a covert and later an open confrontation between Maskhadov's secular separatist regime and Islamist opposition under al-Hattab and Basayev. The second step came in August 1999, when the combined Chechen-Arab forces invaded Dagestan with an aim to expand territorial control and to secure a corridor to the Caspian Sea. The terrorist offensive in

Dagestan occurred at a time of intensified fighting in northern Afghanistan, which sparked concerns that *Talibs*, once they overpowered the Northern Alliance, would continue their advance into former Soviet Central Asia, towards the Caspian.

The major strategic outcome of al Qaeda's involvement in Chechnya was the progressive Alqaedanization of the conflict with implications going well beyond North Caucasus. As Sullivan notes:

> Al Qaeda and its loose confederation of affiliates have successfully converted local struggles in the Philippines, Indonesia, Pakistan, Afghanistan, Saudi Arabia, Yemen, Algeria, Morocco and Iraq into full-blown insurgencies, while adopting the Chechen struggle to stimulate the transition from local jihads into the seeds for a global insurgency.[76]

Today, the international security and intelligence community has to face the consequences of that transformation. The end of anti-Soviet jihad in Afghanistan in 1989 released the first wave of indoctrinated and experienced mujahideen insurgents that stimulated Islamic insurgency throughout the 1990s. In the first years of the twenty-first century, their place was taken by the Chechen veterans. The isolated "hot spot" burning somewhere in the North Caucasus is still firing deadly sparks, the effects of which are felt in many parts of our turbulent world.

Notes

[1] 'V Sochi i Apape Byli Predotvrashcheny Terakty "Al Kaedy — NAK" [Al Qaeda's Terrorist Attacks were Prevented in Sochi and Anapa — National Antiterrorist Committee], *RIA Novosti*, October 14, 2008.

[2] V. V. Vitiuk, "Osnovnye Etapy Razvitia Terrorirzma v Rossii" [Major Phases of the Development of Terrorism in Russia], *Terrorizm v Sovremennom Mire: Istoki, Sushchnost', Napravleniya i Ugrozy*, [Terrorism in the Contemporary World: Origins, Nature, Trends and Threats], ed. V. V. Vitiuk and E. A. Pain (Moskva: Institut Sotsiologii RAN, 2003), 265.

[3] Rohan Gunaratna, *Inside Al Qaeda. Global Network of Terror* (Melbourne: Scribe Publications, 2002), 134.

[4] Marat Iordanov, *Delo N 666. Terror* [Case N 666. Terror] (Makhachkala: Iupiter, 2002): 169–76.

[5] Extracts of the interview with the officer, who worked uncover in Chechnya for over six years were published in Andrei Serenko, '"Predatel'stvo v Raznykh Formakh i Vidakh,'" [Betrayal of Different Forms and Types], *Nezavisimaya Gazeta*, December 7, 1999, 14.

[6] Ibid. Serenko, "Predatel'stvo v Raznykh Formakh i Vidakh," 14.

[7] Gennadiy Troshev, *Moya Voina. Chechenskiy Dnevnik Okopnogo Generala* [My War. The Chechen Diary of the Trench General] (Moskva: Vagrius, 2004), 11.

[8] Anatoliy Voznenikov, *Natsional'naya Bezopasnotst'": Teoriya, Politika, Strategiya* [National Security: Theory, Politics, Strategy] (Moskva: Modul, 2000), 207.

[9] Russian sources note that al-Hattab was born in Jordan and has Chechen origins. Troshev, *Moya Voina*, 228.

[10] Gunaratna, *Inside Al Qaeda*, 68, 135.

[11] Troshev, *Moya Voina*, 228.

[12] Jason Burke, *Al Qaeda. Casting a Shadow of Terror* (London and New York: I.B. Tauris, 2003), 133.

[13] Gunaratna, *Inside Al Qaeda*, 135; Voznenikov, *Natsional'naya Bezopasnotst'": Teoriya, Politika, Strategiya*, 207.

[14] '"Afghan' Chechens in Afghanistan," *The News*, August 19, 1995, http://www.rawa.org/reports3.html#Hek (accessed November 18, 2008).

[15] Gunaratna, *Inside Al Qaeda. Global Network of Terror*, 135.

[16] The presence of the Fatah unit highlighted close links between Chechen separatists and the Palestinian terrorists, including the HAMAS. Zakhar Gelman, '"Terroristy ne Znaiut Granits,'" [Terrorists Do not Know Boundaries] *Rossiiskya Gazeta*, October 2, 2004, http://www.rg.ru/2004/10/02/xamas-chechen.html (accessed September 9, 2005).

[17] Voznenikov, *Natsional'naya Bezopasnotst': Teoriya, Politika, Strategiya*, 207.

[18] Brian Glyn Williams, "The "Chechen Arabs": An Introduction to the Real Al-Qaeda Terrorists from Chechnya," *Terrorism Monitor* (by the Jamestown Foundation), Vol. 2 (1), May 5, 2005.

[19] For more detailed analysis see Evgenii Novikov, '"A Russian Agent at the Right hand of Bin Laden?'" *Terrorism Monitor* (by the Jamestown Foundation), Vol. 2 (1), May 5, 2005.

[20] Anne Speckhard, Kharta Ahkmedova, '"The Making of a Martyr: Chechen Suicide Terrorism,'" *Studies in Conflict and Terrorism*, N 29 (2006), 445–6.

[21] Vasiliy Surikov, '"Rossiiskie Naemniki: Vymysel i Pravda'" [Russian Mercenaries: Lies and Truth], *Nezavisimaya Gazeta*, June 27, 2000, 9, 11.

[22] Troshev, *Moya Voina*, 230.

[23] '"FSB: Unichtozhen Glavny Predstavitel'Al Kaidy' na Severnom

Kavkaze," [The FSB: The Main Representative of Al Qaeda in the North Caucasus was Killed], *RIA Novosti*, December 16, 2005.

[24] Sharon LaFraniere, "How Jihad Made its Way to Chechnya," *Washington Post*, April 26, 2003, http://www.washingtonpost.com/ac2/wp-dyn/A39482-2003Apr25?language=printer (accessed September 15, 2004).

[25] Troshev, *Moya Voina*, 169.

[26] Speckhard, Ahkmedova, "The Making of a Martyr: Chechen Suicide Terrorism," 446.

[27] '"Voina s Terrorom Brosayet Novy Svet na Chechenskiy Konflikt'" [The War with Terror Projects a New Light on the Chechen Conflict], *NEWSru.com*, December 11, 2001, http://www.newsru.com/russia/11dec2001/inopressa.html (accessed May 7, 2004).

[28] Ibid.

[29] Troshev, *Moya Voina*, 231.

[30] Ibid., 230–1.

[31] *The Defense and Foreign Affairs Handbook on Azerbaijan*, 2nd edition (Alexandria: The International Strategic Studies Association, 2007), 51–3.

[32] MGB Gruzii: Boyeviki v Pankissi Finansirovalis' 'Al'-Kaidoi' [Georgia's Ministry of State Security: Militants in Pakissi were Funded by Al Qaeda], *RIA Novosti*, January 14, 2003.

[33] Jean-Charles Brisard with Damien Martinez, *Zarqawi. The New Face of Al-Qaeda* (Cambridge: Polity Press, 2005), 174–75.

[34] Oleg Petrovskiy, 'Pankisskie Laboratorii 'Al Kaedy' [Al Qaeda's Pankissi Laboratories], *Utro.ru*, January 16, 2003, at: http://www.utro.ru/articles/print/20030116032133122071.shtml (accessed September 24, 2004); 'Ben Laden Finansiroval Proizvodstvo Ritsina v Gruzii' [Bin Laden Financed the Ricin Production in Georgia], *NEWSru.com*, January 14, 2003, http://www.newsru.com/world/14jan2003/pank.html (accessed April 30, 2004).

[35] Brisard with Martinez, *Zarqawi*, 174–75.

[36] Graham Allison, *Nuclear Terrorism. The Ultimate Preventable Catastrophe* (New York: Times Books, 2004), 31–2.

[37] Ibid., p. 31.

[38] "Moscow Unwinds the Subject of 'Chechen Ricin,'" *KavkazCenter*.com, January 23, 2003, http://www.kavkazcenter.com/eng/content/2003/01/23/820_print.html (accessed January 15, 2009).

[39] *NEWSru.com*, April 15, 2004, http://www.newsru.com/russia/15apr2004/poison_print.html (accessed September 10, 2004).

[40] "V Chechne Naideny Dokumenty s Tekhnologiei Sozdaniya 'Gryaznoi Bomby'" [Documents on the 'Dirty Bomb' Making Technology were found in Chechnya], *Izvestia.ru*, December 1, 2005, http://www.izvestia.ru/russia/3024562_print (accessed December 2, 2005).

[41] A quote from Yossef Bodanskiy's *Chechen Jihad: Al Qaeda's Training Ground and the Next Wave of Terror* (New York: Harper, 2007) was taken from book review published in the *Defense & Foreign Affairs Strategic Policy*, Vol. XXXVI (1) (2008), 26.

[42] Andrei Sedov, "Oligarkh-Emigrant Boris Berezovskiy: U Boyevikov uzhe Est' Atomnaya Bomba," [The Oligarch-Emigrant Boris Berezovskiy: The Militants already have Nuclear Bomb], *Komsomol'skaya Pravda*, February 8, 2005, http://www.kp.ru/daily/23456/36589/print (accessed February 8, 2005).

[43] For more detailed analysis of these units see Tamara Makarenko, "Chechen Militants Threaten Increased Terrorism," *Jane's Intelligence Review*, 15 (05) (May 2003), 27–9.

[44] For more details on 055 Brigade see Gunaratna, *Inside Al Qaeda*, 58–60.

[45] Ilia Maksakov, "Grozny Ispol'zuyet Yazyk Il'timatumov," [Grozny Uses the Language of Ultimatums], *Nezavisimaya Gazeta*, October 23, 1998, 1; Troshev, *Moya Voina*, 258.

[46] Maksakov, "Grozny Ispol'zuyet Yazyk Il'timatumov," 1; Ilia Maksakov, "Sanktsiya na Primenenie Sily," [Sanction for the Use of Force] *Nezavisimaya Gazeta*, December 18, 1998, 5.

[47] Maksakov, "Grozny Ispol'zuyet Yazyk Il'timatumov," 1.

[48] Speckhard and Ahkmedova, "The Making of a Martyr: Chechen Suicide Terrorism," 445.

[49] Dmitriy Gornostayev, "Bin Ladena Gotovy Prinyat' v Chechne?" [Bin Laden May be Welcomed in Chechnya?], *Nezavisimaya Gazeta*, December 8, 1998, 1–2.

[50] Leonid Gankin, "Chechne Teper' Vsie po Talibanu," [From Now on Everything is like the Taliban for Chechnya], *Kommersant*, January 18, 2000, 11.

[51] Viktor Baranets, "Skol'ko Platyat Boevikam za Terakt?" [How Much Militants are being Paid for a Terrorist Act], *Komsomol'skaya Pravda*, September 2, 2004, http://www.kp.ru/daily/23352/31751/print/ (accessed September 3, 2004).

[52] *Krasnaya Zvezda*, September 18, 2004, http://www.redstar.ru/2004/09/18_09/1_01.html (accessed September 20, 2009).

[53] Yossef Bodanskiy, "Russia's Chechnya Terrorism Highlights Broader Links and Objectives, Linking to anti-US and Palestinian Terrorism," *Defense & Foreign Affairs Daily*, XXII (186), November 29, 2004, http://128.121.186.46/gis/online/Daily/Archives/DailyNov2904.htm (accessed January 25, 2009).

[54] Gunaratna, *Inside Al Qaeda*, 59.

[55] *NEWSru.com*, March 5, 2002, http://www.newsru.com/world/05mar2002/boeviki_print.html (accessed September 10, 2004).

56 "The Situation in Afghanistan and its Implications for International Peace and Security," Report of the Secretary-General A/61/799-S/2007/152, released on March 15, 2007, 2.

57 Martin Chulov, *Australian Jihad. The Battle Against Terrorism from Within and Without* (Sydney: MacMillan Australia, 2006), 143.

58 Wong Chun Wai and Charles Lourdes, "Seeking Clues to JI-Chechen Link," *The Star*, September 27, 2004, http://thestar.com.my/news/stroy.asp?file=/2004/9/27/nation/8988071&sec=nation (accessed January 16, 2009).

59 H. John Pool, *Militant Tricks. Battlefield Rules of the Islamic Insurgency* (Emerald Isle: Posterity Press, 2005), 38.

60 Roddy Scott, "Was Khattab Poisoned by the Russian Security Service?" *Jane's Intelligence Review*, 14 (6), June 2002, 24; Sharon LaFraniere, "How Jihad Made its Way to Chechnya," *Washington Post*, April 26, 2003, http://www.washingtonpost.com/ac2/wp-dyn/A39482-2003Apr25?language=printer (accessed September 15, 2004). One article showed a figure of 1,200 militants. Mark Galeotti, "Peace on Chechnya Agenda," *Jane's Intelligence Review*, 14 (4), April 2002, 48.

61 Yossef Bodanskiy, "Re-Targeting the Caucasus," *Defense & Foreign Affairs Strategic Policy*, Vol. XXXV (10), 4–5.

62 *Rossiiskaya Gazeta*, December 17, 2004, at: http://www.rg.ru/printable/2004/12/17/fsb.html (accessed September 9, 2005).

63 Other figures suggested that the total number of terrorist groups in Chechnya was around 70 to 90. Andrei Pipipchiuk, "Bor'ba s Terrorizmom Prodolzhaetsya," [The Struggle with Terrorism Continues], *Krasnaya Zvezda*, April 3, 2007, http://www.redstar.ru/2007/04/03_04/1_02.html (accessed April 4, 2007; "Na Uchete Pravookhranitel'nykh Organov Chechni Nahodiyatsya 34 Bandgruppy," [34 Bandit Groups are on the Registry of Chechnya's Law Enforcement Agencies], *RIA Novosti*, October 14, 2006.

64 Bodanskiy, "Re-Targeting the Caucasus," 4.

65 "Sem' Ekstremistskih Gruppirovok Oruduiut v Dagestane—MVD Respubliki" [Seven Extremists Groupings are Active in Dagestan—The Republican Ministry of Internal Affairs], *RIA Novosti*, November 20, 2008.

66 "Bolee 35 Teraktov Presecheno s Nachala Goda v Rossii," [More than 35 Terrorist Acts were Thawed in Russia since the Beginning of the Year], *RIA Novosti*, October 14, 2008.

67 "V Rossii v Etom Gody Predotvrashcheny 884 Terakta," [884 Terrorist Acts were Prevented in Russia This Year], *RIA Novosti*, November 21, 2006.

68 "Chleny 'Al'-Kaidy' Deistvuiut na Territorii Chechni i Dagestana—MVD RF," [Members of Al Qaeda are Active on the Territory of Chechnya and Dagestan—Ministry of Internal Affairs of the Russian Federation], *RIA Novosti*, January 21, 2009.

[69] As an illustration see Simonsen Spidlove, *Terrorism Today. The Past, the Players, the Future,* 2nd edition (Prentice Hall: Pearson, 2004), 160–2.

[70] For example, see John Russel, "Exploitation of the 'Islamic Factor' in the Russo-Chechen Conflict before and after 11 September 2001," *European Security,* 11 (4) (Winter 2002), 96–109.

[71] For more detailed analysis see Omar Ashour, "Security, Oil, and Internal Politics: The Causes of the Russo-Chechen Conflicts," *Studies in Conflict & Terrorism,* N 27, 2004, 127–43.

[72] Voznenikov, *Natsional'naya Bezopasnotst': Teoriya, Politika, Strategiya,* 207.

[73] Brisard and Martinez also make this point. See Jean-Charles Brisard with Damien Martinez, *Zarqawi. The New Face of Al-Qaeda* (Cambridge: Polity Press, 2005), 168.

[74] Burke, *Al Qaeda,* 234.

[75] LaFraniere, "How Jihad Made its Way to Chechnya."

[76] John P. Sullivan, 'Terrorism, Crime and Private Armies,"' *Networks, Terrorism and Global Insurgency,* ed. Robert J. Bunker (London and New York: Routledge, 2005), 72.

9

The History of Terrorism and its Analysis in Melanesia: Implications for Security and Policy

Scott Flower

Australia has a long-term interest in the security and stability of countries in the Southwest Pacific region (the region). Since September 11, 2001 (9/11), there has been much hype about the potential for Islamic terrorism in the Melanesian part of this so-called "arc of instability."[1] A view pervading much of the literature is that Papua New Guinea (PNG), the Solomon Islands and Vanuatu pose significant security risks; as weak or failing states they are susceptible to penetration by terrorists who could use these countries to conduct training or attacks in the region.[2] However, the current literature fails to adequately detail the nature of specific terrorist threats that might exist, or discuss the nature of Islam among the region's burgeoning Muslim populations. This chapter reviews and critiques the current literature on terrorism in Melanesia. It presents for the first time, a detailed overview of events relevant to terrorism in the region using new data collected during fieldwork to the region in 2007. It also highlights key issues that warrant further research in order to improve analyses of terrorism in the region.

In 2005, a media arm of the Chechen Mujahideen posted a detailed story on the Muslims of Vanuatu to its website.[3] In 2007, a Papua New Guinean Muslim convert spoke of a conspiracy against Muslims in respect to the execution of Saddam Hussein, stating that PNG Muslims "had always backed Hussein as they shared the same ethnicity."[4] In 2008, Premier of the Solomon Islands' Western province spoke out against the government's attempt to establish ties with Iran on the basis that, "Iran is associated with the work of terrorism."[5] This chapter represents an initial attempt to explain what these and other similar events might mean for the regional security environment in respect to Islamic extremism and terrorism. It presents three issues relevant to academics, analysts, and policy makers responsible for evaluating the security environment in the region.

As Thayer's chapter demonstrates, the literature review and event data illustrates a somewhat narrow analytical emphasis on Islamic terrorism in the region. This reduces the scope of enquiry and limits current understandings of the broader social and psychological dimensions of extremism that are likely to be a precursor to terrorist violence. The literature also highlights the tenuous conceptual associations between terrorism, extremism, Muslims and Islam that confound current assessments of the region. Unlike existing research, this chapter focuses on the potential sources of threat. These potential threats include the region's increasing number of Islamic conversions and the processes and motivations facilitating Islamic conversions that in turn may lead to politically motivated violence (terrorism). Additionally, the broader context of religious change in the region over the last thirty-years has tended toward religious fundamentalism more generally, particularly within Christianity.

Lessons from history and theories of individual/collective identity can explain how pathways to Islamic conversion might affect the security environment. The chapter argues for a closer examination of domestic environments in Melanesian countries themselves; focusing particularly on the role of international Islamic organizations, (including embassies of Muslim nations and International NGOs/aid organizations such as the Islamic Development Bank) and individuals from overseas (such as Islamic missionary group Tablighi Jamaat) as they are likely to have the greatest influence on the threat environment. The Australian government believes the global terrorist threat is likely to persist for a generation.[6] Therefore, an analytical framework that enables the analysis of the potential terrorist threat over the longer term is required. This chapter represents the first step in that process.

Terrorism and Melanesia: a review and critique of the literature

Despite the proliferation of "terrorism studies" and "terrorism experts" since 9/11, there remain few substantial detailed analyses of Islamic terrorism in Melanesia, or of how such terrorism might evolve or function. Whilst there have been a number of attempted terrorist attacks by Islamic extremists in Australia, there is no history of actual or attempted terrorist attacks by Islamic extremists in Melanesia, and no strong evidence of terrorists being recruited or trained in the region.[7] The current literature overlooks this lack of precedent, and tends towards representation of Melanesia as a security risk without outlining the specific security scenarios of potential concern. For the sake of clarity, the security concerns in the current literature regarding Melanesia and terrorism can be summarized as follows:

1. The possibility of a terrorist attack (against Australian territory, Australian interests in a Melanesian country or against a Melanesian country) that is planned and executed by overseas terrorists coming to a Melanesian country with no involvement of locals.

2. The possibility of a terrorist attack (against Australian territory, Australian interests in a Melanesian country or against a Melanesian country) involving terrorists from overseas that includes the use of locals. Potential scenarios include an attack that is decided and directed from outside a Melanesian country using local extremists to conduct the attack; or an attack that originates in a Melanesian country but draws on the support and expertise of extremists outside of the country to facilitate the attack.

3. An attack (against Australian territory, Australian interests in a Melanesian country or against a Melanesian country) planned and executed by local extremists without any connection to Islamic extremists from outside ("home-grown" terrorism).

Prior to 9/11, concerns over threats to regional security from Islamic terrorism were virtually non-existent in security related literature, with the exception of two cases regarding Melanesia's susceptibility to penetration by Islamic actors. The Australian government of the mid-1980s was concerned about Melanesian independence groups receiving financial and military training support from Libyan

Islamic nationalist (and then supporter of international terrorism), Colonel Gaddafi, while others asserted that Ayatollah Khomeini was behind the 1987 coup in Fiji.[8] Libya, (among other Muslim countries) did offer help to establish the Islamic Society of PNG (ISPNG) as early as 1982. PNG's expatriate Muslims, however, were cautious about being associated with Gaddafi and took only limited and indirect assistance in the form of an electronic typewriter, a photocopying machine and US$3,000 in cash.[9] These early concerns over PNG links to Gaddafi may have stemmed from a visit to PNG by an advisor to Elijah Muhammad of the American based Nation of Islam in November 1986.[10]

Prior to 9/11, no Pacific or security scholars foresaw the possibility of Islam becoming a threat to the region's security. Issues of Islamic extremism and terrorism received no mention. Focus instead was given to threats of conflict from socio-economic disparity, the erosion of cultural values, land disputes and poor governance. Other transnational security issues with linkages to terrorism such as money laundering, goods, people and gun smuggling, illegal sale of passports and cyber crime were mentioned but not addressed in detail.[11]

Australian media coverage of terrorism in the region to date has done little to enhance our knowledge of this subject. The majority of media reporting has covered surface issues, at times tended towards hysteria, and has presented negative stereotypes of Islam and Muslims rather than a balanced view.[12] The tone of media coverage has marginalized Muslims in the region, many of whom would not support the small number of extremists who claim the Koran legitimizes their use of indiscriminate violence to achieve political or religious objectives.

Media hysteria has been counterproductive for research in this area, resulting in many Muslim communities closing ranks for fear of being misrepresented. Australian government analyses and press releases regarding the threat from terrorism in the Pacific have further exacerbated the lack of balanced reporting through bias and appear hindered by the lack of a coherent conceptual framework. Whilst Australian government documents acknowledge that Islamic extremism is a "complex problem because it not only engages reason but also religious faith," the Australian government has failed to develop a comprehensive analytical policy framework to examine this "complex problem" as it relates to Melanesia.[13]

Current policy pronouncements also fail to adequately address the broader social causes of terrorism in the region, or how global terrorists might materialize in Melanesia.[14] To be fair, the Australian government has recognized the potential for "local conflicts" involving Muslim communities to "become fertile sources of recruits for terrorist networks."[15] However, such analyses provide no further explanations or material evidence as to how global Islamic terrorism might align itself with Melanesian social and/or political conflicts.

Furthermore, because terrorist threats in the Pacific tend to be assessed from the perspective of threats to Australia, there are few hypotheses regarding possible threats to domestic security in Melanesian countries themselves. The Pacific Islands Forum Secretary Greg Urwin has mentioned the possibility of domestic security threats from terrorism in Pacific states, citing the "possibility of sabotage or attack against tourist industries" such as a Bali style attack, but provided no detail on what such threats might be.[16] An equally important question to consider is, could the growth of Muslim communities in Melanesia lead to the development of new forms of domestic communal violence, and could such violence draw upon Muslims from outside the region for support?

Literature which highlights Melanesians' awareness and views about the "war on terror" and the degree to which they feel threatened by terrorist groups is largely absent.[17] This angle of investigation has not yet invoked research interest despite anthropological data showing that locals in remote areas are aware of the war on terrorism as a result of print and radio media. Additionally, it appears that some Melanesians empathize with Osama bin Laden's anti-imperialist/anti-Western agenda.[18] Security assessments may more accurately reflect the situation in Melanesia if they accounted for the long-held belief held by Melanesians that their society has declined as a result of foreign influences. Anti-imperialist and/or anti-Western sentiments "dovetail nicely with Islamic fundamentalism, which provides a narrative to explain the decline from a perceived earlier and better society."[19]

In the securities studies literature, two general approaches are used to examine terrorism in the Pacific, these being the weak/

failing/failed state approach, and critical security studies. The latter approach sheds little light on the potential terrorist threat scenarios or how terrorism might become operational because it uses a discourse analysis approach.[20] Such analyses do little to enrich an understanding of the core security issues at stake as the methodology focuses on the power relations between states and the framing of the threat, rather than concentrating on evaluating the actual security threats themselves. The weak/failing/failed state paradigm is more commonly found in literature analyzing terrorism in the Pacific; however these analyses are relatively limited in number and restricted in scope.

Based on the limited literature, a general shared view suggests that although there is currently no specific terrorist threat in Melanesia, issues of poor governance and limited resources may potentially be exploited by terrorist networks. Specifically, concerns are expressed about weak and failing states becoming attractive to terrorists because they have weak security institutions and a limited capacity to monitor movements of people, materiel and money.[21] As one commentator put it, "because the region around Australia is fragile, it is in Australia's interests to ensure that these weak nations do not descend into criminality or chaos and become launching pads for terrorists."[22]

An interesting oversight in the weak/failing state assessments is the lack of explanation around how terrorist groups might enhance their capabilities to attack a key target country by establishing themselves in Melanesian states. The assessments also fail to explain how and why terrorist groups might evaluate and preference particular Pacific states as the foci for operations. The logic of the failing/weak state paradigm is unsuccessful in addressing potential terrorist threats because the model is focused on the explanation of why and how failed/weak states are prone to other problems such as ethnic conflict.[23] This does not easily translate into why such states are equally susceptible to "the risk of transnational terrorists taking advantage of them" as a result of the ethnic conflict itself, especially if the parties engaged in a particular existing ethnic conflict lack an Islamic element or population.[24]

The analytical weaknesses of the weak/failing state model to assess terrorist opportunities becomes more obvious when the conceptual symptoms of failing states are operationalized into performance criteria and indices that clearly fail to link internal security issues (ethnic conflict) to the transnational Islamic terrorist security dimension.[25] In stark contrast to the view that Melanesia is a potential terrorist haven, some academics and Pacific Island leaders see concerns over terrorism as a smokescreen for an ulterior Australian agenda (intervention), or as simply not worthy of concern when considering Islamic terrorism.

Some Pacific politicians claim that "the Pacific is free of terrorism," while some academics assert that the likelihood of foreign terrorists escaping detection in the Pacific is virtually zero on the basis that "there is no local constituency for terrorism, and that the arrival of outsiders in small personalized Pacific societies would not go unnoticed."[26] However, the Solomon Islands case where a radical Muslim (with criminal associations) lived in the country and espoused extremist views for a long time show that outsiders can go unnoticed in island communities and they will only be noticed through the support of Australian security agencies.[27] Meanwhile, another smaller group of Australian commentators argue that the terrorist threat from the region is minimal due to barriers of distance, limited transport infrastructure, and poor Information and Communication Technology (ICT), thus making any covert operational use of the region by terrorists fanciful.[28]

Evidence provided in this chapter demands that this skepticism warrants reassessment. While the more alarmist government and media scenarios of terrorist threats from Melanesia are undoubtedly inflated, the latter perspective of a completely benign security environment is also incorrect. Further research and analysis is required to better understand potential threat scenarios and how they should be managed. Analytical effort should focus on the social environments conducive to the development of threats, rather than the top-down state-centric approach used to date.[29] Future research should seek to examine the potential for threats to develop within the region, rather than focusing exclusively on how to strengthen states to block or manage threats from outside the region.

As highlighted in the events below, areas of general security concern as well as the potential for communal conflict should be considered when assessing terrorist threats in the region. The potential for communal conflict is especially important given there is a history of tension and small physical attacks involving Muslim minorities in PNG and the Solomon Islands.[30] To date, Melanesian governments have demonstrated both a lack of capacity and the will to guarantee the protection of Muslim minorities when attacked by Christians, and at times have even used their own police force to attack Muslims.[31] If violence were to escalate it could potentially lead Muslim's to take responsibility for their community's security into their own hands. The potential for such a security situation emphasizes the need for a deeper assessment of the region's future internal security dimensions with particular note taken of the religious changes that are taking place. Such assessments need to extend beyond currently held concerns, which have focused on Melanesia becoming a staging point for attacks against Australia (or its interests).

Context and historical events: Islam, Muslims and terrorism in Melanesia

Religion and religious beliefs are powerful drivers of Melanesian social and political behavior. As people in Melanesia convert to Islam they enter new social relationships and social networks that have regional and global connections. Depending on the nature of the individual, it is the material and/or ideological influences of these new relationships and networks that have the potential to change the threat environment. The following section outlines the general nature of Melanesian religion by situating Islam and the Muslims of the region within the context of current Melanesian religious trends. It discusses the influence of Muslim nations and non-governmental organizations (NGOs) in spreading Islam in the region, and considers the security implications of such organizations. It then presents terrorism-related historical events on a country-by-country basis in order to flesh out how such events are related to Islamic extremism. In so doing, the section highlights the importance of focusing greater analytic attention on the links between domestic and international dimensions.

A focus on domestic factors is required as some security analysts view the growth of Islam or the presence of Islamic minorities with concern. For example, some analysts argue that the peaceful growth of Muslim populations today provides no guarantee of stability over the long term despite the process of proselytism and expansion appearing innocent.[32] While it is true that Islamic proselytism can be "a jihad for hearts and minds (non-violent struggle)," it can also be seen as a first stage in what may escalate into something more political or militant.[33] This section explores potential future scenarios by explaining the factors that may create an environment conducive to terrorism in the region. These factors include the facilitation of international terrorists, or the recruitment and radicalization of local minority Muslims. The section provides a useful basis for evaluating threats because it explores what terrorist activities might be *possible* and determines the degree to which such possibilities are likely.

Significant religious change is occurring in Melanesia with a clear trend over the last thirty years towards fundamentalist Christian religions.[34] When the attraction of new converts to Islam in Melanesia is viewed in this broader religious context, it becomes clear that future research should seek to understand the nature of fundamentalism in the region, rather than focusing more strongly on Islam as a source of threat. Specifically, the following fundamentalist dimensions should be assessed to help predict how such beliefs might drive behavior affecting security:

1. The literal interpretation of holy texts (Bible/Qur'an).
2. A viewpoint based on moral absolutism (good versus evil).
3. A tendency against the separation of religion and the state.
4. The importance of religious legitimacy for political leaders.[35]

Religious beliefs are important to security analysis because Islamic fundamentalism provides a unique set of beliefs that "draws political power from the realm of religion and offers a religious approach to political power."[36] Future studies should include an assessment of beliefs as these may grow into an ideology or narrative that justifies Melanesians using violence for religious and/or political purposes.

By way of example, many Papua New Guineans are "already of the view that religion has a political function whereby divine power is a necessity that averts misfortune and ensures prosperity."[37]

Religion in Melanesia "permeates much of politics and many political players invoke religion as part of the political process."[38] This view is similar to the narrative and ideology of many Islamic extremist groups, however, security analysts who focus on Melanesia are yet to effectively incorporate religious influences into their work and rarely draw on comparative history as a means of exploring the behavior of Muslim minorities. Analyses using comparative history could seek to examine the factors behind Fijian Muslims' decision not to pursue a separate political identity based on religion as a means of generating useful inferences regarding the probability of the politicization of Islam in other Melanesian countries. An alternative approach would be to examine the history of Islamic extremism among regional neighbors such as Indonesia to uncover potential indicators of extremist activity in Melanesian countries.[39]

Since 9/11 there has been a rapid growth (from a small base) in conversions to Islam in Melanesia. Islam's growth however, is still less than its competing fundamentalist Christian rivals, and Christian churches still significantly dominate the religious landscape in Melanesia with approximately ninety-five percent of Melanesians identifying themselves as believers of Christian faiths.[40] The data on growth is only briefly presented below because the underlying reasons for Islam's burgeoning appeal and the geographic spread of new Muslim communities have been discussed by the author elsewhere.[41]

Since 2000, Sunni Islam in PNG has grown from 749 adherents to approximately 4000 in 2008 with growth predominantly occurring in the highlands and in Port Moresby.[42] A further 300 Ahmadi Muslims live in West New Britain and Chimbu. In 1998 the Solomon Islands had only twelve Muslims, however, by 2008 there were between 2000–4000 Muslim converts.[43] In a recent article Moore outlines the religious change underway in the Solomon's of which increasing Ahmadi and Sunni populations belong (ratio of the population being 1:1).[44] Beginning in 1978, the Vanuatu Muslim population had remained static and focused in one village (120 Muslims). However, increased foreign assistance for Vanuatu's Muslim minority over the last eight years has led to a recent significant increase in conversions. Islam has continued to grow and is claimed to have spread to all of Vanuatu's main islands, with over 500 followers.[45]

It is somewhat surprising that Indonesia, (the world's most populous Muslim nation), has played a very limited role in supporting the growth of Islam in Melanesia, and has not at any time proactively engaged in supporting the Islamic proselytism effort.[46] A further unexpected finding from fieldwork is that almost all of the Islamic missionaries to Melanesia come from Australia, rather than Indonesia, Malaysia, or Saudi Arabia.[47] The majority of foreign political support for Islam and Muslims in the region comes from Malaysia.[48] As an example, individuals requesting information on Islam from the ISPNG in Port Moresby have the information posted to them by the Malaysian embassy in Port Moresby.[49]

The annual financial reports of the Muslim associations in the region fail to capture where donations come from or the value of those foreign funds. Based on communications between Melanesian Muslim groups and Saudi religious organizations, however, it would appear that the majority of financial/material support comes from Saudi Arabia. It is likely that Saudi Embassy officials in Canberra disburse money to Melanesia's Muslim communities but there is no oversight of Saudi disbursements by the Australian government and no transparent reporting by the Saudi's.[50]

One of the greatest financial contributors/coordinators in the region has been Ahmad Tatonji a director of The Safa Trust Inc based in Virginia, USA.[51] The Safa Trust Inc was closely associated with the SAAR Foundation in the United States, which was funded by Saudi billionaire Sheikh Al-Rajhi. In 2002, US investigators discovered that the Safa Group and Al-Rajhi transferred money in convoluted transactions through a network of inter-related organizations designed to prevent investigators from tracking the ultimate recipients. It is likely that the vast majority of Safa money went to legitimate charitable purposes. Whilst it is unlikely any money from Totonji/Safa ever went to extremists/terrorists in Melanesia, US investigators have traced some Safa transactions using affiliated charities and companies under its control to individuals and organizations linked to al Qaeda, Hamas and other associated terrorist groups.[52]

More recently governments have acted to uncover the links between financial matters and terrorism in the region. In February

2003, Sheikh Abdul Magied (a Muslim cleric from Sudan) was deported from Fiji because he overstayed his visa. Magied had lived in Fiji for eighteen years and rumors at the time suggested that the deportation may have also been linked to a $30,000 dollar "gift" from a wealthy Saudi Arabian to help Fijian Muslims celebrate Ramadan.[53] However, it is likely that Magied's deportation was not simply for receiving a "gift" but rather the result of Magied's alleged surveillance of the American embassy in American Samoa with a Saudi government employee in August 2002.[54]

The regional financial links to terrorism require further investigation. In 2001, Peebles' assertion that terrorists were operating in the Pacific and that "a number of island countries may be facilitating their work...through offshore banking services" lacked supporting evidence.[55] However his claims deserve more scrutiny given the Habib Bank Ltd (with a branch in Suva) was one of three banks used to transfer large amounts of money under the guise of "aid" to fund the 10 August 2006 UK aircraft bomb plot.[56]

Melanesian Muslim communities also receive money and material from Australian Muslims for missionary and humanitarian efforts and for the building of new mosques. For example, money from Australian Muslims can be donated as a result of advertisements placed in Australian Muslim media which provides bank details for people to place donations.[57] Other material contributions raise the awareness of Islam in the region; for example, Muslim Aid Australia delivered potable water purification systems and reconstruction support to Gizo after a Tsunami hit the Solomon Islands in April 2007.[58]

In addition to the financial, material and political support from Islamic countries and NGOs, the nature and activities of Muslim missionaries to the region is an area that warrants significant research attention. Muslim missionaries that have the intention to recruit and radicalize individuals are in a good position to do so as they have significant influence on converts and tend to work in small groups that are conducive to influencing group psychology and individual radicalization.[59] This dimension of Islam's growth in Melanesia deserves attention because although it is difficult to generalize about converts, some born Muslims argue that converts to Islam often have a higher degree of zealousness than born

Muslims and strive to prove their degree of commitment to their chosen faith.[60]

Islamic proselytism is known as "dawah" and Muslim missionary groups to the region are referred to as Tablighi Jamaat (TJ). These dawah groups use TJ methods and travel in groups of four to six men with the most senior Muslim appointed as Emir (leader).[61] TJ is a formal organization based in India that was established to support Islamic mission. However TJ does not actively coordinate global missionary efforts. It provides doctrine, an effective missionary methodology, and can provide a social network via its annual international conferences.[62]

Since the late 1990s, between two and four of these groups make regular visits to each country each year. The Muslim missionaries in Melanesia, (known as Da'iyah), fund themselves (as part of service to Allah) and organize their own mission groups without notice or approval of TJ, yet they do use the missionary techniques and methods of the TJ.[63] Da'iyah are committed Muslims who generally live in Australia, although occasionally some travelling in the region are from New Zealand and Fiji. Although the Tablighi Jamaat Da'iyah are generally citizens/residents of Australia, ethnically and parochially Da'iyah generally are of South Asian descent (Pakistani, Indian and Bangladeshi Muslims).[64]

The history of the TJ in the region shows that the majority of missionary visits are by peaceful religious people who aim to strengthen the faith of already practicing Muslims. However the view that TJ does "not aim to convert non-Muslims but rather transform nominal Muslims to become real and better Muslims" is not accurate for Melanesia. Some analysts of TJ state that it "remains to be demonstrated whether dawah (missionary) organizations such as TJ serve as a cover for terrorists" however, such claims deserve re-evaluation given recent events.[65]

A number of detailed accounts now highlight how terrorist networks and proselytizing networks, (whilst not directly connected in an organizational sense) are affiliated in terms of social and personal contacts based on shared religious and political goals. There are now a number of cases where TJ members have delivered Islamic extremists to Pakistani based Harakat-ul Jihad offices, and used the TJ network as cover to access visas, transport, accommodation and food.[66] For example, the British converts to Islam that attempted to bomb aircraft flying from England to America were members of the TJ groups.[67] It is worth noting that the Tablighi Jamaat is not currently listed as a terrorist organization by the Australian government. However, four of the six criteria set by the Australian government for assessing whether groups are to be labeled "terrorists" could be viewed as relevant to the TJ.[68]

Terrorism-related events in Melanesia's history

Prior to 9/11 there was already a perception that Islam was undergoing significant growth in Melanesia albeit from a small base and that there would be security implications. In 2000, a group of major Christian churches in PNG released a public briefing paper titled, "The Incursion of Islam into Papua New Guinea: A Warning."[69] The following section details potential terrorism-related events in each country and their importance to future analyses of terrorism in the region. The country-specific events relate to areas of concern such as people and weapons smuggling, border control, recruitment and radicalization, and the potential for religious/communal violence.

The situation in Melanesia is as interesting as it confusing. There has been a substantial amount of reporting on events regarding Islam and the growing Muslim populations with some reports being potentially terrorism related. However, much of the reporting on terrorism matters is difficult to verify and often includes baseless, distorted or inflated claims. For example, as of October 2005 the Memorial Institute for the Prevention of Terrorism (MIPT) knowledge database listed Laskar Jihad (LJ) as operating in the Solomon Islands. However, MIPT does not disclose the source of this information and did not state why terrorists might be in the Solomons or what they are doing there.[70] MIPT most likely decided to list LJ because they misunderstood a statement by Solomon Islands Finance Minister, Peter Boyers who stated on July 8, 2005 that "Jemaah Islamiyah and Laskar Jihad was a real presence in the region" despite Boyers referring to West Papua as the location elsewhere in his speech.[71]

The angle of the story was picked up by the *Solomon Star* newspaper and within days there was new media coverage alleging that teenage Solomon Islanders were being approached for recruitment by "radical Islamic militants" from Indonesia to attend training camps.[72] These allegations were denied by Felix Narasia, (a local Muslim leader) who added that while it was good to be alert to the possibility of outsiders the government should not change its focus from local terrorists (referring to criminal gangs) in the Solomons. It is not entirely clear whether this chain of reports influenced the Australian government to raise its concerns with the Royal Solomon Islands Police in August 2005, requesting them to monitor the activities of Muslims in the country.[73] It is highly likely that the Australian government's concerns were and continue to be about the possibility of Melanesian Muslims being radicalized.

A variety of radicalization environments exist in addition to those relating to the Tablique Jamaat mentioned. Specifically there are Melanesian examples of prison conversions and the overseas education of converts. Both expose vulnerable converts with limited knowledge of Islam and the Koran to extremists looking for recruits. The examples below do not prove that terrorists/extremists are actively engaged in Melanesia but rather indicate the possible opportunities for such individuals in each environment. First there is scope for Melanesians to be recruited or radicalized in prisons because prisons in the region are relatively easy for outsiders to access and lack effective visitor registers, vetting controls, and monitoring capabilities. For example, one prison conversion of an ex-Malaitan Eagle Force member has occurred in the Solomon Islands at Rove prison, and there is no reason why other conversions could not occur in a similar manner in other Melanesian countries.[74]

The justice system and jails in the region are poorly managed and many are overcrowded with inmates who have often been detained for long periods without trial due to capacity constraints within domestic legal systems. Individuals in such systems are extremely susceptible to conversion efforts because inmates are counseled and supported by the missionary. The potential for prison conversions and radicalization has become an issue in US and Australian prisons, with a recent example of a prison in New South Wales experiencing the conversion of approximately forty aboriginal inmates to Wahhabi Islam.[75]

Conversions like those among aboriginal inmates might occur in Melanesian jails given the profiles of aboriginal converts included factors such as perceived disenfranchisement, colonial oppression, discrimination, black theology and limited economic opportunities; all issues for Melanesian inmates. As one Australian aboriginal Muslim convert claimed, "it's very, very simple to convert someone that's oppressed to become an oppressor."[76] Of further relevance to the Melanesian case, (given the high number of criminal gangs in Melanesian countries) is research that shows a correlation between radicalized inmates and their former membership of gangs.[77] This research indicates a higher probability of "crossover" from gang member to Islamic extremist, confirming prisons as a potential source of security threats.

In respect to overseas Islamic education, approximately twenty-five individuals from PNG, Solomon Islands and Vanuatu have been selected over the last twenty years to attend madrassas and Muslim universities in Saudi Arabia, Malaysia, Pakistan and Fiji.[78] Some of these students have received financial support from the Islamic Development Bank under the bank's "supporting Muslim minorities" program.[79] The Australian and PNG security agencies have concerns about the possibility of the students attending overseas education becoming security risks.[80] The Australian government clearly views overseas Islamic schools as a risk because it has cancelled the passport of one student (an Australian citizen) who was studying at Medina University in Saudi Arabia, which is the university where a handful of Melanesian students are currently studying.[81]

Numerous reports speak to the reality of the region's problems with border controls including people and weapons smuggling, each of which impact on the ability of potential terrorists to move freely and obtain materiel. For example in April 2006, a PNG Defence Force Intelligence Service officer reported that people smugglers were successful in gaining illegal entry into Australia for two to three people per month, and individuals of Pakistani, Arab and Indian origin were paying AU$1500 for facilitation.[82] On August 20, 2007, PNG police sought an Indonesian suspected of producing ammunition, drugs and fake documents. Police believed they were investigating an operation that could be part of a bomb and drug manufacturing network for terrorism activities on the basis that they found gunpowder, primers, chemicals, equipment for forging passports, pre-paid mobile phone cards, instruction manuals and precision tools.[83]

The potential for religious and/or communal violence to involve Islam in Melanesia is real and could include a number of scenarios that have negative connotations for the security environment. Religious conflict is one of many forms of violent conflict in the region. In April 2004 religious violence in Vanuatu over "religious differences" broke out on Tanna Island involving up to 400 people in two communities. Twenty-five villagers were seriously injured and a Christian church was burned to the ground.[84] The largest potential risk in terms of terrorism is posed by conflict involving the growing Muslim communities in the region.

Although unlikely, it is possible that attacks by Christians on Muslims in the region could lead Islamic extremists overseas to travel to support local Muslims (as in Iraq and Chechnya). Information on the plight of minority Muslims in the region is available to such extremists via the Internet as exampled by the earlier cited case of the Chechen mujahideen website posting an article on Vanuatu Muslims. Reports of other attacks and discrimination faced by Muslims in Melanesia have also been communicated to Muslims and extremists in other countries via websites and print media.[85] Even if communal violence fails to develop, the fact that contact information for Muslims in the region is available online creates opportunities for Islamic extremists overseas to locate and utilize local Muslims, whether to facilitate travel or procure other needs.

Conclusion

The presence or growth of Islam in Melanesia is neither a necessary nor sufficient condition for declaring a terrorist threat exists in the region. It is simplistic and incorrect to argue that a greater number of Muslims equals a proportionally greater degree of terrorist threat. Despite the detail of this chapter there remain no conclusive reasons why Melanesia's "weak/failing states" and growing Muslim populations pose a *significantly* increased terrorist threat. Whilst there are areas susceptible to the efforts of potential terrorists, and while it is *possible* that extremists could use Melanesian countries to conduct training or attacks in region it is *unlikely* to occur at any stage in the near future based on the evidence available.

It is unlikely that Melanesia's Muslim minorities will self-radicalize given most individual's lack of ICT access. Furthermore, Muslim communities are very small minorities in their respective countries and therefore have a strong interest in maintaining a low profile. Muslims of Melanesia are unlikely to do anything that would incite violence as long as the minority group remains relatively weak. Therefore, the most likely avenue of potential radicalization in Melanesia is from visiting outsiders such as missionaries. Missionary groups such as the Tablique Jamaat deserve greater attention because they are influential on new converts, generally espouse fundamentalist Islamic beliefs, and operate in an environment susceptible to social-psychological control and manipulation.

Even under these conditions, the willingness of a convert to use violence is at the end of a radicalization continuum and is not a point easily reached by believers. Even if individuals undergo some form of radicalization, they are unlikely to escalate to the level of actually conducting politically-motivated violence. The key issue for analysts and policy makers is to understand the environmental drivers of recruitment and radicalization and intervene in those areas. To further explore these areas future research should focus on common features that are necessary but not sufficient for radicalization such as social, educational, and economic circumstances of Muslims, the role of identity and adoption of ideology/belief systems by converts, group dynamics and the broader social and political environment of Muslim communities.

Analyses that scrutinize these areas will provide the best basis for assessing which developments lead to an environment conducive to radicalization and provide justifications for violence by members of a minority group. The threat from Islamic extremism and terrorism in Melanesia is materially the same as the threat faced by other countries with Muslim minorities. In those countries, counter-terrorism efforts have proved that the best security interventions need to counter the radicalization process and not the size of Muslim populations or their growth rates.[86]

Notes

[1] R. Ayson, "Australia's Arc of Instability," Paper. Annual Meeting of the International Studies Association (Honolulu, Hilton Hawaiian Village, 2003).

[2] Barker has branded Melanesia "a launching pad for terrorism," while Wainwright et al. called the region a "Petri dish" for terrorism; G. Barker, "Army decision Just Right," *Australian Financial Review*, August 28, 2006, 62; Elsina Wainwright, *Our Failing Neighbour: Australia and the Future of the Solomon Islands* (Canberra, Australian Strategic Policy Institute, 2003), 13.

[3] Kavkaz Center, "Muslims in Vanuatu," Kavkaz Center 2006, http://www.kavkazcenter.com/eng/content/2006/12/14/6845.shtml   (accessed January 10, 2007).

[4] The National, "Sunni-Muslim Community Dismayed over Saddam's Execution," *The National* (Port Moresby 2007), 6.

[5] "Lokopio slams ties with Iran," *Solomon Star Newspaper* (Honaiara, 2008), http://solomonstarnews.com/index2.php?option=com_content&task=view&id=4481&pop=1&page=0&Itemid=26 (accessed December 30, 2008).

[6] P. Varghese, "Islamist Terrorism: The International Context," speech given by the Director-General of the Office of National Assessments to the Security in Government Conference, Canberra, May 11, 2006; and J. Howard, "Address to the ASPI Global Forces 2006 Conference—Australia's Security Agenda," Hyatt Hotel, Canberra, September 26, 2006, Prime Minister of Australia, http://www.pm.gov.au/media/speech/2006/speech2150.cfm (accessed on February 26, 2007).

[7] T. Cameron, "Conviction and Sentence for Terrorism Offences Upheld," Attorney-General for Australia, http://www.attorneygeneral.gov.au/www/ministers/robertmc.nsf/Page/RWP7F0A6F85B945F5B5CA2573B70008A342 (accessed January 5, 2008); and "Benbrika and five followers found guilty," *The Age*, http://www.theage.com.au/national/benbrika-and-five-followers-found-guilty-20080915-4h38.html?page=-1 (accessed September 17, 2008).

[8] B. Bohane, "Freedom Forces Find Strength in a New Unity of Purpose," *The Sydney Morning Herald* (14 March 2001), 12; and P. Stenhouse, "Militant Islam Sets Sights on the Pacific," *The Sydney Morning Herald*, circa 1987.

[9] M.A. Choudry, "My Memories of Islam in PNG," (personal communication) (2007), 5.

[10] Y. Salmang, "Fair Visit," Post Courier, Port Moresby (November 14, 1986), 4; Y. Salmang, "Religious Visitors," Niugini Nius, Port Moresby, November 13, 1986, 5.

[11] R. Anere, R. Crocombe, R. Horoi, E. Huffer, M. Tuimaleali'ifano,

H. Van Trease, and N. Vurobaravu, *Security in Melanesia: Fiji, Papua New Guinea, Solomon Islands and Vanuatu* (Suva, Pacific Islands Forum Secretariat, 2001).

[12] N.A. Kabir, *Muslims in Australia: Immigration, Race Relations and Cultural History* (London, Kegan Paul, 2005), 249-317.

[13] Australian Department of Foreign Affairs and Trade, "Transnational Terrorism: The Threat to Australia," (Canberra, Commonwealth of Australia, 2004), 104.

[14] See "AusAID, Core Group Recommendations Report for a White Paper on Australia's Aid Program: Companion Volume," (Canberra, Commonwealth of Australia, 2005); and "AusAID, Counter-Terrorism and Australian Aid," (Canberra, Commonwealth of Australia, 2003).

[15] Australian Department of Foreign Affairs and Trade, "Transnational Terrorism: The Threat to Australia," (Canberra, Commonwealth of Australia, 2004), 106.

[16] D. Hegarty, "Interventionism, Regionalism, Engagement: New Forms of Security Management in the South Pacific," SSGM Working Papers, No. 3 (Canberra, Research School of Pacific and Asian Studies, 2004), 6.

[17] S. Simpson, *A Brief History of Terrorism in the South Pacific* (Suva, Fiji Human Rights Commission, 2004), http://www.ecrea.org.fj/webpages/publications_files/Papers/42.doc (accessed December 10, 2006).

[18] D. Moretti, "Osama Bin Laden and the Man-eating Sorcerers: Encountering the 'War on Terror' in Papua New Guinea," *Anthropology Today*, 22: 3 (2006): 13–17.

[19] O. Roy, *Globalised Islam: The Search for the new Ummah* (London, Hurst & Company, 2002), 156.

[20] See D. Lambach, "Security, Development and the Australian Security Discourse about Failed States," *Australian Journal of Political Science*, 41: 3 (2006): 407–418; and B.K. Greener-Barcham and M. Barcham, "Terrorism in the South Pacific? Thinking Critically About Approaches to Security in the Region," *Australian Journal of International Affairs*, 60: 1 (2006): 67–82.

[21] Elsina Wainwright, *Our Failing Neighbour: Australia and the Future of the Solomon Islands* (Canberra, Australian Strategic Policy Institute, 2003), 14.

[22] G. Barker, "Army Decision Just Right," *Australian Financial Review*, August 28, 2006, 62.

[23] See B. Reilly, "State Functioning and State Failure in the South Pacific," *Australian Journal of International Affairs*, 58: 4 (2004): 479–493; J. Rolfe, "Oceania and Terrorism: Some Linkages with the Wider Region and Necessary Responses," Working Paper No. 19/04 (Wellington, Centre for Strategic Studies, 2004); T. Kabutaulaka, "'Failed State' and the War

on Terror: Intervention in Solomon Islands," (Honolulu, East-West Centre, 2004); R. Rotberg, *State Failure and State Weakness in a Time of Terror* (Washington D.C., Brookings Institution Press, 2003); Elsina Wainwright, *Our Failing Neighbour: Australia and the Future of the Solomon Islands* (Canberra, Australian Strategic Policy Institute, 2003); S. Windybank, S and M. Manning, "Papua New Guinea on the Brink," Issues Analysis No. 30 (Sydney, Centre for Independent Studies, 2003); and ASPI, Beyond Bali (Canberra, Australian Strategic Policy Institute, 2002).

[24] D. Peebles, Pacific Regional Order (Canberra, ANU E Press, 2005), 50.

[25] R. Rotberg, ed., *When States Fail: Causes and Consequences* (Princeton, Princeton University, Press, 2004); and Failed States Index 2006, The Fund for Peace: Promoting Sustainable Security,
http://www.fundforpeace.org/programs/fsi/fsindex2006.php   (accessed October 26, 2006).

[26] J. Panichi, 2003, "Muslim Cleric Expelled from Fiji," ABCOnline (broadcast 12.10pm, 26 February 26, 2006), http://www.abc.net.au/worldtoday/stories/s793452.htm (accessed September 18, 2006); I. Scales, "Seizing the Policy Initiatives for Governance in the Solomon Islands," Solomon Islands Update: Crisis and Intervention (Canberra, Research School of Pacific and Asian Studies 2003), 2; R. May in D. Hegarty, "Interventionism, Regionalism, Engagement: New Forms of Security Management in the South Pacific," SSGM Working Papers, No. 3 (Canberra, Research School of Pacific and Asian Studies, 2004), 6.

[27] Islamic radical Bassam Tiba was recently arrested in the Solomons to be extradited to Australia to face murder charges. Tiba had stated to SI police that he was in SI to help build a mosque for the local Muslim community; J. Inifiri, "Aussie arrested here on murder," *Solomon Star Newspaper*, Honiara (October 30, 2008), http://solomonstarnews.com/index2.php?option=com_content&task=view&id=4406&pop=1&page=0&Itemid=26 (accessed November 12, 2008).

[28] Urban and Hughes understate the ICT dimensions of threat. For example, Internet chat sites such as the Papua New Guinea Tourist Forum have been used by a number of South Asian individuals requesting travel and immigration information: http://www.voy.com/5898/218.html, http://www.voy.com/5898/70.html,   http://www.voy.com/5898/100.html, http://www.voy.com/5898/98.html,   http://www.voy.com/5898/97.html, http://www.voy.com/5898/207.html,   http://www.voy.com/5898/194.html, http://www.voy.com/5898/79.html, http://www.voy.com/5898/99.html (accessed October 14, 2006).

One Pakistani intending to travel to PNG claimed to be transiting in East Timor at the time of posting (The Papua New Guinea Tourist Forum,

http://www.voy.com/5898/185.html) which led another chat site participant to voice suspicions over the volume of interest shown by potential
Pakistani travelers. This participant was concerned enough about the individual's intentions, and posted an alert to the site warning other legitimate
users that these Pakistanis were "not genuine tourists." The full text of the
posting is: "All these Pakistanis asking about PNG visas on this site are
obviously not genuine tourists and are only looking to get a back door into
Australia. They are hoping that somebody reading this forum will offer to
help them get into PNG illegally. Stop being so gullible everybody. How
many Pakistani tourists have you seen in PNG recently???" (The Papua
New Guinea Tourist Forum, http://www.voy.com/5898/99.html). Farooq
(PNG Tourism Forum chat site participant) requested visa and travel information to PNG. It may only be coincidence however Farooq's email address is mantiqsys@msn.com. Mantiqi is the name for the geographic and
functional cells that make up Jemaah Islamiyah (JI). Farooq, "Info About
PNG Visa," Papua New Guinea Tourism Forum, September 20 2003,
http://www.voy.com/5898/194.html (accessed October 14, 2006).

   Mantiqi IV encompasses Australia and PNG and has been claimed
to have a primary focus on fundraising for terrorism rather that training
for or conduct of terrorist operations. See Department of Foreign Affairs
and Trade, *Transnational Terrorism: The Threat to Australia* (Canberra, Commonwealth of Australia, 2004), 50; and Parliamentary Joint Committee on
Intelligence and Security, *Review of the Re-listing of Al-Qa'ida and Jemaah
Islamiyah as Terrorist Organisations* (Canberra, Commonwealth of Australia, 2006), 21. See H. Hughes, "Aid Has Failed the Pacific," *Issue Analysis*
No. 33, May 7, 2003 (Sydney, Centre for Independent Studies, 2003); and P.
Urban, "Stop Propping Up the Basket Cases," *The Australian* (September
19, 2006), 14.

   [29] E.Y. Shibuya, "Pacific Engaged or Washed Away? Implications of
Australia's New Activism in Oceania," *Global Change, Peace & Security*, 18:
2 (June, 2006), 71–81.

   [30] For example, for assaults against Muslims in PNG see T. Thomas,
"Group Escapes anti-Muslim Mob," *Papua New Guinea Post Courier*, Port
Moresby (2002), 1; For violence between Christians and Muslims in the
Solomon Islands see D. Marau, "Priest attacked, police want Muslim
leader," *Solomon Star Newspaper*, Tuesday 30 December 2008; For arson
attacks on Mosques see M. Daure, "Arson Attack on Hohola Mosque,"
The National (8–10 December, 2002), 8; and ABC. "Arsonists Target PNG
Mosque," ABC Online (7 November, 2002), http://www.abc.net.au/news/
newsitems/200211/s721500.htm (accessed October 12, 2006).

   [31] Based on interviews conducted by Flower at the Hohola Mosque
in Port Moresby during 2007. Interviews with a number of PNG Muslim

converts included the then Secretary-General of the Islamic Society of PNG; fieldwork notebook No. 1, 54–56.

[32] B. Batley, *The Justifications for Jihad: War and Revolution in Islam* (Canberra, Strategic and Defence Studies Centre, 2003).

[33] A.M. Zin, *Islamic Da'wah (Mission): The Definition, Conception and Foundation* (Kuala Lumpur, Penerbitan Pustaka Antara, 1991), 14–15; P. Stenhouse, "Ignoring Signposts on the Road: Da'wa; Jihad with a Velvet Glove," *Quadrant* 51: 6 (2007): 40–60.

[34] P. Gibbs, *Globalization and the Re-Shaping of Christianity in the Pacific Islands*, ed., M. Ernst (Suva, Pacific Theological College, 2006).

[35] R. Eves, "Cultivating Christian Civil Society: Fundamentalist Christianity, Politics and Governance in Papua New Guinea," State Society and Governance in Melanesia Discussion Paper Series 2008: 8), 1–27.

[36] J. J. G. Jansen, *The Dual Nature of Islamic Fundamentalism* (Ithaca, Cornell University Press, 1997).

[37] P. Gibbs, "Political Discourse and Religious Narratives of Church and State in Papua New Guinea," State Society and Governance in Melanesia Working Paper 2005/1 (Canberra, Research School of Pacific and Asian Studies, 2005), 3.

[38] R.G. Crocombe, *The South Pacific* (Suva, University of the South Pacific, 2001), 217–223.

[39] On religion, see J. Ali, "Islam and Muslims in Fiji," *Journal of Muslim Affairs*, 24:1 (2004), 144. In one example of an alternative approach, Fealy argues that Islamic radicalism in Indonesia is not rising; see G. Fealy, "Islamic Radicalism in Indonesia: The Faltering Revival?" *Southeast Asian Affairs*, 31 (2004): 104–121.

[40] See M. Ernst, ed., *Globalization and the Re-Shaping of Christianity in the Pacific Islands* (Suva, Pacific Theological College, 2006).

[41] S. Flower, "Muslims in Melanesia: putting security issues in perspective," *Australian Journal of International Affairs*, 62:3 (2008): 408–429.

[42] See National Statistical Office of Papua New Guinea 2002, Papua New Guinea 2000 Census: Final Figures, Port Moresby; and S. Marshall, "Growing numbers convert to Islam in PNG," November 17, 2008, http://www.abc.net.au/news/stories/2008/11/17/2422255.htm (accessed November 18, 2008).

[43] Department of State, Annual Report on International Religious Freedom 2006, US Government Printing Office, Washington, 2006 www.state.gov/g/drl/rls/irf/2006/71311.htm (accessed December 12, 2006), 225. Interviews with M.B. Masran during October 2007. Also see "Ahmadiyyat In Solomon Islands," Ahmadiyya Muslim Association of Australia, http://www.ahmadiyya.org.au/sol/maini.htm, 2005 (accessed September 18, 2006).

[44] C. Moore, "Pacific view: the meaning of governance and politics in the Solomon Islands," *Australian Journal of International Affairs* 62:3 (2008): 386–407.

[45] M.L. Ahmadu and Z.M. Shuaibu, *A Short Introduction to Islam and Muslims in Vanuatu* (Kuala Lumpur, Regional Islamic Da'wah Council of Southeast Asia and the Pacific, 2004), 22–23.

[46] The complete record of ISPNG annual general meetings over the last twenty-five years mentions the degree of support received from Muslim countries. The only support from Indonesia appears to be the donation of US$100,000 to construct the Port Moresby mosque and the occasional donation of money for mosque expenses and food for the poor; see Flower's fieldwork notebook no.1 (2007).

[47] See Flower's fieldwork notebook no.1 (2007).

[48] The issue of establishing Islam in PNG was dealt with at the highest level of government and instigated by the Prime Minister of Malaysia in 1982; M. A. Choudry (President of the ISPNG), Notes from meeting between Dr. Mahathir Mohammed, Prime Minister of Malaysia and M A Choudry (20 October 1982), 1.

[49] Muslim converts in PNG showed Flower some of the information packs sent to them from the Malaysian embassy in Port Moresby—the envelopes had the embassy address on them; see Flower's fieldwork notebook no.1 (2007).

[50] M. Franklin, "DFAT Denies Overseeing Saudi Funding," *The Australian*, January 20–21, 2006, 6.

[51] A. Totonji to M.A. Choudry, RE: Dawah Budget cuts in Riyadh, Personal Communication, 3 November 1995.

[52] V.D. Comras, "Al Qaeda Finances and Funding to Affiliated Groups," *Strategic Insights*, 4:1 (2005), http://www.ccc.nps.navy.mil/si/2005/Jan/comrasJan05.asp#references (accessed June 14, 2007).

[53] J. Panichi, "Muslim Cleric Expelled from Fiji."

[54] Islamic Human Rights Commission, 2003, "Bannings and Deportations in the Pacific: Racial Profiling in Fiji and American Samoa," July 25, 2003, http://www.ihrc.org.uk/show.php?id=748 (accessed January 10, 2007).

[55] D. Peebles, "Pacific Regional Order," (Canberra, ANU E Press, 2001), 31.

[56] Habib Bank Ltd, Habib Bank Ltd (Fiji) website, http://www.habibbankfiji.com/ (accessed December 1, 2006). S. Ahmed, and M. Ahmed, "Quake Money Used to Finance UK Plane Bombing Plot," *Daily Times*, http://www.dailytimes.com.pk/default.asp?page=2006/08/12/story_12-8-2006_pg1_1 (accessed December 1, 2006). BBC News, "Airlines Terror Plot Disrupted," BBC News website, posted Thursday, August 10, 2006, 14:16

GMT 15:16, http://news.bbc.co.uk/1/hi/uk/4778575.stm (accessed December 1, 2006).

[57] For example, through requests in Australian Islamic media the ISPNG raised US$26,400 as at October 2006 for the purchase of land for a mosque in Lae. See "Appeal for Lae Islamic Centre," *Queensland Muslim Times* (July 2005), 19; and M.F. Jiffry, "PNG Mosque Appeal," *Queensland Muslim Times*, http://newsletter.qmt.org.au/06oct/1 (accessed November 14, 2006), 1.

[58] Muslim Aid Australia, "Muslim Aid Flies Team to Solomons," April 4, 2007, http://www.muslimaid.org.au/Article.aspx?Id=48 (accessed April 5, 2007).

[59] C. McCauley and S. Moskalenko, "Mechanisms of Political Radicalization: Pathways Toward Terrorism," *Terrorism and Political Violence*, 20 (2008): 415–433.

[60] I. Yusuf, "Falling into the whirlpool of radical Islam," *The Age*, August 25, 2008, 15.

[61] K. Murad, Da "Wah Among Non-Muslims in the West," (Leicester, The Islamic Foundation, 1986).

[62] M.K. Masud, ed., *Travellers in Faith: Studies of the Tablighi Jamaat as a Islamic Movement for Faith Renewal* (Leiden Brill, 2000).

[63] Flower's fieldwork notebook no.1, pages 34–36.

[64] Masud, *Travellers in Faith*, 30.

[65] A. Ali, "Islamism: Emancipation, Protest and Identity," *Journal of Muslim Minority Affairs* 20:1 (2000): 11–28. B. Metcalf, "Travelers' Tales in the Tablighi Jama'at," *The Annals of the American Academy of Political and Social Science*, 588:1 (2003), 146.

[66] A. Collins, *My Jihad: The True Story of an American Mujahid's Amazing Journey* (New Delhi, Manas Publications, 2006), 7–9.

[67] R. Ford, "Converts and Young Mother Among Accused," *The Australian*, posted August 23, 2006, http://www.theaustralian.news.com.au/printpage/0,5942,20223047,00.html (accessed September 21, 2006).

[68] For example, four of the characteristics of other proscribed terrorist organizations are: evidence of their engagement in terrorism, ideology and links to other terrorist groups or networks, links to Australia, threats to Australian interests; see "Parliamentary Joint Committee on Intelligence and Security, Review of the Re-listing of Al-Qa'ida and Jemaah Islamiyah as Terrorist Organisations," (Canberra, Commonwealth of Australia, 2006).

[69] Islamic Human Rights Commission, Islamophobia in Papua New Guinea (2000), http://www.ihrc.org.uk/show.php?id=42 (accessed October 3, 2006).

[70] Memorial Institute for the Prevention of Terrorism (MIPT), "Laskar

212   *Scott Flower*

Jihad," MIPT Terrorism Knowledge Base, http://www.tkb.org/Group.
jsp?groupID=4402 (accessed November 16, 2006).

⁷¹ Solomon Islands Broadcasting Corporation, 2005, "Finance Minister Claims Islamic Militants Plan to Recruit Solomon Islanders," Radio SIBC, 0903 hours, 08 July 2005, http://www.sibconline.com.sb. (accessed 25 October 2006).

⁷² Solomon Islands Broadcasting Corporation, "Islamic Society Pioneer Denies Knowledge About Recruitment Plans by Islamic Extremist Groups," Radio SIBC, 1529 hours, 08 July 2005, http://www.sibconline.com.sb. (accessed 25 October 2006).

⁷³ A. Wate, "Australia Worry at Local Muslims," Solomon StarNews, 08 August 2005,
http://www.solomonstarnews.com/?q=node/4057 (accessed 12 October 2006).

⁷⁴ The conversion of David Samo (now Muhammad Sabir David Samo), was by Ahmadiyya leader Musa Bin Masran M.B. Masran, "Ahmadiyyat In Solomon Islands," Ahmadiyya Muslim Association of Australia, http://www.ahmadiyya.org.au/sol/maini.htm (accessed 18 September 2006), 5–6. Samo was in prison for his alleged involvement in the murder of Selwyn Seki and was awaiting trial at the time of conversion Solomon Islands Broadcasting Corporation, "Witness Gives Evidence in Saki Murder Trial," SIBC News, October 17 2005, http://www.tutuvatu.com/news.html (accessed January 25, 2007).

⁷⁵ R. Kerbaj, "Radical Brainwashing Aborigines in Prison," *The Australian* (August 17, 2006), http://www.kooriweb.org/foley/news/2006/august/aust17aug06.html (accessed October 21, 2006).

⁷⁶ Ibid.

⁷⁷ D. Van Duyn, "Prison Radicalization: The Environment, the Threat and the Response," Statement to Senate Homeland Security and Governmental Affairs, September 19, 2006, http://hsgac.senate.gov/_files/091906VanDuyn.pdf (accessed October 4, 2006), 2–4.

⁷⁸ For PNG see Flower's fieldwork notebook no.1; for Solomon Islands see A. Wate, "Muslim Groups Refute Claims," *Solomon's Star Newspaper*, August 10, 2005 http://www.solomonstarnews.com/?q=node/4127 (accessed October 12, 2006); for Vanuatu see S. Joy, "Muslims in Vanuatu," *Vanuatu Daily Post* (October 19, 2004),http://www.news.vu/en/living/religion/muslims-in-vanuatu.shtml (accessed July 2, 2007).

⁷⁹ IDB, "Scholarships for Muslim communities in IDB non-member countries," IDB Website, http://www.isdb.org/english_docs/idb_home/scholarship_MuslimMinorities_CPO.htm#50 (accessed October 16, 2006).

⁸⁰ B. Orere, "Muslims Open Up New School in Oro," *Post Courier*, April 1, 2004, 5.

[81] R. Ackland, "Meanwhile, down south one slips past the keeper," *Sydney Morning Herald,* July 18, 2008, 15. See Flower's fieldwork notebook no.1

[82] Barlow, K., "Australian Officials Involved in People Smuggling: PNG Informer," ABC Online, Wednesday 19 April, http://www.abc.net.au/worldtoday/content/2006/s1619024.htm (accessed 19 January 2007).

[83] H. Yakham, H and C. Faiparik, "Indons Upset over Report," *The National* (22 August 2007), 7.

[84] The Christian church was burned to the ground by followers of the John Frum movement, see N. Squires, "Cargo Cult's Feud with Prophet Fred's Sect Splits Pacific Island," Vanuatu News Port Vila Press Online (May 07 2004),
http://www.news.vu/en/living/religion/cargo-cults-feud-with-pro.shtml (accessed 2 January 2007).

[85] Al-Mujaddid, "PNG Muslims Interfaith Dialogue," *Queensland Muslim Times Newsletter* (May 2005), 19; and S. Sandbach, "Events in Papua New Guinea," (1997), http://www.ihrc.org.uk/show.php?id=119 (accessed 14 September, 2006).

[86] This view is supported by assessments conducted by the Netherlands General Intelligence and Security Service, From Dawa to Jihad: The Various Threats from Radical Islam to the Democratic Legal Order (2004), www.minbzk.nl/contents/pages/42345/fromdawatojihad.pdf (accessed 15 September 2006), 6.

Part III

The Australian Experience

10

Echoes of Distant Thunder: Musings on a History of Terrorism in Australia

Sean Brawley and Ian Shaw

In their work *Terrorism in Perspective,* Griset and Mahan observed:

> The United States has a long history of political violence,
> but until recently, few scholars characterized the experi-
> ence as terrorism. This limited perspective has resulted in a
> lack of systematic knowledge and research about terrorism
> throughout the history of this country.[1]

An Australian historian could delete "United States" and insert
"Australia" into this quote and the contention would remain valid.
Australia does have a long history of politically motivated violence
that few in the general public, government or academia have labeled "terrorism." Shortly after the Bali Bombings of 2002, which
killed 88 Australians, Australian Broadcasting Corporation (ABC)
radio commentator Terry Lane provided a good example of this
understanding of the Australian past:

> We don't have any history of terrorist activity in Australia,
> in fact I think the one and only terrorist activity in Australia
> was the Hilton Hotel bombing, and that was decades ago.[2]

Indeed, for many Australians, the Hilton Hotel bombing remains the only terrorist attack on Australian soil in the nation's history. The incident occurred in February 1978; a bomb detonated in a garbage bin outside the Hilton Hotel in Sydney while the Commonwealth Heads of Government Regional Meeting (CHOGRM) was convening inside. The more recent attacks on Australians and Australian interests overseas (notably the Bali Bombings in October 2002 and the Australian Embassy bombing in Jakarta in September 2004) and a number of high profile terrorism-related prosecutions within Australia have only seemed to perpetuate such notions that Australia was once safe from politically motivated violence but that the nation's splendid isolation is evaporating.

If one applies the Australian Government's 2002 definition of terrorism — an action or threat "made with the intention of advancing a political, religious or ideological cause" with the aim of "coercing, or influencing by intimidation, the government...or intimidating the public or a section of the public" — then it can be asserted that Australia has a long history of terrorism.[3] There are numerous events in Australia's past that can be examined through the lens of terrorism studies. At the same time, care must be taken in identifying events and labeling them correctly. The existence of terrorist methods does not necessarily mean a terrorist act has been committed. For example, a survey of the Australian press in the twentieth century shows that the construction and detonation of Improvised Explosive Devices (IEDs) has occurred with surprising regularity. The overwhelming majority of these incidents, however, have not been connected to terrorist acts. It is not the device but the motivation and intention behind its use that marks a terrorist act.

In November 1998, twenty-seven explosive devices were sent through the mail addressed to senior officials of the Australian Taxation Office (ATO) and the Human Rights and Equal Employment Opportunity Commission. One of the devices exploded at the Canberra mail center injuring several people.[4] This campaign, the largest letter bomb campaign in Australian history, was, however, not politically motivated. Rather it was the actions of a disgruntled ATO employee. Other incidents are not so clear-cut. In the early 1980s, a campaign of violence and intimidation was directed at the Family Court of Australia. Its results included the shooting death of a judge, the bombing of the homes of two judges resulting in injury and death, and the bombing of the court's registry in Parramatta. Some scholars have asserted that these attacks were a terrorist campaign set against the broader agitation against the court conducted by fathers' right groups.[5] The fact that no one has ever been arrested for these crimes militates against a firm conclusion.

Other incidents in Australia's past have simply been forgotten and therefore deserve sustained research to make a classification. What was the motivation behind a bombing campaign in the north Queensland town of Townsville in 1933? Why was the home of the Crown Prosecutor one of the targets?[6] Was it simply the work of a "disgruntled ratepayer" that led to a series of attacks including a car bombing directed at the Town Clerk of Burwood Council in Sydney in November 1937?[7] Who planted a high explosive (HE) bomb detonated by an alarm clock on a Qantas Catalina flying boat in Sydney Harbour in August 1949? Was it connected to an earlier sabotage threat by "communists" unhappy that the airline was transporting small arms and ammunition in its cargo to Singapore to assist the British in the struggle against "communist terrorists"?[8] Closer examination of these incidents through media reports and police reports from the time will help in deciding whether such events are episodes in the history of Australian terrorism.

The authors are currently completing the first general history of terrorism in Australia.[9] The history will attempt, in part, to distinguish genuine terrorist acts from other acts of violence. Yet the history of terrorism in Australia is not simply a list of violent acts. Terrorism has exerted an influence on Australia in others ways that deserve exploration. How, for example, have the Australian people engaged with the words "terrorism" and "terrorist"? Why were these terms often used to describe events and individuals overseas but infrequently used to label similar events within Australia? Why did a New South Wales premier pen a romantic poem in the 1880s titled the "Beauteous Terrorist"?

Finally, much of Australia's terrorism history is not simply a domestic story: it connects with terrorism beyond the nation's shores. Western Australia was a refuge for Latvian revolutionaries in the 1900s, and was a training ground for Japanese cultists in the 1990s.[10] Australia provided diaspora support for the terrorist activities of the Irish Republican Army, the Palestinian Liberation Organization and the Liberation Tigers of Tamil Eelam. It is these transnational connections that comprise the dominant theme in the history of Australian terrorism—the echoes of distant thunder.

A framework for a history of terrorism in Australia

This chapter represents something of a work in progress report for the general history being completed by the authors. It is organized around some of the content and methodological issues that we argue are crucial in such an undertaking. The main driver for this chapter is the consideration of a historical framework for the study of terrorism in Australia.

In 2007, Koschade was the first Australian scholar to attempt to create an historical framework for organizing and exploring the history of terrorism in Australia. He alerted scholars and practitioners to the importance of history to terrorism studies in Australia, arguing that "Without such a context, the field is deprived of a basis for both quantitative and qualitative analytical methodologies and techniques that aim to understand, explain, and predict terrorism."[11]

Koschade identified three key periods in the history of terrorism. They are:

1. Early Terrorism: 1868–1915
2. International Terrorism: 1960–circa 1990
3. Twenty-first Century Islamic Extremism: circa 1990–Today

While Koschade's framework is an important contribution because it began a long-needed discussion, it is problematic because it tends to concentrate on actual incidents to chart the course of this history. Further, these events are selected because of their parallels—in form or intent—with contemporary acts and understandings of terrorism. A deeper investigation of Australia's past throws up more events worthy of consideration and, as a consequence, challenges the neat categories Koschade has created. As well as identifying other events in the periods identified, there is also much to be said about Australia's terrorism history between 1915 and 1960 when Koschade suggests something of a historical lacuna. Finally, as noted, terrorism's impact on Australia cannot always be simply characterized by attacks on Australian soil or Australian citizens.

The terrorist Ned Kelly?

Under his framework Koschade identifies Henry O'Farrell's 1868 attempt to assassinate the Duke of Edinburgh at the Clontarf picnic grounds on Sydney Harbour as the first terrorist act in Australian history. The connections of this act with the broader concerns of Irish nationalism and the Fenian Brotherhood give the event its status as a terrorist act and highlight the transnational connections that dominate in Australian history.[12] Despite later rejections of the validity of his claims, O'Farrell would insist that he was "instructed from abroad" and that the aim of the attack was that of the wider "Fenian organization" — "to strike terror into the English people (or aristocracy), believing that to be the most effectual mode of bringing about the independence of Ireland."[13]

The ending of Koschade's first period in 1915 is marked by Mullah Abdullah and Muhammad Gul's attack on the Broken Hill/Silverton picnic train in 1915.[14] The two Muslim men (from present day Afghanistan and Pakistan) saw the Ottoman Empire's entry into the Great War and the Caliphate's declaration of jihad as a call to arms. Four Broken Hill residents were killed and seven wounded. The two perpetrators were also killed in the ensuing gun battle.

In the wake of the September 11 attacks, the Broken Hill incident has gained renewed importance for some Australians. Erroneously, some have asserted on websites and in other forums that the attack was the first terrorist attack in Australia. They imply that the Islamic connection to the events provides some evidence from the past of the danger of the Islamic threat and points to the dangers of an Islamic minority in Australia.[15]

Not only are the Clontarf and Broken Hill incidents the bookends of Koschade's first category, they are also identified as the only incidents of the period 1868 to 1915. Are there no other incidents to chronicle the period between 1868 and 1915? Could we argue, for example, that the infamous Victorian bushranger Ned Kelly was a terrorist and his famous "Jerilderie Letter" a manifesto?
In the Jerilderie Letter, Kelly wrote:

It will pay Government to give those people who are suffering innocence, justice and liberty. If [sic] not I will be compelled to show some colonial stratagem which will open the eyes of not only the Victoria Police and inhabitants but also the whole British army and now [sic] doubt they will acknowledge their hounds were barking at the wrong stump....And that [Constable] Fitzpatrick will be the cause of greater slaughter to the Union Jack than Saint Patrick was to the snakes and toads in Ireland...I give fair warning to all those who has reason [sic] to fear me to sell out and give £10 out of every hundred towards the widow and orphan fund and do not attempt to reside in Victoria but as short a time as possible after reading this notice, neglect this and abide by the consequences, which shall be worse than the rust in the wheat in Victoria or the druth of a dry season to the grasshoppers in New South Wales. I do not wish to give the order full force without giving timely warning. But [sic] I am a widows [sic] son outlawed and my orders must be obeyed.[16]

Looking from abroad, the Glasgow *Herald* noted that the Kelly Gang—"who for some time have been creating much terror amongst the peaceable inhabitants of Victoria and New South Wales" were "splendidly organized and armed" and helped by "sympathisers."[17] The Leeds *Mercury* was insistent that Kelly's capture and execution bought "an end to the reign of terror."[18] When Kelly's armor toured Ireland in 1897, the *Belfast News-Letter* noted the bushranger has been "the terror of Australia."[19] Further, in the aftermath of Kelly's capture another chapter was written in the history of counter-terrorism. The Jerilderie Letter was suppressed and bushranger-themed plays banned for fear they might encourage public unrest.[20] These actions did not, however, prevent the popularity of a fictionalized account of bushranging written by Rolf Boldrewood. In one scene in *Robbery Under Arms*—which became one of the great colonial novels—an aspiring bushranger warns a member of the outlaw gang: "You fellers don't think you're going on for ever and ever, keepin' the country in a state of terrorism, as the papers say."[21]

And what about Ben Hall, another famous Australian bushranger? Long before Kelly at Jerilderie, Hall raided towns and in
one case held the town of Canowindra for several days twice. His
public support also provoked a counter-terrorist response from the
authorities which included the destruction of his home and property and the arrest and indefinite remand without charge of individuals suspected of an association with the gang.[22] It is interesting that
both Kelly and Hall's activities were taking place at a time when
Europe's anarchists and communists were compiling manifestos resisting the state and calling for and inspiring many acts of terrorism
in Europe and abroad. Is Kelly's construction of his motivation in
the Jerilderie letter that far removed from the famous Russian "terrorist" Stepniak's definition of a terrorist: "the defender of outraged
humanity, of right trampled under foot"?[23]

Pemulwuy: Australia's first terrorist?

Another reason for challenging Koschade's 1868 to 1915 chronology is that it suggests that there was no terrorist act committed in
Australia before O'Farrell's actions at Clontarf. In identifying 1868
as a starting point, Koschade is perhaps too influenced by the here
and now and therefore fails to appreciate earlier examples of terrorism in Australian history. We would assert that a better starting
place for the study of terrorism and counter-terrorism in Australian
history is in the British colonization of the continent in the late eighteenth century.

The colony of New South Wales was established during a turbulent period in European history. At the center of this maelstrom
was the French Revolution. To resist the internal and external forces
of counter-revolution, the Jacobin Republic formed the Committee
of Public Safety. The committee was charged with defending the
Republic by whatever means necessary. Between 1793 and 1794 the
committee unleashed the "Reign of Terror." "The Terror" sought
out Royalist counter-revolutionaries. Presumed enemies of the Republic were subjected to a wave of executions aimed at not only
removing the immediate threat but ensuring that no French citizen
would dare consider opposing the state.[24]

The beginnings of modern notions of terrorism are often said to be found in the state-sanctioned political violence of the late eighteenth century. Robespierre was the first man in history to be labeled a *"Terroriste."*[25] The terror had a lasting impact across the English Channel in Britain and the shockwaves (in part personified by Scottish Jacobins) reached its colonies on the other side of the world.[26] Interestingly, the early colonial history of New South Wales shows a pre-"terror" terror being unleashed by another regime seeking to maintain its revolution.

Despite the protestations of scholars like Windschuttle, the waging of a "war" on the frontiers of white settlement in Australia has been accepted as an appropriate historiographical approach to the investigation of the early encounters between the British colonizers and indigenous Australians.[27] Most recently these ideas, which had been constructed first around ideas of Aboriginal resistance (first enunciated by scholars like Reynolds), have been supported by the contribution of military historians such as Connor and Grey.[28]

The early frontier history of New South Wales does have the odd engagement, such as the Battle of Richmond Hill in 1795, but looking at this broader frontier encounter through the lens of military history is simply not satisfactory. This is not to say that the Windschuttle version of history is better; it is not. But it is interesting that when this early history of New South Wales is examined through the notions of state-sponsored terrorism, terrorism and counter-terrorism, the evidence appears more powerful than when it is used in these earlier interpretations.

Early colonial records hold many examples of the desire of the newly arrived British to instill "terror" in the local indigenous population as a means of securing the new settlement's survival. Like Robespierre, Governor Arthur Phillip saw terror as a tool to sustain his revolution in New South Wales. As early as 1790, Phillip suggested the Crown would need to "infuse an universal terror" against some Aboriginal communities to ensure the survival of the colony.[29] Royal Marines Captain Watkin Tench was originally ordered to take 50 men, kill a number of Aboriginal men and remove their heads. Bodies would be left displayed as a warning to others — a ritual not far removed from the public performance of the guillotine in France.[30] In the mid-1790s Lieutenant-Governor William

Patterson, who was responsible for the security of the new colony, sent marine units onto the Cumberland Plain with the orders to "Destroy as many as they could meet with of the wood tribe…and, in the hope of striking *terror*, to erect gibbets at different places, whereon the bodies of all that they might kill were to be hung."[31]

Unable to resist British colonization through their traditional war parties—as highlighted by the Battle of Richmond Hill which showed the folly of traditionally armed Aboriginal men standing before massed British firepower—the Eora and Dharug people were quickly compelled to adopt new measures. Connor notes that "Aborigines developed tactics for frontier warfare that differed from the tactics used in their traditional warfare."[32] These new clandestine tactics demonstrate that Aboriginal resistors sought to replicate the British strategy of "infusing an universal terror."

Henry O'Farrell therefore is not the first Australian terrorist. The first Australian terrorist in the modern sense of the word is the Eora man Pemulwuy. Quickly identifying the British military as a hard target, Pemulwuy concentrated his efforts on the soft civilian targets that the British military were charged to protect. White settlers on the outskirts of the British colony were the targets. This might involve the indiscriminate killing and wounding of white settlers (regardless of age or gender), killing stock, stealing food and other supplies (including guns and ammunition) for sustenance, and the destruction of white homes and crops through the use of fire.[33]

Having had some success on the frontier, Pemulwuy then launched a bold attack on the center of British power; Sydney Town itself. This he did with an audacious raid on Brickfield Lane (present day George Street). The attack showed that the Crown's forces were stretched and resulted in some consideration being given to the colonists forgoing the Hawkesbury district or perhaps even Parramatta.

In the British response to Pemulwuy we see the first counter-terrorism measures being implemented in Australia. The military concentrated its efforts on protecting the civilian soft targets. At the same time, mobile forces were established to try and interdict and disrupt the attacks. Those Aboriginals with more "moderate" dispositions toward the British were pressured to give up Pemulwuy and his followers. When this strategy did not work all Aboriginals were banned from Sydney Town in the hope of placing further pressure on the indigenous community. Further, proscriptive rules and regulations were placed on Aboriginal communities lest they be identified as enemies of the State.

Pemulwuy's terrorist campaign was ultimately a failure. He was killed by the British in 1802. Having removed the head of this terrorist cell (both figuratively and literally—his head was preserved and sent to England) the power of the group declined despite the continuing activities of his son. His techniques, however, would continue to be practiced in Aboriginal resistance to white colonization. A Proclamation by Governor Lachlan Macquarie in 1816 demonstrates the continuing concerns of the Colony:

> Whereas the ABORIGINES, or Black NATIVES of this Colony, have for the last three Years, manifested a strong and sanguinary Spirit of ANIMOSITY and HOSTILITY towards the BRITISH INHABITANTS residing in the Interior and remote Parts of the Territory, and been recently guilty of most atrocious and wanton Barbarities, in indiscriminately murdering Men, Women, and Children, from whom they had received no Offence or Provocations; and also in killing the Cattle, and plundering and destroying the Grain and Property of every Description, belonging to the Settlers and Persons residing on and near the Banks of the Rivers Nepean, Grose and Hawkesbury, and South Creek, to the great Terror, Loss and Distress of the suffering Inhabitants....

Terror (indiscriminately applied) remained a tool that could be used by the State to counter these campaigns:

> And although it is to be apprehended that some few innocent Men, Women, and Children may have fallen in these Conflicts, yet it is earnestly to be hoped that this unavoidable Result, and the Severity which has attended it, will eventually strike Terror amongst the surviving Tribes, and deter them from the further Commission of such sanguinary Outrages and Barbarities.[34]

Regulations continued to build the colony's counter-terrorist approach to its Aboriginal inhabitants. No Aboriginal person was permitted within one mile of any town, village or farm owned by "a British subject while carrying a weapon of any description." The *Sydney Gazette* would later define Aboriginal weapons as "implements of Terror."[35] Not more than six unarmed Aboriginal people were allowed to "lurk or loiter about any Farm in the Interior, on Pain of being considered Enemies, and treated accordingly." Those who were "peaceable, inoffensive and honest" would be "furnished with Passports or Certificates to that Effect," and might also have been offered land grants and support.[36]

There are other episodes in early Australian colonial history that can also be examined through the lens of state-sponsored terrorism, indigenous terrorism and counter-terrorism. In Tasmania the "Black War" of 1823–31 can easily be seen as a terrorist campaign and here we see the term "terror" being used to describe not the activities of the British military but the activities of Aboriginal groups.[37] The events on the Liverpool Plain of New South Wales in the 1830s provide another example as does the "Cullinlaringo" massacre in Central Queensland in 1861 when nineteen Europeans were killed.[38] Into the late nineteenth century, the Northern Territory witnessed concerted terror campaigns against white colonials. Several pastoral concerns collapsed through financial ruin caused by the destruction of pastoral lands and cattle killing.[39] State sponsored terrorism—as a tool of counter-terrorism—also continued to be deployed on the frontier into the twentieth century, ending with the Conniston Massacre of 1928.[40]

Writing on Australian frontier colonialism in the early 1990s, Morris noted that "the culture of terror that sustained conquest and dispossession remains an important yet unanalysed dimension of the colonial process."[41] Morris is correct but the investigation of Australian frontier colonialism also needs to explore how Aboriginal resistors to white domination came to see what, by today's definitions, are clearly terrorist acts as important weapons in their armory of resistance.

It is important to note that in early colonial Australia the phrase "terrorist" is used but it is rarely used to refer to acts of politically motivated violence. Still under the shadow of the French Revolution and its contextualization by the likes of Edmund Burke, the term is often used with poetic flourish to identify those who are seen to figuratively stand in the way of the colony's development. When the Sydney *Gazette and Advertiser* speaks of "terrorists" in Sydney Town in March 1829 it is a metaphor for the bureaucrats of the Governor's office.[42] When a few months later the same paper reports "willful terrorist knocked down in a moment" it is a metaphor for Sydneysiders' fears about their tenure over title deeds.[43] More generally, any individual or group that threatens the colony or Britain might be labeled a "terrorist." The *Hobart Town Courier* of 2 May 1829 for example refers to "terrorists" as the doomsayers talking down the British economy.

Revolutionary terrorism

In light of this re-interpretation of frontier relations in the new colony of New South Wales, Koschade's first category becomes redundant. Further, there are other events that predate 1868 that are worthy of attention and classification. Reflecting the enduring association of the phrase "terrorist" with the French Revolution, in December 1847 the *Maitland Mercury and Hunter River General Advertiser* reported "The Last of the Terrorists" had died.[44] In the late 1840s, however, several European societies were seen to face a new reign of terror and a new generation of terrorists. The "terrorists" now had fellow travelers in "communists" and "socialists."[45] Even before the revolutions of 1849, fears of a new reign had even reached Hobart. In November 1847 the "peace of the town had been disturbed in an unusual manner." Five hundred members of the Tailors Union were organizing against non-union members and making "threats of no ordinary character." Eight of the "terrorist" ring-leaders were brought before the Magistrate's court.[46]

Reports of the Eureka Stockade made mention of "terrorists" though the terrorists were not those individuals in "open rebellion" but the members of the press who were championing their cause; "It is the safety of the public that demands the utmost care lest, if guilty, they escape their just punishment through the influence of terrorists…."[47] The influence of these terrorists was seen as justification enough for yet another development in counter-terrorism in Australia. In dealing with the rebels, the Crown suspended Habeas Corpus to secure the convictions of the ringleaders.

These two examples show that the phrase "terrorist" still had close association to the French Revolution and continued to be constructed around those who threatened, in whatever form, the safety of the British Empire and the status quo.[48] The *Hobarton Mercury* in September 1855, for example, suggested that those who advocated universal male suffrage were "terrorists."[49]

Despite the fixation with Ireland and the Fenian "terrorists" (an association that some extended to the activities of the Kelly Gang) in the 1870s, the rise of the so-called "Terrorist Party" in Russia at the end of that decade altered the way many Australians thought about terrorism and terrorists in the late nineteenth century. In the 1880s the terms generate romantic associations in the minds of many Australians. A terrorist is a revolutionary seeking to end despotic oppression such as that exercised in Russia. One such Australian was New South Wales Premier Sir Henry Parkes who captured his regard for the Russian terrorist Sophia Perovskaia in his poem "The Beauteous Terrorist."[50] In 1882 the Brisbane *Courier* had associated terrorism with little more than the "dynamite and the knife" of the Fenians.[51] By 1886 the same paper appeared to find more sympathy with Henry Parkes' characterization and suggested that a terrorist was "a man of lofty ideals and philanthropic impulses."[52]

In the last years of the nineteenth century, the Australian romance with terrorists waned. While Sophie Perovskaia's life remained worth studying in the opinion of the members of the Women's Equal Franchise Association, terrorists were no longer individuals to be praised for the strength of their convictions.[53] The continuing outrages of Irish nationalists and the Boers resisting British rule in South Africa were terrorists not deserving of any empathy (though support for Irish nationalism remained strong within the diaspora). Further, the rise of anarchists and the increasingly indiscriminate nature of terrorist attacks saw the term regain the negativity that had been associated with Robespierre and the French Revolution. Terrorists were increasingly seen as a material and physical danger to the British Empire, and by extension, to Australia.

Anti-Asian terrorism

Before categorizing the twentieth century, there is yet another category that precedes Koschade's first: anti-Asian terrorism. While its
origins are often informed by industrial matters, its racial dimension is what makes it distinctive and enduring. An examination of
Gold Rush history in mid-nineteenth century Australia provides
much circumstantial evidence to support the contention that concerted campaigns against Asians and Asian interests in Victoria,
New South Wales, and later Queensland, can be classified as acts
of terrorism. One could explore such a theme through examinations of the Lambing Flat Riots in New South Wales in 1861, or the
anti-Chinese campaigns on the Palmer River in the 1870s. Such incidents and events are, however, simply the best remembered of
these efforts. Anti-Asian incidents at Hanging Rock in 1852, Ben-
digo in 1854, and Buckland River in 1857, are but three more, less
well-remembered, examples.[54]

    Anti-Asian violence does not end on the gold fields.[55] Further,
the threat of such violence or the threat of violence by a racially
distinct "fifth column" was one of the motivations for adopting the
White Australia Policy. The first report of the 1915 Broken Hill incident in the Melbourne *Argus* identified the perpetrators as "Asi-
atic."[56]

    Coordinated campaigns of violence and intimidation grew in
the wake of the White Australia Policy's demise in the 1970s. The
most notable of these campaigns is the one orchestrated by Jack
Van Tongeren and the Australian Nationalists Movement in the late
1980s. The campaign used assault, intimidation and fire-bombing
to attempt to drive Asian interests out of Western Australia.[57] Since
September 11, anti-Asian sentiment has increased in some circles
constructed around the dominance of Islam in Southeast Asia.

    Anti-Asian activity is interesting because it lends itself to
the label "home-grown" in comparison to the transnational
flavor of much of Australia's terrorism history. The more recent
manifestations, however, demonstrate an interesting transnational
connection. While its origins were closer to home, strong American
influences can be gauged in much of the anti-Asian activity that
took place in the 1980s and beyond. *The Turner Diaries* inspired the

operational approach of van Tongeren.[58] Further, with the demise of the Australian Nationalists Movement and National Action, many of the new groups which have appeared in their wake have strong American connections such as the Church of the Creator and RAHOWA (Racial Holy War against the Mud Races), and White Aryan Resistance.[59]

More generally the militia phenomenon in the United States which was a contributing factor in the Oklahoma City bombing has inspired Australian adherents to form American-style militias with titles like the A.U.S.I. Freedom Scouts, the Confederate Action Party and The Loyal Regiment of Australian Guardians. These organizations merge traditional home-grown xenophobia with an American operational approach. Of course these recent militias were not the first of their kind in Australian history as scholars including Andrew Moore and Keith Amos have demonstrated.[60]

Anti-Asian campaigns have not been the only forms of ethnic or racially motivated terrorism in Australian history. There are other cases from Australia's past deserving examination and classification. During the Great War a number of homes and businesses of German families were bombed in Mosman, a north shore suburb of Sydney.[61] In one case a family narrowly escaped with their lives.

In Queensland, tensions within and beyond the Italian community in Innisfail in the 1920s and 1930s led to a series of bombings and murders. In ten years, there were reportedly eleven murders, thirty bombings, and numerous counts of blackmail and extortion. Police tried to downplay any suggestions of an organized terrorist campaign. Under the title "Northern Terrorists," the Brisbane *Courier Mail* reported that the Commonwealth refused to become involved because it believed it was simply a family-feud and not the work of the "Black Hand…or any other terrorist society."[62] The press, however, were not convinced. Tensions were seen to exist between nationalities, and the "terrorist blackmailers and gunmen" were creating a grave feeling of unrest and jeopardizing local industry.[63] In March 1934 the Brisbane *Courier Mail* reported Commonwealth intervention at Innisfail. The Commonwealth Investigation Branch (the forerunner of the Australian Security Intelligence Organisation) had a "close watch," not on a Mafia organization but a new organization called the "Lancer Corps." It was suggested that this group had "arisen out of the Black Hand terrorist campaign" and was constituted by British/Irish Australians as a counter-revolutionary force—not dissimilar to other right-wing militia groups in Australia during the interwar period. Its members sought from the Defence Department a machine gun so that its members could train with the weapon to protect their homes.[64]

In approaching ethnic or racially motivated crime it is useful to recall Hamm's caveat: "Not all acts of terrorism can be considered hate crimes, and hate crimes are not necessarily terrorism unless such prejudiced violence has a political or social underpinning."[65] Nonetheless, further examination of ethnic and racial violence in Australia through the lens of terrorism studies is justified.

Industrial terrorism

The rise of the union movement in the late nineteenth century appeared to some sections of the Australian community to contain the same sorts of terrorists who bid ill to the British Empire. With European and American examples before them, terrorist acts in industrial disputation became more common in Australia. To the conservative press, labor leaders were seeking to follow in the paths of Robespierre and unleash terror on Australian streets. Queensland labor leader and parliamentarian John Coyne was identified during the 1912 general strike in Brisbane as a "baby terrorist."[66]

There are many cases of industrial unrest in Australia during the period from the 1890s to the 1930s that include what can be classified as terrorist acts. In 1925, the Melbourne *Argus* labeled this phenomena "Industrial Terrorism" and its meaning extended beyond the withdrawal of labor as a way to coerce capital.[67] Examples include the 1897 bomb-throwing campaign unleashed against mining interests at Lucknow near Orange in central western New South Wales. Media reports noted: "It is thought in Sydney that the object of the bomb-throwing was not so much to cause injury as to intimidate the men at work."[68] In 1899, the Lumper Strike at the Fremantle Docks was notable; the strikers became "terrorists" when they attacked the docks and physically scared away the remaining "free labourers."[69]

The town that might be considered the "terrorist" capital of Australia in the early twentieth century was the NSW mining town of Broken Hill. As well as the 1915 picnic train incident, concerted bombing attacks were not an unusual tool of industrial campaigns there. One such campaign took place in January 1909 and included the destruction of an ice cart that was supplying mine management and attacks at the Block 10 Mine. One attempt to destroy the mine did not succeed and the police were able to recover the "primitive bomb of most deadly character" which "consisted of a piece of brass piping packed with explosive, and attached to a short length of fuse." The bomb did not detonate but "if it had exploded the result would probably have been disastrous."[70] More bombs exploded in Broken Hill in April of the same year.[71]

Once again much of the influence for inspiration and approach came from overseas, notably the activities of the American-formed International Workers of the World (IWW) and its antecedents. It is during the Great War that terrorist acts as a weapon of industrial disputation in Australia reach their height. Back in Broken Hill, the local media became a new target. As IWW agitation in the town increased, Broken Hill's newspaper the *Daily Miner* became the subject of attack for its media reporting of industrial disputes. On 19 February 1917, "shortly after the close of an open-air I.W.W. meeting" the paper's offices were bombed. Undeterred, the paper kept printing and the office was bombed again on 25 February 1918.[72]

The IWW's resort to violence on industrial matters was also extended to the debate on whether Australia should adopt conscription. An attempt was made at Beaconsfield in Tasmania in October 1916 to blow up a hall in which a pro-conscription meeting was taking place. The gelignite and shrapnel filled bomb, which it was hoped would weaponize the hall's gas generating plant, did not achieve the outcome hoped by its perpetrators but still managed to leave one man seriously injured.[73] In response to such incidents the Minister for Defence, the former Union official Senator George Pearce insisted: "There was…no place in Australia for men who put bomb, knife and bullet before the Ballot Box."[74] Fears of an attack on the Australian Prime Minister saw his security increased. One IWW member insisted from his soap box in the Sydney Domain: "What is William Hughes shaking for if he is sure of his position? Why does he want detectives to guard him? I suppose that he thought someone would throw a bomb. We don't waste bombs unless there is something to waste them on."[75]

The IWW campaign, which included the murder of a policeman, culminated in an arson attack on Sydney in 1916 following the arrest and imprisonment of one of their number.[76] Twelve members of the IWW were arrested. In pronouncing their sentence the presiding judge observed:

> ...these misguided fanatics and terrorists engaged in a plot to intimidate the authorities charged with the administration of justice in New South Wales, and not only conspired but carried our their plot by deliberately starting numerous fires, the effects of which might readily have been the burning down of the whole city of Sydney and the destruction of hundreds of lives.[77]

The IWW period also saw another development in Australian counter-terrorism. Elevating the IWW beyond the simply criminal, the Commonwealth asserted its jurisdiction in having the IWW declared illegal under the 1914 Commonwealth Crimes Act which could proscribe "unlawful associations." This proscription allowed the government to also close down the IWW paper and its other public activities; acts that lessened the power of the organization to continue its activities. The formation at the same time of a Commonwealth "Counter Espionage Branch" as well as "Special Branches" in state police forces created the capability for government to monitor and act against such organizations.[78]

Industrial terrorism continued in Australia into the interwar period. For example, in 1923 milk supplies in Victoria were threatened when "terrorists" launched a campaign against cheap milk sellers. The campaign included the contamination of supplies with the "possible serious detriment to consumers."[79] In 1928, a waterside dispute in Melbourne saw a bombing campaign directed at the homes and hostels hosting "volunteer" wharf labor and several "well known business men." The bombing of a Greek club saw twenty men injured and one woman died from illness caused by another attack. Police assumed the same bomb makers ("communists") were responsible for the 1931 bombing of the home of the leader of the Victorian state parliamentary opposition Sir Stanley Argyle and threats made against another politician.[80]

In 1929, the New South Wales legislative assembly introduced "drastic legislation" to "suppress terrorism." The legislation aimed at curbing the power and influence of some unions by suppressing mass picketing and union "terrorist methods."[81] In April 1931 five prominent Sydney residents including the manager of the Bank of New South Wales and the managing director of the *Sydney Morning Herald* were sent mail bombs "arranged so that they might explode when opened." The bombs were allegedly sent by a "secret organisation." A member of this secret society came forth and claimed they had been recruited from abroad and blackmailed to deliver the letters. Police later reported that the devices could not have been detonated and the incident was a "stunt."[82]

The last industrial terrorist act of this period appears to have occurred in Sydney in 1938. The home of a union organizer involved in an industrial dispute at the Lidcombe Abattoir was bombed. The blast killed two people.[83]

During the Great War and the Russian Revolution, the IWW "terrorist anarchy" in Australia helped to remove any lasting vestiges of romantic and sympathetic associations with the word "terrorist" in the eyes of the media and the general public.[84] Industrial disputes in the coal industry in 1920 saw the *Argus* alleging that the coal union was engaged in "terroristic soviet methods."[85] Much was made of the fact the IWW "methods must harm any cause, good or bad":

> To burn a man's house down and himself inside it, or to blow him to pieces with gelignite, may silence him effectually enough, but will convince neither him nor anybody else of anything but the necessity of society's joining hands to stop the game.[86]

During the interwar years, the terms "terrorism" and "terrorist" gained, in Australia, their more modern association with indiscriminate attack and the killing of innocents. Further, the "terrorist" moved from Europe to be more closely associated with the colonized world. Fuelled by Australian xenophobia, the terrorist became a non-European in the years before World War II. Through the interwar period, the Australian media regularly reported on terrorist campaigns—notably those conducted by nationalists in India. In 1932, the *Canberra Times*, reporting on the murder of an American tourist in the Middle East, noted that the perpetrators were "Arab Terrorists." It is out of this narrower construction of the term "terrorist" that the idea that Australia does not suffer from terrorism grows. An Australian writing to the *Nambour Chronicle* in October 1935 observed: "Terrorism, that fateful word probably conveys little if anything to you in Australia, but to those who have lived in India, and particularly in Bengal, it has a wealth of meanings, none of them pleasant."[87] Protected by the White Australia Policy, Australians appeared to believe that they were safe from the worst cases of terrorism.

That terrorism was not perceived as a major problem for Australia by the late 1930s is also evidenced by the Commonwealth's response to the first international initiatives to prevent terrorism. Such calls emerged in the League of Nations in the wake of the assassination of King Alexander of Yugoslavia. The incident provoked calls from some member nations for the creation of a "Convention for the prevention and punishment of terrorism" which would in turn lead to the establishment of an "international criminal court" which would exercise jurisdiction over terrorism cases. Australia however declined to be a signatory to such a proposed convention: "So far as British countries are concerned the convention is unnecessary for British laws already discourage and punish terrorist activities."[88] In 1930s Australia, therefore, home-grown "terrorists" were groups of youths such as the gangs at Bondi and the "Terrorist gang in Redfern" that threatened local communities with petty crime and demanding money with menaces.[89]

International terrorism

During the late 1930s, the words "terrorist" and "terrorism" were returned to Europe to describe some of the individuals and actions associated with the rise of fascism. Germany, for example, was being subjected to "Nazi Terrorism."[90] With the onslaught of war

Australians were fighting against "terrorist dictatorship."[91] The "terrorist tactics of the Axis forces" were witnessed by Australian troops in the Middle East, Greece and Malaya.[92] Within the nation, fears of fifth column activity by the small Japanese community saw another milestone in the history of Australian counter-terrorism. Internment had already been used as a tool during the Great War but during the Pacific War the government moved to not only intern naturalized British subjects but Australian-born of Japanese ancestry. Further, at the war's conclusion, all Japanese, including Australian citizens, were deported to Japan.[93]

With the end of war, terrorism and terrorists found a new home in Southeast Asia. Readers of the *Canberra Times* were informed in November 1945 of a "mysterious terrorist organisation" operating in Malaya. A headline the following February read: "Indonesian Terrorists Worse than Japs."[94] Further, the association between terrorism and Russia returned with the Cold War and fears about the expansionary activities of the Soviet Union. "Communist Terrorists," who had been reported on from time to time in the interwar period, were the new threat and it was the presence of these terrorists in Malaya which resulted in the Australian military embarking on its first war on terror in 1950 as a contribution to the Malayan "Emergency."

The 1940s and 1950s were quiet decades in the history of terrorism in Australia. While further research is necessary, the most significant incident was a campaign directed against Qantas Airways. In August 1948, "suspected sabotage" delayed the departure of a Qantas Constellation flight from Sydney to Singapore via Darwin. The aircraft had in its cargo "a quantity of small arms and ammunition" and police believed the threat was made by "communists" who wished to stop the British in Malaya receiving any assistance. A year later, a Qantas flying boat in Sydney Harbour was destroyed by a high explosive set off by an alarm clock. Unable to solve the cases, police dismissed the latter as the work of a "crank who had a grudge against the airline."[95] It is interesting to note that unsolved cases with some terrorist credentials are often later discounted by the police as "stunts" or the work of a "crank." Such conclusions may well be correct but several cases deserve further research.

Australia's postwar mass migration program also had a significant impact on the nation's terrorism history. The alleged Black

Hand campaigns in Queensland in the 1920s and 1930s were recalled with allegations that the organization had established itself in Melbourne and subjected the local Italian community to a "reign of terror."[96] More important, the expansion of the immigration program to southern and Eastern Europe brought new immigrants, many of whom maintained close connections with political struggles at home. It is the postwar migration scheme that brought to Australia the men who would form the largest terrorist organization on Australian soil during the 1960s. Stuart Koschade's chapter on the Croatian Revolutionary Brotherhood provides an insight into what followed.

The decade of the 1960s marked the beginning of Koschade's second period in the history of terrorism in Australia. Following a descriptor often used in terrorism studies literature, Koschade labeled the category: "International Terrorism: 1960–Circa 1990."[97] The label "international" is somewhat misleading in the Australian context given the early transnational connections in the nation's terrorist past.[98] This said, its wide use and the association of "international" with "modern" gives it a wider credence that an Australian study would be foolish to overturn. However, the chronology might be extended back into the 1940s to capture its origins from an Australian perspective, and extended ahead to the 1990s rather than "circa 1990." Including the 1990s would catch episodes such as Aum Shinrikyo's (Supreme Truth) Western Australia training ground and its 1994 Sarin gas attack on the Tokyo underground railway system.[99]

The second era in Australia's terrorism history is also notable because the international terrorist situation produced a range of local responses. Multinational corporations and government departments began to make contingency plans about how they might deal with a terrorist attack on their assets.[100] Responding to the changed international situation and the increasing level of terrorist activity on Australian soil, the period was also marked by the Commonwealth Government making more serious efforts to counter terrorism.

In addition to Croatian separatist terrorism, there were significant terrorist campaigns launched in Australia during the 1970s and

1980s. Most of these attacks were the echoes of distant thunder. Australia became a site of most of these terrorist activities simply because both sides of the conflict were represented.

Emerging from the hotbed of terrorism that was Beirut in the 1970s, the Justice Commandoes of the Armenian Genocide launched a campaign against Turkish interests in Europe in the late 1970s. In 1980, the group expanded its operations to North America and Australia. The campaign in Australia commenced with the assassination of the Turkish Consul General and his driver/bodyguard on a quiet Sydney street in December of that year. In 1986 a man was killed while attempting to set the timer on a bomb which aimed to blow up the offices of the Turkish consulate in Melbourne.

Australia also became a site for the wider conflict between Israel and the Arab World. The terrorist attack made on the 1972 Munich Olympic Games, by a militant Palestinian group, unleashed terror campaigns all over the world. Australia was caught up in these events in September 1972 when mail bombs directed to the Israeli Embassy in Canberra and the Consulate-General's offices in Sydney were detected. Reflecting the "international" dimension, the bombs had been mailed in Amsterdam.

In December 1982, the Israeli consulate in Sydney and the nearby Hakoah sports club at Bondi were bombed. In the wake of the attacks, the Palestine Liberation Organization and previously unheard of group "The Organisation for the Liberation of Lebanon from Foreigners" claimed responsibility. Australian police and security authorities and the Israeli government all believed the attack was more likely the work of the 15 May Organization, a Palestinian terrorist group based in Baghdad and sponsored by the Iraqi government. It was assumed the "bomb-maker" (suspected to be Mohammed Rashid who was later jailed for his part in an attempt to blow up a Pan Am flight from Los Angeles to Tokyo) flew into Australia, planted the bombs, and then left.

The attack was not the first time a terrorist incident in Australia had been linked to the Iraqi government. One clear and somewhat bizarre example of state-sponsored terrorism perpetrated by a foreign government on Australian soil was the so-called "Iraqi Dates" incident of 1978. An Iraqi diplomatic official attended a Sydney meeting of the Assyrian Universal Alliance and on his departure presented to the organizers a box of dates. The hydrochloric acid that laced the dates did not cause death but injured several people including one child who suffered permanent throat damage.

The Hilton hotel bombing in 1978 was the most infamous terrorist act on Australian soil in this period of international terrorism. Its relative success, the indiscriminate nature of the attack, the fact it killed innocent Australian citizens, and the fact that British/Irish Australians were originally found guilty of the attacks before their convictions were quashed helps to ensure its legacy and perhaps explains why Lane remembered it as the only terrorist attack in Australian history.

The attack was constructed as another example of Australian soil becoming the site of international terrorism because the Indian Prime Minister was present at the Commonwealth Heads of Government Meeting and the series of anti-Indian terrorist attacks (including attacks on property and several stabbings) that preceded the meetings were connected to demands for the release from an Indian prison of Ananda Marga sect spiritual leader Prabhat Ranjan Sarkar. The incident also provoked further changes in how the Commonwealth government sought to counter terrorism including a new federal agency and a new state-commonwealth consultative body to respond to acts of Terrorism.[101]

A number of the campaigns in the "International Terrorism" period produce the opportunity for the historian to engage in the pastime of "virtual history." What would have happened if Croatian separatist terrorist Viko Virkez had not turned himself and his co-conspirators into Lithgow police hours before the commencement of a major bombing campaign in 1981? If the terrorists who planted and detonated the Hakoah Club bomb had placed the car closer to one of the key structural pillars the explosion would have succeeded in destroying the building, killing scores of the patrons. If the bomb placed beside the Turkish Consulate in Melbourne in 1986 had exploded as planned, police forensic experts subsequently calculated that the number of casualties, killed and injured, on busy Toorak Road would have been in the hundreds. How different would Australia's terrorism history be if these events had succeeded in the way their perpetrators had planned?

Home-grown

These transnational terrorist campaigns—directed mostly at foreign assets and individuals—also had an impact on "home grown" organizations and issues. Protest against conscription and the Vietnam War, for example, saw some radical elements of the anti-war movement advocating violence and carrying out attacks against the offices of American corporations, the Commonwealth Department of Labour and National Service, and military bases. Organizations such as the People's Liberation Army and the Draft Resistance Group are worthy of closer study to further highlight the nature of their campaigns and examine how their rhetoric and operations were influenced by the broader international climate of the era.

The late 1970s also saw the birth of home-grown eco-terrorism. Attacks were directed at Atomic Energy Commission establishments and later on the Franklin Dam hydro-electricity project in Tasmania. A hijacking (one of the new tactics of the international terrorism era) was also attempted in connection with the Franklin Dam campaign.

In the "International Terrorism" category, Koschade does hold the sub-category of "Domestic Terrorism." In responding to transnational issues such as the environment or the Vietnam War they are domestic only in the sense that their membership was Australian born and they were focused on the Australian context. As reflected in the two examples above, most of this activity was inspired by left wing political causes arising from the new social movements of the 1960s. They are, as a result, in stark contrast to the right-wing anti-Asian terrorist activity of the 1980s. Given this study's earlier findings, making a claim for "Domestic Terrorism" in the 1970s is less engaging. The term "Left-Wing Terrorism" has been adopted in several international studies and appears more relevant here.[102] Further, given that the examples listed in the international category are dominated by ethnic and nationalist issues, the re-emergence of ideology as a dominant force for action suggests that these events are deserving of their own category.

The war on terrorism

Koschade completes his framework with the category "twenty-first Century Islamic Terrorism." September 11 ensured that the "New Terrorism" category some scholars suggested in the late 1990s to characterize the activities of groups like al Qaeda would be quickly superseded.[103] While reflective of the international attention given to the efforts of al Qaeda and other Islamic terrorists groups, the term "Islamic Terrorism" does suggest that terrorism in the twenty-first century is the domain of one religious faith and consequently demonizes all adherents of that faith. Our study has decided to place this period in the history of terrorism in Australia under the title "The War on Terror." In the same way a scholar of World War II is afforded some flexibility in how they approach their subject, this label perhaps more usefully represents the period and the far-ranging consequences that jihadi or religious terrorism (to borrow two more unsatisfying labels) has unleashed. In the Australian context the weight of effort expended by the state in counter-terrorism is but one example. The legal ramifications as discussed in Lynch's chapter in this collection are another theme, as are the broader strategic consequences discussed in Reynolds' chapter.

Because of the magnitude of September 11 and the subsequent "war on terror," the scholar chronicling the history of this period in Australia's terrorist past faces an embarrassment of riches, even when confronted by the Australian government's thirty-year archive rule. Court reports, for example, are very useful sources as exampled by the trials of people such as Jack Roach, Faheem Khalid Lodhi, Jack Thomas and Zekky Mallah.

That Australia became a target for jihadi terrorist attack is proven by the considerable efforts by al Qaeda, Lashkar-E-Toiba and Jemaah Islamiyah to establish operational and support cells in this country. These efforts took Australian citizens to Afghanistan to meetings with Osama bin Laden and brought personalities such as French terrorist Willie Brigitte to Australia.

Events such as the Bali Bombings of 2002 and the Australian embassy bombing in Jakarta in 2003 saw Australians subjected to a style of attack they had witnessed first hand in the 1980s. The degree to which these efforts reflected the failure of Australian citizens and foreign nationals to establish jihadi operational terrorist cells in Australia in the years preceding these attacks will be an important focus of a broader study.

Again, there is much opportunity for historians to engage in virtual history. For example, what would the result have been if Indian national Mohammed Abdul Afroz Razzak's plan to hijack and crash an airliner into the southern hemisphere's tallest concrete reinforced building—the Rialto Towers in Melbourne—had not been called off in favor of a new plan (aborted at the last moment) to hijack a plane in Manchester and crash it into the British Houses of Parliament on September 11?[104]

A new framework for studying Australia's terrorist past

Having traversed 220 years of Australian history through the lens of terrorism, a more complicated picture has been presented than is suggested by Koschade's original framework. While perhaps not "waves" as in Rapoport's definition of the term, our new categories do mark the important periods and themes in a history of terrorism in Australia. The framework we will utilize as we complete our study therefore is as follows:

1. State-sponsored terrorism as a tool of colonization, 1788 to the early twentieth century
2. Terrorism as a tool of Aboriginal resistance, 1790 to the early twentieth century.
3. Revolutionary Terrorism, 1840s to 1890s
4. Anti-Asian Terrorism, 1860s to 1990s
5. Industrial Terrorism, 1890s to 1930s
6. International Terrorism, 1940s to 1990s
7. Left-wing Terrorism, 1970s to 1980s
8. The War on Terror, 1990s to today

As noted, there are a number of themes within these categories. The transnational influences that have shaped Australia's experience of terrorism are apparent throughout. These can be explored in a number ways such as the conduct of foreign terrorist campaigns on Australia's shores, transnational influences on approach and method within acts committed within Australia, and the important and enduring theme of community support and sustenance. The history of Australian counter-terrorism is also a theme that carries through all of these categories.

Conclusion

Much is to be gained by Australian historians re-calibrating the nation's history and examining it through the lens of terrorism and counter-terrorism. Such an exercise is more than simply another contribution to the "Terror Factory" that has emerged around the world since September 11?[105] It does not contribute to a wider enterprise conducted by the government and media that allegedly makes Australians more alarmed than alert. The lack of systematic knowledge and research about the history of terrorism in Australia does leave the general public believing foolish ideas that before the "war on terror" Australians had never known terrorism and the Hilton bombing was the only terrorist attack to predate 2002; or that the 1915 Broken Hill incident is somehow indicative of the nature of jihadist threat to Australia in the twenty-first century. Understanding the nature of the nation's relationship with terrorism in the past should also better assist government and those agencies charged with the nation's protection to better understand and deal with future threats. Might, for example, the successful experience of the Croatian Revolutionary Brotherhood and the unsuccessful experience of Jemaah Islamiyah provide case studies that could help to understand the ingredients for the successful creation of foreign terrorist cells in the Australian environment? This can hardly be viewed as Australian historians selling out their academic freedom and independence in the service of the state. Critical terrorism history must remain the touchstone of such work. As noted, this chapter does represent work in progress. Further research will produce a more complete understanding of terrorism in Australian history. On with the work...

Notes

[1] Pamela L. Griset and Sue Mahan, *Terrorism in Perspective* (Thousand Oaks: Sage, 2003), 85.

[2] Terry Lane, transcript of the "National Interest," ABC Radio National, 28 April 2002, http://www.abc.net.au/rn/nationalinterest/stories/2002/541944.htm (accessed 12 September 2006).

[3] Commonwealth of Australia, Security Legislation Amendment (Terrorism) Act 2002, http://www.comlaw.gov.au/ComLaw/Legislation/ActCompilation1.nsf/0/18BFD93E176C8F0ACA256F7100572147/$file/SecLegAmTerrorism2002.pdf (accessed 1 July 2008).

[4] *Illawara Mercury*, 27 April 2000.

[5] Therese Taylor, "Australian Terrorism: Traditions of violence and the Family Court Bombings," *Australian Journal of Law and Society*, 8 (1992): 1–24.

[6] *The Canberra Times*, 13 July, 1933.

[7] *The Canberra Times*, 12 November, 1937.

[8] *The Canberra Times*, 1 September, 1949.

[9] The history of terrorism and its impact in Australia is a neglected field of study. The existing work is very patchy and tends to appear as contextual background in popular studies by journalists or academic studies by political scientists. See for example James Crown, *Australia: The Terrorist Connection* (Melbourne: Sun Books, 1986) and Jenny Hocking's *Beyond Terrorism: The Development of the Australian Security State* (Sydney: UNSW Press, 1983). There are specific historical studies that examine certain episodes in Australia's past and these are noted in this chapter where appropriate. The only attempt to provide a broader understanding over the *longue durée* of Australian history is Kevin Baker's *Mutiny, Terrorism, Riots and Murder: A History of Sedition in Australia and New Zealand* (Kenthurst: Rosenberg, 2006). As noted in the title, however, the work does examine its subject more though the lens of sedition than terrorism. For a useful introduction to the field of terrorism studies in Australia consult Stuart Koschade, "An Assessment of Terrorism Studies in Australia: Recommendations and Future Directions" in *Proceedings Research Network for a Secure Australia — Closed Counter-Terrorism Workshop* (Melbourne University, 2006).

[10] For an introduction to the Latvian theme consult FG Clarke, *Will-o'-the-wisp: Peter Painter and the Anti-tsarist Terrorists in Britain and Australia* (Melbourne: Oxford University Press, 1983).

[11] Stuart Koschade, "Constructing a Historical Framework of Terrorism in Australia," *Journal of Policing, Intelligence and Counter Terrorism* 1/2 (2007).

[12] For discussions of the incident and the Fenian movement in Australia consult Malcolm Campbell, *Ireland's New Worlds: Immigrants, Politics, and Society in the United States and Australia, 1815–1922* (Madison: University of Wisconsin Press, 2008); Robert Travers, *The Phantom Fenians of New South Wales* (Kenthurst: Kangaroo Press, 1986); and Keith Amos, *The Fenians In Australia, 1865–1880* (Sydney: UNSW Press, 1988).

[13] *Liverpool Mercury*, 19 May, 1868.

[14] For a brief recent analysis see Baker, 192–194. Abdullah acted as the imam of the Broken Hill mosque. See Shahram Akbarzadeh and Abdullah Saeed, *Muslim Communities in Australia* (Sydney: UNSW Press, 2001), 29. For a contemporary account see *Barrier Miner*, 2 January, 1915; *Argus*, 2 January, 1915 and *Northern Territory Times and Gazette*, 7 January, 1915.

[15] For an example of these opinions see the web site "Australian Islam Monitor." http://islammonitor.org/index.php?option=com_content&task=view&id=1917&Itemid=97 (accessed 2 January, 2009).

[16]   http://www.slv.vic.gov.au/collections/treasures/jerilderieletter1.html (assessed 4 July, 2008).

[17] *Glasgow Herald,* 11 August, 1880.

[18] *The Leeds Mercury,* 28 August, 1880.

[19] *Belfast News-Letter*, 7 October, 1897.

[20] Australian Defence Force Academy Professor of English Paul Eggert examined the notion of Kelly as terrorist in a 2005 seminar paper "The Terrorist's Voice: Ned Kelly, Rolf Boldrewood and Peter Carey." He concluded "the so-called domestic terrorists of today have their forebears in this country's history, from which depressingly little has been learnt," http://www.unsw.adfa.edu.au/news/archives/2005/nov_3_2005.html.

[21] Rolf Boldrewood, *Robbery Under Arms*, ed. Paul Eggert and Elizabeth Webbey (St Lucia: University of Queensland Press, 2006), 347.

[22] John Hirst, *Freedom on the Fatal Shore* (Melbourne: Black Inc, 2008), 404–405.

[23] Cited in Walter Laqueur, *Voices of Terror: Manifestos, Writings, and Manuals of Al Qaeda, Hamas, and Other Terrorists from Around the World and Throughout the Ages* (New York: Reed Press, 2004), 89.

[24] For discussions of the Terror see David Andress, *The Terror: The Merciless War for Freedom in Revolutionary France* (New York: Farrar, Straus, and Giroux, 2006).

[25] The term "terrorist" would remain first and foremost associated with the French Revolution. Under the title "The Last of the Terrorists" *The Maitland Mercury & Hunter River General Advertiser* of 18 December 1847 reported the death of one of the last of the revolutionary figures.

[26] Perhaps because he did not see the revolutionary government as legitimate the Anglo-Irish thinker Edmund Burke was quick to use the term

"terrorist" but associate it with those who opposed rather than supported the state. For a discussion of the term's crossing of the English Channel in the late eighteenth century see Lee Griffith, *The War on Terrorism and the Terror of God* (Grand Rapids: Wm. B. Eerdmans Publishing, 2004), 12. For a study of the French Revolution's impact on Britain consult Chris Evans, *Debating the Revolution: Britain in the 1790s* (London: I.B.Tauris, 2006). For the impact on the fledgling colony of New South Wales consult John Gascoigne, *The Enlightenment and the Origins of European Australia* (Cambridge: Cambridge University Press, 2002).

[27] See Keith Windschuttle, *The Fabrication of Aboriginal History* (Sydney: Macleay Press, 2002).

[28] John Connor, *The Australian Frontier Wars, 1788–1838* (Sydney: UNSW Press, 2002); and Jeffrey Grey, *A Military History of Australia* (Melbourne, Cambridge University Press, 2008), 28–40.

[29] Cited in Alan Atkinson, "Conquest," *Australia's Empire*, ed. Deryck M. Schreuder and Stuart Ward (Oxford: Oxford University Press, 2008), 42.

[30] Henry Reynolds, *The Other Side of The Frontier: Aboriginal Resistance to European Invasion of Australia* (Melbourne: Penguin, 1982), 87.

[31] David Collins, "An Account of the English Colony in New South Wales," *Monthly Review*, November (1798), 253.

[32] Connor, *Australian Frontier Wars*, xii.

[33] For an introduction to Pemulwuy consult Eric Willmot, *Pemulwuy: The Rainbow Warrior* (Sydney: Weldons, 1987).

[34] *Sydney Gazette and New South Wales Advertiser*, 18 May, 1816.

[35] *Sydney Gazette and New South Wales Advertiser*, 32 October, 1818.

[36] *Sydney Gazette and New South Wales Advertiser*, 18 May, 1816.

[37] Naomi Parry, "'Many deeds of terror': Windshuttle and Mosquito," Evatt Foundation *Papers*, August 2003, http://evatt.labor.net.au/publications/papers/110.html (accessed 10 September 2007).

[38] See Roger Milliss, *Waterloo Creek: The Australia Day Massacre of 1838, George Gipps and the British Conquest of New South Wales* (Sydney: UNSW Press, 1994); and Greg de Moore, *Tom Wills: His Spectacular Rise and Tragic Fall* (Sydney: Allen and Unwin, 2008), 114–120.

[39] Tony Austin, *Simply the Survival of the Fittist: Aboriginal Administration in South Australia's Northern Territory, 1863–1890* (Darwin: History Society of Northern Territory, 1992), 20–24.

[40] Henry Reynolds, *Why Weren't We Told?: A Personal Search for the Truth About Our History* (Melbourne: Ringwood, 1999), 111–112.

[41] Barry Morris, "Frontier colonialism as a culture of Terror," *Power, Knowledge and Aborigines*, ed. Bain Attwood and John Arnold (Melbourne: La Trobe University Press, 1992), 72.

[42] Sydney *Gazette and Advertiser,* 19 March, 1829.

[43] Sydney *Gazette and Advertiser* 20 June, 1829.

[44] *Maitland Mercury and Hunter River General Advertiser*, 18 December, 1847.

[45] *The Courier,* 17 January, 1849.

[46] *The Courier,* 27 November, 1847.

[47] *Moreton Bay Courier,* 24 March, 1855.

[48] *The Moreton Bay Courier,* 6 May, 1858.

[49] *Hobarton Mercury* 5 September, 1855.

[50] Henry Parkes, *The Beauteous Terrorist and Other Poems* (Melbourne: George Robertson and Company, 1885).

[51] Brisbane *Courier,* 8 Dec, 1882.

[52] Brisbane *Courier,* 2 August, 1886.

[53] Brisbane *Courier,* 8 April 1889; *Courier,* 21 January, 1896.

[54] Humphrey McQueen, *A New Britannia* (St Lucia: University of Queensland Press, 1994), 33.

[55] See a selection of the essays in Ann Curthoys and Andrew Markus, eds., *Who are Our Enemies? Racism and the Australian working class* (Sydney: Hale and Iremonger, 1978).

[56] *Argus*, 2 January, 1915.

[57] Consult Steve James, "The Policing of Right-Wing Violence in Australia," *Police Practice and Research,* 6/2 (2005): 103–119; Judith Bessant, "Political crime and the case of young neo-nazis: A question of methodology," *Terrorism and Political Violence,* 7/4 (1995): 94–116; and Jack Van Tongeren, *The ANM Story* (True Blue Aussie Underground, 2004).

[58] See Michael Bradley, "True-Blue White Australians: Ongoing support for a White Australia, 1966–1998," BA Hons Thesis, University of New South Wales, 1998.

[59] For a study of such right wing groups consult Andrew Moore, *The Right Road?: A History of Right-Wing Politics in Australia* (Melbourne: Oxford University Press, 1995).

[60] Andrew Moore, *The Secret Army and the Premier: Conservative Paramilitary Organisations in New South Wales, 1930–32* (Sydney: UNSW Press, 1989); and Keith Amos, *The New Guard Movement, 1931–1935* (Melbourne: Melbourne University Press, 1976).

[61] *The Mercury,* 14 March, 1916; *Argus* 8 January, 1917.

[62] *Courier-Mail,* 12 January, 1934. The Black Hand was a criminal society connected to the Mafia. For a discussion of the Black Hand's activities in Queensland see Eugenie Navarre, *The Cane Barracks Story* (Carindale: Glass House Books, 2007); William A. Douglass, *From Italy to Ingham: Italians in North Queensland* (St Lucia: University of Queensland Press, 1995); and Ross Fitzgerald, *The People's Champion, Fred Paterson: Australia's Only*

Communist Party Member of Parliament (St Lucia, University of Queensland Press, 1997).

[63] *Courier-Mail*, 12 January, 1934.

[64] *Courier-Mail* 12, 14 and 15 March, 1934.

[65] Cited in Donald Altschiller, *Hate Crimes: A Reference Handbook* (Santa Barbara: ABC-CLIO, 2005), 178.

[66] Nambour, *Chronicle and Northcoast Advertiser*, 20 April, 1912.

[67] *Argus*, 21 January, 1925.

[68] Brisbane *Courier*, 24 September, 1897.

[69] *West Australian*, 16 March, 1899.

[70] *Northern Territory Times and Gazette,* 22 January, 1909.

[71] *Northern Territory Times and Gazette,* 16 April, 1909.

[72] *Argus*, 19 February, 1917 and 25 February, 1918.

[73] *Argus*, 23 October, 1916; and *Mercury* 24 October, 1916.

[74] *Argus*, 26 October, 1916.

[75] *Argus*, 12 October, 1916.

[76] For further detail consult Ian Turner, *Sydney's Burning* (Sydney: Alpha Books, 1969).

[77] *The Mercury*, 5 December, 1916.

[78] See Jenny Hocking, *Terror Laws: ASIO, Counter-Terrorism and the Threat to Democracy* (Sydney: UNSW Press, 2004), 15-19; and Mark Finnane, "The Public Rhetorics of Policing in Times of War and Violence: Countering Apocalyptic Visions," *Crime Law and Social Change*, 50/1-2 (2008): 7-24.

[79] *Argus*, 24 January, 1923.

[80]*Canberra Times*, 23 November, 1928; *Argus*, 4 Dec 1928 and 21 May, 1929; and *Canberra Times*, 11 November, 1931.

[81] *Northern Territory Times*, 27 September, 1929.

[82] *Canberra Times*, 29 April, 1931.

[83] *Canberra Times*, 23 and 27 April, 1938.

[84] *The Mercury*, 8 February, 1916.

[85] *Argus*, 10 July, 1920.

[86] *Mercury*, 24 October, 1916.

[87] *Nambour Chronicle*, 25 October, 1935.

[88] *Canberra Times*, 10 February, 1938.

[89] *Canberra Times*, 16 May, 1936.

[90] *Canberra Times*, 20 August, 1936.

[91] *Canberra Times*, 26 June, 1942.

[92] *Canberra Times*, 11 April, 1942.

[93] Sean Brawley, *The White Peril: Foreign Relations and Asian Immigration to Australasia and North America, 1919-1978* (Sydney: UNSW Press, 1995), 168-169. Griset and Mahan characterize the internment of Japanese Americans during the Pacific War as "another infamous example of overzealous

counterterrorism at the expense of cherished American values." *Terrorism in Perspective*, 289.

[94] *Canberra Times*, 12 November, 1945 and 7 February, 1946.

[95] *Canberra Times*, 7 August, 1948 and 30 August, 1949.

[96] *Canberra Times*, 20 June, 1951.

[97] For examples of the use of this descriptor see Brian Jenkins, ed., *International Terrorism: A New Mode of Conflict* (Crescent Publications, 1975); Yonah Alexander, ed., *International Terrorism: Political and Legal Documents* (Dordrecht Martinus Nijhoff Publishers, 1992); and Charles W. Kegley, *International Terrorism: Characteristics, Causes, Controls* (New York: St. Martin's, 1990).

[98] David Rapoport is another scholar who has extended the international past World War II. See "The Four Waves of Modern Terrorism," *Attacking Terrorism: Elements of Grand Strategy*, ed. Audrey Cronin and J. Ludes (Washington DC: Georgetown University Press, 2004), 46-73.

[99] Other historians have also stretched the chronology of "modern terrorism" back to the 1940s. See for example William F. Shughart, "An Analytical History of Terrorism, 1945-2000," *Public Choice*, 128 (2006), 7-39.

[100] For an example see Sean Brawley, *Beating the Odds: Thirty Years of the Totalizator Agency Board of New South Wales* (Sydney: Focus Book, 2004), 133.

[101] Hocking, *Terror Laws*, 88.

[102] See for example Shughart, "An Analytical History of Terrorism"; Donatella de Porta, "Left-Wing Terrorism in Italy" *Terrorism in Context*, ed. Martha Crenshaw (University Park: Penn-State Press, 1995), 105-159; and Brent L. Smith, *Terrorism in America, Pipe Bombs and Pipe Dreams* (Albany: State University of New York, 1994), 24.

[103] See for example Walter Laqueur, *The New Terrorism: Fanaticism and the Arms of Mass Destruction* (New York: Oxford University Press, 2000).

[104] Razaak was later arrested in Bombay and convicted of the conspiracy to commit the hijacking at Manchester on September 11. See Angel Rabasa and Cheryl Benard, *The Muslim World After 9/11* (Santa Monica: Rand Corporation, 2004), 308.

[105] *Sydney Morning Herald*, 9 June, 2007.

11

Australia's History of Terrorism: Institutionalized Discrimination and the Response of the Mob

Luke Howie

Analyses of the history of terrorism are receiving more attention in the post-9/11 world.[1] The increasingly important role of history in understanding terrorism and how it might be prevented and mitigated represents important progress towards Australia's evolving counter-terrorism capabilities. This new attention to the history of terrorism brings necessary baggage and debates surrounding the meaning and contested nature of history. As a non-historian, I argue that these broader debates about the nature of history provide a crucial location from which rigorous studies of terrorism can be launched by both historians and non-historians alike. It is in this spirit that I write this chapter where I argue that many responses to acts of terrorism and political violence in Australia have been characterized by discrimination, prejudice, and racism. I intend to suggest that, in the aftermath of terrorism and political violence, actions that would be considered unacceptable in other contexts in liberal democracies such as Australia are tolerated and encouraged by large segments of the Australian community and supported by institutional scaffoldings such as law enforcement and intelligence organizations, government departments, and the media.

I use for the title of this chapter the suggestive term "mob" quite deliberately. Its origins lie in the philosophy of Hannah Arendt and the "authoritarian character" outlined by Erich Fromm.[2] "Mob" embodies the crowd, aggressiveness, anonymity, savagery, de-humanization, and the decline of reason. Gustave Le Bon once famously wrote that when in a crowd the average citizen can "descend several rungs in the ladder of civilisation."[3] I attempt to exercise this conceptualization of the mob to frame the response of people and institutions in Australia to terrorism. I use "mob" to refer to the faceless, sometimes mindless, always glib, and often violent crowds that sometimes gather for unspoken but mutually understood purposes. These purposes often appeal to some notion of common sense for identifying risk and danger in a racial, political, social and cultural group. Perhaps controversially, I argue that the mob may be a spontaneous crowd like the one that gathered on the Sydney beachfront in December 2005 and violently attacked people they deemed to be from the Middle East, or it may be the governmental, security and policing organizations that help form the social and cultural scaffolding for people living in Australia.

There are many moments in this chapter where I could choose to "make something out of it" or "downplay the significance." I hope the reader will indulge me as I err on the side of seeing the insidious behind the incidences described here. Some, I argue, are potentially alarming examples of discrimination and prejudice. Others may well be accidents and mistakes or mitigated by extenuating circumstances. I ask that the reader consider these instances to be moments of conjecture and critical examination rather than hyperbolizing on my part. There are other moments where it may seem that I am oversimplifying and ignoring other complexities such as class, politics, and security when exploring prejudice along racial, religious and nationalist lines. Whilst I intend to account for a variety of complexities as I write, I also intend to focus, zero-in on, and analyze discriminatory and prejudicial moments in the history of responding to terrorism to Australia. I do this in the hope of bringing several shady and gloomy events into the light so that they may be interrogated with a rigor that was absent when they occurred.

I have ordered this chapter in the following way. First, I explore the problem of complexity. I argue that whilst I attempt to illuminate the discriminatory and prejudicial attitudes underlying the history of terrorism in Australia, there are always complexities that problematize glib and oversimplified analyses and responses. Second, I identify three examples from Australia's history of terrorism to explore institutionalized discrimination and mob-like responses. These examples, the Irish threat, friendly terrorism, and the Muslim threat, are linked through their translation from global threats to local consequences and the discriminatory and prejudicial responses they elicited. In concluding, I argue that the media plays a central role in interpreting global threats as local consequences. Media reporting, especially reporting that relies heavily on certain "experts" and official spokespeople, is crucial in articulating terrorism threats and the groups that should be held responsible.

Complexities in Australia's history of terrorism

There are complexities in each of the scenarios that I explore in this chapter. Whilst I argue that there have been numerous incidences involving terrorism and political violence in Australia that have resulted in some form of discrimination targeting groups of people perceived to be collectively responsible, I also attempt to acknowledge, without detracting from my key arguments, that there were other contributing factors that resulted in this perception. As such, discrimination and prejudicial attitudes do not manifest independently of other social, political and institutional forces. On some occasions, the response to terrorism has appeared to be plainly discriminatory. On other occasions, discriminatory and prejudicial overtones have manifested as subtle differences in how some groups of people are treated or portrayed in the media as risky, subversive and dangerous. When this has occurred it has often been accompanied by complexities such as politics, social trends, class struggles, international wars both hot and cold, and policing and intelligence imperatives. As such, rarely are there instances when it can be said that there was brutal, mindless racism in response to terrorism.

Mol and Law argue that much of the recent research and theory into various aspects of social science, cultural studies, critical theory, and some philosophy has represented a "revolt against simplification."[4] The world of the twenty-first century is certainly far more complex than its depiction in media representation and some academic discourse. It is a world that resists attempts to tame it and tie it down. If analysts, theoreticians and researchers attempt too tightly to constrain realities in understanding issues and events, simplification can often become a barrier to understanding. For Mol and Law: "There is complexity if things relate but don't add up, if events occur but not within the processes of linear time, and if phenomenon share a space but cannot be mapped in terms of a single set of three-dimensional coordinates."[5] Such complexity is evident in much of Australia's history of terrorism.

There are, generally speaking, alternative explanations for the seemingly discriminatory and prejudicial situations explored in this chapter. As I explore anti-Irish discrimination in Australia's history, I am aware also of the class consciousness involved in early Australian trade unionism and the entangling of Australia's Irish diaspora and Catholicism. I acknowledge that despite such overt racism as embodied in the NINA (no Irish need apply) signs that once littered Australian cities, the problem was likely always more complex than merely race or nationality.[6] Equally, I am aware that there were good reasons for Australia's intelligence and policing agencies focusing almost exclusively on left-wing and pro-communist threats and almost condoning the similarly violent or worse subversive threats posed by fascist and right-wing elements. The latter would have been more formidable allies had the communist threat materialized. I am also aware that the recent Dr. Mohammed Haneef terror scare that culminated in the Federal Police commissioner calling for a media blackout is perhaps not as alarming as it first appears.[7] It could be argued that the Australian Federal Police (AFP) have a difficult and thankless job to do in an unforgiving media environment that works to accentuate their failures whilst merely reporting their successes.

Many of these complexities are historically situated and form the contexts for the events that I describe in this chapter. Irish settlers in Australia left behind (or perhaps did not leave behind) a legacy of sectarian, nationalist, racial and religious violence that resulted in uprisings, guerrilla warfare and terrorist violence when allowed to fester in the United Kingdom during the twentieth century.[8] The communist threat, and an associated tolerance of apparent fascist threats in Australia, formed a miniature theater for the much broader socio-political and cultural implications of the Cold War and the various regional stand-offs between the US, the Soviet Union and their respective satellites.[9] And, as Anne Aly's earlier chapter demonstrates, the 9/11 terrorist attacks, the so-called "war on terror" and the global language of jihad—misunderstood as it is—are important global forces that have local consequences for counter-terrorism policing in present day Australia.[10]

There are also important complexities that emerge from my subjective position as a non-historian that deploys a particular version of history in developing social and cultural theory to be used for analyzing contemporary terrorism. In an earlier chapter, Sean Brawley and Ian Shaw express reservations with Stuart Koschade's suggestions for using selective events in history to make comparisons and parallels with present day understandings and acts of terrorism. I argue, however, that Koschade's suggestions are an effective way of illuminating the present by—in a necessarily problematic way—gesturing towards the past. It may be that both Koschade and I are too optimistic in this shared belief that specific historical occurrences can illuminate how present-day terrorism is understood and engaged with in Australia, but it is nonetheless a convention of some brands of sociology and critical cultural studies to engage with history in this way. These are disciplines in which I have been trained and of which so-called critical terrorism studies undoubtedly form a part. As such, I intend for the narratives, analysis, and descriptions contained in this chapter to be viewed as an attempt to contextualize the present-day "war on terror" as it has manifested in Australia by exploring some of Australia's history of terrorism. The cases that I introduce in this chapter are designed for this particular purpose. The same descriptions and narratives would likely be inappropriate for many other types of historical analysis. There are other historically situated concerns, issues, concepts and "realities" that may rightly inform such an analysis but many of these are beyond the most pressing and present-day concerns that I attempt to address in this paper.[11]

Yet, in acknowledging such complexities, I do not intend to generate "ever more complexities until we submerge in chaos" and I suggest that the simple dichotomy of complex and simple is itself a monumental simplification.[12] As such, I do draw a line in the sand. The NINA signs were a horrible and racist gesture that should never have been tolerated, the Australian security state should have hounded and interrogated right-wing groups with the same vigor as left-wing groups, and the AFP were engaged in some careless policing when they arrested a man whom most insiders believed had precious little connection to terrorism.[13] Whilst none could be described as bold bigotry, none are clean of discriminatory and prejudicial innuendo. I want to shed light on these scenarios and illuminate some events that those who value Australia's security and freedom may find deeply concerning.

Australia's history of terrorism

As Brawley and Shaw have detailed in an earlier chapter, Australia's history of terrorism and political violence is more strange and detailed than most imagine. Whilst Australia certainly has first-hand experience with terrorism, the overwhelming majority of incidences involving terrorism in Australia have been in response to incidences occurring overseas. In the complex and globalized media and image saturated world of the twenty-first century events like "9/11," "7/7," and the Bali bombings have had significant local consequences. September 11, 2001 is seen as a watershed year in the history of terrorism and I argue that it has become a lens through which all terrorism can be interpreted. The focus of this chapter is the sometimes discriminating and prejudicial response of the "mob" following acts of terrorism. September 11 has provided an illustrative platform for such an analysis. Poynting and Noble have documented many cases of anti-Arab and anti-Muslim discrimination in post-9/11 Australia.[14] Others have explored the fear, anxiety and discriminatory attitudes of some in an Australian population caught in the crossfire of the mediated global "war on terror."[15] The mob-like responses of some groups cast a dark light on "multicultural" Australia. The institutional responses to the Dr. Mohammed Haneef terror scare serve as a mirror for this mob response. Despite scarce and abstract evidence of any wrongdoing by Haneef, much was made of this brief moment when he was considered, mistakenly, to be "public enemy number one."[16] This matter was made all the more disturbing by policing organizations continuing to stake their claim that Haneef was a dangerous man long after it was determined that the courts of liberal-democratic Australia would not convict him of terrorism offences.

These contemporary examples continue a trend of foreign terrorism and political violence resulting in discriminatory, prejudicial, and racist outcomes in Australia. I have chosen three examples that I explore in this chapter. These are organized under three headings: anti-Irish, pro-Right, and anti-Islam.

Anti-Irish: "No Irish Need Apply"

The Irish were among the first Europeans in Australia and have been described as Australia's first white minority group.[17] From the time of arrival the Irish were seen as a subversive element, "bearers of the Jacobin contagion" and "ideologically and physically dangerous traitors."[18] Many Australians were displeased with the slow pace of political progress especially in contrast to progress in America. Imagery of the Boston Tea Party and the Declaration of Independence were frequently invoked to accentuate lackluster political growth.[19] This created a political space that was seen as ripe for Irish radicalism and republicanism. Irish discontent and activism in America was viewed by some to be a glimpse into Australia's future. Articulate members of the Irish community in Australia were often able to give voice to the grievances of the colonists. Irish-Catholic politician and literary critic Daniel Deniehy publicly praised the American constitution, and Irish-Protestant George Higinbotham "threatened an American-type breakaway" if administrators in England did not cease unreasonably intervening in colonial affairs.[20]

In short, it was believed that the Irish were subversive and radical in America and Britain and would be subversive and radical in Australia. Anti-Irish racism and discrimination was common place. These sentiments were epitomized by the many employment advertisements that ended with the initials NINA: No Irish Need Apply.[21] According to O'Farrell, it was believed that "Celtic Irish were of vastly inferior racial stock" and likely to be "crafty and cunning liars."[22] Some examinations of Australia's history of terrorism and political violence have sought to demarcate so-called Irish or Fenian violence from otherwise Catholic-Protestant violence or Trade Union-Employer violence.[23] I suggest that such distinctions are problematic as Irishness was not easily separable from Catholicism and early Australian trade unionism.

Perhaps the most well known political assassination attempt in Australia's history was the attack on Prince Alfred, Duke of Edinburgh, in 1868 at Clontarf in New South Wales. Prince Alfred, the son of Queen Victoria, arrived with a small fleet of escorting ships and stepped on shore to jubilation and an altogether grandiose welcome. Australians were insecure about their geographical location on the outer fringes of the British Empire and a royal visit provided elation at the idea that Australia was perhaps less marginalized than some believed—so too could Australian colonists bask in the everydayness of British royalty enjoyed in England. The crowd was sent into a mass of frenzy and shock with the assassination attempt by an Irishman, Henry James O'Farrell, who shot the Prince in the back with a pistol. The attack sparked wild rumors that quickly spread throughout the cities. Among the stories was the lingering myth that the Prince had been killed as an early victim in an Irish uprising. O'Farrell, after declaring at his trial that the Prince would find a Fenian waiting for him when he arrived for his tour of New Zealand, left a note to be opened after his death. In this note he stated that he was not a Fenian and had had no affiliations with the group.[24] This did not prevent sections of the policing and Protestant communities in Sydney and Melbourne declaring there to be an Irish threat. O'Farrell was also a devout Catholic.[25] The intertwining perceptions of Catholicness and Irishness became a hotbed for unfounded Fenian plots and "sectarian ill-feeling."[26] As Coogan argued, the equation "Irish + Catholic = Agitation" was etched firmly into the psyche of many in Australia around this time.[27]

For Coogan and Dunn it was clear that any Fenian links to the attempt on the Prince's life were "mistaken."[28] Despite O'Farrell perhaps playing to the crowd by initially not disputing the Fenian charge, it was noteworthy that he was drunk at the time of the assassination attempt and also had a history of mental illness:

His brother died in a lunatic asylum, but O'Farrell died on the gallows because the premier of the day, Henry Parkes, was an unscrupulous practitioner of the brutal doctrine… a hanging generates much valuable political capital. Even though the Prince's life was saved, at the risk of their own, by two Irish bystanders, the O'Farrell incident generated huge anti-Irish feeling in both Australia and New Zealand.[29]

Anti-Catholic and anti-Irish sentiment spread rapidly throughout Australia following the attempt to kill the popular Prince. Public "indignation meetings" that discussed ways to prevent Irish revolution and violence were held in many parts of the country.[30] It was a problem that was being tackled in Britain and had been reported extensively in the Australia media. Ultra-British and ultra-Protestant groups became more active and attracted many new members and many Irish Catholics and Irish-Protestants were attacked in the streets by vigilante gangs.[31] There is an eerie similarity between the response of the mob to this so-called Irish violence and the response of the mob more than a century later at Cronulla beach:

> On December 11 2005, images from Australia, a country rarely the focus of world media, flashed around the globe…. They made an ugly picture: a violent, frenzied mob of 5,000 "white" Australians, fuelled by alcohol, attacking anyone of "Middle Eastern appearance" that they could find near Sydney's Cronulla beach.[32]

The reasons for these attacks differ depending on who you ask. According to Poynting the Cronulla riots were supported by deeply discriminatory and prejudiced attitudes.[33] Under this view the attacks at Cronulla, and those that targeted people who were deemed to be Irish some 137 years earlier, represent something that is rarely witnessed—a majority group seeking to put a minority group "back in their place." For others, the Cronulla riots were merely drunken Aussie youth, blowing off some steam as an understandable response to so-called Lebanese gang activity in the region. More alarmingly, the Cronulla riots were dubbed by the Federal Member for Cook, Bruce Baird, as revenge for the Bali bombings.[34] This was despite there being no known involvement of anybody of Lebanese descent in these attacks leaving one to believe that Baird sees a connection between Lebanese Muslims, terrorism and 5000 white rioters attacking people they thought were foreign at Cronulla beach.

This is the nature of the "mob." It will rarely act with sound reason, but it will never be short of justifications. It privileges the use of aggression and violence over the need for understanding and compromise. The images of distraught and regretful young Australians as they faced court for their roles in the Cronulla riots should serve as a reminder that the crowd can make otherwise well-adjusted and socially responsible people act as though they have descended into the security and anonymity of uncivilized mob behavior.[35] Not all were so regretful however, and all Australians should be alarmed that neo-fascist groups saw the Cronulla riots as an ideal opportunity to recruit new members and spread propaganda.[36]

Pro-right: "friendly" terrorism

During the 1990s, as wars raged across the Balkans, aggressive and sometimes violent confrontations occurred between people living in Australia who identified with particular ethnic and cultural groups involved in this international war.[37] I witnessed this violence first hand in the streets and school yards of Melbourne and Geelong when groups of young people rallying under their particular flags engaged in their own displaced version of the Balkan conflict. Some of these young people would openly declare their admiration and allegiance with the radical Croatian group, Ustashi.[38] Steve Bozic, a secondary school teacher in Western Sydney, also experienced this first hand.[39] What began with senior students with Croatian parents at his school ignoring his directions and refusing to talk to him, soon culminated in bricks and bottles being thrown at his home and confrontations in the school-yard. In one instance a fifteen-year-old boy arrived at one of Bozic's classes wearing Ustashi insignia and another boy declared "I shouldn't talk to you—in fact I should hit you."[40] Bozic's wife whom also worked at the secondary school was routinely confronted by thirteen-year-old Croatian students declaring that they were Ustashi. It perhaps goes without saying that in a post-9/11 world, students declaring their links to Islamic terrorism would be treated far more seriously than these incidences were.

This was not the first occasion where the media and the government showed little concern for the need to confront Balkan war inspired violence. According to Hocking there have been many attacks in Australia involving the Australian Yugoslav communities including two serious bomb blasts at Yugoslav travel agencies in Sydney that injured sixteen people and caused significant property damage.[41] As documented in Koschade's chapter in this collection, there had also been circulating rumors of Ustashi-linked groups carrying out operations from Australia. This was seemingly confirmed when in September 1963 the Yugoslav government announced the arrest of "nine Yugoslav exiles" who were "recruited and trained in Australia" for specific roles in carrying out acts of terrorism.[42]

Despite repeated concerns being expressed by the Yugoslav government, the Australian government took no action. In 1972, nineteen Croatians were arrested crossing the border into Bosnia heavily armed. Of these nineteen men, nine had lived in Australia. In response, the Commonwealth Attorney General, Ivor Greenwood, denied that there was any evidence of Croatian terrorism being launched from Australia. With the election of the Labor Party later that year, the new Attorney-General Lionel Murphy was presented with information "which suggested that the earlier disclaimers were not correct."[43] It now seemed to be a matter of common knowledge that Croatian terrorism had long been entrenched in Australia: "Murphy claimed in the Senate on March 13, 1973 that the previous government had deliberately suppressed evidence of the operations of Croatian extremists in Australia, and he soon became convinced that ASIO had done likewise."[44]

In a leaked ASIO report that was dated "July 1972," Croatian terrorism was argued to be fractured, limited and without organizational support. The idea that the Ustashi were the "dominant force" in groups of Croatian extremists in Australia was also considered by ASIO to be "a fascist conspiracy theory" peddled to "receptive sections" of the Australian community.[45] With the visit of the Yugoslav prime minister imminent, Murphy visited the

Canberra offices of ASIO and examined a number of documents that discussed the threat posed by Croatian nationalism. Two of these documents proved to be especially significant: one discussing the presence of Croatian terrorist training camps in Australia, and another that discussed the decision of ASIO to withhold information about Croatian terrorists from the government. This document also stated that any future ASIO statements about Croatian terrorists in Australia "should not be at variance with those made by the previous [conservative] government."[46] This prompted Murphy to "visit" ASIO's Melbourne offices, alarmingly described as a "raid" by most of Australia's media. In the aftermath of this incident Murphy believed that organizations such as ASIO needed to be more accountable to ministerial controls. He argued:

> The necessity for such controls is demonstrated by the history of such organizations here and overseas. Characteristically, from time to time they exceed, and misuse, their powers. The expectation that they will do so creates a climate of apprehension and an inhibition of lawful political activity even at the highest levels of government.[47]

Bizarrely, it was later discovered that from the time the "raid" occurred, ASIO considered Lionel Murphy a security risk and an "agent of influence for the Soviet Union."[48] It may be that Murphy was more of a threat to the freedom that ASIO had come to enjoy than to Australian national security.

This was not the first occasion that ASIO demonstrated a particular political logic in responding to terrorism from the Right. According to Cain, ASIO had been hostile to the labor movement and the Australian Labor Party since its inception.[49] Indeed, an exorbitant amount of attention had been paid by intelligence and policing organizations in Australia to left-wing, labor, and Irish movements whilst comparatively little concern had been shown towards the comparatively worse or more threatening actions of right-wing, fascist and neo-fascist groups, individuals and organizations. Cain floated the possibility that in many respects the Cold War era intelligence circles considered right-wing groups to be "kindred spirits" that could serve as ideological allies "together pursuing, with a view to suppressing, the dreaded Communists."[50] This was a trend carried over from before World War II when Italian Fascists and German Nazis were permitted to operate with little intervention or monitoring in Australia. In some instances the members of these groups were "given the party card with the fascist oath" and their details were sent to foreign sponsors and registries in Europe.[51] Anti-fascist organizations that arose in Australia in response, were far smaller, less organized, and were without international sponsorship yet were subject to far more scrutiny and surveillance. This was despite fascist groups receiving direct sponsorship from the Italian and German governments.

In these descriptions of right-wing terrorist activities in Australia, we see an institutional response that mirrors the aggression, anonymity and lack of reason that is characteristic of the spontaneous mobs that targeted Irish people in 1868 and Middle Easterners in 2005. When government, security, and policing institutions fail to facilitate the pursuit of all security threats with equal vigor, and when these same institutions allow dangerous and subversive groups to flourish, these institutions exhibit all of the mindless and dehumanizing characteristics of the "mob."

Anti-Islam: the importance of being Mohammed

September 11 sparked a spate of anti-Muslim and anti-Arab incidents and attacks in the US. These included the heckling of a Lebanese man who had run the arts center at the World Trade Center as he was searching for survivors, the chasing of a Wyoming mother and her children from a "Wal-Mart" because they appeared Muslim, and the firebombing of a mosque in Texas.[52] An Egyptian worker won a payout for discrimination after being fired from a restaurant because his manager believed that having someone who appeared Muslim as a staff member would be bad for business.[53] As Freyd argues:

> Surely we know that all Arabs or all Muslims are no more responsible for the horrific tragedy than are all Irish or all Christians responsible for terrorism in Northern Ireland.

> Surely we do not want to repeat acts reminiscent of our own
> history of severely mistreating innocent Japanese Ameri-
> cans during World War II. Surely we do not want to engage
> in the same sort of racism and hatred of innocent people
> that we find so abhorrent in other lands.[54]

According to Manning, post-9/11 Australia is similarly a country
where Islamophobia has "run riot" and where people appearing
to be Muslim, who fit an image of Islam, are subjected to prejudice
and discrimination.[55] Khatab and Bouma argue: "The attacks of 11
September 2001, along with the Gulf War and the tragic events that
have followed it have given new life to the identification of Islam
with violence. Islam and its adherents have become noticeable."[56]

The Russell Street bombing in Melbourne on March 27, 1986
provides an illustration of institutionalized processes that sought to
attribute blame for "terrorism" to Muslims and Arabs. Melbourne's
The Age newspaper on March 28, 1986 ran a front-page story where
crime writer Bob Bottom declared that the Russell Street bombings
were likely the work of Palestinian Liberation Organization (PLO)
terrorists.[57] Bottom reported that police were looking for an "Arab-
looking suspect" who had connections to international terrorism.[58]
Several months later the Immigration Minister, Chris Hurford, con-
demned this claim as an "unfair slur on all Arab-Australians."[59] The
four Victorians who were later charged with these bombings were
not Arab and had no links to the PLO. In this way the Russell Street
bombings bear an odd similarity to the Oklahoma City bombings
perpetrated by anti-government and anti-establishment activist
Timothy McVeigh. Not only were Arab and Muslim terrorists assumed to be responsible for the Oklahoma City bombing in the immediate aftermath, but Jordanian-American Abraham Ahmad was
detained, strip-searched and interrogated at length at Chicago's
O'Hare Airport and again when he arrived in London after being
released. As Hanania described the incident:

> Imagine police in security uniforms surrounding you,
> handcuffing you and, in front of the hundreds of other
> passengers waiting to board the flight, marching you off
> like a criminal. You're then placed in a small room and

ordered to strip your clothes. Your bags are removed from the plane. No one will tell you why you are being detained, or what you have done… sitting thousands of miles away in a Chicago airport, Ahmad, who happens to be Middle Eastern, a Palestinian born in Jordan, "looked" the part and was immediately arrested because he "fit the profile."… Abraham Ahmad was stopped because he had dark skin, a tightly cropped beard, black curly hair and looked Arab.[60]

Tragically, this was not the end of Ahmad's ordeal. After detaining him for four hours at O'Hare Airport, security officials purchased Ahmad a replacement ticket to London so he could continue his journey. On arrival he was again detained, strip-searched, hand-cuffed, and deported to Washington DC. News reports of his arrest and deportation broke in the United States and media crews surrounded his small home in Oklahoma. Unlike Richard Jewel, the man initially accused of carrying out the 1996 Atlanta Olympics bombing, Ahmad was not issued an apology once it became apparent that he had nothing to do with the bombing. In the Jewell case:

…the FBI and the government issued a formal apology to Richard Jewell, the man they had once said was a suspect in the equally as horrific but less destructive bombing at Olympic Park in Atlanta. Jewell was at least at the scene of the bombing and had collected "souvenirs" from the deadly explosion there. Jewell obviously has one thing going for him, an advantage that even Timothy McVeigh probably enjoys. He doesn't look like an Arab.[61]

In December 2005 in Australia, a terror scare flashed across the pages of *The Sydney Morning Herald* declaring that Arabs and Muslims in Sydney's suburbs were under close scrutiny in search of potential terrorists.[62] According to Lague and Pitt's article, "Sections of the Lebanese community are suspected of links with Islamic terrorist movement Hezbollah." The authors cited a "confidential Immigration Department cable" that called for scrutiny to be placed on all "Arabs" entering the country on short-term visas. However, this cable, according to then Immigration Minister Nick Bolkus, was "routine" and some "eighteen months old."[63] The then chairwomen of the NSW Ethnic Communities Council described the claims as "almost a case of direct discrimination." She added: "It is like claiming all Italians are members of the Mafia or all Chinese are members of the Triads, and very hurtful to the Lebanese community, who have come to Australia to get away from the politics of their country."[64] It is significant in this context that of the 250000 Lebanese people in Australia at the time more than half were Christian and only around thirty-seven percent were Muslim. Whilst Lague and Pitt acknowledged that there was no "official connection" between the 50000 Shi'ites in Australia and Hezbollah there was "unofficial connections."[65] This attention is difficult to understand given that the media, ASIO and the federal government turned mostly a blind-eye to far more threatening connections and activities being carried out by radicalized Croatian groups in Australia.

Mohammad Hassanien's case was a strange chapter in the history of terrorism in Australia. Hassanien reportedly entered Australia on May 7, 1996 with a false passport. On June 1 he was arrested and deported and later described in *The Age* as "A man closely linked to an international terrorist organization responsible for many bombings and the massacre of 18 tourists at a Cairo hotel."[66] Hassanien was scooped up in a joint operation between the Federal Police and ASIO called Operation Dynamo and whilst his activities in Australia have never been revealed, a "source" claimed that he was not "here for a holiday." It was claimed that Hassanien, who "is of Middle Eastern origin," was a member of a terrorist organization that sought to "promote the Islamic religion in its fundamental form."[67] In offering analysis of the terrorist threat to Australia, Federal Police agent Steve Kelson argued that soft targets were the primary focus of terrorists in general, and the goal of Hassanien's particular terrorist organization was "attention-seeking."[68]

As this story continued to feature prominently in Australia's newspapers, an alarming development was reported. Birnbauer and Murdoch wrote in *The Age* that "The fingerprints of the terrorist suspect Mohammad Hassanien were found on documents in the possession of a man suspected of making the bomb that shook New York's World Trade Center in 1993."[69] They added that Hassanien had been trying to avoid "Egyptian and Danish intelligence" agencies and that the head of Interpol in Copenhagen had indeed confirmed that there were links between Hassanien and the World Trade Center bombings in 1993.[70] Birnbauer and Murdoch concluded the article with a comment that appeared almost in passing: "After being deported to Denmark, he (Hassanien) was charged over offences relating to a false passport and was released."[71] In *The Sydney Morning Herald* of the same day, Riley revealed that Hassanien, who had been reported to be someone of interest to law enforcement and intelligence authorities throughout the world, was in fact wanted by no one.[72] Riley reported that despite Hassanien being branded a "suspected terrorist" by the AFP and linked by ASIO to international terrorist groups he was not regarded by Interpol in Copenhagen to be a "terrorist."[73] In fact he had been acquitted of charges relating to terrorism. He was also not wanted by the FBI despite widespread claims in the Australian media that he was.

In the days that followed his release in Denmark, many of the journalists who contributed to the demonizing of Mohammad Hassanien reported on many significant problems with the investigation into his activities. These journalists began to ask some difficult questions. Ellingsen reported that Hassanien was actually protected under political asylum in Denmark and his deportation from Australia did little more than send him home.[74] A Copenhagen police spokesperson said of Hassanien; "We don't think he poses any risk…As far as we are concerned, he is a free man with a clean slate."[75] It was revealed in this article that at his acquittal for terrorism offences in April 1996, the trial judge criticized the Danish secret service for trying to bring a conviction with such little evidence. A feature appeared in *The Age* newspaper on June 22, 1996 that sought to investigate why a seemingly innocent man was deported as a terrorist. The journalists reported on a number of inconsistencies between the threat that Hassanien posed and the way he was portrayed by Australian law enforcement officials. Birnbauer et al., reported on how the AFP had claimed that Hassanien's only criminal conviction—for arson—was politically motivated.[76] According to Danish authorities however, this was simply not true. The arson conviction related to a revenge attack against a friend's ex-wife. Further conjecture surrounds what happened when Hassanien was arrested and how the police came to believe he was a threat. Earlier reports indicated that he had pulled a knife on police, a story that a young man from a local mosque who was with Hassanien at the time disputes. It is also believed that it may have been Egyptian intelligence who tipped off Australian police—a group with considerable interests at stake in reacquiring somebody under political protection in a European country. The media coverage of the Hassanien incident and the embarrassment that it cause attracted the attention of the Attorney-General who berated the AFP. The federal police association responded by arguing that the officers should be commended. Hassanien went into hiding in Denmark and became a figure of ridicule following reports in Denmark that a Melbourne television station had referred to him as "the world's most wanted terrorist."[77] Regardless of what occurred in this strange chapter in the history of terrorism in Australia, "Hassanien fits perfectly into a world where facts and fiction blur and truth can be shaped like clay."[78]

Of course, the case of Mohammad Hassanien is familiar. The recent "Dr Haneef" case bears a strong resemblance. The Dr Haneef case became well known to Australians after the Queensland-based, Indian-born doctor was detained for ill-defined terrorism offences. However, it would seem that Dr Mohammed Haneef had even fewer connections than Mohammad Hassanien to terrorism. Amongst the comical analysis in the media of terror threats and dangers that the detaining of Haneef sparked—always mitigated with "if" he is a terrorist "then…"—the facts are difficult to find. On June 30, 2007 an amateurish attempted terrorist attack took place at Glasgow Airport. On July 2, 2007 a so-called link was determined between the attacks and Mohammed Haneef and he was subsequently arrested and detained without charge. There was a frenzied journalistic response as perhaps there should be. Button's article in *The Age* was alarmingly titled "They Swear to Save Lives."[79] He described how British police were "desperately trying to establish a common denominator" between the failed Glasgow attack and Haneef. Crawford and Hudson reported that people were ringing hospital switch boards to ensure that family and friends were not being treated by terrorists.[80] Pemberton, writing in *The Australian*, in noting that policing authorities had "not yet made a link" between Haneef and the attempted attacks in Glasgow bizarrely concluded:

But the timing of events, the acknowledged British source of advice and the fact one of the men arrested, Mohammed Haneef, was a registrar at Gold Coast Hospital in Southport, so a doctor, who had trained in India before coming to Australia from Northern England, suggest a direct connection.[81]

Does it suggest a direct connection? Hardly. Muslims can at least be grateful that circumstantial evidence that would place perhaps hundreds of Australian doctors in a position of "direct connection" with terrorism would not stand-up to legal scrutiny. Analysis such as this, book-ended with claims that "We may have dodged a bullet," works to feed anti-Islamic sentiment in Australia.[82] Arab and Muslim leaders were once again forced to defend themselves against the myth of "Islam = terrorism" and Islamophobia once again found a sturdy platform. Despite the further reports of possible police bungles in handling the case, secret plots to make the charges stick, and Haneef's total exoneration of any wrongdoing, the damage had already been done—once again.[83]

Dr. Haneef's story is quite different to that of Dr. John Di Palma, an Innisfail based doctor who was arrested in 2007 after a "steel bunker" was found at his bushland property containing "50 military-style weapons" that included four automatic assault rifles, two Uzis, shotguns and 100,000 rounds of ammunition as well as silencers and a bullet proof vest—enough to arm a small guerrilla army.[84] Dr. Di Palma received a two year wholly suspended sentence because a district court judge considered Di Palma to be someone with "a deep and almost lifelong interest in firearms."[85] Why was there no Dr. Di Palma terror scare? I wonder about the outcome of this case had Dr. John Di Palma been a Muslim.

As Anne Aly's chapter rightly points out, what it means to be Muslim was radically changed by 9/11. I suggest the sense of victimhood that Aly describes as characteristic of Muslim diaspora throughout the world—a victimhood that is brought into sharp focus by the stories of Mohammad Hassanien and Mohammed Haneef—is, in the case of Australia, mirrored in the "host" population. The character of the white/anglo/Australian victim was breathlessly occupied by various media commentators and some "experts" and perhaps by around 5000 rioters on Sydney's Cronulla beach in late 2005.[86] Yet the events at Cronulla also demonstrate that the victim is rarely passive—it is a cornerstone of pop-psychology that when the human animal is threatened we will either "fight" or "fly."[87] Partly for this reason, racist, discriminatory, and mob-like responses will ensure that new generations of Australian Muslims have a reason to fight or fly. This could make a major act of terrorism in Australia more likely.

Conclusion: global terrorism, local consequences

The "mob" has played an important role in shaping the history of terrorism in Australia and will likely help shape the consequences of terrorism in the future. Moreover, the mob-like responses that have been characteristic of Australia's history of terrorism make terrorism in Australia more likely. Responding to violence with violence rarely achieves an outcome that does not result in more violence.[88] Events like the Cronulla riots, restrictive counter-terrorism laws, and other mob-like responses may yet prove to be spectacular "own-goals" in the "global war on terror."

There are strange similarities between the three scenarios that I have outlined in this chapter. These seemingly disparate threats, the Irish threat, the Croatian threat, and the Arab threat, all originated in global threats of terrorism and political violence. Yet, all of these global threats have had significant local consequences. The Australian, indeed the world's media, have long been efficient in translating foreign threats into local concerns. Often this mediated translation has worked to sensationalize, spectacularize, and exaggerate the threat posed by terrorism and terrorists. What Grant Wardlaw has described as "breathless journalistic hyperbole" can be seen to play a central role in the dissemination of discourses encoded with discriminatory and prejudicial stereotypes and overtones.[89] Yet, I do not intend to lay responsibility at the feet of the media—to do this would be to simplify the problem. Experts and official spokespeople who contribute to those media discourses also contribute to wildly glib and discriminatory public and institutional responses to terrorism. In identifying some of these deficiencies of the media at times of terror, I would be remiss if I did not also acknowledge times when the media rightfully adopts the position of cornerstone for democratic criticism.

One such example is provided by Wright and Marriner writing for *The Age* at the height of the Dr. Haneef counter-terrorism parody: "He is not the defendant. He is not the accused. He is a suspect, an unsatisfactory term loaded with whatever innuendo you might wish to pile upon it—which, in this new age of international terrorism, can be a very big load indeed."[90] Haneef was a victim of a mob mentality and a paranoia that is reinforced by the memory of the 9/11 terrorist attacks and the resulting "global war on terror." The targets of the mob have changed since European settlers first displaced indigenous populations. Whether they are Irish, communist, Lebanese or Muslim, the discriminatory response of the mob has been and will continue to be common.

Notes

[1] Jenny Hocking, *Terror Laws: ASIO, Counter-Terrorism and the Threat to Democracy* (Sydney: University of New South Wales Press, 2004); Kevin Baker, *Mutiny, Terrorism, Riots and Murder: A History of Sedition in Australia and New Zealand* (New South Wales: Rosenberg, 2006); and Walter Laqueur, *No End To War: Terrorism in the Twenty-First Century* (New York: Continuum, 2003).

[2] Hannah Arendt, *The Origins of Totalitarianism* (New York: Harcourt, Brace and World, 1951); Erich Fromm, *The Fear of From Freedom* (London: Routledge, 2008/1942), 140-141.

[3] Gustave le Bon, *The Crowd: A Study of the Popular Mind* (Atlanta: Cherokee, 1982).

[4] Annemarie Mol and John Law, "Complexities: An Introduction," *Complexities: Social Studies of Knowledge Practices*, ed. Annemarie Mol and John Law (Durham: Duke University Press, 2002), 1-22.

[5] Ibid, 1.

[6] Tim Pat Coogan, *Wherever Green is Worn: The Story of the Irish Diaspora* (New York: Palgrave, 2000); Tim Pat Coogan, *The I.R.A.* (London: Harper Collins, 2000).

[7] Samantha Maiden and Nathalie O'Brien, "Keelty Calls for Media Terror Blackout," *News.com.au*, January 30, 2008, http://www.news.com.au/story/0,23599,23131030-421,00.html, 2008 (accessed January 14, 2009).

[8] Ibid.

[9] For fragments of some of these complexities see Andrew Lynch's chapter in this book, "The Use of History by Lawyers in Debating Responses to Terrorism," as well as Edward Herman and Noam Chomsky, *Manufacturing Consent: The Political Economy of the Mass Media* (New York: Pantheon, 2002); Frank Cain, *The Australian Security Intelligence Organisation: An Unofficial History* (Essex: Spectrum Publications, 1994), ix; Mark Finnane, *Police and Government: Histories of Policing in Australia* (Melbourne: Oxford University Press, 1994); Kevin Baker, *Mutiny, Terrorism, Riots and Murder*.

[10] For an account of this language of jihad, common Western misunderstandings surrounding the religious meaning of jihad, and the politicization of Islam, see Sayed Khatab and Gary Bouma, *Democracy in Islam* (London: Routledge, 2007).

[11] This includes the long history of Irish oppression in the United Kingdom, the long struggle of post-colonials, colonials and satellite states during the Cold War, the evolution of ethnic threats, the equating of Islam with violence as outlined, for example, in Sayed Khatab and Gary Bouma, *Democracy in Islam*, 202.

[12] Annemarie Mol and John Law, "Complexities."

[13] This was recently confirmed by a report released by the Australian Government that was prepared by John Clarke QC (see ABC News, "Report Concludes Haneef was Innocent," December 23, 2008, http://www.abc.net.au/news/video/2008/12/23/2454058.htm, 2008 (accessed January 14, 2009).

[14] Scott Poynting and Greg Noble, "Living With Racism: The Experience and Reporting by Arab and Muslim Australians of Discrimination, Abuse and Violence Since 11 September 2001," Report to The Human Rights and Equal Opportunity Commission, April 19, available at http://www.hreoc.gov.au/racial_discrimination/isma/research/UWSReport.pdf, 2004 (accessed January 15, 2005).

[15] Here I use "crossfire" in a metaphorical sense and my thoughts go out to those literally caught in the war on terror's crossfire. For accounts of fear, anxiety and discrimination in response to terrorism in Australia, see Anthony Burke, *Beyond Security, Ethics and Violence: War Against the Other* (London: Routledge, 2007); Anthony Burke, *Fear of Security: Australia's Invasion Anxiety* (New York: Cambridge University Press, 2008); Andrew Lynch, Edwina MacDonald, and George Williams, eds., *Law and Liberty in the War on Terror* (Leichhardt: Federation Press, 2007); Sharon Pickering, Jude McCulloch and David Wright-Neville, *Counter-Terrorism Policing: Community, Policy and the Media* (New York: Springer, 2008); and Sayed Khatab and Gary Bouma, *Democracy in Islam*.

[16] Herald Sun, "Behind the Plot," *Herald Sun*, July 4, 2007, 4; Carly Crawford and F. Hudson, "Aussie Swoop as Police Believe They Have Cracked a Ring of…TERROR DOCTORS," *Herald Sun*, July 4, 2007, 1; and G. Pemberton, "Bombs Aimed at the Heart of Democracy," *The Australian*, July 4, 2007, 14.

[17] Robert Hughes, *The Fatal Shore* (London: Pan, 1988).

[18] Robert Hughes in Tim Pat Coogan, *Wherever Green is Worn*, 430.

[19] Geoffrey Partington, *The Australian Nation: Its British and Irish Roots* (Melbourne: Australian Scholarly Publications, 1997), viii.

[20] Ibid.

[21] For a broader and more detailed account of anti-Irish racism and discrimination, see Patrick O'Farrell, *The Irish in Australia: 1788 to the Present* (Sydney: University of New South Wales Press, 2000).

[22] Ibid, 247.

[23] Kevin Baker, *Mutiny, Terrorism, Riots and Murder*; Paula Hamilton, *No Irish Need Apply: Aspects of the Employer-Employee Relationship Australian Domestic Service 1860-1900* (London: Australian Studies Centre, Institute of Commonwealth Studies, University of London, 1985).

[24] Ibid, 65.

[25] Robert Travers, *The Phantom Fenians of New South Wales* (Kenthurst: Kangaroo Press, 1986).

[26] Kevin Baker, 65.

[27] Coogan, *Wherever Green is Worn*, 448; Coogan, *The I.R.A.*

[28] Coogan, *Wherever Green is Worn*, 449; Cathy Dunn, "The Attempted Assassination of Prince Alfred at Clontarf 1868," http://www.shoalhaven.net.au/~cathyd/history/prince.html, 1998 (accessed April 11, 2006).

[29] Coogan, *Wherever Green is Worn*, 449.

[30] Dunn, "The Attempted Assassination of Prince Alfred."

[31] Ibid; Kevin Baker, *Mutiny, Terrorism, Riots and Murder*; and Coogan, *Wherever Green is Worn*.

[32] Scott Poynting, "What Caused the Cronulla Riot?" *Race & Class*, 48: 1 (July, 2006), 85.

[33] Ibid.

[34] Australian Associated Press, "Neo-Nazi's in race Riots: Police," *The Sydney Morning Herald*, December 12, 2005, http://www.smh.com.au/news/national/neonazis-in-race-riots-police/2005/12/12/1134235970427.html, 2005 (accessed February 2, 2007).

[35] Natasha Wallace, "Life in Tatters as Court Mops Up After Lifesaver Attack," *The Sydney Morning Herald*, January 20, http://www.smh.com.au/news/national/life-in-tatters-as-court-mops-up-after-lifesaver-attack/2006/01/19/1137553712920.html, 2006 (accessed November 4, 2008).

[36] Liam Houlihan, "Gang Makes Death Threats to Cops," *Herald*

Sun, December 14, available at http://www.news.com.au/heraldsun/story/0,21985,24796470-661,00.html, 2008 (accessed January 5, 2009); Nadav Shlezinger, '"Victory in Cronulla,"' *The Review*, January, 2006, http://www.aijac.org.au/review/2006/31-1/cronulla311.html, 2006 (accessed November 8, 2008).

[37] Events like these were aptly described in an earlier chapter by Brawley and Smith as "the echoes of distant thunder."

[38] For an account of the Ustashi see Lewis Kent, *Beware of Genocide!: Short History of Ustashi Crimes and Their Activities in Australia* (East Brunswick: Yugoslav Settlers' Association of Australia, 1964).

[39] T. Hewett, "Renewal of Hostilities Spills Over into Teacher's Life," *The Sydney Morning Herald*, July 15, 1992, 11.

[40] Ibid.

[41] Jenny Hocking, *Terror Laws*, 40.

[42] Ibid.

[43] Ibid, 41.

[44] Ibid.

[45] Ibid.

[46] Ibid, 42.

[47] Lionel Murphy in Jenny Hocking, *Terror Laws*, 42-43.

[48] Jenny Hocking, *Terror Laws*, 43.

[49] Frank Cain, *The Australian Security Intelligence Organisation: An Unofficial History*, ix.

[50] Ibid, 13.

[51] Ibid, 14.

[52] Jennifer Freyd, "In the Wake of Terrorist Attack, Hatred May Mask Fear," *Analyses of Social Issues and Public Policy*, 2: 1 (2002), 5.

[53] Ibid; L.M. Sixel, "EEOC Suit Claims Firing Prompted by Terrorism Fear," *Houston Chronicle*, available at http://www.chron.com/cs/CDA/printstory.mpl/business/sixel/206095, 2003 (accessed March 22, 2004).

[54] Jennifer Freyd, "In the Wake of Terrorist Attack," 5.

[55] Peter Manning, *Us and Them: A Journalist's Investigation of Media, Muslims and the Middle East* (Milsons Point, NSW: Random House, 2006), 3.

[56] Sayed Khatab and Gary Bouma, *Democracy in Islam*, 201.

[57] Bob Bottom, "Revenge Motive Traced," *The Age*, March 28, 1986, 1, 6.

[58] Ibid, 1.

[59] Joseph Wakim, "Guilty Until Proven Innocent," paper presented at the Restoration for Victims of Crime Conference, September, Melbourne, http://www.aic.gov.au/conferences/rvc/wakim.pdf, 1999 (accessed January 10, 2008).

[60] Ray Hanania, "Innocent Terror Suspected Haunted by Memories," *Arab American View Newspapers Online*, available at http://www.hanania.com/aaview/col101096.htm, 1996 (accessed February 14, 2006).

[61] Ibid.

[62] D. Lague and H. Pitt, "Terrorism Alert: Sydney Suburbs Under Scrutiny," *The Sydney Morning Herald*, December 7, 1995, 1.

[63] Joseph Wakim, "Guilty Until Proven Innocent."

[64] H. Pitt, "Terrorist Alert Hurts Muslims," *The Sydney Morning Herald*, December 8, 1995, 6.

[65] D. Lague and H. Pitt, "Terrorism Alert."

[66] B. Birnbauer and J. Koutsoukis, "Terrorist Suspect Expelled," *The Age*, 18 June, 1996, 1.

[67] Ibid.

[68] The Age, "Terrorist Group Deals in Bombs, Political Killing," *The Age*, June 18, 1996, 8.

[69] B. Birnbauer and L. Murdoch, "Hassanien Link to Trade Centre Bombing," *The Age*, June 20, 1996, 2.

[70] Ibid.

[71] Ibid.

[72] M. Riley, ""Terrorist" Not Wanted, Says FBI," *The Sydney Morning Herald*, June 20, 1996, 8.

[73] Ibid.

[74] Ellingsen, "The Man We Deported: Not Bad, Just Mad," *The Sydney Morning Herald*, 22 June, 1996, 30.

[75] Ibid.

[76] B. Birnbauer, Ellingsen, J. Button, M. Daly, J. Koutsoukis and R. Dunn, "Mission Improbable," *The Age*, June 22, 1996, 15.

[77] Ibid.

[78] Ibid.

[79] J. Button, "They Swear to Save Lives," *The Age*, July 4, 2007, 1.

[80] C. Crawford and F. Hudson, "Aussie Swoop as Police Believe They Have Cracked a Ring of...TERROR DOCTORS," *Herald Sun*, July 4, 2007, 1.

[81] Greg Pemberton, "Bombs Aimed at the Heart of Democracy," *The Australian*, July 4, 2007, 14.

[82] Ibid.

[83] Hedley Thomas and Andrew Fraser, "Police Wrote in Haneef Diary," *The Australian*, July 23, available at http://www.theaustralian.news.com.au/story/0,25197,22117157-601,00.html, 2007 (accessed February 5, 2008); Michael McKenna and Kevin Meade, "Terror Evidence May be Lost After Bungle," *The Australian*, July 10, 2007, http://www.theaustralian.news.com.au/story/0,20867,22047319-601,00.html, 2007 (accessed February 5, 2008); Hedley Thomas, "Secret Plot to Keep Haneef Jailed," *News.com.au*, November 2, http://www.news.com.au/story/0,23599,22688346-2,00.html, 2007 (accessed February 2, 2008).

[84] Tony Wright and Cosima Marriner, "Guilty Until Proven Innocent?"

The Age, June 14, http://www.theage.com.au/news/in-depth/guilty-until-proven-innocent/2007/07/13/1183833770690.html, 2007 (accessed February 19, 2008).

[85] Ibid.

[86] Greg Pemberton, "Bombs Aimed at the Heart of Democracy"; Media Watch, "Front Page—Jones and Cronulla," available at http://www.abc.net.au/mediawatch/transcripts/s1574155.htm, 2005 (accessed January 14, 2008. Be sure to follow the hypertext links to the audio files for Alan Jones' radio program shortly before the Cronulla riots.

[87] For an account of the behavioral responses to violence and terrorism see Henry Fischer III, "Terrorism and 11 September 2001: Does the "Behavioural Response to Disaster Model" Fit?" *Disaster Prevention and Management*, 11: 2 (2002), 123-127.

[88] R.G. Frey and Christopher Morris, eds., *Violence, Terrorism, and Justice* (New York: Cambridge University Press, 1991).

[89] Grant Wardlaw, "Terrifying, But Not Necessarily Terrorism," *The Age*, March 29, 1986, no page number available. Peter Manning, *Us and Them*.

[90] Tony Wright and Cosima Marriner, "Guilty Until Proven Innocent."

12

The Croatian Revolutionary Brotherhood: Action Kangaroo

Stuart Koschade

The exploits of right-wing Croatian extremist groups in Australia between the 1940s and 1970s have not been appropriately examined within the Australian history or terrorism studies literature. During this period, Croatian separatists established a number of different groups in Australia, with some boasting memberships in the thousands. The more violent of these groups waged campaigns of terrorism in both Australia and Yugoslavia. Of these groups, the most active and violent, was known as the *Hrvatsko Revolucionarno Bratstvo* (HRB, Croatian Revolutionary Brotherhood), which launched two incursions from Australia into the Socialist Federal Republic of Yugoslavia (SFRY) between 1963 and 1972. This chapter will provide the first detailed study of what was the largest terrorist organization to ever operate within Australia, specifically focusing on the group's "Action Kangaroo" incursion in 1963. The chapter will frame this operation and the development of the HRB within a wider context of Croatian extremism, demonstrate the significance of this operation, and conclude by discussing the government responses that resulted in the decline of the HRB and other violent Croatian separatist groups in Australia.

Origins of the HRB—the Ustasha

The *Ustasha* (insurgent) was a Croatian separatist movement that sought independence from Serbian control following the establishment of Croatia within the Kingdom of Serbs, Croats, and Slovenes under the Serbian King Alexander from 1929.[1] Following Croatia's inclusion, the Kingdom of Yugoslavia banned all nationalist parties and introduced increasingly Draconian measures (including the dispossession of all political rights).[2] As a result, the Croatian Party of Rights founded the Ustashi movement, led by Dr Ante Pavelic, who commenced revolutionary activities against the Kingdom of Yugoslavia. Shortly after becoming the leader of this separatist movement, Pavelic was forced into exile where he pledged his allegiance to the Internal Macedonian Revolutionary Organization (IMRO).[3] Bolstered by support from fascist Hungary and Italy, as well as from the IMRO until its defeat in 1930, the Ustasha movement undertook guerrilla operations and assassinated Yugoslav officials both within the Kingdom and internationally.[4] Reflecting their willingness and ability to project their cause beyond Yugoslavia, they were accused of conspiracy with the IMRO in the assassination of King Alexander in Marseille in 1934. Pavlic was held directly responsible for the assassination.[5]

On April 8, 1941, pre-empting the Axis incursion into Yugoslavia, the Ustasha and members of the Croatian Peasants Party led an invasion into Yugoslavia in a revolt against Serbian rule of Croatia. After two days, the Croatian forces had gained control of Yugoslavia. The Croat Colonel, Slanko Kvaternik, declared the independence of Croatia on behalf of the exiled Ustasha leader Pavelic.[6] Following the arrival of the Axis forces and the return of the Ustasha leader, Hitler installed Pavelic as *Fuhrer* of Croatia. Pavelic's regime was as barbaric as (if not worse than) the Nazi regime that installed it.[7] Following its installation, Pavelic's regime massacred 330,000 Jews, Muslims, Serbs, and Gypsies within Croatia, and exported thousands to Nazi concentration camps.[8]

In the wake of the newly established Fascist government's oppressive rule, a widespread anti-Fascist campaign began in July of 1941 to oust the Ustashi and German forces from Yugoslavia. Joseph Broz Tito, the commander of the People's Liberation Army of Yugoslavia and Partisan Detachments, led this campaign. The initial success enjoyed by Tito was countered by Germany in *Fall Weiss* (Plan White) and *Operation Schwarz* (Operation Black). Both of these operations inflicted heavy casualties upon the Partisans, but sufficient numbers were able to escape both German offensives and continue their operations. By 1945, with the support of the Red Army and the Royal Air Force Balkan Air Force, the Partisans consolidated control of Belgrade.[9]

Following the fall of the Fascist Ustashi government in the Independent State of Croatia in 1945, the victorious forces led by Josip Tito installed the SFRY. While many of the Ustashi hierarchy fled Europe for the shores of countries such as the United States (US), Argentina, Canada, and Australia, some remained in Europe and set about organizing resistance movements to overthrow the newly established SFRY. The most prolific of these movements was the *Hrvatsko Otpor Pokret* (Croatian Resistance Movement, CRM). The CRM conducted physical and weapons training in Italy, Austria, and France. Further, the CRM attempted to coordinate the resistance against Tito's SFRY.[10] The operations of the CRM and similar movements enjoyed very little success in their endeavors, ultimately resulting in the obliteration of most of these Europe-based movements by 1950. The failure of the Europe-based Ustashi movements and the pursuit of their members led to further emigration from Europe. It was clear that a successful Croatian separatist campaign had to be developed and launched from a position of strength. In nations such as the US, Argentina, Canada, and Australia, these groups found this relative security and refuge.

The rise of Australia-based Ustashi movements

Immediately following the collapse of the fascist Croatian state in 1945, members of the hierarchy of the Ustashi government, pursued by the Socialist regime for their brutal war crimes against Serbs, Jews, and Gypsies, escaped and migrated to Spain, Argentina, Canada, and Australia. In many of these countries, the Ustasha alumni began creating terrorist organizations that aimed at the destruction of the SFRY and the liberation or reinstallation of Croatia. The membership and resolve of these groups were strengthened further, following the flight of CRM members in the late 1940s and early 1950s.

The most prolific of these organizations was the *Hrvatski Oslobodilacki Pokret* (Croatian Liberation Movement, HOP), which was established in 1956 by the exiled Ante Pavelic. The HOP doctrine and ideology was based on the original Ustashi principles set out by Pavelic in 1933.[11] The headquarters of the HOP was in Buenos Aires, Argentina, where Pavelic was exiled. Aided by the wide diffusion of former Ustashi members as well as the widespread emigration of displaced Croats, the HOP established twenty-five branches around the world including in Canada, the US, Europe, and Australia.[12]

In the period between October 1945 and August 1967, approximately 68,000 Yugoslavs entered Australia. This estimate includes all ethnic groups from the state of Yugoslavia, the major groups being Serbs and Croats. This figure does not include "stateless persons," who at the time would have included a large number of Croatian émigrés. The Australian Government estimated that during this period approximately 30,000 of the 68,000 émigrés were Croatian.[13]

Aided by this strong Croatian diaspora in Australia, the newly emigrated former Ustashi members established the Australian section of the HOP following its foundation by Pavelic in 1956. The Australian branch of the HOP was the leading body of the various Australia-based Croatian movements and was supported by groups such as the Australian Croatian Association in Melbourne.[14] By 1964, the Australian HOP branch had up to 5,000 members.[15]

The HOP in Australia was a predominantly political movement, the aim of which was the total severance from the SFRY and independence from Tito-Communist interference and control.[16] The group was led in Australia by Fabian Lokovich, a former leader of the Ustashi Youth Movement and bodyguard to Pavelic during the Ustashi regime.[17] The former Ustashi officer Srecko Blaz Rover, who was heavily involved in a number of violent Croatian separatist movements, would later head the HOP.[18]

Following the group's inception, the HOP began conducting military training in Australia, and was attended by members of the other Croatian separatist organizations. These camps, later described by the Australian Government as "Picnic Camps," usually took place for a week in the summer in the Wodonga region of Victoria. These camps usually served as an annual meeting for HOP members from all over Australia, with the attendance usually numbering around 100.[19] HOP members armed with .22 caliber rifles guarded the camps wearing army fatigues and tank tops emblazoned with the Croatian shield.[20] Perhaps the most significant of these camps was in 1962 near Wodonga in Victoria.[21] In close proximity to this camp, the Australian Citizen Military Forces (CMF) were undertaking maneuvers using their standard issue armament in addition to armored vehicles. This CMF group was approached by HOP members who were in turn given a demonstration of the equipment and weapons. Photos of HOP members holding CMF weapons and sitting on armored vehicles were subsequently published in the HOP magazine, *Spremnost*, in an article entitled "Today on the River Murray; Tomorrow on the River Drina."[22]

While the HOP in Australia conducted training camps, had significant connections to the extensive international HOP network, and espoused its aims of overthrowing the Tito's SFRY, the organization did not appear to possess the intention to forge this rhetoric into action. This trait seemed endemic within a vast majority of these separatist organizations. A number of HOP members lost faith in this and other organizations through this lack of action. One such group to emerge in the wake of this inaction was the HRB. As reported by the Australian Commonwealth Police, the HRB was the most violent of the Croatian independence groups. The HRB was established on June 9, 1961, by five Croatian émigrés following their dissatisfaction with the HOP's lack of militancy and revolutionary action.[23]

The Croatian Revolutionary Brotherhood

The HRB was established by four Croatian émigrés: Jure Maric, Ilija Tolic, Josip Oblak, and Geza Pasti. Jure Maric arrived in Australia from Austria on September 13, 1958, and worked as a fitter. Maric was naturalized as an Australian citizen on August 1, 1963.[24] Pasti, a former Ustashi officer, arrived in Australia in February of 1954.[25] Ilija Tolic left for Australia in 1958, while Oblak arrived in Australia around the same time.[26]

Maric, Pasti, Oblak, and Tolic were highly active within the Australian Croatian community. As well as being members of the HOP,

Oblak, Tolic, and Maric were members of the Croatian-Australian Association, the Jure de Frantic Croatian Association, and the United Croats of Oceania group.[27] Tolic, who was a forester by trade but made a living as a factory worker in Australia, was the secretary and later president of the Jure de Frantic Croatian Association.[28] Oblak was also a member of the Croatian Club in Fremantle.[29] Like the HOP, these Croatian groups were political movements supporting the separation of Croatia from the SFRY. These groups would (to a degree) support violent separatist activity but not undertake it. These four men were among the section of the Croatian community who had become frustrated at the HOP's lack of support and training for terrorist and revolutionary operations in Croatia.[30]

On June 9, 1961, Maric, Pasti, Oblak, and Tolic attended a lecture in Sydney led by the leader of the *Hrvatski Narodni Otpor* (Croatian National Resistance, HNO), Srecko Blaz Rover. Rover, a former Ustashi officer, was among the first émigrés to organize Ustashi movements in Australia following his arrival in 1950.[31] The Australian Commonwealth Police believed that Rover's lecture deepened Maric, Pasti, Oblak, and Tolic's dissatisfaction at the lack of revolutionary and violent action taken by the two major Croatian separatist organizations (the HOP and HNO).[32] Maric claimed that Rover's lecture was a "Funerary Oration to the Late Croatia." Agitated, the four men drove to an outer Sydney suburb and began to discuss the idea of the formation of a covert organization for the liberation of Croatia through insurgent and terrorist means.[33] During this meeting, the four men created the HRB, which was to expand into Europe using the remnants of the networks that existed, and finally extend into Croatia.[34] The principles of the organization were later set out as follows:

> The HRB—as shown in its title—is a fighting organisation of all the Croatian patriots who have set themselves the task of liberating the Croatian people from the foreign yoke and of restoring the State of Croatia within its ethnic and historical boundaries.[35]

The Australian Branch of the HRB was codenamed Command Post Number Four, with Maric holding the position of General Secretary or Commander of Committee Number Four.[36] Area Command

One was Croatia and Area Command Two was Europe (primarily in Germany and Italy), whence operations into the SFRY would be launched. Area Command Three was Fascist Spain where a significant number of the Ustashi hierarchy had fled following the fall of Pavelic's regime.[37] The role of Area Command Four was to raise funds for the operations through the Croatian community in Australia. In addition to this role, Area Command Four recruited and trained HRB operatives to lead incursions into the SFRY.[38]

After just three years from its formation, the HRB Area Command Number Four boasted a membership of between one and two hundred members, with some Australian Government estimates as high as 500.[39] Every member of each of the international commands of the HRB was issued with a membership number. The membership number allocation for Australian members ranged from 61 to 1000. By 1967 the Australian membership numbers 61 to around 330 had been issued. The numbers 1 to 60 were for members of the European command.[40] Each of these members would have taken the "Oath of the Croatian Revolutionary Brotherhood":

> I swear by Almighty God and things that are most sacred to me to fight, until the end of my life, for the liberty and sovereignty of the Croatian People. By voluntarily joining the ranks of the Croatian Revolutionary Brotherhood, I pledge myself to obey and carry out without demur any orders and instructions given to me and to serve loyally the Brotherhood's revolutionary principles.
>
> I pledge myself to keep any secrets entrusted to me and not to disclose anything that might damage the interests of the Brotherhood and of the Croatian People.
>
> If I offend against this oath and the Brotherhood's Revolutionary Principles, my penalty, under the organization's laws, shall be death. So help me God.[41]

On their acceptance into the Brotherhood, members were given their membership number and were assigned to a *Stozher*. A stozher was a division of the Area Command and were established in most major cities. Shortly after the creation of the HRB in 1961,

Maric sent Pasti to Melbourne to establish stozhers both there and in Geelong.[42] The Australian command was made up of four stozhers by the mid-1960s:

1. Stozher 1: Sydney;
2. Stozher 2: Wollongong;
3. Stozher 3: Melbourne and Tasmania; and
4. Stozher 4: Geelong.[43]

Each stozher had a commander, who was a senior member of the HRB and reported to Area Command Four.

During the early 1960s, the HRB meetings took place in the home of Maric and later at Rudolf Franjic's residence at 63 First Avenue, Warrawong. Franjic was another senior member of Area Command Four.[44] These meetings were usually held once a fortnight.[45] At these houses, new members undertook the Oath of the HRB.[46]

The HRB maintained a high level of secrecy and was largely unknown within either the Yugoslav (Serbian and Croatian) community or by the Australian Government. In a document entitled *Croatian Revolutionary Brotherhood: Maintenance of Secrecy—Fundamental Duty of Revolutionaries—Principle of Secret Operation*, issued by Jure Maric and Geza Pasti, the pair outlined the operational security procedures of the HRB as follows:

a) Membership of the Brotherhood is not to be mentioned in public places;

b) Do not tell even your friends anything that you do not want the Croatian People's enemies to find out;

c) A task allotted to one is to be accepted and carried out without demur;

d) Any suspicions, suggestions, alterations or amendments are to be passed on only to the superior without anybody else's presence, while it is the latter's duty to pass it on to his superiors and properly competent officials of the organisation, who after a thorough examination of the material submitted, make their decision.

e) Any printed propaganda material designated for Brotherhood members must never and nowhere be allowed to fall in the hands of persons who are not members of the Brotherhood.

f)   Maintenance of contacts is effected by coded correspondence, by personal conversation [section missing];

g)   The official title of the organisation must never be mentioned without specific approval of the Supreme Headquarters;

h)   It is strictly prohibited to discuss the Brotherhood in any manner, even in a whisper, in the presence of outsiders;

i)   It is permitted and necessary to propagate, by spoken word and with the pen, the ideas of the Croatian Revolution as propounded by the Brotherhood, but it must never be stated openly or hinted that it is our organisation that stands behind them.

j)   In propounding and propagating revolutionary ideas, principles, thoughts and programs, the source from which the matter has been taken must never be given.[47]

These operational procedures allowed the group to remain clandestine, to recruit from within more conservative separatist organizations, and to train with relative freedom.

In a secretive booklet published by the HRB entitled *Kletva* (The Vow), the details of the HRB's operational structure were disclosed. This organization (in theory) was based around an extremely compartmentalized military structure with the terrorist strike force of the Brotherhood consisting of a three-man cell called a *Troika*.[48] The troikas of the HRB were "the units which will carry the burden of the Croatian revolution," and were "mobile and can easily be placed among the people. The troika is not a fighting unit and should not openly fight with the enemy."[49] The troika was composed of a commander, an intelligence officer, and an explosives expert trained in mines, time-delay explosives, booby traps, and other weaponry.[50] According to the *Kletva*, to ensure maximum security within the cell, the troika was formed from individuals who share strong family or friendship ties to each other so that a spy could not be placed within the cell and the members were less likely to betray the group. The only person who had contact with any other members of the HRB was the commander, who communicated with the *Roj* commander.[51] According to Marijan Jurjevic

> A roj is composed of four troikas. The roj commander is responsible to the vod commander, a vod being composed of four rojs. The vod is again part of a larger group, four vods making a satnija, the commander of which is known as a satnik, who commands nearly 200 men. Each satnik is responsible to a bojnik. These bojna, composed of four satnija are again part of a larger group, the stozher. The commanding officer of the stozher, the stozernik or colone, is in control of over 3,000 men.[52]

This structure was how the HRB was to operate inside the SFRY during a sustained campaign. According to the Kletva document, the individuals making up the troika should not know or communicate with the individuals of other troikas. This was to ensure the security of each cell.[53] In 1963, the HRB deployed its first set of troikas to the SFRY in an operation entitled "Action Kangaroo."

Action Kangaroo

The first operation of Area Command Four was codenamed "Action Kangaroo" and involved the insertion of three troikas into the SFRY. The objective of these troikas was to instigate revolutionary dissent among the Croatians and carry out terrorist activities against the SFRY Government.[54] The planning for this operation was largely undertaken by the high-ranking members of Area Command Four, such as Maric, Pasti, Oblak, and Tolic, as well as individuals such as Josip Senic, Rocque Romac, and Adolf Andric. The logistics of the operation were also developed in consultation with Area Command Two.[55]

The proposed operation used three troikas. The first troika consisted of Ilija Tolic, Josip Oblak, and Rade Stojic. The second troika was made up of Mika Fumic, Kremsimir Perkovic, and Stanko Zdrilic. Drazen Tapsanji, Vladimir Leko, and Branko Podrug were the members selected for the final troika. The members of these troikas were selected along the operational guidelines outlined in the Kletva. The troika members were very close associates; for example Tolic and Oblak were two of the four founding members of the HRB, and Fumic and Perkovic were from the same village in Croatia.[56]

The inclusion of Oblak and Tolic in the cell is quite significant, as they were two of the founders of the group and among the highest-ranking members of the HRB. Like Oblak and Tolic, Leko was from Sydney, while the rest of the group was based in and around Melbourne and the regional areas of New South Wales (NSW).[57] A majority of these members travelled to Australia from refugee camps in Austria and Italy at different times.[58] Tapsanji had lived in Melbourne for around eight years before gaining Australian citizenship in the same year that he joined the HRB.[59] By contrast, Stojic left Italy for Australia in October 1962, just one year before the operation was launched.[60] In the months following Stojic's arrival in Australia and establishment in Geelong, he joined the HRB.[61] Perkovic arrived in Melbourne around 1959, followed by Zdrilic, who arrived in Sydney in 1960.[62] Mika Fumic also settled in Melbourne, where he worked in a glass factory.[63]

Shortly after arriving, all of these individuals joined either the HOP or the HRB. By 1963, all nine were members of both organizations. Due to the covertness of the group, the HOP was unaware of its members' ties to the HRB and was largely unaware of its existence, allowing the HRB relative ease in recruiting the more extremist members of the HOP.[64] For example, Zdrilic was recruited from the HOP by HRB member Petar Brajkovic in 1960.[65] The discord between these groups was evident when the HOP discovered that Pasti was involved with the HRB and was consequently removed from not only the HOP committee but the HOP itself.[66] The Melbourne HRB members involved in Action Kangaroo were recruited, trained, or assisted by Viktor Vicic, Ivan Smolcic, Stjepan Sefer, Luka Bilonic, and Petar Brajkovic.[67]

The headquarters for the training of the Sydney stozher was the Sydney Catholic Office at 121 Queen Street, Woollahra. This office was run by Priest Rocque Romac.[68] Romac arrived in Australia in August of 1955, and in 1957 became chaplain to the NSW Croatian community.[69] The Commonwealth Police believed that Romac had joined the HRB shortly after its inception in 1961.[70] Within his Catholic office, Romac ran a Croatian club.[71] On September 15, 1962, Romac established a library in the Catholic offices where Josip Senic, a senior executive within the HRB, was appointed an honorary librarian by Romac.[72] Using this position, Senic instructed HRB members (including the nine members of the incursion cell) in military and combat as well as Croatian separatist indoctrination.[73] Throughout this training, Senic took care to ensure the lessons remained clandestine from both the public and from individuals within the Catholic offices. Between 1962 and 1963, Zdrilic and Podrug were regularly instructed in map-reading, mines, explosives, and hand-to-hand combat and assassination techniques in this library.[74]

The nine insurgents received instruction on topography and map-reading at the home of HRB leader Jure Maric who resided at 138 Cabbage Tree Lane, Fairy Meadows, NSW.[75] In addition to the instruction, Adolf Andric prepared:

1. Topographic signs used by the Yugoslav military
2. A manual of 20 pages concerning guerrilla warfare in Yugoslavia,
3. A document concerning the types of poisons and acids for to be used for assassinations and in the overall revolutionary struggle, and
4. Documents outlining potential targets for terrorists in Yugoslavia.[76]

In addition to this training, Mika Fumic and Ilija Tolic attended a week long HOP camp in 1962, where they were told, along with all the members, "Today you are emigrants on the Murray River, tomorrow you will be on the Drava."[77]

On completion of their preliminary training in Australia in early 1963, the nine members sporadically left Australia for Europe to undertake their operation, assembling in Stuttgart in the Federal Republic of Germany (FRG). On arrival in Stuttgart, the nine insurgents rallied with Area Command Two, where they received advanced lessons in the handling, construction, and use of arms and explosives.[78] This instruction was given by HRB Area Two command member Niko Kovacic (who lived in Stuttgart), who instructed the group in pistol shooting in a forest in the vicinity of the Hotel Bahnhof.[79] Kovacic told Podrug that "In Yugoslavia you must shoot, so that they see and hear that the Croatian emigrants are not forgetting their homeland."[80] The additional training, support, and accommodation in Stuttgart was provided by Area Command Two members Marijan Simundic and Slavko Saric.[81] The group was also assisted in Germany by Franko Orlovich and Nada Glavic, also members of Area Command Two.[82]

Following the training in Stuttgart, the group travelled to Milan, Italy, where they received further training and instruction in relation to crossing the Italy-Yugoslavia border safely. They were individually briefed on their roles within the operation and were instructed to place pieces of paper with the letters "HRB" written on them in the pockets of the Yugoslav military officers they assassinated.[83]

The group was well versed in its objectives and was provided with a list of approved targets. The list included names of Yugoslav public and political figures marked for assassination. The troikas were also to target critical infrastructure within northern Yugoslavia (their designated area of operations) such as major bridges, public buildings, and factories, as well as railroads and reservoirs.[84] In addition, the troikas were to target army officers and police (and procure their arms), to rob stores if cash was required, to locate the addresses of Yugoslav leaders and military storage facilities, burn down hotels, and kill foreign tourists.[85] The final objective was to focus on the Croatian villages and provincial enterprises in northern Yugoslavia, spreading anti-Communist propaganda and promoting civil unrest.[86]

The group was armed and supplied with ammunition by members of Area Command Two.[87] On their crossing of the border, the group carried between them 15 kilograms of explosives, 100 detonators, 100 meters of fuse wire, 6 Italian Biretta pistols with 450 rounds of ammunition, 2 daggers, and 4 radios.[88]

The group moved further west from Milan and rallied at Monfalcone near the Italian-Yugoslav border.[89] By this stage of the operation, the HRB members from Area Command Four had become distressed and dissatisfied at the lack of weapons, ammunition, and resources that Area Command Two had provided them with.[90] Despite these concerns, the three troikas of Action Kangaroo slipped across the Yugoslav border just after midnight on the morning of

July 7, 1963.[91] The moon was bright, but the cloud cover was sufficient to provide the group with adequate cover from the Yugoslav security forces.[92] Immediately after their insertion, the cell broke contact with Area Command Two, but continued with their mission.[93] Following the group's successful insertion into the Communist country, the nine men split into their troikas and headed east towards Croatia.[94]

The first troika was made up of Tolic, Oblak, and Stojic. In the court proceedings that followed the cell's capture, the SFRY government claimed that Tolic, who was the overall commander of the operation and the commander of his troika, led his troika through Slovenia from the Italian border.[95] Late at night while its residents were asleep, Tolic, Oblak, and Stojic arrived in the village of Ljubljanica, approximately 356 kilometers from Monfalcone. Ljubljanica is situated near the town of Derventa, in Bosnia and Herzegovina. Tolic's family resided in this town, and the group sought refuge and assistance from them. On their arrival, Tolic showed his brother, Mate Tolic, their array of weapons and explosives and informed him of his mission.[96] Mate Tolic allowed the men to stay overnight. Ilija's mother, Danica Tolic, cooked food for the trio and washed their clothes. Ilija proposed a plan to destroy local infrastructure and proposed that Mate should assist the troika in destroying the Ljubljanica electricity transformer, to which Mate replied "I refuse to bring evil on myself and my village. Don't you realise Ilija, that things here are not as you were told they were. Go back to where you came from brother."[97] Following this refusal Mate asked the trio to leave. Tolic's mother had advised Mate to report her son's presence and intentions to the People's Militia.[98]

These discussions with his brother may have prompted Tolic to reconsider his actions. This, combined with the fact that Area Command Two had under-supplied and under-supported the men from Area Command Four, resulted in the troika abandoning its mission, leaving Ljubljanica and attempting to return to the Italian border.[99] Ilija Tolic later stated in court proceedings in Rijeka that "I made up my mind to go back. I gave up every activity. I dragged Oblak and Stojic further and further towards the Italian border. And then the end came."[100] Tolic, Oblak, and Stojic were apprehended in the city of Rijeka, in Croatia, approximately 277.5 kilometers from

Ljubljanica, and just over fifty kilometers from the border with Italy.[101]

The second troika was made up of Fumic, Perkovic, and Zdrilic. This troika headed to a village outside Brinje, about 154 kilometers from their Monfalcone insertion point, where Fumic and Perkovic had family. The two families sheltered the troika. Fumic's sister-in-law, Danica, and Perkovic's sister Zora, travelled into Brinje, where they purchased shoes for the three men so that they could move around more easily. While the families claimed that they were unaware of the purpose of the trio's arrival, Zora hid her brother's Beretta pistol in the cellar of her home.[102]

Fumic's troika was apprehended at Koper, about 126 kilometers west of Brinje, within days of leaving his family's village.[103] The significant distance west into Slovenia indicates that Fumic's troika was also attempting to return to the Italian border. This strongly suggests that Tolic's troika was communicating with Fumic's troika using the radios that each of the troikas carried.

The Podrug, Tapsanji, and Leko (who was carrying 5 kilograms of explosives and 14 detonators with him) troika headed east like the other two troikas; however, it is unclear where the trio travelled to before receiving orders from Tolic to return to the Italian border.[104] The troika was apprehended in the mountainous Gorski Kotar region within Croatia on a road outside Karlovac by members of the People's Militia.[105]

The Action Kangaroo members were arrested within a fortnight of entering the SFRY by the *Uprava Drzavne Bezbednosti/Sigurnosti/Varnosti* (State Security Administration, UDBA) and associated SFRY forces.[106] All nine members were arrested between July 19 and 22, 1963 in the towns of Koper, Rijeka, and Karlovac.[107] All had Australian travel documents or passports on them when arrested, creating considerable embarrassment for the Australian Government.[108]

Pasti (also an Australian citizen) left Australia for Area Command Two around the time the troikas were discovered and arrested by the UDBA and SFRY forces, possibly when Area Command Two lost radio communication with the group.[109] After arriving in the FRG, Pasti was arrested and charged on October 3 by German police with the illegal possession of a firearm (which he procured in

Italy) and with being a member of a secret organization (which was an offence in the FRG).[110] Pasti pleaded guilty to both charges, was sentenced to seven months imprisonment, and deported. During the proceedings of the trial, Pasti informed the court that he was the organizer of the training for the nine men in Yugoslavia.[111]

On September 20, 1963, the SFRY Government announced that nine men from Australia (two with Australian passports) were arrested during a terrorist operation against the SFRY.[112] The trial began in March of 1964 in Rijeka and ended on April 19, 1964.[113] At the close of the trial, Oblak and Tolic received sentences of fourteen years, Tapsanji received a sentence of thirteen years, Leko, Stojic, and Podrug received sentences of twelve years, Fumic and Perkovic received sentences of six years, and Zdrilic received a seven year sentence.[114] Fumic, Perkovic, and Zdrilic received lighter sentences after they renounced their actions and the HRB.[115]

Following the trials of the nine HRB members, those who assisted the troikas were also punished through court proceedings in Rijeka. Mate Tolic was sentenced to ten months imprisonment for sheltering his brother. Maria Tolic, Zora Perkovic, and Danica Fumic received sentences of seven months for harboring the HRB members.[116]

While causing embarrassment to the Australian government (particularly with regard to the Spremnost photos), the operation had a similar effect on the HRB. In an open letter to Area Command Four from Franjo Turk and Josip Senic, both members of the European command, stated "we continue to be attacked, vilified and spat upon because of the nine Brothers who have so tragically ended in the Operation Kangaroo."[117] The HRB set out to rectify this embarrassment by distributing a circular giving a description of the aborted operation, pointing out the mistakes that were made and the lessons that were learned. The circular then advocated further operations aimed at sabotage and guerrilla warfare within Yugoslavia.[118] The unsuccessful operation ensured significant attention from the Australian Government, forcing the HRB underground. Despite the subsequent lack of operational activity, the operation, assisted by the distributed circular, appears to have served as a catalyst for the Croatian separatist movement in Australia.

Croatian separatism post-1963

A number of Croatian separatist groups formed following the HRB's Action Kangaroo and a number of existing groups became more violent in their modus operandi. Following the formation of many of these new groups, a number engaged in a violent campaign against Yugoslav officials, interests, and individuals within Australia. Various small-scale incidents of political violence appeared in the early-to-mid 1960s against Yugoslav institutions such as the Consulate-General and the Yugoslav Settlers Association. By 1966, this violence escalated to death threats, stabbings, and attempted murders.

In the mid to late 1960s, the Ustashi activities in Australia had advanced into the realm of terrorism. On September 17, 1966, a parcel bomb exploded prematurely in a parcel chute in the General Post Office (GPO) in Melbourne. The parcel was addressed to Marijan Jurjevic, a Yugoslav who had set out to publicize the Ustashi group's activities since the early 1960s.[119] Between January 1967 and November 1971, seven separate bombings were carried out against:

1. The Yugoslav Consulate-General in Double Bay;
2. The Yugoslav National Day ball;
3. The Yugoslav Consulate-General in Sydney;
4. The Yugoslav Embassy in Canberra;
5. The Yugoslav Consulate-General in Melbourne,
6. A Serbian Orthodox Church; and
7. A Yugoslav travel agency in Sydney.[120]

The HOP military camps continued into the 1970s, when the Ustashi groups had to constantly increase and revise their security measures due to increased attention from the Australian Government's intelligence and law-enforcement arms.[121] By this stage, the HOP had established the *Saveza Hrvatske Ujedinjene Mladezi Svijeta* (Croatian United Youth of the World, SHUMS) and the *Hrvatska Maldez* (Croatian Youth) movements, and trained with automatic weapons and high-powered explosives in remote areas of Victoria and South Australia.[122] SHUMS was led by Srecko Blaz Rover, who had earlier also led the HOP and the *Hrvatski Narodni Otpor*

(Croatian National Resistance, HNO), a Melbourne-based group with links to the HNO headquarters in Spain.[123] The Secretary of SHUMS was Zdenko Marincic, who arrived in Australia in early 1970. In 1972, Marincic flew to Frankfurt, West Germany, without any form of permit or visa, and was subsequently refused entry. Marincic returned to Australia and was arrested after concealing a rifle in his luggage, as well as four silencers concealed in a toy koala.[124] Rover was also directly involved in this violence. In 1967 Rover constructed a bomb disguised as an expensive-looking pen, which seriously injured a young Yugoslav at a Yugoslav National Day Ball.[125]

Further separatist groups emerged during this period, including the Australian branch of *Ujedinjen Hrvati Njemacki* (UHNj, United Croats of West Germany). This group was formed around June 1971 in Sydney, and was led by Jakov Suljack. In October of 1972, Suljack was arrested and charged with another count of assault and possession of an unlicensed pistol.[126] Suljack's commitment to the liberation of Croatia was clear: in the 1971 November–December edition of the "Croatian Call," he stated: "It is our duty to support the Croatian liberation struggle…for without a bloody shirt there will be no independent state of Croatia," echoing the frustrations of Maric, Oblack, Tolic and Pasti in 1963. The meetings for the Australian branch of the UHNj were held at the Irish National Association's Ulster room in Sydney.[127]

On April 6, 1972, simultaneous bombings were executed against the Australia and New Zealand Bank's Migrant Advisory Centre in Melbourne, and the residence of pro-Yugoslavian figure, Jurjevic.[128]

As stated in a report by the Attorney General's Department, on September 16, two explosive devices were detonated, the first at the Adriatic Travel Agency, in George Street, Sydney. The second device, also on George Street, was detonated inside the General Trade and Tourist Agency. Sixteen people were injured in the second explosion, two of whom were injured critically.[129] A third explosive device was removed from the Adriatic Travel Agency.[130]

In 1972, the HRB become known as the *Hrvatska Ilegalan Revolucionarna Organizacija* (Croatian Illegal Revolutionary Organisation, HIRO).[131] By this stage the size and structure of the group had advanced dramatically, spanning every state and territory in the country.[132] In June 1972, six Australian citizens and three others who had previously lived in Australia entered Yugoslavia through Austria as part of a larger group of Croatian terrorists. This represented the HRB's second Australia-launched incursion into Communist Yugoslavia.[133] All but one of these Australian insurgents were either killed or tried and executed by SFRY security forces.[134] One of these insurgents killed was Adolf Andric, the HRB member who had instructed the members of the Action Kangaroo operation.[135]

As has been seen with a majority of terrorist campaigns, the mounting success of these groups and their operations ultimately resulted in their downfall. The grandeur and frequency of the separatist operations and attacks of 1972, in addition to the 1963 incursion into Yugoslavia, posed serious questions as to the level of the Australian Federal Government's response to anti-Communist terrorism. The inability of authorities to act also exposed organizational and collaborative weaknesses between the state and federal authorities investigating these groups. The change in government in 1972 leveled severe measures against the Croatian groups. [136] Subsequent to a greater counter-terrorism focus against groups such as the HNO and the HRB, an inquiry was established by the Whitlam Government under Justice Hope, leading to a much sharper focus on accountability within Australia's security agencies. This in turn led to a much harsher response from agencies such as the Australian Security Intelligence Organization, and the decline of groups such as the HRB.[137]

Conclusions

Although Croatia's independence in 1991 has ensured that the cause of groups such as the HRB will not resurface, the initial success of the robust response from the security and intelligence arms of the Australian Government from 1972 to 1974 (although not examined in detail here) demonstrate the success of the approach in this case. Future research that focuses on the effects of this response on the Croatian community, as stated above, may provide valuable insights into contemporary approaches and engagement with the Islamic community in efforts to counter the threat of Islamic extremism.

The HRB represents the largest terrorist organization to operate within Australia. The violent operations undertaken by the HRB and other separatist groups represent the longest and most sustained terrorist campaign within Australia's history. The HRB's Action Kangaroo served as a catalyst for Croatian separatist terrorist in Australia, but also around the world. The lack of attention given to this group and its inaugural operation within historical and terrorism studies research, points to a greater need to uncover and understand the historical foundations and responses to terrorism and extremism within Australia. The sparse literature on groups such as Aum Shinrikyo and its operations in Australia, as well as operations by the Palestinian May 15 Organization and its Australia-based support networks, are indicative of this requirement. Such research will no doubt have significant applications to the strategic, political, and legislative challenges posed by the threat of Islamic extremism in Australia, and future threats posed by Australia-based terrorist networks and organizations.

Notes

[1] Marcus Tanner, *Croatia: A Nation Forged in War* (New Haven: Yale University Press).

[2] The name of the Kingdom changed following the dissolution of Croat rights.

[3] Criminal Investigations Branch, *Brief History of "Ustashi" Movement till end of War in 1945* (Melbourne Victoria Police, 1964).

[4] Walter Laqueur, *Terrorism* (London: Weidenfeld & Nicolson, 1977).

[5] Dave Davies, *The Ustasha in Australia* (Melbourne: Communist Party of Australia, 1972), 1-2.

[6] Criminal Investigations Branch, *Brief History of "Ustashi" Movement till end of War in 1945* (Melbourne Victoria Police, 1964).

[7] Dave Davies, *The Ustasha in Australia* (Melbourne: Communist Party of Australia, 1972), 1-2.

[8] Marcus Tanner, *Croatia: A Nation Forged in War* (New Haven: Yale University Press, 1997).

[9] The Balkan Air Force established as a part of the British Royal Air Force. John Lampe, *Yugoslavia as History: Twice there was a Country* (Cambridge: Cambridge University Press).

[10] Central Intelligence Agency, *The Croatian Resistance Movement* (Langley: Central Intelligence Agency, 14 June 1984).

[11] This essentially outlined the sanctity, sovereignty, and superiority of the Croatian Nation. Attorney General's Department, *Draft Press Statement on Croats* (Canberra Attorney General's Department, 1964).

[12] Attorney General's Department, *Draft Press Statement on Croats* (Canberra Attorney General's Department, 1964).

[13] Prime Minister's Department, Briefing *Notes for the Prime Minister: The Yugoslav Community in Australia* (Canberra: Prime Minister's Department, 13 December 1967).

[14] Victoria Police, *Victorian Police Report On Croatian Movements in Australia* (Melbourne: Victoria Police, 1964).

[15] Attorney General's Department, *Draft Press Statement on Croats* (Canberra Attorney General's Department, 1964).

[16] Department of Immigration, *Meeting at the Department of Immigration on the 25th November, 1963 Concerning Activities of Croatian Migrants* (Canberra: Department of Immigration, 1963).

[17] British Embassy, *Memorandum to Department of External Affairs: Trial of Yugoslav Emigrants in Rijeka* (Canberra: Department of External Affairs: Canberra, 22 April 1964). Mark Aarons, *War Criminals Welcome: Australia, a Sanctuary for Fugitive War Criminals Since 1945* (Melbourne: Black Inc, 2001), 407.

[18] Lionel Murphy, *Senate Hansard: Croatian Terrorism*, 27 March 1973.

[19] Criminal Investigations Branch: Special Branch, *Brief History of "Ustashi" Movement till end of War in 1945* (Victoria Police: Melbourne, 1964).

[20] House of Representatives, Question No. 280, 27 August 1964.

[21] Lionel Murphy, *Senate Hansard: Croatian Terrorism*, 27 March 1973.

[22] *Spremnost*, January-February 1963.
The Drina is a river on the border of Bosnia and Herzegovina and Serbia and Montenegro.
The official government position on this event (which became extremely embarrassing following the 1963 HRB incursion into the SFRY) was that the local CMF commander saw and took the opportunity for a low scale recruiting drive.

[23] Commonwealth Police, *Report to Commissioner: Croatian Revolutionary Brotherhood: Execution of Search Warrants* (Canberra: Commonwealth Police Force, 17 October 1967).
Mark Aarons, *War Criminals Welcome: Australia, a Sanctuary for Fugitive War Criminals Since 1945* (Melbourne: Black Inc, 2001), 412.

[24] Commonwealth Police, *Report to Attorney General's Department: Croatian Revolutionary Brotherhood* (Canberra: Commonwealth Police, 25 Janu-

ary 1967).

[25] Mark Aarons, *War Criminals Welcome: Australia, a Sanctuary for Fugitive War Criminals Since 1945* (Melbourne: Black Inc, 2001), 404.

[26] *The Sydney Morning Herald*, 6 September 1963.

[27] Croatian Australian Association, *Meeting Minutes: No. 38 Emergency Closed Meeting of the Executive of the Croatian Australian Association* (Wollongong, Croatian Australian Association, 8 April 1960).

Jure de Francetic Croatian Association, *Meeting Minutes: Committee Meeting No. 1* (Warrawong, Jure de Francetic Croatian Association, 26 January 1958).

[28] *Politika*, 16 April 1964.

Politika, 17 April 1964.

[29] Mark Aarons, *War Criminals Welcome: Australia, a Sanctuary for Fugitive War Criminals Since 1945* (Melbourne: Black Inc, 2001), 411.

[30] Ibid, 413.

[31] Ibid, 412, 420, 397.

[32] Commonwealth Police, *Report to Commissioner, Croatian Revolutionary Brotherhood: Execution of Search Warrants* (Canberra: Commonwealth Police Force, 17 October 1967).

[33] Ibid.

[34] Attorney General's Department, *Draft Press Statement on Croats* (Canberra Attorney General's Department, 1964).

[35] Commonwealth Police, *Report to Commissioner, Croatian Revolutionary Brotherhood: Execution of Search Warrants* (Canberra: Commonwealth Police Force, 17 October 1967).

[36] Ibid.

[37] Ibid.

[38] Josip Senic, Letter to Jure Maric, 21 July 1966.

[39] Attorney General's Department, *Draft Press Statement on Croats* (Canberra Attorney General's Department, 1964).

Attorney General's Department, *Disturbances in the Yugoslav Communities* (Canberra: Attorney General's Department, 29 July 1964).

[40] Commonwealth Police, *Report to Commissioner: Croatian Revolutionary Brotherhood: Execution of Search Warrants* (Canberra: Commonwealth Police Force, 17 October 1967).

[41] Ibid.

[42] Ibid.

[43] Ibid.

[44] Franjic arrived in Australia on December 12, 1949, and was later naturalized November 9, 1965.

Attorney-General's Department, *Minute Paper: Croatian Revolutionary Brotherhood: Issue of Search Warrants* (Canberra: Attorney-General's Department, 13 February 1967).

[45] Commonwealth Police, *Report to Commissioner: Croatian Revolutionary Brotherhood: Execution of Search Warrants* (Canberra: Commonwealth Police Force, 17 October 1967).

[46] Attorney-General's Department, *Minute Paper: Croatian Revolutionary Brotherhood: Issue of Search Warrants* (Canberra: Attorney-General's Department, 13 February 1967).

[47] Jure Maric & Geza Pasti, Duplicate Handout: Croatian Revolutionary Brotherhood: Maintenance of Security—Fundamental Duty of Revolutionaries—Principle of Secret Operation.

[48] This formation is very similar to the military organization of the Stern Gang who operated in Palestine in the late 1930s and early 1940s.

[49] Cited in "The Geli Men: The Ustasha & Croatia," Bertrand Peace Foundation, 3.

[50] Cited in Marijan Jurjevic, *Ustasha Under the Southern Cross* (Melbourne: M. Jurjevic, 1973).

[51] Marijan Jurjevic, *Ustasha Under the Southern Cross* (Melbourne: Marijan Jurjevic, 1973), 41.

[52] Ibid, 39.

[53] Ibid, 41.

[54] *The Sydney Morning Herald*, 6 September 1963.

[55] Department of External Affairs, *Memorandum to Prime Minister's Department: Activities of the Croatian Revolutionary Brotherhood* (Canberra: Department of External Affairs, 27 May 1964).

[56] *Politika*, 17 April 1964.

[57] *The Sydney Morning Herald*, 6 September, 1963.

[58] Ibid.

[59] *Politika*, 16 April 1964.

[60] Australian High Commission, *Inward Cablegram to Department of External Affairs: Unclassified: Terrorist Trail* (London: Australian High Commission, 15 April 1964).

[61] Attorney General's Department, *Briefing Sheet: Questions for the Attorney General* (Canberra: Attorney-General's Department, 7 August 1964).

Australian High Commission, *Inward Cablegram to Department of External Affairs: Restricted: Terrorist Trial* (London: Australian High Commission, 22 April 1964).

[62] Ibid.

[63] Australian High Commission, *Inward Cablegram to Department of External Affairs: Unclassified: Terrorist Trial* (London: Australian High Commission, 15 April 1964).

[64] Attorney-General's Department, *Draft Statement: Yugoslav Immigrant Organisations* (Canberra: Attorney-General's Department, 1964).

[65] Prime Minister's Department, *Briefing Sheet: Questions for the Prime*

Minister (Canberra: Prime Minister's Department, 7 August 1964).

[66] Attorney General's Department, *Draft Press Statement on Croats* (Canberra Attorney General's Department, 1964).

[67] Department of External Affairs, *Memorandum to Prime Minister's Department: Activities of the Croatian Revolutionary Brotherhood* (Canberra: Department of External Affairs, 27 May, 1964).

[68] Australian High Commission, *Inward Cablegram to Department of External Affairs: Restricted: Terrorist Trial* (London: Australian High Commission, 22 April 1964).

[69] Mark Aarons, *War Criminals Welcome: Australia, a Sanctuary for Fugitive War Criminals Since 1945* (Melbourne: Black Inc, 2001), 418.

[70] Ibid, 418.

[71] Ibid, 409.

[72] Ibid, 417.

[73] Ibid, 417.

[74] Mark Aarons, *War Criminals Welcome: Australia, a Sanctuary for Fugitive War Criminals Since 1945* (Melbourne: Black Inc, 2001), 417. *The Sydney Daily Mirror*, 5 September 1963.

[75] Attorney-General's Department, *Minute Paper: Croatian Revolutionary Brotherhood: Issue of Search Warrants* (Canberra: Attorney-General's Department, 13 February 1967). "Crime Intelligence, Croatian Revolutionary Brotherhood" (Sydney: New South Wales Police, 17 March 1967).

[76] Commonwealth Police, *Draft of Report to Attorney-General: Croatian Brotherhood: Documents Seized from Adolf Andric of Geelong* (Canberra: Commonwealth Police, October 1967).

[77] Australian High Commission, *Inward Cablegram to Department of External Affairs: Unclassified: Terrorist Trial* (London: Australian High Commission, 15 April 1964).

Politika, April 17 1964.

The Drava is a major river in that runs from Italy and forms the border of Croatia and Hungary.

[78] Mark Aarons, War Criminals Welcome: Australia, a Sanctuary for Fugitive War Criminals Since 1945 (Melbourne: Black Inc, 2001), 409.

[79] British Embassy, *Memorandum to Department of External Affairs: Trial of Yugoslav Emigrants in Rijeka* (Canberra: Department of External Affairs, April 22 1964).

Jure Maric, Address Book: Exhibit 215 (Commonwealth Police, 1964). *Politika*, 17 April 1964.

[80] *Politika*, 16 April 1964.

[81] Marijan Simundic was later assassinated on September 13, 1967.

Department of External Affairs, *Memorandum to Prime Minister's Department: Activities of the Croatian Revolutionary Brotherhood* (Canberra: Department of External Affairs, 27 May 1964).

82 Ibid.

83 Mark Aarons, *War Criminals Welcome: Australia, a Sanctuary for Fugitive War Criminals Since 1945* (Melbourne: Black Inc, 2001), 409.
Politika, 16 April 1964.

84 *The Sydney Daily Mirror*, 5 September 1963.
British Embassy, *Memorandum to Department of External Affairs: Trial of Yugoslav Emigrants in Rijeka* (Canberra: Department of External Affairs, 22 April 1964).

85 Ibid.

86 *The Sydney Daily Mirror*, 5 September 1963.

87 British Embassy, *Memorandum to Department of External Affairs: Trial of Yugoslav Emigrants in Rijeka* (Canberra: Department of External Affairs, 22 April 1964).

88 Mark Aarons, *War Criminals Welcome: Australia, a Sanctuary for Fugitive War Criminals Since 1945* (Melbourne: Black Inc, 2001), 409.

89 *Politika*, 16 April 1964.

90 Ibid.

91 Mark Aarons, *War Criminals Welcome: Australia, a Sanctuary for Fugitive War Criminals Since 1945* (Melbourne: Black Inc, 2001), 409.

92 Ibid.

93 *Politika*, 16 April 1964.

94 Aarons, *War Criminals Welcome*, 409.

95 Australian High Commission, *Inward Cablegram to Department of External Affairs: Restricted: Terrorist Trial* (London: Australian High Commission, 20 April 1964).
Politika, 17 April 1964.

96 Ibid.

97 Ibid.

98 Ibid.

99 *Politika*, 16 April 1964.

100 *Politika*, 17 April 1964.

101 *The Sydney Morning Herald*, 6 September 1963.

102 *Politika*, 17 April 1964.

103 *The Sydney Morning Herald*, 6 September 1963.

104 *Politika*, 16 April 1964.

105 Ibid.

106 Aarons, *War Criminals Welcome*, 410.

107 *The Sydney Morning Herald*, 6 September 1963.

108 Aarons, *War Criminals Welcome*, 410.

109 Attorney General's Department, *Draft Press Statement on Croats* (Canberra Attorney General's Department, 1964).

110 Australian Security Intelligence Organisation, *Memorandum to Prime Minister's Department: 9728* (Melbourne: Australian Security Intelligence

Organisation, August 1964).

[111] Attorney General's Department, *Draft Press Statement on Croats* (Canberra Attorney General's Department, 1964).

[112] Ibid.

[113] Attorney General's Department, *Draft Press Statement on Croats* (Canberra Attorney General's Department, 1964).

Politika, 19 April 1964.

[114] Ibid.

[115] Ibid.

[116] *Politika*, 19 April 1964.

[117] Turk was a high ranking member of Area Command Two. Following the 1963 operation Senic travelled to Europe to take up a position in Area Command Two.

Josip Senic & Franjo Turk, Open Letter to Croatian Revolutionary Brotherhood Command Post No. 4, nd.

[118] Commonwealth Police, *Report to Commissioner: Croatian Revolutionary Brotherhood: Execution of Search Warrants* (Canberra: Commonwealth Police Force, 17 October 1967).

[119] Dave Davies, *The Ustasha in Australia* (Melbourne: Communist Party of Australia, 1972), 6-9.

[120] Attorney-General's Department, *Croatian Nationalist Activities in Australia—Annexure D: Significant Incidents Within the Yugoslav Community in Australia 1964-1972* (Canberra: Attorney-General's Department, 5 July 1972).

[121] Marijan Jurjevic, *Ustasha Under the Southern Cross* (Melbourne: M. Jurjevic, 1973), 38-41.

[122] Ibid.

[123] Lionel Murphy, Senate Hansard: Croatian Terrorism, 27 March 1973.

[124] Ibid.

[125] Ibid.

[126] Ibid.

[127] *Croatian Call*, November-December 1971.

Lionel Murphy, Senate Hansard: Croatian Terrorism, 27 March 1973.

[128] Dave Davies, *The Ustasha in Australia* (Melbourne: Communist Party of Australia, 1972), 7.

[129] Attorney-General's Department, *Croatian Nationalist Activities in Australia—Annexure D: Significant Incidents Within the Yugoslav Community in Australia 1964-1972* (Canberra: Attorney-General's Department, 5 July 1972).

[130] Cited in Jenny Hocking, *Beyond Terrorism: The Development of the Australian Security State* (St. Leonards: Allen & Unwin, 1993).

[131] The HIRO will be referred to as the HRB.

[132] Commonwealth Police, *Croatian Illegal Revolutionary Organisation* (Canberra: Commonwealth Police Force, 1972).

[133] Croatian Terrorism: Senate Hansard, 27 March 1973.

[134] Ibid.

[135] Marijan Jurjevic, *Ustasha Under the Southern Cross* (Melbourne: M. Jurjevic, 1973), 39.

[136] Jenny Hocking, *Terror Laws: ASIO, Counter-Terrorism, and the Threat to Democracy* (Sydney: University of NSW Press, 2004), 127-129.

[137] Tony Wright, "Playing Catch up: When Terrorism First Struck Australia, ASIO was Looking the Other Way," *The Bulletin*, 123, 6483 (2005), 21-25.

13

The Use of History by Lawyers in Debating Responses to Terrorism

Andrew Lynch

The almost total absence of any Australian laws dealing with terrorism before September 11, 2001 means that the steady legislative activity of federal and state governments in the wake of the events of that day is only too understandable.[1] In the five year period immediately following the attacks on New York's Twin Towers and the Pentagon building in Washington, DC, the Australian Commonwealth Parliament alone had passed thirty-seven new laws directly addressing the terrorist threat.[2]

The Commonwealth's legislative responses to terrorism have been wide-ranging in scope and include many sensible, and probably overdue, measures to protect the security of significant sites and dangerous substances. These laws have attracted little controversy. The same cannot be said, however, of the introduction of a suite of new terrorism crimes, preventative civil orders which roughly append to the orthodox framework of criminal justice and some of the enhanced powers conferred upon Commonwealth agencies, particularly the Australian Security Intelligence Organisation (ASIO).[3]

Understandably, lawyers have been very central to Australia's public and parliamentary debates over the need for and content of many of these anti-terrorism measures. However, there are two notable limitations on the perspectives that they are able to bring to those conversations. The dominant one is, of course, the inevitable lack of access to security information—and the inability to sensibly analyze it even if it were available.[4] Not only is this an understandable deficiency, but it is also one which is shared with the majority of non-government actors—most notably the media—in their scrutiny of new proposals to increase the powers of the state in order to meet the threat of terrorism. Ultimately, lawyers, along with the media, other "civil society" stakeholders, and the general public, must accept at face value much of what is conveyed to them by the government about the present security climate or at least leave challenges on that score to defense specialists or political deliberation.

This does not, however, insulate from sensible critique the justifications given for particular proposals relative to the threat as it is presented by the government. The issues of necessity and proportionality are still ones against which new initiatives can be meaningfully assessed. But the quality of contributions to public debate in this vein, hinges upon the second limitation under which Australia's legal community has labored. The other factor which constrains legal debates about terrorism measures is lawyers' grasp of the history of politically motivated violence and particularly how that might impact significantly on what we propose to do about the current threat. Unlike the classified nature of national security information, the resource of historical analyses of past experience, both here and in overseas jurisdictions facing a more sustained threat of terrorism, is theoretically available—but it is one which lawyers either do not have the time or expertise to draw upon as profitably as they might.

This reflects, of course, Australia's very fortunate lack of much terrorist experience and the absence of any earlier legislative attempts to protect the community.[5] By way of contrast, lawyers in the United Kingdom—the jurisdiction to which the Commonwealth government has most often looked for inspiration when proposing new counter-terrorism measures—do not have this difficulty. The decades of escalating legal responses to the terrorist activities emanating from the conflict in Northern Ireland means that the legislative proposals of the British government post-September 11 have been subjected to a very well-rounded scrutiny from the legal community.[6] Practitioners and legal academics—not to mention the police and government departments—have already seen many similar policies in action and subjected them to frank appraisal.[7] In that jurisdiction, there is a much keener awareness of what measures will work—which will prove largely symbolic—and also how the curtailment of some civil liberties may serve merely to alienate moderate members of the community and aggravate the problem.[8]

In the absence of any domestic experience of legislating against terrorism, Australian lawyers have had to look overseas or to make analogies from our own past—neither of which may be entirely ideal in their efforts to debate with the government about its laws. In this chapter I aim to consider how lawyers have engaged with history to this end in discussing modern terrorism and our responses to it. My assessment is that so far these experiences demonstrate that much closer collaboration between legal commentators and historians would enhance the quality of debate as well as the substance of any resulting counter-terrorism laws.

History as legal precedent

The first way in which history informs and shapes legal responses to terrorism is within the very traditional preoccupation which the law has with "precedent." Under the common law method, lawyers are trained to meet new scenarios by identifying the most suitably analogous legal precedent and to take guidance from that. If the past and present situations do not lend themselves to being meaningfully distinguished, then today's law will be approached by a court through the prism of that earlier experience.

However, case authorities in Australia with any relevance to the kind of legal changes introduced by the federal government since September 11, are hardly thick on the ground. There are, however, two particular areas—the proscription of organizations and the preventative detention of individuals—where earlier judicial and legislative experiences have been invoked in recent debates over new anti-terrorism laws.

1. Proscription of Organizations

Interestingly, the current discussion over who should be banning organizations in modern Australia draws on not one, but two competing models from Australia's previous efforts to stamp out communism. Since 2004, the Commonwealth Attorney-General has, under Division 102 of the Criminal Code, possessed the power to proscribe organizations if satisfied they are in some way connected to terrorist activity.[9] The consequence of proscription is that criminal sanctions apply to a range of activities conducted by individuals in relation to the organization. We might presume that these activities should be unmistakably terrorist in character, but the provisions do not provide any limiting factor in that respect. This has been a source of criticism of several of the offences.[10] Indeed the possible scope of their application was startlingly demonstrated when in 2007 an innocent man, Dr Mohamed Haneef, was charged with providing "support" to a terrorist organization simply because, before leaving the United Kingdom for Australia, he had given a SIM card to a relative later implicated in a terrorist attempt. The charge was eventually abandoned but only after Dr Haneef's liberty had been seriously transgressed.[11]

Additionally, and even more controversially, are the so-called "status" offences. It is a crime to be a member—formal or informal—of a terrorist organization.[12] It is also an offence to "associate" with people in such an organization where it can be shown that doing so "assists" the group to exist or expand in some way.[13] It is these amorphous offences—not dependant upon any criminal *activity* as such but which may be triggered by close social and family networks—that have attracted significant concern as provoking "a substantial increase in fear, a growing sense of alienation from the wider community and an increase in distrust of authority" in Muslim and Arab Australian communities.[14]

The conferral of this discretion to ban organizations upon a member of the Executive has strong echoes of the Menzies government's attempt to meet the danger of communism by passage of the *Communist Party Dissolution Act* in 1950. That law banned the Australian Communist Party outright and provided the Governor-General with a power to declare unlawful any "affiliated" organizations the continued existence of which would be prejudicial to the security and defense of the Commonwealth.

In 1951, the Act was invalidated 6:1 by the High Court for the principal reason that it usurped the Court's own power of judicial review under the Constitution.[15] While the legislation allowed

review of an entity's link to communism, the threat which it posed
to national security as determined by the Parliament (in the case
of the Communist Party itself) or as assessed by the Governor-
General (under the proscription mechanism) was completely
unexaminable. Yet that was the key fact upon which reliance on the
Commonwealth's constitutional power to make laws with respect to
defense depended.[16] By effectively providing for the connection of
the law to the source of its own power to be determined *exclusively*
by the opinion of the legislature or executive, the Act disregarded
the High Court's authority as the ultimate arbiter of constitutional
validity.[17]

There is little doubt that the new regime in Division 102 of the
Criminal Code for the proscription of terrorist organizations avoids
the defect of the Menzies government's legislation since the discretion of the Commonwealth Attorney-General is subject to at least
bare judicial review. Even if the earlier Act were passed in the same
terms today, the case of *R v Toohey; Ex parte Northern Land Council*
has since exposed the Governor-General's discretion (which is, of
course, almost always exercised in accordance with ministerial advice) for examination in accordance with the principles of admin-
istrative law.[18]

Regardless of the legal basis for the decision in the *Australian
Communist Party* case, it is regularly referred to by many who have
very serious concerns over whether the conferral by Division 102
of a discretion upon the Minister is the *appropriate* mechanism by
which organizations should be banned. On this broader question,
the High Court's decision provides some rather enigmatic support,
namely through the leading judgment of Justice Dixon, who was
elevated to the Chief Justiceship just a year after the case was decided.

In finding the proscription power under the *Communist Party
Dissolution Act* to be invalid for want of a process of judicial review,
Dixon was explicit on the dangers of the Executive arm of government. His Honour said, in what is surely the most famous passage
from the case:

> History and not only ancient history, shows that in countries
> where democratic institutions have been unconstitutionally

superseded, it has been done not seldom by those holding the executive power. Forms of government may need protection from dangers likely to arise from within the institutions to be protected.[19]

Wariness as to the possible misuse of Executive power clearly underlies the Court's decision, and the case has come to represent more generally the role of the law in acting as a brake upon this sort of thing. Justice Dixon hinted at the Court's powers in this regard when he said of the Constitution that it

> ...is an instrument framed in accordance with many traditional conceptions, to some of which it gives effect...others of which are simply assumed. Among these I think that it may fairly be said that the rule of law forms an assumption.[20]

The suspicion that there may be more to this statement than meets the eye was confirmed by two of the present Court's influential members, Justices Gummow and Hayne when, in 1998, they said the occasion has yet to arise for consideration of all that may follow from it."[21]

The Attorney-General's power of proscription has been the subject of two major reviews. While the Parliamentary Joint Committee on Intelligence and Security declared itself unpersuaded that a judicial, rather than executive-based, system of proscription was a "practical or more effective method," the specially convened Security Legislation Review Committee, under the auspices of the Attorney-General's Department, was divided on the issue.[22] In its July 2006 report, some members of that Committee thought the Attorney-General should retain this power while others favored instead the adoption of a judicial process along the lines put in place by the Bruce-Page government in its efforts to ban communist organizations in the 1920s.[23]

Part IIA was inserted into the Commonwealth *Crimes Act* in 1926 by the Bruce-Page government as a response to public fears of Bolshevism arising after disruptive strike action by unions.[24] The Part creates a range of criminal offences by virtue of an individual's connection to an "unlawful association"—essentially defined as one which encouraged or advocated overthrow of the Constitution or the Commonwealth by force, violence or destruction of property. The derivative offences include membership and fundraising, but were mostly effective only in hampering efforts by communists to rent premises for meetings or distribute materials through the post. Originally, the unlawfulness of a body was only determined as a necessary element in the prosecution of individuals under these derivative offences.[25] However, to provide a more lasting ruling, the Part was amended by the Lyons government in 1932 by the inclusion of section 30AA which enabled the Attorney-General to independently seek a court declaration that a body was an "unlawful association."[26]

Use of the judicial process in Part IIA was only ever attempted once, in respect of the Friends of the Soviet Union (FOSU) over 1935–37. Douglas describes the history of this highly unsatisfactory episode—which eventually culminated in abandonment of the application by the Commonwealth, whose case Menzies described as "hopeless."[27] With the settlement of this litigation, the government lost interest in the Act. Today's advocates for judicially-determined proscription in respect of "terrorist organisations" under Division 102 of the Criminal Code have pointed to s 30AA as a favorable precedent—despite (or perhaps because of) the fact that the legislation is ambiguous in several respects and the process would seem likely to render the banning of organizations much more difficult than is presently the case.[28]

Ultimately, the debate over the current proscription regime in Division 102 is suffused with, but barely assisted by, our knowledge of the past. Both prior and competing models devised in response to the communist threat spectacularly failed to facilitate the policy behind their enactment. In current debates over how the power should be exercised and by whom, the past looms large—but not in a way which provides much helpful guidance. The new Commonwealth Attorney-General has recently indicated his qualified support for those proposals to subject his discretion to additional checks, though his predecessor was clearly opposed to surrendering the power of proscription to the judicial arm.[29] But while no fundamental change is to be made to the proscription regime, the continued presence of the unlawful association's provisions in Part IIA inevitably challenges assertions that the executive alone should have the power to ban organizations.

More broadly, the divide over whether a power of proscription should even *exist* is heavily shadowed by these earlier attempts to deal with communism. However, it is far from clear that this provides a comparable paradigm to today's issues. One reason for this is the practical difficulties which must attend any attempt to prosecute individuals for "membership" offences in respect of the type of "organizations" we aim to thwart these days.[30] The centrality of organized structures to understanding the nature of the terrorist threat was significantly diminished by the circumstances of the 2005 London bombings. Although the four suicide bombers responsible had links with others who have since been arrested in relation to the attack, it appears that the plot was home-grown rather than the implementation of an edict delivered from the higher command of al Qaeda. Terrorist violence appears today to be not so much "organized" as inspired or facilitated through "shared values, common socialization, effective bonds and modern communication"—making it far less susceptible to rigid offence categories of "directing" or "supporting" a terrorist organization.[31] Indeed, Sloan has stressed that the use of decentralized and cell-like groups has been critical to the effectiveness of many recent terrorist strikes, particularly against governments who persist in thinking and acting themselves only in terms of "an organizational doctrine characterized by a ladder hierarchy, top-down command and control, bureaucratic layering and jurisdictional complexity."[32] As Peppler observes in his earlier chapter, this is all in clear distinction from the highly structured nature of communist activity in the mid-twentieth century.

An even more complex question is whether the present security situation amounts to a conflict the nature of which justifies detention by the state of those citizens it believes are intent on causing it harm. This is the other area of current debate where past legal precedent has been brought to bear.

2. Detention

Australia has experience of detaining persons merely on the basis of suspicion during times of armed conflict and it did so during both World Wars. While much criticism is directed to the forced internment by the United States government of Japanese-Americans during WWII and the decision of the United States Supreme Court in *Korematsu v United States* which upheld that as valid, little recognition is given to the High Court's finding that Australian versions of that policy—laws granting the Executive an unfettered discretion to detain "disaffected or disloyal" persons—were constitutional.[33]

Interestingly, the High Court itself has recently been trying to make sense of its own history in this regard. In a 2004 challenge to the indefinite detention of stateless persons denied asylum by the Commonwealth, some of its members had cause to consider whether the war-time detention cases were correctly decided as being within the scope of the Commonwealth's power to make laws with respect to defense. Justice McHugh defended the precedential value of those cases and, maintaining that the purpose of the detention was protective rather than punitive, saw "no reason to think that this Court would strike down similar regulations if Australia was at war in circumstances similar to those of 1914-1918 and 1939-1945."[34] Justice Kirby, on the other hand, derided them as embarrassing, and "of doubtful authority in the light of legal developments that occurred after they were written"—essentially the Court's own decision in the *Communist Party* case.[35] At first glance this seems a little disingenuous since most of the majority Justices in the *Communist Party* decision were prepared to admit, during a time of actual war, an exception to the need for judicial review of the constitutional facts upon which executive power depended. The lack of a conflict on this scale ensured that the *Communist Party Dissolution Act* fell outside that exception.[36] But Winterton has also questioned the reasoning underlying the war-time detention cases and their status as an exception to the reasoning in the *Communist Party* case.[37]

In 2005, little over a year after these judicial musings on the validity of those earlier detentions, the Commonwealth Parliament introduced twin schemes for preventative detention and control orders for suspected terrorists. These two schemes are obviously different from each other, and they both possess numerous safeguards which clearly distinguish them from the war-time detention laws. However, at their core, both involve the State in depriving individuals of their liberty without judicial adjudication of guilt.

Control orders allow obligations, prohibitions and restrictions to be imposed on an individual "for the purpose of protecting the public from a terrorist act."[38] The list of conditions available for inclusion in control orders bears strong similarities with that operating in the United Kingdom, and ranges from very minimal intrusion on an individual's freedom to a significant deprivation of his or her liberty.[39] Under section 104.5(3) of the Criminal Code, the order can include prohibitions or restrictions on the individual:

- being at specified areas or places;
- leaving Australia;
- communicating or associating with certain people;
- accessing or using certain forms of telecommunication or technology (including the Internet);
- possessing or using certain things or substances; and
- carrying out specific activities (including activities related to the person's work or occupation).

The order can also include the requirement that the person:

- remain at a specified place between certain times each day, or on specified days;
- wear a tracking device;
- report to specified people at specified times and places;
- allow photographs or fingerprints to be taken (for the purpose of ensuring compliance with the order); and
- if the person consents—participate in specified counseling or education.

Unlike preventative detention orders, control orders stop short of imprisoning the subject in a state facility. Nevertheless, an order incorporating either a prohibition or restriction on the person being at specified areas or places, or a requirement that he or she remain at specified premises between specified times each day or on specified days, may well amount to "detention" in all but name and might even effectively result in house arrest. A person who contravenes any of the terms of a control order to which he or she is subject commits an offence with a maximum penalty of five years jail.[40]

Under section 104.4 of the Criminal Code, control orders may be obtained by the Australian Federal Police from a federal court which is satisfied on the balance of probabilities that:

- "making the order would substantially assist in preventing a terrorist act"; or
- "that the person subject to the order has provided training to, or received training from, a listed terrorist organisation."

Additionally, the court must be satisfied that each of the obligations, prohibitions and restrictions to be imposed on the individual are "reasonably necessary, and reasonably appropriate and adapted, for the purpose of protecting the public from a terrorist act." In determining these matters, the court must take into account the impact of the obligations, prohibitions, and restrictions on the person's circumstances—including financial and personal.

The purpose of preventative detention orders is rather different and they purely permit detention of individuals—for a maximum of forty-eight hours at the Commonwealth level but with a possible extension of up to two weeks with State and Territory involvement. An order may be made for one of two purposes: prevention of an imminent terrorist attack or preservation of evidence relating to an attack in the last 28 days. For an order to be made for the first purpose, the issuing authority (which is an individual rather than a court) must be satisfied that there are reasonable grounds to suspect that the person either:

- "will engage in a terrorist act";
- "possesses a thing that is connected with the preparation for, or the engagement of a person in, a terrorist act"; or
- "has done an act in preparation for, or planning of, a terrorist act."

The authority must also be satisfied that the making of a preventative order would "substantially assist in preventing a terrorist act from occurring"; and detaining the subject for the period for which the person is to be detained is "reasonably necessary" for this purpose.

In respect of neither the control nor preventative detention orders, is there any requirement to charge the individual with a criminal offence—let alone establish guilt as to the same. Indeed the Attorney-General admitted at the time the new orders were introduced, "If you work on the assumption that only those people who could be convicted of an offence are subject to a control order then you wouldn't have control orders."[41] Can the immediate context justify this quite radical departure from orthodox principles of criminal justice?[42]

Obviously, all hyperbole and rhetoric aside, we are not presently in a "war" comparable to the two world wars. Thus the broadest expansion of the defense power in times of "hot war" which was recognized in the *Communist Party* case does not arise. But then, nor is the present legislation as extreme as that encountered by the Court in its examination of the *Communist Party Dissolution Act*. The real issue is whether our present security needs are sufficient to enliven the Commonwealth's defense power so as to provide legislative support for the deprivation of liberty, including forms of detention, of persons merely perceived to constitute a threat to the state. The presence of various checks and balances in relation to both orders is a significant factor but ultimately cannot be determinative.

This question fell open for discussion amongst the High Court in hearing the constitutional challenge to Australia's first control order over Jack Thomas.[43] In this case, six of the seven Justices upheld the constitutional validity of the control order regime in Division 104 of the Criminal Code on the basis that it is at least supported by the Commonwealth's power to legislate on defense.[44] The scope of the defense power is, of course, undoubtedly a legal question, but it is difficult to deny that it is closely bound up with very large historical and political ones. So much became clear when members of the Court questioned counsel in the case about the nature of the present security climate, its similarity to past conflicts—"hot" and "cold"—and the meaning of "war" itself.

Thomas' lawyers argued that the Commonwealth's power to make laws with respect to defense cannot be used to respond to the threat of terrorism, at least not so far as that calls for something beyond resort to the navy or military—both referred to in the grant of power. This rather technical reading met with a fairly cool response from the bench with Justice Callinan being the most unreceptive member. His Honour said:

> These circumstances are absolutely unique. I know in history of no other situation in which nationals living within…their own national community, actually set out clandestinely to destroy other people in the community. I just cannot think of any situation in which that has ever occurred before and occurring in many countries throughout the world and done by people, moreover, who have demonstrated that they do not care whether they live or die themselves. It is a unique combination of circumstances…That is why the defence power has to be the most flexible of all the powers.[45]

This bleak assessment was initially disputed by Justice Kirby who responded:

> There is, of course, a lot of writing on the background of terrorism and many historians have traced acts of terrorism back to the Middle Ages and many assert that the pirates of the high seas, many of them British, were the terrorists of their time, and in the early 1890s there was the great movement of anarchists, the communists were called terrorists and certainly all of the colonial liberation movements were called terrorists in their time, and many of the people who fought in those were willing to die for their cause. So I do not think it can be said that this is entirely unique.[46]

But Justice Callinan insisted at this point that the present situation was unprecedented "because it crosses international borders… and you cannot identify the enemy."[47] This appeared to complement Justice Hayne's invocation of von Clausewitz's theory of war on the first morning of hearings so as to challenge counsel as to the need for an external aggressor in order for a state of war to exist.[48] The following morning, the judge asked again why the "central conception [is] not the pursuit of ideological or political aims through forces…why confine it to internationalism?"[49] The attempt by Thomas' counsel to maintain that the defence power is limited to use of the navy or military against external aggressors appeared to collapse in the face of statements from other members of the bench who found it "presupposes purity which may not be present" and is "rather simplistic."[50]

Several remarks from members of the Court in the *Communist Party* case had stressed the purpose of the power as directed towards "external enemies" or "war with an extra-Australian nation or organism," to which the members of the *Thomas* majority responded in different ways in their final judgments.[51] Justices Gummow and Crennan tempered this limited portrayal of the power with evidence from English history to confirm the capacity of national governments to protect against violent unrest.[52] For his part, Callinan J stated simply that "insufficient critical attention" was given by the *Communist Party* majority to the scope of the power to encompass responses to internal dangers posed by non-state actors and aspects of Dixon J's opinion in particular were "questionable."[53] On this issue, his Honour stated a clear preference for the "more perceptive" approach of the dissenting judge in the earlier case, Chief Justice Latham.[54]

However, the reduction of "war" to a core concept—or, on another view, to effectively collapse "war" and "terrorism" into each other, does little to simplify the question of the extent to which responses to threats somewhere on the continuum between war and peace may be supported by the defense power.[55] The *Communist Party* case, which takes place at a time which we might think is roughly analogous, actually offers very little direct guidance on the scope of the defense power in a scenario such as the present. While it establishes that, short of total war, the Executive's opinion as to the threat to the nation cannot alone determine the reach of that power, the case offers only a rather muted indication of how the courts themselves will view the breadth of the power outside of the total war paradigm.

Members of the Court clearly differed over the usefulness of the historical record. Justice Callinan adopted from the start a view that the present situation was exceptional and that the Commonwealth's use of its legislative power over defense was justified to a greater extent than when meeting the challenges of the Cold War since the "evidence…here goes beyond that."[56] While this is not quite as explicit in his eventual judgment, during the hearings, his Honour seemed to be ready to distinguish the High Court's rejection of the

Communist Party Dissolution Act not merely on purely legal grounds but *historical* ones also.

Seeking to make this distinction clear for the Court, the Commonwealth Solicitor-General laid out quite plainly the reasons behind Australia's present "particular vulnerability":

> The first is the ready availability today of explosive substances, highly toxic poisons, germs and other weapons or things which can be used as weapons. That is the first matter. The second matter is that it contains cities with very large localized populations and of necessity many people are frequently concentrated in a small area. The third factor is the very high value our society places on human life. A society which had no regard for human life including that of its own members would not suffer from the vulnerability that our society does suffer from. The fourth matter is the dependency of modern society on a variety of types of infrastructure. The fifth is the high value placed by our society on a number of iconic structures, to use the modern cliché. The sixth is that infrastructure and iconic structures can easily be destroyed by explosives. Water supplies can be poisoned and in other ways great damage can be done to infrastructure and human life by individuals. The seventh matter is the particular vulnerability of aviation and, to a lesser degree, ships, buses and trains. The eighth is the growth of fanatical ideological movements which compass the destruction of western civilisation and, in particular, of Australia, or elements of it. The archetypical examples of the combination of factors I have referred to, or some of them, are the events of 9 [sic] September 2001, the events of Bali, Madrid, London, Nairobi and Dar es Salaam, Jakarta. One could go on at great length.[57]

In contrast, Kirby J (in dissent) stated that "analysis of the defence power in the present case should proceed on a parallel footing" to that in the *Communist Party* case. His Honour noted that even though Australian forces had landed in Korea during the Korean War at the time that the Communist Party Dissolution Bill was introduced into Parliament this was not sufficient to enliven

the defense power. Similarly, his Honour found that, despite political rhetoric using the language of war, the events identified in
the *Thomas* case did not constitute a "war-like environment" for the
purposes of the defense power.[58]

In the end, the Court held in *Thomas v Mowbray* that the current threat enables the State to impose restrictions upon the liberty
of individuals, possibly amounting to substantial deprivations, despite the Commonwealth admitting that Australia is in a situation
of relative peace. There need not be external threats or war between
nations—the defense power also applies to protecting the public
from terrorist acts.

The *Thomas* hearings make it clear that the judiciary is not immune to the diversity of historical and political understandings
which exist about terrorism and conflict more generally. These pose
a significant challenge in the production of clear legal answers to
questions about the validity of legislative and executive responses
to the threat of terrorist activity.

The historical yardstick

The second, and probably more common, use to which history has
been put in debates about new counter-terrorism laws is as a yard-
stick for determining whether they are excessive. This is particularly so in respect of the definition of "terrorism."

It is widely acknowledged that a perfectly acceptable definition is impossible to achieve though the Australian one is certainly
better than most others.[59] Definitions are regularly tested by asking whether a particular figure or group now widely appreciated
as fighting for liberation would be caught within their provisions.
Nelson Mandela is the classic example, and Mahatma Ghandi is
another—and indeed Justice Kirby in the *Thomas* hearings drew on
both to express concern over the scope—or at least the extended
jurisdictional reach—of Australia's terrorism definition.[60] Testing of
this sort is very valuable—especially in a country which has had to
create offences from scratch.
This hypothetical application of laws to episodes from the past
demonstrates not just their width but also the political malleability
of "terrorism" more generally. This is reinforced by current uses of

the "terrorism" label by despotic regimes to crush legitimate opposition as in, for example, Zimbabwe.

One response to this is to abandon any effort to define terrorism as a legal concept and all specific criminal laws which would depend upon it. And while this approach has its adherents, it seems neither politically realistic nor consistent with international obligations.

These same considerations—as well as immense practical difficulties of identification—also scuttle arguments that if we have a definition it should come with an exemption for actions carried out in a "just cause." In January 2007, an English court rejected arguments made by human rights lawyer Geoffrey Robertson that the definition of terrorism should be read down so as not to apply to a Libyan dissident seeking to facilitate the overthrow of Colonel Gaddafi's regime.[61] In March that year, the United Kingdom's Independent Reviewer of terrorism laws similarly rejected the calls from some parliamentarians for amendment of the statutory definition to the same end.[62]

Despite the difficulty of attempting to devise a legal framework which distinguishes between terrorists and "freedom fighters," history is an essential tool for both ensuring effectiveness and enabling vigilance about the way in which law attaches consequences to terrorism. It is for this reason that we must be wary about proposals which might inhibit the free expression of material which debates these questions as part of the historical record.

The relationship between history, terrorism, and law was made abundantly clear when, again in the UK, the Blair government initially introduced its offence of "glorifying" terrorism. The law was to apply to discussion of any terrorist act occurring in the last twenty years and also to other historical events further in the past as identified by a list prepared by the Home Office.[63]

As some were quick to point out, this proposal might have exposed the Irish leader Bertie Ahern to a five year jail term for commemorating the Easter Uprising of April 1916—except inexplicably that was an event deemed by the Home Office not to qualify as a "terrorist act" despite it falling easily within the UK definition of the term.[64] One critic opined that now "the Crown Prosecution Service must be staffed with experts in William the Conqueror, the Black Prince, the New Model Army, the Gordon rioters, the Tolpuddle Martyrs."[65]

Thankfully, common sense prevailed and although in 2006 the glorification offence was enacted it was much tighter than originally planned—in particular it required an intention or recklessness as to whether the remark induced others to commit a terrorist offence.[66] Importantly, both the twenty-year time limit and the government list of terrorist acts in history were dropped.

Australian law does not have a glorification offence but it does enable the Attorney-General to proscribe an organization which praises the doing of a terrorist act where there is a risk that might have the effect of leading a person (regardless of age or mental impairment) to engage in a terrorist act.[67] Intent is irrelevant. This framework has also been transferred into the national classification legislation for books and films, despite a number of inquiries having expressed concern over the width of the concept of "advocacy."[68] That, combined with the lack of clear and express protections for academic analysis and artistic work, sits uneasily with ensuring frank discussion of episodes from history which have involved political violence.[69] Those conversations are essential not just in themselves but particularly to debates over the introduction of new anti-terrorism laws and should be brought to the fore more, not less.

Conclusion

The legal profession engages with history all the time—but when governments start to legislate in an area which they have not needed to address until now then there is a clear need for broader historical expertise. The creation of Australian responses to terrorism has been an exercise which has involved looking to overseas jurisdictions for inspiration, but it is vital that we also understand how those other nations have developed the laws which they have if we are to implement them appropriately.

Historians are in a strong position to make meaningful contributions to contemporary policy debates over Australia's national security strategies and the way in which these are promoted through changes to the criminal justice system and general legal landscape. The legal profession, which has so far borne the bulk of the responsibility for engaging with the government on these issues, would welcome the greater engagement of historians.

Notes

[1] There was no law at national or state level which criminalized terrorist activity. The only legislation of this type in existence was in the Northern Territory: *Criminal Code Act* (NT) Pt III, Div 2. Additionally, there was some legislation passed pursuant to international obligations in respect of particular terrorist acts such as hi-jacking or aircraft: *Crimes (Aviation) Act 1991* (Cth).

[2] Andrew Lynch and George Williams, *What Price Security? Taking Stock of Australia's Anti-Terrorism Laws* (Sydney: UNSW Press, 2006).

[3] *Criminal Code* (Cth) Div 101-103; *Criminal Code* (Cth) Div 104-105; and *Australian Security Intelligence Organisation Act 1979* (Cth) Pt II, Div 3.

[4] This is not to say that lawyers are completely unable to make these arguments, see: Christopher Michaelsen, "Antiterrorism Legislation in Australia: A Proportionate Response to the Terrorist Threat?" *Studies in Conflict & Terrorism* 28 (2005), 321.

[5] This is not to dispute the case which can be made for a long history of terrorism acts on Australian soil (see Stuart Koschade, "Constructing a Historical Framework of Terrorism in Australia: From the Fenian Brotherhood to Twenty-First Century Islamic Extremism," *Journal of Policing, Intelligence and Counter Terrorism* 2 (2007): 54) but even so, major attacks upon the civilian population are largely unknown in this country.

[6] See particularly, David Bonner, *Executive Measures, Terrorism and National Security—Have the Rules of the Game Changed?* (Aldershot: Ashgate, 2007); Laura K Donohue, *The Cost of Counterterrorism—Power, Politics, and Liberty* (New York: Cambridge University Press, 2008); Conor Gearty, "11 September 2001, Counter-Terrorism and the Human Rights Act," *Journal of Law and Society 32 (2005),* 18; Clive Walker, *Blackstone's Guide to the Anti-Terrorism Legislation* (Oxford: Oxford University Press, 2002).

[7] Two very useful works of this sort are Laura K Donohue, *Counter-Terrorist Law and Emergency Powers in the United Kingdom 1922-2000* (Ballsbridge: Irish Academic Press, 2001); and Clive Walker, *The Prevention of Terrorism in British Law* (Manchester: Manchester University Press, 1986).

[8] Ibid; and David Bonner, *Emergency Powers in Peacetime* (London: Sweet & Maxwell, 1985).

[9] *Criminal Code Amendment (Terrorist Organisations) Act 2004* Sch 1, cl 1.

[10] This is particularly so in respect of *Criminal Code* (Cth) s 102.5; see Security Legislation Review Committee, *Review of Security and Counter-Terrorism Legislation* (2006), 117-118; Parliamentary Joint Committee on Intelligence and Security, Parliament of Australia, *Review of Security and Counter Terrorism Legislation* (2006), 74-75.

[11] *Criminal Code* (Cth) s 102.7; A full account of this incident is available in The Hon John Clarke QC, *Report of the Inquiry into the Case of Dr*

Mohamed Haneef (Canberra: Commonwealth of Australia, 2008). See also the discussion of the case in the chapter authored by Luke Howie in this book.

[12] *Criminal Code* (Cth) 102.3.

[13] *Criminal Code* (Cth) 102.8.

[14] Security Legislation Review Committee, n 10, 142.

[15] *Australian Communist Party v Commonwealth* (1951) 83 CLR 1.

[16] Under section 51(vi) of the Commonwealth Constitution, the Parliament has the "power to make laws for the peace, order, and good government of the Commonwealth with respect to the naval and military defence of the Commonwealth and of the several States, and the control of the forces to execute and maintain the laws of the Commonwealth."

[17] George Winterton, "The *Communist Party* Case" in *Australian Constitutional Landmarks* ed. HP Lee and George Winterton (Cambridge: Cambridge University Press, 2003), 108, 132-3.

[18] (1982) 151 CLR 342.

[19] (1951) 83 CLR 1, 187.

[20] Ibid, 193.

[21] *Kartinyeri v Commonwealth (Hindmarsh Island Bridge Case)* (1998) 195 CLR 337, 381.

[22] Parliamentary Joint Committee on Intelligence and Security, Parliament of Australia, *Inquiry into the proscription of "terrorist organisations" under the Australian Criminal Code* (2007), 44. The Security Legislation Review Committee was required to review the operation of the initial package of anti-terrorism laws by an amendment to Security Legislation Amendment (Terrorism) Bill 2002 (Cth) forced by the opposition parties. Its composition was statutorily prescribed.

[23] Security Legislation Review Committee, n 10, 99-100

[24] An excellent history of the origins and subsequent use of Part IIA is given in Roger Douglas, "Keeping the Revolution at Bay: The Unlawful Associations Provisions of the Commonwealth *Crimes Act*," *Adelaide Law Review* 22 (2001), 259.

[25] The only person to have been convicted of an offence under Part IIA is Harold Devanny who was acquitted on appeal: *R v Hush; Ex parte Devanny* (1932) 48 CLR 487.

[26] Initially application could be made to the High Court or State Supreme Court. The power has reposed exclusively in the Federal Court since 1979.

[27] Douglas, "Keeping the Revolution at Bay," 24, 282 (fn 75).

[28] See Douglas, "Keeping the Revolution at Bay," 24.

[29] See "Australian Government response to PJCIS Inquiry into the proscription of terrorist organisations under the Australian Criminal Code—December 2008": http://www.ag.gov.au/www/agd/agd.nsf/Page/

Publications_AustralianGovernmentresponsetoPJCISInquiryintothepro-
scriptionofterroristorganisationsundertheAustralianCriminalCode,   December 2008. Cf. 21, Parliamentary Joint Committee on Intelligence and
Security, above n 29, 40.

[30] See Security Legislation Review Committee, above n 10, 64-65.

[31] Andrew Goldsmith, "Preparation for Terrorism: Catastrophic Risk
and Precautionary Criminal Law" in *Law and Liberty in the War on Terror*,
ed. Andrew Lynch, Edwina MacDonald and George Williams (Sydney:
Federation Press, 2007), 70-1.

[32] Stephen Sloan, "Foreword: Responding to the Threat" in *Networks,
Terrorism and Global Insurgency* ed. Robert J Bunker (Abingdon: Routledge,
2005), xxiv-xxv.

[33] For *Korematsu v United States* 323 US 214 (1944). See the cases of *Lloyd
v Wallach* (1915) 20 CLR 299; *Ex parte Walsh* [1942] ALR 359; and *Little v
Commonwealth* (1947) 75 CLR 94.

[34] *Al-Kateb v Godwin* (2004) 219 CLR 562, 588.

[35] *Al-Kateb v Godwin* (2004) 219 CLR 562, 620-22.

[36] The Act received royal assent on 20 October 1950 when Australian
troops were already fighting in the Korean war, but the Court did not regard the nation as being on a war footing: (1951) 83 CLR 1, 196 (Dixon J).

[37] Winterton, above n 16, 128-9.

[38]Commonwealth Criminal Code s 104.1. The expression "terrorist
act" is given a lengthy, multi-partite definition in s 100.1 of the Code.

[39] Prevention of Terrorism Act 2005 (UK) s 1(4).

[40]Commonwealth Criminal Code s 104.27.

[41] "Control order for protection: Ruddock" (28 August 2006), <http://
news.ninemsn.com.au/ article.aspx?id=125661&print=true> at 13 September 2007. The United Kingdom Court of Appeal echoed some agreement
with this when it recently pronounced that "a control order is only appropriate where the evidence is not sufficient to support a criminal charge."
Secretary of State for the Home Department v MB [2006] EWCA Civ 1140,
[53].

[42] See generally, Lucia Zedner, "Seeking Security by Eroding Rights:
The Side-stepping of Due Process," *Security and Human Rights* ed. Benja-
min J Goold and Liora Lazarus (Hart Publishing, Oxford 2007), 265.

[43] Thomas had trained in Afghanistan with al Qaeda before the 2001
terrorist attacks. He was detained by the Pakistan ISI and questioned by
that organization and the CIA before being formally interviewed by Australian authorities. He was charged under the Commonwealth Criminal
Code with terrorism offences over a year after his return to Australia in
2003. For a full account of the circumstances regarding Thomas' activities, court trials and then subjection to a control order, see Andrew Lynch,

"Maximising the Drama: "Jihad Jack," the Court of Appeal and the Australian Media," *Adelaide Law Review* 27 (2006), 311.

⁴⁴ Justice Hayne did, however, join Justice Kirby in dissent on the actual result of the case, those two Justices finding that the law breached the constitutional separation of judicial power.

⁴⁵ *Thomas v Mowbray* [2006] HCATrans 661 (6 December 2006).

⁴⁶ Ibid. In his judgment, Kirby J also noted: "Terrorism is not a new phenomenon. Conduct sharing features now associated with "terrorism" has occurred for centuries." He went on to cite the bombing at the Sydney Hilton Hotel during a Commonwealth Regional Heads of Government Meeting in 1978, and the government established review that followed it, as the clearest example of an instance that "terrorism" had been addressed by the Federal Government prior to the 2005 terrorism laws: *Thomas v Mowbray* [2007] HCA 33, [158].

⁴⁷ *Thomas v Mowbray* [2006] HCATrans 661.

⁴⁸ *Thomas v Mowbray* [2006] HCATrans 660. See also *Thomas v Mowbray* [2007] HCA 33, [422] (Hayne J).

⁴⁹ *Thomas v Mowbray* [2006] HCATrans 661.

⁵⁰ Ibid., Gummow J and Heydon J respectively. See also *Thomas v Mowbray* [2007] HCA 33, [436]-[437] (Hayne J).

⁵¹ (1951) 83 CLR 1, 194 (Dixon J). (1951) 83 CLR 1, 259 (Fullagar J).

⁵² *Thomas v Mowbray* [2007] HCA 33, [140]-[142].

⁵³ *Thomas v Mowbray* [2007] HCA 33, [583]. *Thomas v Mowbray* [2007] HCA 33, [589].

⁵⁴ Ibid; cf. [244] (Kirby J). This part of Callinan J's opinion echoes many of the comments he made in his delivery of the Sir John Latham Memorial Lecture on 3 May, 2005: IDF Callinan, "International Law and Australian Sovereignty" *Quadrant* (July-August 2005), 9.

⁵⁵ *Thomas v Mowbray* [2006] HCATrans 661.

⁵⁶ Ibid.

⁵⁷ *Thomas v Mowbray* [2007] HCATrans 76 (Mr David Bennett QC). Kirby J quoted these factors in his judgment, accepting that "[a]ll of these elements represented potential dangers to Australia's constitutional system which, in given circumstances, this country would be entitled to protect and defend itself from": *Thomas v Mowbray* [2007] HCA 33, [253]-[254]. However, His Honour concluded (in dissent) that the measures in Division 104 cannot be supported by the defence power: [266]-[267].

⁵⁸ *Thomas v Mowbray* [2007] HCA 33, [241]-[243].

⁵⁹ See Ben Golder and George Williams, "What is "Terrorism"? Problems of Legal Definition" *University of New South Wales Law Journal* 27 (2004), 270.

⁶⁰ *Thomas v Mowbray* [2006] HCATrans 660.

[61] *R v F* [2007] 3 WLR 164.

[62] Lord Alex Carlile, *The Definition of Terrorism* (2007), 43-45.

[63] Simon Jeffrey, "Q&A: the glorification of terrorism," *Guardian Unlimited*, 2006, http://politics.guardian.co.uk/terrorism/story/0,,1710371,00.html (accessed 13 September 2007).

[64] George Jones, "MPs attack "vague" law of glorification," *Daily Telegraph* (London), 16 February 2006, 4. Alan Travis and Rosie Cowan, "Anti-Terror Laws: Clarke's draft bill proposes new offence of glorification," *The Guardian*, 16 September 2005, 4

[65] Simon Jenkins, "This is an act of censorship worthy of Joseph Goebbels," *The Guardian*, 23 September 2005, 32.

[66] *Terrorism Act 2006* (UK) s 1.

[67] *Criminal Code* (Cth) s 102.1.

[68] *Classification (Publications, Films and Computer Games) Amendment (Terrorist Material) Act 2007*. Security Legislation Review Committee, above n 10, 73; Parliamentary Joint Committee on Intelligence and Security, above n 10, 71; Senate Standing Committee on Legal and Constitutional Affairs, Parliament of Australia, *Report on Classification (Publications, Films and Computer Games) Amendment (Terrorist Material) Bill 2007 [Provisions]* (2007) 16.

[69] The law merely says that "a publication, film or computer game does not advocate the doing of a terrorist act if it depicts or describes a terrorist act, but the depiction or description could reasonably be considered to be done merely as part of public discussion or debate or as entertainment or satire": *Classification (Publications, Films and Computer Games) Act 1995* (Cth), s 9A.

14

Australian Regional Strategy, Terrorism, and the Risk of Asymmetric Warfare

Wayne Reynolds

Robert Engell was perplexed by Iraq: "Powerful actors have failed to achieve their objectives against weaker opponents." Shock and awe had taken the battlefield in minimal time but the Americans had failed to win the peace. To Engell the Iraq conflict was not explained by the war on terror but was symptomatic of the strategic context since the end of the Cold War—"the conflicts of the new millennium seem ever more bewildering, complex and asymmetric."[1]

It is the contention in this paper that the global "war on terror" is very much a part of the strategic realignment of the United States after the Cold War. The resultant activism displayed by Australia, especially under Howard, has focused largely on the threat posed by international terrorists. A focus on September 11 and al Qaeda, however, provides only a partial understanding of the transformation that is shaping the security environment in the region.

Terrorism has been a minor problem within Australia. In 1979, Justice Hope could conclude that Australia was protected by its geography and "fortunate in not having disaffected domestic political or separatist groups who resort to terrorism." Jenny Hocking noted over a decade later that Australia had developed a "comprehensive strategy of domestic counter-terrorism" but there was still considerable ambiguity about the understanding of terrorism.[2] The Bali bombing in 2002 removed any such ambiguity. Large numbers of Australians were killed and the intelligence service was found to be wanting. It had been too narrowly focused on the domestic scene.

The struggle against terrorism is a largely a regional one, but the dimensions of the threat and the means of combating it, require a much broader assessment of the security picture. Much Australian defense planning has long assumed that major threats are conventional and have come from states. To the extent that there is a debate historically, it has been about the relative merits of continental defense as opposed to forward defense. The war on terror provides another chapter in that broader debate. This paper will argue that regional strategy has long been based on the assumption that Australia was a "Principal" and that it should have a leadership role in any security structures. Defense planning to 2015, as one group of analysts wrote in the year that General Cosgrove led Australian troops into East Timor, was based on "Maintaining the Strategic Edge."[3] It is a question of how that is done. Putting boots on the ground in the region and moving to embrace the notion of "military operations other than war" could distort defense preparedness. The "war on terror," like Vietnam, could embroil Australia in an asymmetric conflict.

US post-Cold War policy

There has been too much emphasis on the revolutionary nature of the new threats. Huntington, for example, has raised serious questions about the clash of cultures and this in turn has refocused debate on the issue of failed states.[4] There has been much discussion herein about the end of the Westphalian system itself. Some have seen a clear link between globalization and fragmentation.[5] The nature of peacekeeping operations have accordingly come into sharp focus with calls to address the horrors of the 1990s in Rwanda, Somalia and the former Yugoslavia, which have led to a demand for intervention by the world community to address the conflicts within states from which spring potential terrorist threats.[6]

It is important, however, to place the terrorist threat into the context of US strategy. Traditionally terrorism as a threat has ranked well below nuclear and conventional threats. While there have been threats from non-state actors in the past, they have been seen as problems to be dealt with by police or the intelligence services. Indeed a feature of American planning before Vietnam was the assumption that air power and the possible use of tactical nuclear weapons would overwhelm a Chinese or North Vietnamese conventional attack.[7] Whatever the lessons of Vietnam were, a departure from this defense thinking was not one of them.

Global strategy and conventional conflict are, arguably, the proximate causes of the current terrorist threat. George Friedman, the founder of the Statfor intelligence company, summed up the American dilemma in Iraq by suggesting that "The US held the most valuable geography in the Middle East, but the forces there were too busy defending themselves from guerrillas to be in a position to threaten neighbouring countries."[8] Terrorism here is a reaction, geographically located, to American strategy. That strategy pre-dated September 11 by over a decade.[9] The dramatic collapse of the Warsaw Pact after 1989 presented historic opportunities for the United States to "shape" the strategic environment.[10] The objectives of the new US strategy were the promotion of rapid globalization and the identification of potential threats to the process.[11] To Defense Secretary William J. Perry, the US would need to adopt a form of "preventative defense," a means of projecting military power ashore in an attempt to defend US interests.[12] This thinking was reflected in the American Quadrennial Defense Reviews either side of 9/11 which assumed that any threat to American interests abroad would have to be "asymmetric." There would be no peer competitor facing the United States until well after 2010. Therefore the adjustments to American strategy not only predicted asymmetric threats by rogue states and terrorist groups but also identified the area that such a problem would arise. To Stephen J. Flanagan, a former staffer in the National Security Council, the objective of US strategy would be to focus on an area stretching from the Middle East to South Asia. In this "southern arc" the US could expect to face "powerful asymmetrical threats" from a diverse set of regional players who were essentially those left out of the new global order — Iran and Iraq.[13]

There would be little to be expected from the UN which had its peacekeeping role premised on "strategic consent among the disputants about the role of the intervening force."[14] The UN was simply not suited to coping with the many complex challenges posed by a rapidly globalizing world, and one in which there was one superpower. It would fall to the US to refashion NATO as a global partner and to convince important regional allies to "begin blending their security policies and defense planning" with those of the Pentagon.[15] To that end NATO, on its fiftieth anniversary in 1999, was tasked with conducting missions beyond Europe. The arrangement was sealed at the Washington Summit that year with the initiation of the NATO Defense capabilities Initiative.[16] There was, in short, a call for a "global NATO," something that was to become a reality four years later when the organization intervened in Afghanistan as part of George W. Bush's war against terror.[17]

The focus on terrorist threat in the aftermath of 9/11 has confused the debate about the forms of response to it. It was American strategy to shape the global strategic environment and to focus on the arc of instability that determined the course of action pursued by the Clinton and Bush Administrations. The likely nuclear and terrorist responses were factored in as rational reactions to that strategy.[18] Intelligence was held hostage to a strategy. There was indeed confusion even before the war started. Scott Ritter wrote scathingly about the goals of US intelligence when UNSCOM inspections were pressured to focus not on WMD targets but on those to do with regime change. Presidential palaces contained Baathists, not WMDs.[19]

The war on terror is now a reality in Iraq but it was one that arose from planning to wage conventional a conflict, albeit one that was a case study of the Revolution in Military Affairs (RMA). The problem was that it did not prepare for what Marine General Charles Kulak calls the "three bloc war" — high intensity combat together with low intensity peacekeeping and humanitarian assistance.[20] Belatedly, General Petraeus and Frederick Kagan, key proponents of the recent troop "surge," looked to the behavior of another empire. Britain had fought an insurgency in Malaya but called it an "Emergency." But empires, as John Keay reminds us, are about division and chaos. British hegemony in the Middle East was not without many examples of gross mismanagement.[21] No one in Washington is talking about a change to grand strategy. The 2004 RAND study on the future security of the Middle East noted that

> The discussion of asymmetric war is largely a product of the 1991 Gulf War, but it has many historical antecedents and is embedded in the process of strategic innovation. Asymmetric conflict has been a frequent occurrence in the Middle East. The wars of decolonization were essentially asymmetric, pitting insurgent forces against conventional armies.[22]

The current "surge" in Iraq is about winning the neighborhood and the insurgent action is coming largely from forces within the neighborhood. Here lies a key problem in the assessment of terrorism: the United States has stressed the global nature of the al Qaeda threat.[23] The question is whether a terrorist threat in Australia's neighborhood draws inspiration from an international challenge mounted by al Qaeda. Rohan Gunaratna has been the leading advocate of this thesis. Ironically Gunaratna is a native of Sri Lanka, a state with an enduring secessionist struggle. But his work on al Qaeda has squarely put the focus on the "global network of terror," re-releasing his 2002 in 2005 to include a "post-Bali preface and comprehensive details of Jemaah Islamiyah's infiltration of our region."[24] In similar vein Sally Neighbour's award-winning work sought to study "the trail of terrorism from Afghanistan to Australia."[25] Zachary Abuza too saw a problem with the spread of "militant Islam" in the region, while Alan Dupont noted that in the 2003 defense review the "real threats" were not from conventional actors but largely from "strategic terrorism" and that Australian security interests were not "determined by geography."[26] Former ASIO head Dennis Richardson stressed, as he took on the post as Australian's ambassador in Washington, that it "was a mistake to compartmentalize attacks in Bali, London and elsewhere without recognizing the growing common global links between them."[27]

In seeking partners in that struggle, the US may become hostage to complex and intractable conflicts which are regional, based on local grievances, and involve state actors. The cases of the Islamic insurgencies in Chechnya and Palestine come to mind. Despite being caught without major allies in Vietnam, US strategy through the Cold War was to avoid being drawn into asymmetric conflicts. The use of terrorist violence to meet national objectives has been the subject of a recent study by the Indian hawk Brahma Chellaney. Chellaney opines that Pakistan has used jihad "as a relatively cheap way" to keep Indian forces tied down in Kashmir but that counter-terrorism emerged as an "important platform for strategic coopera-tion" between India and the United States." For Chellaney the "les-son is to not turn the war against terrorism into an ideological battle to serve one's strategic interests."[28] The question here is whether the question had occurred to anyone in Canberra.

Australian regional planning and defense policy

Unlike India, Australia has benefited by an alliance with the sole superpower after the collapse of the Soviet Union. The war on ter-ror, however, according to Rod Lyon of Australian Strategic Policy Institute, will see a need for allies to "behave more proactively than they did in the Cold War."[29] But the war on terror, or the war on al Qaeda, has also presented a historic opportunity to engage Ameri-can power directly into the "arc of instability" to Australia's north. Australian policy-makers have long debated the balance of prepar-ing expeditionary forces for coalition warfare and the forces for re-gional defense. Contemporary Australian strategy faces a similar dilemma — defense preparation is based on a possible deployment in the Middle East as well as the region. The modern iteration of this dual policy was declared by Howard in October 2006: "Quit Iraq and you hand victory to Jemaah Islamiah."[30]

Australia has predictably embraced American strategy with respect to the war on terror. American threats have become Aus-tralian threats in all forms of that war. Australia will play a role in the conduct of American Eurasian strategy with earmarked forces for the Middle East; it will continue to play a major role in nuclear non-proliferation through the Proliferation Security Initiative, the Global Nuclear Energy Partnership and missile defense, and in the war on terror. The question is not how Australia will fight al Qaeda in the region. The question is one of what is Australia's regional policy. Here one can assume that despite the change of government in December 2007 the broad directions of policy since 1941 will remain.

There are historic opportunities now to extend ANZUS and UKUSA and to explore the dimensions of a trade agreement that gives access to North American Free Trade Area. And there are opportunities to bring powerful allies into Australia's backyard.

Historically, Australia—mindful that the Anglo-American alliance prioritized northern adversaries—embraced a regional doctrine of engaging the strategic "arc of islands" that circle Australia's long coastline to the north.[31] Possession of key bases from Cocos to the New Hebrides was demanded and Australia asserted its rights as a "Principal" in any discussions affecting the area. The proposition that Australia should take a lead in regional security goes back to the original conception of Australasia. The notion was regional and embraced a large area of the South West Pacific. In fact, the British gave it an exact location in latitude and longitude.[32] Before Federation there was talk of an Australian "Monroe Doctrine." By World War II Australia's first bilateral treaty, the Australia-New Zealand Agreement or "ANZAC Pact," enshrined the proposition that the South Pacific Dominions were "principal powers" in the region. Evatt even secured amendment of the UN charter to ensure that "regional enforcement action" was a key function of the World Organization's security function. By 1948 Australia's key defense arrangement, albeit one ignored by historians, ANZAM, was put in place. ANZAM, the British Commonwealth defense arrangement, recognized Australian regional leadership in any future war.[33]

The concept of a strategic arc was largely abandoned, however, by the failure to engage British or American support throughout the Cold War.[34] The Timor deployment in 1999 was a watershed in Australian regional strategy but it also occurred as American thinking on the role of its key allies crystallized at the Washington NATO Summit the same year.[35] Allies here were to be encouraged to adopt a new strategic concept that would see their forces operate with those of the US well beyond their traditional borders. Such forces would operate pre-emptively employing technologies produced by the Revolution in Military Affairs. So armed, they would be, as Kugler saw it, "reconfigured as regional hubs for power projection."[36] And where were these "regional hubs"? Senator John McCain's former national security adviser, Anthony Cordesman, identified the "core partners" to be NATO, Japan, Australia, Canada, South Korea, Egypt, Britain and Saudi Arabia.[37] John Bolton would later call for Australia to join NATO, an idea that proved most attractive to Downer.[38]

Australia might have shared in the so-called intelligence failure with respect to the decision to invade Iraq, but if history is any guide, Australia's intelligence was sound. Policy in Canberra was based on United States strategy and good intelligence was about understanding that strategy. Former ASIS officer, Warren Reed, here argued that the decision to invade Iraq was based on American Eurasian strategy and it was one in which "intelligence has played the role of handmaiden to policy."[39] Andrew Willkie, a former analyst with the Office of National Assessments, even suggested that the British and Australians "needed to treat the US more as a focus of intelligence" and that it was "no accident that the National Security Council of Cabinet in Australia included the US in its National Foreign Intelligence Assessment Priorities."[40]

It is not a new predicament for Australian policy makers. Spender, Australia's ambassador to Washington in the 1950s, spent considerable effort studying US grand strategy. In a lengthy analysis written on Christmas Eve 1957, a crucial time in the evolution of Western nuclear strategy, he cabled Canberra that:

> It is my belief that the question of limited wars is likely to be the one which in practice will be most critical for countries such as Australia. Unfortunately there is even more obscurity in this field than in regard to global strategy…it was conceivable that political conditions in Asia might make it necessary for the US to avoid the use of tactical nuclear weapons.[41]

Spender was in front of the game, and his dilemma is not without relevance now. Following US grand strategy in the post-Cold War world is not surprising given the historic strength of the alliance. The question now is whether Australia is going back to older strategic assumptions, such as those before 1962, about regional security.[42] The answers go the core of the so-called war on terror.

Much has been written about the global threat posed by al Qaeda, but it raises the question of whether the war on terror is really a global one or whether it is ultimately reducible to a number of regional conflicts. Following the October 2002 Bali attacks, Secretary of State Colin Powell, immediately called for Australia to "stay the course in its global war on terrorism." The same day the *Australian* ran the headline "Bin Laden bankrolled Bashir CIA told."[43] Zachary Abuza reported within six weeks that "almost every Southeast Asian terrorist group fought in Afghanistan in the 1980's."[44]

Yet in October 2005, when there was another explosion in Bali, the assessment had shifted. Few agreed with former president Abdurrahman Wahid that elements of the TNI or Indonesian army were involved in the first Bali attack but there was now a concession that the threat may have been the work of local factors. Bruce Hoffman from RAND explained that since 2001 al Qaeda had "mutated" into four hierarchical levels from with a "loose al-Qa'ida network" in various regions.[45] Australian journalist Paul McGeough had observed this transformation in the parent conflict in Iraq itself where "The notion of a bin Laden chain of command has been superseded by a sort of McDonald's of terrorism franchise."[46] Peter Alford concluded from his study on the Islamic-based insurgency in the Southern Philippines that the insurgency was an "essentially local and grass roots affair."[47]

What was clear was that Indonesia did not seem to take the threat seriously enough. Indeed there were doubts from the beginning. After September 11, Harold Crouch argued that Indonesian terror groups, such as Laskar Jihad or the Front to Defend Islam, lacked sophisticated networks.[48] Kirsten E. Schulze saw Laskar Jihad as a product of "a very specific Indonesian situation—the conflict in Ambon."[49] Clive Williams too argued after Bali 2002 that Megawati had been "in denial about terrorism except where it can be used as an excuse for cracking down on separatists."[50]

The Australian reaction to the terrorist attacks, by contrast, was both decisive and followed the American script. The Australian Federal Police and ASIO were sent to Bali in 2002, and friends in APEC and the World Bank were brought on board to press Indonesia to crack down on terrorism. In early 2004, Australia moved to establish the "regional flying squads" from the Federal Police and to promote the new Indonesian Centre for Law Enforcement and Cooperation with the Indonesian police, which had been separated from the military in 1998.[51] These were pragmatic measures but were undertaken against a stubborn refusal by the Howard Government to sign the ASEAN 1976 Treaty of Amity and Co-operation, which had embodied ASEAN's commitment to nonaggression. Behind this declaratory policy was a concern that Australia would be surrendering its "justified intervention" in Timor, as former defense analyst Peter Jennings saw it.[52] Paul Dibb also pointed to the danger of signing a regional security pact "for the first time in our history" that did not include the United States.[53] But American support was never in doubt. Howard was in Washington when a second deployment of troops was sent Dili. He briefed US Defense Secretary Donald Rumsfeld and Secretary of State Condoleezza Rice stating that Canberra "must take the lead in dealing with political instability in…the arc of instability."[54] The language paralleled that of US planners, but it also harked back to a much older Australian policy.

It is the latter that may well explain the fear in Jakarta that Australian regional policy is predicated on the dismemberment of Indonesia.[55] Greg Sheridan wrote in April 2006 that "East Timor and Papua New Guinea are independent nations but they are really military protectorates…the Indonesian military could easily create vast trouble on the borders of those nations, leading their governments to request our military help. This would be a diabolical mess for Australia."[56]

The relationship with Indonesia was the centerpiece of Australian regional strategy during the Cold War and it was one that was underpinned, after the West New Guinea crisis before 1962, by American thinking on regional security. The post-Cold War period, and the American strategic realignment, has seen an emergence of significant problems for Indonesia. Globalization and the push to introduce Western business practices was very much a part of the 1997 Asian financial crisis, which was particularly severe in Indonesia.[57] Globalization also brought with it the possibility of fragmentation.[58] There was inevitably speculation, following the fate of Yugoslavia, about the fate of Indonesia. The new global order swept away Suharto and installed a number of non-military, and spectacularly unsuccessful, leaders. It also threatened dismemberment with secessionist struggles intensifying particularly in the eastern archipelago—the Moluccas, West Papua and East Timor.

Here the strategic interests of Indonesia and Australia intersect. Canberra's interest in the eastern archipelago was dramatically influenced by the Pacific War. The occupation of the inner arc of islands from Timor, Ambon, New Guinea, and New Caledonia in 1941, was based on an assessment that this barrier was crucial in the event that the Singapore base was lost. In September 1943, the Naval Intelligence Division argued, in an assessment that was to endure well beyond the Second World War, that Bacau airfield in Portuguese Timor, was a crucial possession for Australia, from which offensive air power could control the eastern archipelago as well as provide a defensive screen for the mainland.[59] The Joint Planning Committee reported in June 1945 that "the screen of islands to the north and north-east in enemy hands would constitute a threat to her safety." The committee also concluded, in a script that could have been written for INTERFET [International Force for East Timor] in 1999, that Australia "would need forces capable of amphibious operations to eject an enemy which may obtain lodgement in our northern defense area."[60]

Similar assessments were trotted out thereafter. In 1974, during the lead up to the invasion the following year, the Joint Intelligence Organisation (JIO) pointed to the views of some in Defence that an independent Timor would ensure military access in the event of pressure being exerted by Indonesia. Timor would act to shield the North West approached to Australia in much the same way as Papua shielded the North East. Moreover the base would act as a "significant counter-threat to Indonesian forces and lines of communication in Eastern Indonesia."[61]

The strategic role of Timor has been dramatically enhanced since, with the further development of the North West Shelf energy resources and the changes to Australian regional defense strategy.[62] It is an interesting coincidence that Australia started to develop the North West Shelf at the same time as the Guam Doctrine. This focused thinking in the post-Vietnam era and was to lead to the blueprint laid out in the Hawke period. The focus of interest in the Dibb Report has been on the defense of Australia's northern approaches.

The dominance of sea and air assets in the gap in the island screen in the north western approaches was the centerpiece of this thinking. But the forces that could deny the approaches to Darwin could also be used offensively. The dominance of air and sea assets could be fatal to an island nation like Indonesia. Later Kim Beasley would posit, in his own version of pre-emption, a naval role to combat terrorism and piracy in the archipelago.[63]

Timor was only part of the story. There is a strong suspicion that the former Dutch province of "Eastern Indonesia" and certainly West New Guinea were designed to lay the foundations for a separate state after independence.[64] Evatt had promoted Australia's leading role as a trustee power which was well placed to play an active part in the administration of colonial territories in the region at the end of the Pacific War. Nearly a decade after Indonesian independence, Cabinet received a joint External Affairs and Defence submission from R.G. Casey and Phillip McBride, arguing that Australia should oppose any trusteeship in West New Guinea which had a

> strong Asian element...Christian influence, particularly in education, might be replaced in the West by Islamic teachers. This would help to attract the whole territory towards Asia and away from the South Pacific.[65]

Given the pressure for secession by the South Moluccan Christians, especially on Ambon, and the links between West New Guinea and the islands to the West, there was every chance that rebellion in these islands would yet deliver them to the Australian "arc of islands" strategy. During the outer islands rebellion in 1957, External Affairs Minister R.G. Casey raised the issue with CIA director Allen Dulles of "whether separatism should be deliberately encouraged."[66] Washington may well have entertained fragmentation to 1957, but advised Casey that there would be better mileage in grooming the Officer Corps.

It has become fashionable now to question the nature of Indonesian power and even to ask whether the territorial limits inherited from the Dutch and Portuguese are appropriate. George Aditjondro's "brilliant formula," in Peter King's assessment, is that

Australia should "relate to the archipelago" rather than to the Indonesian state.[67] Clinton Fernandes takes this further and argues that the formation of a number of smaller states in the archipelago along ethnic and religious lines "would not be contrary to the interests of most Australians."[68]

That the state has endured as a single entity has been largely the product of the Cold War. As long as Indonesia was seen as a shield against Chinese aggression, as was the case with a unified Yugoslavia on the borders of the Soviet Bloc, there was an interest in keeping it intact.[69] Significantly, the strategic assessments of Portuguese Timor in 1975 presupposed the need to retain Indonesian friendship. A careful reading of those assessments reveal, however, if that factor is set aside, then there were significant benefits in a strategic partnership between Australia and an independent Timor—especially in the event that force was to be projected into the region.[70]

Peter Hartcher opined in June 2006 that Australia "had acquired an accidental empire...It is not an empire of deliberate Australian expansionism but of failing state implosion." In so doing, he argued, the US was "only too happy" to see Australia take responsibility in a zone that was not of primary strategic importance.[71] The reasons for the historic intervention into Timor have become the source of heated speculation, but the step was one which had immense strategic implications. Timor was historically a part of the island screen and now Howard revived the language of the arc but with the addendum of "instability." It was not a far cry from Evatt's original justification for Australian pre-eminence. Indeed the move into Timor was followed by an active Australian role in the entire screen. New Guinea, the Solomon Islands and Vanuatu were all to be the focus of a much more intrusive interest from Canberra.

The Howard Government has not changed the developing strategic posture in the region—it had long underpinned Australian strategy. What Howard did, however, is use American strategic principles in a regional setting. Pointedly, the appeal from Canberra was not to multilateral action but to the American National Security doctrine of pre-emption. Australia's right to act here was as a "Principal" in the region. Intervention need not be secured through the United Nations under Chapter VIII. He would also forgo signature of the ASEAN Treaty of Amity and Co-operation at the 2004 summit in Laos, which had enshrined the proposition that states did not interfere with matters of domestic jurisdiction.[72]

What has been arguably more significant is the capability that lies behind the Australian rhetoric. The *Defence White Paper* of 2000 foreshadowed a major increase in spending, even though Australia then spent much more on defense than any other state in the region, and one which would provide Canberra with a dramatically enhanced capability to intervene in the island screen. But there was a clear choice in how this would be done. In discussing "Military Operations Other than War" the white paper noted that

> If it is judged that we are likely to be drawn into more low intensity land operations, we need to invest in appropriate capabilities...Whatever the approach taken (defence or regional security), it is clear that an enhanced peacekeeping capability would involve greater resources.[73]

Seven years later the broad outlines of the response were becoming clearer. The 2007 budget allocated defense $22 billion, the biggest since Vietnam and by far the biggest in Southeast Asia. Interoperability and force projection were center stage. Air warfare destroyers would play a part in global nuclear strategy. Abrams tanks and an expanded army would be provided with significant lift capabilities by air and sea.[74]

Greg Sheridan argues that the development of the defense force was largely influenced by the intervention of INTERFET into East Timor in 1999, which had "jolted" the Howard Government out of its acceptance of the "narrow continental defence" doctrine that had been developed under Beasley.[75] But Sheridan overplays the lack of preparedness in 1999. Clinton Fernandes argues that Indonesia's military co-operation in Timor was partly secured by Australian naval superiority, which hunted Indonesian T-209 submarines deployed in the path of INTERFET, and air power, which was "ready to knock out communications as far as TNI headquarters on the outskirts of Jakarta if necessary."[76] To underline this capability, in December 2003 Australian Air Chief Houston stressed a need for "small strike bombers" which could carry the longer ranger American Joint Air to Surface Standoff Missile (JASSM). The *Australian* rightly pointed to this triggering Indonesia's long fears about the potential role of the nuclear capable *FIII* in delivering a strategic strike.[77] To add to Jakarta's concerns, Australia had committed to the American missile defense system, a step which could "destabilise the region."[78] Below that air power came the boots on the ground. In early August 2006 Howard announced a major expansion of the AFP International Deployment Group and the establishment of two additional battalions. Hugh White said that it all indicated that "Howard has transformed the army into an instrument of his policy of engagement in Australia's neighbourhood."[79]

The question that arises here is Indonesia's response to Australia's regional assertiveness and the role that terrorism plays in that response. Not surprisingly Indonesia has pursued asymmetric strategies in its military planning since independence. Robert Lowry reasons that this is the result of experience with external threats by larger powers, the Dutch, Japanese and the British. It is also a pragmatic response to having insufficient resources and an extensive archipelago.[80] During the Confrontation with Malaysia in 1964 and 1965, Sukarno employed both asymmetric strategies in the face of overwhelming force from Britain. Pointedly the British threatened the use of nuclear weapons, deployed aircraft carriers with naval support ships in the Sunda Strait, and prepared plans such as *Addington* to deliver a massive air strike. In the circumstances it was not surprising that Sukarno talked up Indonesian attempts to acquire nuclear weapons. But the actual conflict came down to largely to small-scale military attacks in remote border areas of Kalimantan. Today the Indonesians cannot realistically in the short term counter Australian force projections, especially when such forces are supported by American power. The structure of the army would suggest a reliance on asymmetric warfare and a dependence on local militia, especially where the conflict is essentially sectarian or separatist. Some would see such forces as crossing the line to terrorism.

The intervention in Timor has altered the strategic calculus in eastern Indonesia and the intractable problems in West Papua could result in conflict with little notice. On the eve of Australia's intervention in 1999, Gary Klintworth, a former advisor to the DIO, argued that a united Indonesian archipelago had been seen as a bulwark but it had "always been an unrealistic goal because Indonesia can never be cohesive and stable while it tries to hold on to West Irian, East Timor and Aceh."[81] ASPI Program Director, Peter Jennings, argued that "the biggest cause of Indonesian terrorist opposition to Australia is the leading role we played in liberating Timor in 1999."[82] Paul Kelly was more circumspect but conceded that "East Timor constitutes a new challenge for Australia as a regional power."[83] Paul Keating has no doubts about the issues at stake. He conceded that the administration in Timor was largely in the hands of the military and that it ruled with "insensitivity, brutality and incompetence," but "I was not prepared to make the whole of our complex relationship with 210 million people subject to this one issue."[84]

Damien Kingsbury has documented the factious nature of the armed forces, especially after the accession of Habibie when the "Red and White" faction of ABRI displaced officers loyal to Suharto. He argues that "elements of TNI" then orchestrated violence in Timor "against the explicit wishes of President Habibie."[85] Others assert that there are not only links but that they go to the center of power. John Martinkus writes that the army's elite Kostrad and Koppassus have been involved in bombings and that the Bali bombings of October 2002 could have been perpetrated by Indonesian military intelligence. That claim has been supported by former President Abdurrahman Wahid. Indonesia military intelligence had also penetrated JI, a factor that suggests that it must have been aware of, and possibly complicit in, the Christmas bombings which occurred across the archipelago in 2000—the year following the Timor intervention.[86]

Others believe that sections of the military are involved in terrorist acts but that this is due not to any central command, but rather the lack of it. Alan Dupont argues that decentralization of political and economic power in post-Suharto Indonesia has "reduced Jakarta's control over the activities of the military in general, and Kopassus in particular."[87]

The jury is still out on the fate of post-Soeharto Indonesia. Military rule has endured throughout most of the Cold War and yet after a succession of popularly elected Presidents from across the political spectrum, Indonesians turned to a general, and one with a reputation of Megawati's security minister of being tough on secessionists. "Reformasi" has not removed, as Kevin O'Rourke put it, "the entrenched interests that have blocked democratisation and the rule of law thus far."[88]

Where to from here?

The United States crossed a strategic threshold in 2003 when it invaded Iraq. The move had implications for American global strategy but it also brought in its wake a major insurgency. Significantly the conflict was not one simply of combating terrorism. The invasion was conventional and justified in the name of nuclear counter-proliferation by rogue states.

Australia did not cross a threshold in 2003 when it joined the United States in Iraq. The dispatch of Australian expeditionary forces to that region in support of major allies underlies history since Federation. In the case of Suez in 1956, diplomatic support was given in defiance of world opinion.[89] The threshold that was crossed was in 1999 with the intervention in Portuguese Timor.[90] Significantly, the forces that were dispatched were ready to engage in a conventional conflict with forces that were actively assisted by Indonesian military forces.

There is no gainsaying the strategic significance of the event in Jakarta's eyes— casting Australian regional strategy in terms of engaging "an arc of instability" or having a right of pre-emption in the war on terror plays on Indonesian fears. Sending troops to Timor as a national, as opposed to a UN, contribution has a potentially similar effect. There is, to be sure, a problem that in the past the various UN agencies have lacked the force to deal with such messy internal conflicts. There has also been a failure by ASEAN to act, at least until recently.[91] The challenge though is to persevere with UN action under Chapter VIII as an important part of regional planning. It was to this end that Australia strengthened the UN charter to allow for regional initiatives such as the launching of the South Pacific Commission, the precursor of the current organization that has proved to be so valuable in supporting the intervention in the Solomon Islands.[92] Australia has long assumed a leading role in UN initiatives in trusteeship. Indeed it was through the Trusteeship Council that Evatt attacked the colonial record of the Dutch and

Portuguese. Australia has also assumed the seat on the IAEA Board of Governors as the leading nuclear power in the region. From this position it can help to oversee the orderly development of nuclear power for peaceful purposes and to monitor non-proliferation, especially in Indonesia.[93]

The key approach in the arc of islands will be to pursue "Military Operations Other than War." Conflict may be anticipated but lasting stability will come from a much more comprehensive engagement.[94] To that end, the use of federal police will be crucial, although Indonesians will recall with justifiable bitterness that Dutch anti-insurgency operations in the 1940s were called "Police Actions." An active diplomacy is also crucial, bilateral as well as multilateral. Michael Wesley has recently written that Howard has had surprising success pursuing a low key and essentially bilateral diplomacy, but the refusal to sign TAC on the basis on US alliance commitments was damaging.[95] As it turned out, the fact that US allies South Korea and Japan signed TAC provided a way forward.

Indeed the latter relationship will be crucial. In the late 1990s, Japan was brought into the American attempt to increase the defense capability of allies, especially in NATO, to ensure greater scope for joint operations. Today the Trilateral Security Dialogue with Australia and the United States has provided a framework for coordinating the security interests of the three. Herein, the Japanese, with US encouragement, have developed a formidable force projection capability. Its navy of over 200 vessels is the second biggest in the Pacific.[96] Australia has predictably encouraged Japanese activity in the region. Indeed, this had been foreshadowed by Gareth Evan's initiative in securing Japanese help in ending the Cambodia conflict in the late 1980s.[97]

It is hard then to see how Indonesia can do anything other than go along with the prevailing trends in the region at this time. It may voice concerns about the invasion of Iraq and the meddling of the West in its attempts to avoid declaring JI a terrorist organization, but the trilateral arrangements encompassed by APEC, and the security pacts with Japan and the United States, demand a level of caution on its part. The sullen restraint of the TNI during the historic Timor intervention was testimony to Jakarta's lack of strategic options.

The issue is one of balancing Australian defense policy with Indonesian sensitivities. Indeed it was a concern about regional attitudes that led Kim Beasley to reject a security treaty with Japan. The challenge now is that the doctrine and capability of force projection brings with it a need to embrace Indonesia. The recent security treaty falls short of a formal defense treaty but does provide for expanded military co-operation and intelligence-sharing. But there should be much more scope for comprehensive interaction across a number of areas. Australian universities, for example, could embrace something of the Colombo Plan thinking of the 1950s, when "shaping" of Asian attitudes in the early Cold War was seen as a crucial initiative.[98]

What then of defense policy? Gary Brown argues that the terrorist threat should be met by directing defense spending to a more robust preparation against strategic attacks against domestic targets.[99] But the terrorist threat is a regional one. The current expenditure on defense is not simply a reaction to terrorism. The capacity to project power, implicit in the INTERFET intervention in 1999, and explicit in the Defence White Paper the following year, was based ultimately on the ability to dominate the air and sea routes. It is this capability that would neutralize a conventional threat from Indonesia. Greg Sheridan has argued that Indonesia could make life difficult in New Guinea by prosecuting a low level insurgency, thereby tying down extensive military resources. This analysis ignores the history of such conflict and the interplay in the levels of conflict. In the confrontation, Sukarno adopted an asymmetric war strategy *because* of the conventional and nuclear superiority of his adversaries.[100] Forces were indeed needed to counter low-level threats, but plans such as *Addington* were in place to deliver a decapitating air assault against Indonesian command and control targets. The same assets today would allow an interdiction of movement from Java to Eastern Indonesia from Darwin and block staging through Baucau and Dili.

Asymmetric war has been a feature of conflict in Southeast Asia throughout the Cold War. There is no greater guide to the pitfalls of using concepts of global war and the techniques of modern conventional war to counter it than the engagement in Vietnam. But there are some verities that were then obvious and are still compelling.

First, there is the reality of American global power. The United States has made quite clear that globalization and power projection go hand in hand. What is significant is the strategic repositioning since the end of the Cold War. The American "arc of instability" stretches to Southeast Asia and the war on terror has led to an unprecedented engagement into the island screen to Australia's immediate north.

Second, Australia has long focused on security in the island screen to the north. It has also sought to maintain a strategic dominance in the region by possessing the most advanced weapons. The latter was the prize for regional engagement with major allies. The current debate on the merits of "capability planning" needs to focus on the interaction between global and regional policies. There is certainly something to be said for asking whether the assumption of a role as a regional hub, or John Howard's "US Deputy Sheriff," brings with it a danger that Australia might repeat the path to asymmetric conflict of the type waged in the Malayan Emergency and Vietnam.[101] The way in which Australia pursues the war on terror in the "arc of instability"—the Australian sub-section of the American arc—can trigger an asymmetric response from a threatened Indonesia. The controversies surrounding the RAMSI deployment raise questions of how force is projected and how the diplomatic situation handled. But engagement in the Solomon Islands will prove manageable. Indonesia is another matter.

The economic crisis of 1997 was a reminder just how fragile was the hold of Jakarta over the archipelago. Indonesia could yet become a case study in the downside of globalization-fragmentation. There is therefore every chance that conflict in the region could be asymmetric—whether the product of Jakarta's strategy, rogue elements in the military, or from separatist and jihadist forces. Australia has no option, therefore, in preparing for its own version of the three bloc war. The question is one of balance as thinking is put into how far an A$22 billion budget will go. But if Bali demonstrates anything it is that Australians are much more likely to die in the island to the north than on their own soil. The threat of terrorism is bound up with Australia's strategic choices that have long been evolving but have been given a significant boost since the end of the Cold War.

Notes

[1] Robert Engell, "Explaining US and British Performance in Complex Expeditionary Operations; Civil-Military Dimensions," *The Journal of Strategic Studies*, 29 (December 2006), 1042-43.

[2] Jenny Hocking, *Beyond Terrorism: The Development of the Australian Security Service*, (St. Leonards: Allen & Unwin, 1993), 123, 189.

[3] Desmond Ball, ed., *Maintaining the Strategic Edge: The Defence of Australia in 2015* (Canberra; Strategic and Defence Studies Centre, 1999).

[4] Samuel Huntington, *The Clash of Civilisations and the Remaking of World Order* (Sydney: Simon & Schuster, 1996).

[5] Ian Clark, *Globalisation and Fragmentation: International Relations in the Twenty-First Century* (Oxford: Oxford University Press, 1997).

[6] Alex J. Bellamy, Paul Williams and Stuart Griffin, *Understanding Peacekeeping* (Cambridge: Polity Press, 2004).

[7] Of the eight contingency plans developed by SEATO after March 1957, only three envisaged the sort of conflict that developed in Vietnam —and all of these came relatively late and in reaction to developments in the Sixties that had not been foreseen originally. Damien Marc Fenton, "SEATO and the Defence of Southeast Asia 1955-1965," PhD thesis, Australian Defence Force Academy, 2006, 144.

[8] George Friedman, *America's Secret War: Inside the hidden worldwide struggle between the United States and its Enemies* (London: Little and Brown, 2004), 334.

[9] Kenneth Pollack, from the Council of Foreign Relations, argued that "September 11 convinced many Americans that we needed to be more engaged in the world, to actively seek out threats and destroy them before they can strike us." *The Threatening Storm: The United States and Iraq: the crisis, the strategy, and the prospects after Saddam* (New York: Random House, 2002), xxiii.

[10] *The Global Century: Globalisation and National Security*, eds., Richard L. Kugler and Ellen L. Frost, Vol. 1 (Washington DC: National Defense University Press, June 2001), 4-5.

[11] Kugler, "Controlling Chaos: New Axial Strategic Principles," *Globalisation and National Security*, 872.

[12] Harlan K. Ullman, "Influencing Events Ashore," *Globalisation and National Security*, 502. Alfred Thayer Mahan had argued that modern states needed navies to ensure access to markets and raw materials, necessitating access to bases.

[13] Stephen J. Flanagan, "Meeting the Challenges of the Global Century," *Globalisation and National Security*, 24. See also Seymour J. Deitchman, "Military Power and Maritime Forces," 158.

[14] Michael J. Dziedzic, "Peace Operations: Political-Military Coordination," *Globalisation and National Security,* 318.

[15] Kugler, "Controlling Chaos: New Axial Strategic Principles," *Globalisation and National Security,* 100, 102.

[16] Robert E. Hunter, "Global Economics and Unsteady Regional Politics," *Globalisation and National Security,* 121.

[17] Alan K. Henriksen, "Beyond Global-Regional Thinking," *Globalisation and National Security,* 208. Kissinger cautioned that the United States was "in no better position to dictate the global agenda unilaterally than it was at the beginning of the Cold War." Power, moreover, had become much more "diffuse," a factor that required local allied cooperation. Henry Kissinger, *Diplomacy* (New York: Touchstone, 1994), 809.

[18] Friedman has rightly explained that a major failure of the US was to explain the connection between Iraq and the "broader war." *America's Secret War,* 331.

[19] Scott Ritter, *Iraq Confidential: The Untold Story of America's Intelligence Conspiracy* (New York: I.B. Taurus, 2005).

[20] Charles Kulak, "The Strategic Corporal: Leadership in the Three Bloc War," *Marines Magazine,* 28 (January 1999).

[21] Keay, *Sowing the Wind.*

[22] Nora Bensahel and Daniel L. Byman, *The Future Security Environment in the Middle East: Conflict, Stability and Political Change* (Santa Monica: RAND, 2004), 271.

[23] Derek D. Smith, *Deterring America: Rogue States and the Proliferation of Weapons of Mass Destruction* (Cambridge: Cambridge University Press, 2006).

[24] Rohan Gunaratna, *Inside Al Qaeda: Global Network of Terror* (Melbourne: Scribe, 2005).

[25] Sally Neighbour, *In the Shadows of Swords: On the Trail of Terrorism from Afghanistan to Australia* (Sydney: Harper, 2004).

[26] Zachary Abuza, *Militant Islam in Southeast Asia* (Boulder: Lynne Reinner, 2003). "Straightjacket off as Defence gets real," *Australian,* 27 February 2003, 13.

[27] *Australian,* 6 October 2006.

[28] Brahma Chellaney, "Fighting Terrorism in Southern Asia: The Lessons of History," *International Security,* 26 (Winter 2001): 100-113.

[29] Rod Lyon, "Alliance Unleashed: Australia and the US in a new strategic age," *ASPI Strategy* (Barton: ASPI, June 2005), 32.

[30] *Sydney Morning Herald,* 20 October 2006, 1. For a discussion of Australian regional planning and the role of the Middle East before 1953 see Peter Edwards, *Crises and Commitments: The Politics and Diplomacy of Australia's Involvement in Southeast Asian Conflicts 1948-1965* (North Sydney: Allan & Unwin, 1992), Chapter 7.

[31] See Neville Meaney, *The Search for Security in the Pacific 1901-1914* (Sydney: Sydney University Press, 1976).

[32] John Bach, *The Australia Station: A History of the Royal Navy in the South West Pacific 1821-1913* (Kensington: UNSW Press, 1986); John Moredike, *An Army for a Nation: A History of Australian Military Developments 1880-1914* (North Sydney: Allen & Unwin, 1992).

[33] Wayne Reynolds, "Whatever happened to the Fourth British Empire? The Cold War, Empire Defence and the USA, 1943-1957," *Cold War Britain, 1945-1964: New Perspectives,* ed. Michael F. Hopkins, Michael D. Kandiah and Gillian Staerck (Basingstoke: Palgrave, 2003), 127-142.

[34] Wayne Reynolds, "Labor Tradition, Global Shifts and the Foreign Policy of the Whitlam Government," *Evatt to Evans: The Labor Tradition in Australian Foreign Policy*, ed. David Lee and Christopher Waters (Canberra: Research School of Pacific and Asian Studies and Allen & Unwin, 1997), 110-131.

[35] The US had moved its position on Timor before sent the letter in December 1998 to Habibie advocating a change of approach. In July the US Senate called for a referendum on Timor that should be supervised internationally. Frank Frost and Adam Cobb, "The Future of Timor: Major Current Issues," *Australia's Asia-Pacific Neighbourhood — Challenge and Change: Papers on Indonesia, Papua New Guinea and the Koreas* (Canberra: Department of the Parliamentary Library, 1999), 99. For a contrasting view see Lachlan Colquhoun, "S.E. Asia's jittery security outlook," *The Diplomat*, 5 (April/ May 2006), 26. He argues that, with respect to regional security, "Canberra's ability to make a positive difference was hamstrung by its perceived links to the United States."

[36] Kugler, "Future US Defense Strategy," *Globalisation and National Security*, 381.

[37] Anthony H. Cordesman, "The Military in a New Era: Living with Complexity," *Globalisation and National Security*, 401.

[38] "Downer Commits to NATO Link-up," *Australian*, 9 October 2006.

[39] Lance Collins and Warren Reid, *Plunging Point: Intelligence Failures, Cover Ups and Consequences* (London: Harper Collins, 2005), 229.

[40] Andrew Wilkie, *Axis of Deceit* (Melbourne: Black Inc. Agenda, 2004), 61.

[41] Despatch 5/57, Spender to External Affairs, 24 December 1957, NAA: A1838/269, TS852/10/4/2.

[42] David Capie talks here of the "back to the future trend" as scholars are "rummaging through dusty shelves…to explain contemporary global politics." David Capie review *Contemporary Southeast Asia*. 22 (April 2000), 226.

[43] *Australian*, 21 October 2002.

[44] *Australian,* 11 December 2002.

[45] *Australian,* 27 October 2005.

[46] *Sydney Morning Herald,* 22 March 2004.

[47] *Australian,* 17 October 2005.

[48] "Qaida in Indonesia? The Evidence Doesn't Support Worries," *International Herald Tribune,* 23 October 2001.

[49] Kirsten E. Schulze, "Laskar Jihad and the Conflict in Ambon," *Brown Journal of World Affairs,* IX (Spring 2002).

[50] *Australian,* 14 October 2002.

[51] *Australian,* 5 February 2004. In October Downer announced a doubling of counter-terrorism funds over five years—to $20 million. *Australian,* 6 October 2004.

[52] *Australian,* 30 November 2004.

[53] *Australian,* 20 May 2005.

[54] *Australian,* 17 May 2006.

[55] Peter Hartcher and Tom Allard, "Dire Straits," *Sydney Morning Herald,* 8-9 April 2006.

[56] *Australian,* 6 April 2006.

[57] Philippe F. Delhaise, *Asia in Crisis: The Implosion of the Banking and Finance Systems* (Singapore: John Wiley & Sons, 1998).

[58] Ian Clark, *Globalisation and Fragmentation: International Relations in the Twentieth Century,* Oxford: Oxford University Press, 2002.

[59] "Post-War Defence of Australia," NAA: MP1587/1/0, 218B, Naval Intelligence Division, 22 September 1943.

[60] "Post War defence forces," NAA: A5799, Defence Committee Agendum 107/1945, report to Joint Planning Committee, 45/107, 11 June 1945.

[61] JIO Paper and Defence Planning Division working paper by W.B. Pritchett, 15 August 1974, NAA: A1838/369, 696/5 Part 3. In the event the RAAF and RAN submarines closely monitored Indonesian activities in Timor. NAA: A1838/319, 3038/10/1 Part 38.

[62] Ross Babbage, *A Coast Too Long: Defending Australia beyond the 1990s* (Sydney: Allen and Unwin, 1990), 27. Sending forces into the island screen was an option to counter regional conventional threat. Babbage's Kokoda Foundation criticized later the size of the RAAF, arguing that 80 to 100 planes were not enough to protect the North West shelf. *Sun Herald,* 2 October 2005.

[63] Beasley, "Maritime pirates the next big terror threat" *Australian,* 26 July 2005.

[64] Ken Buckley, Barbara Dale and Wayne Reynolds, *Doc Evatt* (Melbourne: Longman, 1994), Ch. 20.

Submission 1312, "Netherlands New Guinea and Indonesia," Casey and McBride, NAA: A4926, August 1958.

[65] Submission 1312, "Netherlands New Guinea and Indonesia," Casey and McBride, NAA: A4926, August 1958.

[66] Brian Toohey and William Pinwill, *Oyster: The Story of the Australian Secret Intelligence Service* (Port Melbourne: Mandarin, 1989), 70.

[67] King, *West Papua and Indonesia since Suharto*, 152.

[68] Clinton Fernandes, *Reluctant Indonesians: Australia, Indonesia, and the Future of West Papua,* (Melbourne: Scribe, 2006), 132.

[69] Whether that argument still holds is dependent in part on the assessment of China's diplomatic offensive in Southeast Asia and the possibility that the United States has determined on a neo-containment strategy against China. Kwa Chong Guan, "Southeast Asia's Strategic Challenges: Balancing between China and the US," and Ross Terrill, "Taking the Long View: China's Emerging Great Power Role in the Asia-Pacific Region," *Global Forces 2005: Proceedings of the ASPI conference: Day 2-Strategic Challenge* (Barton: Australian Strategic Policy Institute, 2006).

[70] Whitlam's Brief in September 1974 pointed to Australia's interests stemming from the location of Timor "250 miles from Darwin, and near our resources zone and close to major shipping routes." Auseo Brief for Whitlam, 2 September 1974, *Documents on Australian Foreign Policy: Australia and the Indonesian Incorporation of Portuguese Timor 1974-1976* (Canberra: Department of Foreign Affairs and Trade, 2000), 90.

[71] *Sydney Morning Herald*, 30 June 2006.

[72] Craig A. Snyder, "Southeast Asian Perspectives on Australia's Foreign Policy," *Contemporary Southeast Asia*, 28 (August 2006), 329.

[73] *Defence Review—Our Future Defence Force, A Public Discussion Paper* (Canberra; Defence Publishing Service, June 2000), 62.

[74] Paul Dibb, "Planning processes need a reality check," *Defence Report, Australian*, 26-27 May 2007, 2.

[75] Greg Sheridan, *The Partnership: The Inside Story of the US-Australian Alliance under Bush and Howard* (Sydney, University of NSW Press, 2006), 128-131.

[76] Clinton Fernandes, *Reluctant Indonesia: Australia, Indonesia, and the future of West Papua,* (Melbourne: Scribe, 2006), 127-128. Fernandes, however, argues that Australia lacks the economic and military power to influence Jakarta. Clinton Fernandes, *Reluctant Saviour: Australia, Indonesia and the independence of East Timor* (Carlton North: Scribe, 2004), 4.

[77] *Australian*, 6-7 December 2003.

[78] *Sydney Morning Herald*, 6-7 December 2003.

[79] *Sydney Morning Herald*, 28 August 2006. The AFP was to expand by 422 new recruits. At that juncture there were 470 police abroad—out of an establishment of 5361. *Australian*, 26-27 August 2006.

[80] Robert Lowry, *The Armed Forces of Indonesia* (St Leonards: Allen and Unwin, 1996), 3.

[81] *Australian*, 5 January 1999.

[82] *Australian*, 10 September 2004.

[83] *Australian*, 3-4 June 2006.

[84] Paul Keating, *Engagement: Australia Faces the Asia-Pacific* (Sydney: Macmillan, 2000), 129-130.

[85] Damien Kingsbury, "The Reform of the Indonesian Armed Forces," *Contemporary Southeast Asia*, 22 (August 2000), 304.

[86] John Martinkus, *Indonesia's Secret War in Aceh* (Milson's Point: Random House, 2004), 39-41. See too Peter King, *West Papua and Indonesia since Suharto: Independence, Autonomy or Chaos?* (Sydney: UNSW Press, 2004), 152, 167.

[87] Alan Dupont, "Supping with the devil," *The Diplomat*, 2 (June-July 2002), 34.

[88] Kevin O'Rourke, *Reformasi: The Struggle for Power in Post-Soeharto Indonesia* (Crows Nest: Allan & Unwin, 2002), 405.

[89] W.J. Hudson, *Blind Loyalty: Australia and the Suez Crisis* (Melbourne: Melbourne University Press, 1986).

[90] For assessments at the time see "Australia's Asia-Pacific Neighbourhood—Challenge and Change: Papers on Indonesia, Papua New Guinea and the Koreas," Canberra, Department of the Parliamentary Library, 1999.

[91] See "Achieving Security the "ASEAN Way," Alan Collins, *Security and Southeast Asia: Domestic, Regional and Global Issues* (London: Lynne Rienner Publishers, 2003).

[92] Buckley, Dale and Reynolds, *Doc Evatt*, "The Indonesian Revolution and Australian Security."

[93] Indonesia is on SIPRI's list on "countries of strategic nuclear concern." Tanya Ogilvie-White, "Nuclear Issues, Terrorism and Pacific Security," *Securing a Peaceful Pacific*, ed. John Henderson and Greg Watson (Christchurch: Canterbury University Press, 2005), 110.

[94] William Tow refers to a need for "convergent security" which integrates realist and liberal approaches. Tow, *Asia-Pacific Strategic Relations: Seeking Convergent Security* (Cambridge: Cambridge University Press, 2001), 204.

[95] Michael Wesley, *The Howard Paradox: Australian Diplomacy in Asia 1996-2006* (Sydney: ABC Books, 2007).

[96] George Friedman and Meredith Lebard, The Coming War with Japan, New York: St. Marin's Press, 1991. Humphrey McQueen tackled the issue in *Japan to the Rescue: Australian Security around the Indonesian Archipelago during the American Century* (Port Melbourne: William Heinemann Australia, 1991).

[97] Gareth Evans and Bruce Grant, *Australia's Foreign Relations in the world of the 1990s* (Melbourne: Melbourne University Press, 1995).

[98] Professor Shih Choon Fong, the president of the National University of Singapore, has recently warned Australian universities against gaining a reputation as "revenue chasers." *Australian Higher Education*, 6 June 2007. I make this case in Wayne Reynolds, "Beyond White Australia: Australian Education and the Engagement of Asia after the Second World War," *The International Journal of Learning*, 13 (2006) and "Whatever Happened to the Colombo Plan?" proceedings of Hawaii International Education Symposium, January 2007.

[99] *Sydney Morning Herald*, 18 December 2002.

[100] Humphrey Wynn, *The RAF Strategic Nuclear Deterrent Forces: Their Origins, Roles and Deployment 1946-1969* (London: HMSO, 1994).

[101] Wayne Reynolds, "The Wars that were Planned: Australia's Forward Defence Posture in Asia and the Role of Tactical Nuclear Weapons, 1945-1967," *Australian Journal of International Affairs*, 53, 3 (November 1999): 295-309.

Concluding Remarks

Clive Williams MG

I felt privileged to be asked to write a conclusion to such a well-informed range of views on a number of terrorism-related topics. The book contains chapters from 13 writers; some of the authors are well-known—others less so—but all provide insightful analyses. I believe it is valuable to have a mix of material from established academics as well as some of the younger up-and-coming strategic thinkers and historians. To my mind, the lessons to be learned from history are critically important; I will return to that point later.

My own introduction to "academic terrorism" was in 1980 when I chose it as my area of study for a Master's degree in criminology at the University of Melbourne. My supervisor was former head of Commonwealth Police intelligence and Melbourne barrister, Kerry Milte, and my overseas supervisors were Paul Wilkinson and Major General Richard Clutterbuck, both internationally-recognized terrorism experts. At the time, I was working at the Defence Signals Directorate (DSD) in Melbourne. Fortuitously, I had a working relationship with the Victoria Police's Special Operations Group (SOG), which gave me access to their specialized library on politically motivated violence.

I found terrorism so interesting that I tried to make the topic part of my duties in subsequent intelligence positions in Australia and overseas. It was not easy to do that in Australia because the Australian Security Intelligence Organisation (ASIO) jealously guarded this part of its domestic responsibilities from potential competitors like Defence intelligence, where I worked. In earlier years, ASIO had had competition from Police Special Branches, but these branches had been progressively closed down by state Labor governments for exceeding their charters—mainly for keeping files on potentially subversive "left-wing" Labor politicians!

In 1996, I was running a branch in the Defence Intelligence Organisation (DIO) responsible for global issues, and saw this as an opportunity to establish a Counterterrorism Intelligence Cell. The justifiable rationale was that it would provide material to our Special Forces that was beyond the capability of ASIO to produce—information on, for example, terrorist groups' tactics, weapons, and types of explosives used. We disseminated a security-classified weekly email newsletter, and by the nature of these things, soon had a large following of apparently satisfied customers.

About six months after the cell was established, ASIO discovered what we were doing. I was summonsed to a meeting at ASIO and told by a senior manager that the cell had to be closed down because it was intruding on ASIO's legislated responsibility. I pointed out that we were providing operational support to Defence customers of a kind that ASIO was unable to produce. (I should also add that ASIO at that time had no timely emailed product.) A few days later they backed down and said they would not fight the issue provided the newsletters were not provided to non-Defence customers. We agreed and duly lopped those customers from our address list. I should add that Defence itself was not above turf protection or "silo-ing." One senior Defence officer justified silos by describing them as our "cylinders of excellence"!

With 9/11, most of the petty jealousies and turf disputes related to terrorism disappeared, and since then Australia has had a much more holistic approach to threats to our national security. (I note however in 2009 that pressure on budgets might again undermine cooperation and lead to turf protection.)

I resigned from Defence at the end of 2002, and started running graduate courses in terrorism at the Australian National University. I have, in the years since, taught Masters graduate courses at the University of California at San Diego, George Washington University in Washington DC, the UN University in Tokyo, Cheng Chi University in Taiwan, Jakarta University in Indonesia, the University of Sydney, the University of NSW at the Australian Defence Academy, and Macquarie University—and have given more international conference presentations and workshops than I care to remember.

My main focus now is on running three different but inter-related Master's electives: "Terrorism Issues," "Crime, Espionage and Security," and "National Security and Counterterrorism."

It has been an interesting ride, and I have met a great bunch of people in the process—many of whom are authors of these chapters. I should emphasize that I am still learning about terrorism, as I did from reading these excellent book contributions.

To return now to the history aspect; I think that knowledge of the history of terrorism is important to both practitioners and academics.

One of my tasks after the establishment of Air Security Officers (ASOs), popularly referred to by the media as "Sky Marshals," was to give them a two-hour introductory session on the history of air terrorism, with emphasis on Australia-related incidents. DIO had sometimes done hijack debriefs and I had access to other nations' lessons learned. One DIO debrief concerned a hijack that had involved an Australian passenger, Peter Ward, in 1999. An Air India Airbus, Flight IC-814, had been hijacked out of Kathmandu and ended up in Kandahar, where a deal was eventually done with the Pakistani hijackers and the passengers released. Peter's debrief provided valuable information on Islamist hijack methodology, and clearly demonstrated Taliban complicity in the IC-814 hijack. This example and more recent incidents were valuable in determining effective ways of dealing with incidents in the air.

A forgotten historical example, as far as airport screening procedures were concerned, was Ramzi Yousef's use of liquid explosive in 1994. Forgetting that historical example and not having appropriate countermeasures in place could have led to tragedy in 2006 had the UK transatlantic airliner plot not been detected by MI5 and SO13 of the Metropolitan Police. Unfortunately, Operation Overt did not result in the level of convictions that should have eventuated. Political nervousness and US pressure resulted in the perpetrators being arrested prematurely—which weakened the police case against them when they went to trial.

Looking at terrorism from a practitioner-cum-academic perspective, there are two points I would make—keep good historical records of your own experiences for reference purposes (and possibly for your memoirs!) and, more generally, emphasize to students the importance of history in the evolution of terrorism as a political motivator.

I have kept a computer-based chronology of terrorist incidents since 1980, although it includes prior incidents where I have had access to interesting information—an example being the Croatian bombing campaign—aspects of which are covered very competently by Stuart Koschade in his chapter. Few federal government agencies, if any, have maintained a detailed chronology of Australia-related incidents, or can tell you how many Australians have been killed or injured in politically motivated incidents in Australia or overseas. Post-9/11, electronic searching has become easier and there are more databases, but I believe it is still worth maintaining terrorism subject folders. I still make a daily practice of saving articles and images electronically, as well as recording relevant TV programs. A professional intelligence officer is always on the lookout for material on his or her area of interest, and I suggest the same holds true for professional academics.

In my five-day course, "Terrorism Issues," I devote a whole day to the history of terrorism, pre- and post-1968, looking in particular at the influence of radical thinkers and leaders on the evolution of terrorism as a strategy. Terrorism does not win wars, but it can certainly influence political decision makers and can result in outcomes that satisfy terrorists—such as the 1993 Oslo Accords' recognition of the rights of the Palestinians. Terrorism can also have drastic consequences: Bosnian Serb Gavrilo Princip's assassination of the Archduke Franz Ferdinand of Austria in Sarajevo in 1914 set off a chain of events that led to the First World War and the death of twenty million people. Many of today's terrorism problems are of course rooted in historical grievances; the terrorist attacks on India and the Kashmir dispute being a case in point.

History is also important to individual topics of study. Terrorist modus operandi today is based on a long history of trial-and-error, technological breakthroughs, response to effective countermeasures, and the need for publicity among other factors. If you do not understand this process, contemporary terrorists' tactics may not make much sense. Religious extremism is another area where understanding the message and influence of the key theorists is of fundamental importance. Today that includes reading the writings of Dr Ayman al-Zawahiri and Osama bin Laden—all of them. Not just summaries or spin-doctored interpretations!

That said, I will now stop reminiscing and proselytizing, and reflect on the preceding chapters!

Fittingly, the first chapter is by the respected academic, Carlyle A. Thayer. Carl questions the expertise of some of the so-called experts who emerged after 9/11 and about the lack of academic rigor in many of the post-9/11 studies. His chapter is a preliminary report on how better-organized research could add to our understanding of politically motivated violence in Southeast Asia. Carl would like to see multi-disciplinary teams of terrorism specialists working on primary source material to offer inter-alia explanations for the causes of radicalization, and particularly for "home-grown terrorism."

Lucy Resnyansky looks at intersections in social science knowledge and the prevention of terrorism. She notes that the complexity of terrorism and groups of influence make meta-analysis of terrorism a pressing concern. She focuses particularly on the interaction between research and practice. Lucy outlines a social scientific knowledge approach to the prevention of the emergence of terrorism as a social phenomenon. Key aspects in her view are the local perspective, relevance of a broader range of social research, and proactive strategies and constructive solutions.

Sean Brawley was the mover and shaker for this book and without his sterling efforts it would not have happened. His chapter is about transdisciplinarity, signature pedagogy, and the place of history in terrorism studies and counter-terrorism. Sean notes that prior to 9/11 there was a limited body of work in the area of cross-disciplinary terrorism studies. Even in 2009, I am struck by the number of people working on terrorism-related topics in disciplines such as anthropology, sociology, divinity, political science etc., and how little they interact with terrorism researchers working in overlapping areas. Sean concludes that much can be gained from cross-disciplinary approaches, particularly involving historians. Indeed, this book, with its many different perspectives, shows what can be gained by plumbing different backgrounds and expertise.

Brett Peppler is a former Australian Intelligence Corps colleague who has a well-justified reputation for innovative lateral thinking and creative ideas. Brett looks at intelligence pathologies in terrorism analysis, noting that national intelligence priorities can be fickle and that analysts often shoulder the blame for intelligence "failures." His paper argues that terrorism has evolved more rapidly than the Western intelligence community's ability to support effective terrorism analysis. He concludes that systemic weaknesses in culture and practice are largely to blame, but so too are the unrealistic expectations of policymakers. He observes that alternative analysis methodologies are needed to better understand our adversaries' world views and mindsets, especially where counterterrorism problems are characterized by high levels of ambiguity or uncertainty.

Anne Mahmoud Aly considers lessons from the past, drawing from the historical roots of militant Islamic ideology and its influence on contemporary jihadist movements. Jihadist movements are not a new phenomenon; they were born in the declining years of Ottoman imperialism, with the aim of establishing an Islamic order. She discusses the contemporary significance of Dr Ayman al-Zawahiri's writings and speeches, the emerging phenomenon of militant Islamism, al Qaeda's discourse on jihad, the discourse's global appeal, and how it might be countered. She concludes that what is new about contemporary terrorism is the militant Islamists' transmission of their message to a globalized audience, and how well it resonates with some individuals and groups. Many young Muslims now see themselves as the victims and the West as the infidel enemy. In Anne's view, the major failure of the "war on terror" has been its failure to generate a persuasive counter-discourse.

Eamon Murphy looks at combating religious terrorism in Pakistan. He suggests that Pakistan is not a natural home for Islamist extremism, rather its growth has much to do with efforts by competing power groups within Pakistan and the local knock-on effects of the regional policies of foreign governments. Eamon draws upon insights from critical terrorism studies, particularly in relation to the root causes of terrorism and examines how the state itself, in this case Pakistan, can contribute to the rise of religious terrorism. He notes that the application of hard power alone is not the solution to Pakistan's problems—real progress in economic and political reforms is likely to prove a more promising approach to combating Islamist extremism.

Alexey D. Muraviev has a relevant background and special expertise in his chosen topic—al Qaeda's eastern front—the Russian vector in the network's international activity. He notes that al Qaeda's involvement has evolved over three stages since 1992: first, preparation and strategic reconnaissance; second, engagement and establishing control, and; third, declined interest and capacity—but retaining links. The lesson to be learned from this case study is that al Qaeda analyzes its setbacks and is prepared to go back to the drawing board to come up with new approaches. In sum, al Qaeda does not countenance failure and believes it has the time on its side to be able to ultimately prevail.

Scott Flower looks at the history of terrorism and its analysis in Melanesia, and the implications for security and policy. He reviews and critiques the current literature on terrorism in Melanesia, and presents for the first time useful new data collected during field work in 2007. He also highlights areas needing further research. Scott concludes that it is simplistic to argue that growing Muslim populations equate to an increasing threat. They are still very small minority populations in Melanesia. He believes that while some members could be radicalized by travelling preachers, they are unlikely to engage in politically motivated violence. Nevertheless, a key issue for analysts and policymakers is to understand the environmental drivers for recruitment and radicalization—and how best to counter them.

Sean Brawley returns to the fray with Ian Shaw to muse about a history of terrorism in Australia. The authors note how little most Australians know about their own terrorism history. Even when they do know about incidents, much of the obvious critical analysis is missing. "What was the motivation behind a bombing campaign in Townsville in 1933?" "And who planted a bomb detonated by an alarm clock on a Catalina flying boat in Sydney harbour in 1949—and why?" Clearly, much is to be gained by historians examining the nation's history of politically motivated violence prior to the best known past incident, the 1978 Hilton Hotel bombing. Even the Hilton bombing is a stretch for most Australians; anyone born after

1970 tends to frame terrorism within the context of 9/11 and Bali 2002. Much could be gained from examining and analyzing past incidents; in particular, it would allow us to put current threats in context, and temper scare-mongering of the kind experienced under the Howard government.

Luke Howie picks up the theme of the importance of history in his chapter on institutionalized discrimination and the response of the mob. He argues that history provides a platform from which rigorous studies of terrorism can be launched by both historians and non-historians. He uses the term "mob" to describe the faceless, sometimes mindless, always glib, and often violent Australian crowds that sometimes gather for unspoken, but mutually understood, purposes. I was immediately reminded of the "red-neck" youths rioting against Muslims at Cronulla in 2005. Luke goes on to mention that incident. His historical examples include the Irish threat, the Croatian threat, and today's perception of an Arab threat. He concludes that the mob continues to play a significant discriminatory role in our terrorism history; in 2007 it quickly turned Dr Haneef from a cooperative suspect to a dangerous flight-risk. As recently as 2009, poorly-informed mob thinking is making it difficult for the Rudd government to resettle carefully screened Guantanamo detainees in Australia.

Stuart Koschade also takes an historical bent with his examination of the violent activities of the Croatian Revolutionary Brotherhood (HRB) in Australia between the 1940s and 1970s. Of particular note are their incursions into Yugoslavia in 1963 and 1972. Stuart focuses in particular on Operation Action Kangaroo—the 1963 incursion. I worked in Army counterintelligence and MI-11 in the late 1960s and we often helped Police Special Branches by recording the car number plates of suspects attending HRB meetings. The Australian Army also had security problems with HRB members joining the Citizens Military Force (CMF) to gain military training. Stuart says that the robust response of Australia's security agencies had much to do with the HRB's containment and decline. He believes there may be lessons from our past practices that could inform our approach to dealing with contemporary terrorism problems.

Andrew Lynch examines the legal approach to dealing with terrorism in Australia, noting that in the wake of 9/11 the Howard government passed thirty-seven new laws directly addressing the terrorist threat. While some were sensible, Andrew expresses concern over the processes and safeguards which accompany many, particularly the powers to proscribe organizations and issue control orders. The law is, of course, a precedent-based profession, engaging with history on a daily basis. While Australia may take its inspiration for some new laws and powers from overseas, notably the UK, it is important that we understand how they developed. In the UK's case, for example, its legal approach to terrorism was based on its long history of dealing with Fenian terrorism. Andrew believes that the legal profession would welcome the involvement of historians when it engages with the government over the development of relevant Australian legislation. It is also to be hoped that future legislation will see government working more closely with the law community than was the case post 9/11.

The honor of being last goes to Wayne Reynolds who looks at Australian regional strategy, terrorism and asymmetric warfare. He contends that the "global war on terror" is or was very much part of the strategic realignment of the US after the Cold War, and it also shaped Australian strategic thinking. He notes however that asymmetric warfare was a feature of conflict in Southeast Asia throughout the Cold War. He notes the danger of fragmentation in Indonesia; threats to Australian interests could arise from rogue elements in the military, Jakarta's strategy, or from jihadist or separatist forces. Australia therefore has no option but to prepare for its own version of the three bloc war. He observes that Australians are more likely to die on the soil to our north than in Australia. This is borne out by my own statistics which show that Australians are seven to eight times more likely to die overseas from politically motivated violence than they are in Australia.

I think you will agree that there is much food for thought in the preceding chapters, not only for academics, but also for practitioners and those who have a general interest in terrorism and counterterrorism. Some chapters are clearly works-in-progress, while others are supported by a strong body of research.

A common thread throughout is the importance of history, not least because of its influence on the future. One of my intelligence tasks in the 1980s was working on intelligence estimates, which project five years into the future. (Intelligence forecasts look even further into the future and come up with alternative scenarios.) I soon learned from my older and more experienced colleagues that you cannot do effective trend analysis unless you look at the past. The more of the past you have to look at, the more accurate your estimate of the future is likely to be. Looking forward accurately is critically important for Defence in particular, because capabilities that Defence is planning for today may not be operational for many years to come, so you have to get it right.

Regrettably, in Australia today there is a degree of public complacency about terrorism. The media has a short attention span and has long since moved on to climate change and the economic crisis—but terrorism is as significant a national security issue for us now as it was back in 2001, and we ignore its potential social impact at our peril. As terrorism specialists we should also be acknowledging that major changes are occurring in the international environment, including a slow decline in US influence and the rise of competing power blocs.

We should be thinking about what these changes mean for terrorism and counterterrorism—worthwhile topics perhaps for a future study?

About the Authors

Sean Brawley is Associate Professor of History, and Faculty Teaching and Learning Fellow at the University of New South Wales. His research interests include sport and military history. Sean's work in terrorism studies has concentrated on the place of sport in American and Australian reactions to terrorist attacks, and on methodological issues related to the place of history in this field. He is currently researching and writing with Ian Shaw the first general history of terrorism in Australia. Sean is a member of the Australian Research Council Funded Research Network for a Secure Australia (RNSA).

Anne Mahmoud Aly is a post-doctoral research fellow with the Centre for Applied Social Marketing Research at Edith Cowan University, Perth. Her work has explored Australian Muslim identity, terrorism and fear, social dimensions of counter-terrorism, political fear and citizenship. Anne's most recent research looks at the fear of terrorism among Australian Muslims and in the broader Australian community. She has also presented sessions on counter- terrorism, terrorism profiling, and models of terror sustainment to state security agencies and police in Western Australia. Previously, Anne was a senior policy officer in the State Government.

Scott Flower is currently a PhD scholar at the Crawford School of Economics and Government, Australian National University, Canberra. As a consultant, Scott has provided analysis and advice to government and corporate clients on international development and security issues.

Luke Howie is Lecturer in the Department of Behavioural Studies and a member of the Global Terrorism Research Centre (GTReC) at Monash University. He is also a Research Associate at the Australian Homeland Security Research Centre (AHSRC) in Canberra. Luke's research interests include behavioral responses to terrorism, the meanings and consequences of terrorism for business, the relationship between terrorism and city-spaces, post-9/11 popular culture, terrorism and the media, and terrorism and social networking websites.

Stuart Koschade has a background in political science. Since 2002 he has developed a broad area of expertise within the field of terrorism studies. Stuart completed his Honors thesis examining the motivations of specific Al Qaeda soldiers through sources of conflict theory. In 2007, he completed his PhD at the Queensland University of Technology, employing social network analysis to examine a number of terrorist cells that had operated in Australia, including groups such as Aum Shinrikyo, Lashkar-e-Taiba, and Jemaah Islamiyah. During this period, Stuart was a research associate of the Australian Homeland Security Research Center in Canberra. His terrorism studies research has included work on social network analysis of terrorist cells, Islamic extremist ideology, the academic field terrorism studies, and terrorism history in Australia. Stuart has been published in journal such as *Studies in Conflict and Terrorism* and *Policing, Intelligence and Counter Terrorism.*

Andrew Lynch is Director of the Gilbert and Tobin Centre of Public Law and an Associate Professor in the Faculty of Law, University of New South Wales. Andrew researches in the field of Australian federal constitutional law and specializes in the intersection of public law and legal responses to terrorism. He is an author of *What Price Security? Taking Stock of Australia's Anti-Terror Laws* (2006) and a co-editor of *Law and Liberty in the War on Terror* (2007), as well as many journal articles, and conference and seminar papers in these and other areas. Additionally, Andrew has given evidence to a number of parliamentary and non-government inquiries into Australia's counter-terrorism legislative scheme. He writes regularly on public law and terrorism issues in the media.

Alexey D. Muraviev is a strategic affairs analyst and an award-winning lecturer in International Relations and Strategic Studies in the School of Social Sciences and Asian Languages at Curtin University of Technology, Perth, Western Australia. He has written and contributed to over forty publications on matters of national and international security, including two books (one co-authored) and a research monograph. His research interests include problems of modern maritime power, contemporary defense and strategic policy, Russia's strategic and defense policy, Russia as a Pacific power, transnational terrorism, and Australian national security, among others. In 2007 and 2008, the Australian Research Council (ARC) College of Experts nominated Dr Muraviev as an "expert of international standing."

Eamon Murphy is Professor of History and International Relations in the School of Social Sciences and Asian Languages at Curtin University of Technology in Western Australia where he teaches courses on modern Middle East and Indian history and on international relations in South and South West Asia. Recently, he has moved into the field of terrorism studies with particular reference to South Asia and South West Asia. He is currently co-editing *Contemporary State Terrorism* to be published by Routledge in July 2009 and is contributing two chapters on state terrorism in India and Pakistan.

Brett Peppler was a career intelligence analyst from 1978 until 1998 before establishing an independent strategic planning consultancy, Intelligent Futures, which specializes in the fields of futures studies, intelligence, and risk management. He is also a sessional lecturer at universities in Australia and abroad. Brett has been a member of the Australian Institute of Professional Intelligence Officers (AIPIO) since 1992 and a former editor of the Australia Institute's journal. He is currently the Vice President (Programs) on the AIPIO Board. Brett has drawn from his professional experience to contribute to the literature within the disciplines of intelligence, futures studies, and risk management.

Lucy Resnyansky is a research scientist at the Defence Science and Technology Organisation, Australia. She has a Bachelor (Honours) degree in Linguistics (1985) and a PhD in Social Philosophy (1994) from Novosibirsk State University (Russia); and a PhD in Education (2005) from the University of South Australia. She is an Affiliate Researcher with the Centre for Studies in Literacy, Policy and Learning Cultures (LPLC), Hawke Research Institute for Sustainable Societies, University of South Australia. Her research interests are in the areas of social modeling for intelligence and national security; methodological aspects of interdisciplinary research practice; sociocultural implications of technology; and the Internet as a social space.

Wayne Reynolds is Associate Professor of History at the University of Newcastle. He is an Australian foreign relations and defense planning specialist with a focus on nuclear issues. He was invited to edit a volume on Australia and the Nuclear Non-Proliferation Treaty for the Department of Foreign Affairs and Trade's document series. Since his major study on Australia's bid to acquire a nuclear weapon capacity was published in 2001, he has written articles and book chapters on nuclear issues in Canada, Britain, and Australia. He has also published on Asian engagement and the Colombo Plan.

Ian Shaw is Senior Training Officer in the Commonwealth Attorney Generals' Department in Canberra. With degrees from Melbourne, Monash, and Michigan Universities, Ian has worked for most of the last twenty-five years, in both public and private sectors, in the general area of counter-terrorism; an area in which he has both research and practitioner experience. He has published articles in both academic and mainstream media, and also writes on social history. Ian's most recent book is a study of Australian Rules football, entitled *The Bloodbath* (Scribe 2006).

Carlyle A. Thayer is Professor of Politics, School of Humanities and Social Sciences, University College, The University of New South Wales at the Australian Defence Force Academy. He was educated at Brown University, holds an M.A. in Southeast Asian Studies from Yale, and a PhD in International Relations from The Australian National University. In 2008 he spent his sabbatical year first as the Inaugural Frances M. and Stephen H. Fuller Distinguished Visiting Professor of Southeast Asian Studies at Ohio University in the United States, and then as Visiting Fellow in the Strategic and Defence Studies Centre at The Australian National University.

Clive Williams MG has a career background in the Australian Intelligence Corps and Defence Intelligence. He has worked and lectured internationally on terrorism-related issues since 1980. He left Defence in 2002, and has since run terrorism and national security-related Master's-degree courses at the ANU and a number of Australian and overseas universities. He became Visiting Fellow at the ANU's Strategic & Defence Studies Centre in 2002, Adjunct Professor at Macquarie University's Centre for Policing, Intelligence & Counter-Terrorism (PICT) in 2006, and Visiting Professor at the University of NSW at ADFA in 2006.

www.ingramcontent.com/pod-product-compliance
Lightning Source LLC
Chambersburg PA
CBHW020653270326
41928CB00005B/106